British Crime Cinema

The crime film is one of British cinema's most important genres, with hundreds of films produced in the last few decades. British underworld films evoke a compelling atmosphere of tough machismo in seedy low-life locales. Even unpretentious B films contain implicit critiques of social conditions and the hard-boiled surfaces of thrillers like *Hell is a City* and *They Made Me a Fugitive* offer a welcome alternative to the cosiness of most British films of their era. Yet, while American noir and gangster pictures are revered as important cultural documents, their British cousins have been given scant consideration. Why has the history of the British crime film been relegated to an underworld below the critical gaze?

British Crime Cinema is the first substantial study of this neglected genre. Bringing together original work from some of the leading writers on British popular film, and including interviews with key directors Mike Hodges (*Get Carter*) and Donald Cammel (*Performance*), the book follows the progress of the crime film from its first flourishing during black market Britain of the 1940s, through to the resurgence of the gangster cult in the late sixties, and to more recent examples such as *The Long Good Friday*, *Shallow Grave*, and *Face*.

The contributors trace the influence of the Hollywood gangster picture on its British counterpart, and assess the crime film's relationship to the British New Wave. They also explore how many underworld films questioned contemporary social attitudes, subverted feminine stereotypes, represented particular versions of masculinity, and provided an insight into the shifting gender relations of post-war Britain.

Steve Chibnall is Senior Lecturer in Media Studies at De Montfort University, Leicester. **Robert Murphy** is Senior Research Fellow at De Montfort University.

British Popular Cinema series

Series Editors: Steve Chibnall and I. Q. Hunter,
De Montfort University, Leicester

At a time when there is a growing popular and scholarly interest in British film, with new sources of funding and notable successes in world markets, this series explores the largely submerged history of the UK's cinema of entertainment.

The series rediscovers and evaluates not only individual films but whole genres, such as science fiction and the crime film, that have been ignored by a past generation of critics. Dismissed for decades as aberrations in the national cinema and anaemic imitations of American originals, these films are now being celebrated in some quarters as important contributions to our cinematic heritage.

The emergence of cult genre movies from the apparently respectable lineage of British film emphasises the gap between traditional academic criticism and a new alliance between revisionist film theorists and extra-mural (but well-informed) cinema enthusiasts who wish to take the study of British film in unexpected directions. This series offers the opportunity for both established cineastes and new writers to examine long-neglected areas of British film production or to develop new approaches to more familiar territory. The books will enhance our understanding of how ideas and representations in films relate to changing gender and class relations in post-war Britain, and their accessible writing style will make these insights available to a much wider readership.

Books in the Series:

British Crime Cinema
Edited by Steve Chibnall and Robert Murphy

British Science Fiction Cinema
Edited by I. Q. Hunter

Forthcoming titles:

British Horror Cinema
Edited by Julian Petley and Steve Chibnall

The British Historical Film
Edited by Claire Monk and Amy Sargeant

British Crime Cinema

Edited by Steve Chibnall and
Robert Murphy

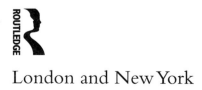

London and New York

First published 1999
by Routledge
11 New Fetter Lane, London EC4P 4EE

Simultaneously published in the USA and Canada
by Routledge
29 West 35th Street, New York, NY 10001

Typeset in Palatino by Routledge
Printed and bound in Great Britain by Biddles Ltd, Guildford and
King's Lynn

British Library Cataloguing in Publication Data
A catalogue record for this book is available from the British Library

Library of Congress Cataloguing in Publication Data
British crime cinema / edited by Steve Chibnall and Robert Murphy
Includes bibliographical references and index.
1. Gangster films–Great Britain–History and criticism.
I. Chibnall, Steve. II. Murphy, Robert.
PN 1995.9.G3B72   1999
791.43`655–dc21   98–49739
                            CIP

ISBN 0–415–16869–4 (hbk)
ISBN 0–415–16870–8 (pbk)

Contents

List of illustrations   vii
Notes on contributors   ix
Acknowledgements   xi

1 **Parole overdue: releasing the British crime film into the
   critical community**   1
   STEVE CHIBNALL AND ROBERT MURPHY

2 **The censors and British gangland, 1913–1990**   16
   JAMES C. ROBERTSON

3 **Spin a dark web**   27
   TIM PULLEINE

4 **Outrage: *No Orchids for Miss Blandish***   37
   BRIAN MCFARLANE

5 **Men, women and money: masculinity in crisis in the British
   professional crime film 1946–1965**   51
   ANDREW CLAY

6 **The higher heel: women and the post-war British crime film**   66
   VIV CHADDER

7 **The emergence of the British tough guy: Stanley Baker,
   masculinity and the crime thriller**   81
   ANDREW SPICER

8   **Ordinary people: 'New Wave' realism and the British crime film 1959–1963**   94
    STEVE CHIBNALL

9   *Performance*: **interview with Donald Cammell**   110
    JON SAVAGE

10 **Mike Hodges discusses *Get Carter* with the NFT audience, 23 September 1997**   117

11 **A revenger's tragedy – *Get Carter***   123
    ROBERT MURPHY

12 **Dog eat dog: *The Squeeze* and the *Sweeney* films**   134
    LEON HUNT

13 **Space in the British crime film**   148
    CHARLOTTE BRUNSDON

14 **Allegorising the nation: British gangster films of the 1980s**   160
    JOHN HILL

15 **From underworld to underclass: crime and British cinema in the 1990s**   172
    CLAIRE MONK

    A filmography of British underworld films, 1939–1997   189
    ANDREW CLAY AND STEVE CHIBNALL, ASSISTED BY SUMAY
    HELAS AND KEVIN WAITE

    Index   242

Illustrations

Figures

1.1	Susan George and Michael York in *The Strange Affair* (1968)	3
1.2	Jayne Mansfield and Anthony Quayle in *The Challenge* (1960)	6
1.3	Derren Nesbitt and Margaret Whitting in *The Informers* (1963)	10
2.1	Richard Attenborough surrounded by racetrack gangsters in *Brighton Rock* (1948)	20
2.2	Richard Burton in *Villain* (1971)	24
3.1	The trade advertisement for *They Made Me A Fugitive* (1947)	31
3.2	Poster for *Spin a Dark Web/Soho Incident* (1956)	35
4.1	*No Orchids for Miss Blandish* (1948)	41
4.2	Hugh McDermott and Zoe Gail in *No Orchids for Miss Blandish* (1948)	43
5.1	Paul Douglas in *Joe Macbeth* (1955)	61
5.2	Francoise Prevost and William Lucas in *Payroll* (1961)	63
6.1	Poster highlighting Diana Dors in *Yield to the Night* (1956)	72
6.2	Odile Versois and Diana Dors in the trade advertisement for *Passport to Shame* (1959)	78
7.1	Stanley Baker with Herbert Lom and Peggy Cummings in *Hell Drivers* (1956)	86
7.2	Stanley Baker in *The Criminal* (1960)	90
8.1	*Offbeat* (1960)	99
8.2	John Crawford and Stanley Baker in *Hell is a City* (1960)	102
9.1	James Fox, Stanley Meadows and John Bindon in *Performance* (1971)	113
10.1	Mike Hodges on the set of *Get Carter* (1971)	119
10.2	Wilfred Brambell and Anthony Newley in Ken Hughes' *The Small World of Sammy Lee* (1963)	121
11.1	Michael Caine and Alun Armstrong in *Get Carter* (1971)	128
11.2	Britt Ekland in *Get Carter* (1971)	130
12.1	Poster for *Sweeney!* (1976)	137
12.2	Anna Nygh in *Sweeney 2* (1978)	142

13.1   Googie Withers and John McCallum in *It Always Rains on Sunday*
        (1947)   151
13.2   Richard Widmark in *Night and the City* (1950)   154
14.1   Bob Hoskins and Dave King in *The Long Good Friday* (1981)   164
14.2   Ray McAnally presides over a fight in *Empire State* (1987)   169
15.1   Jude Law and Sadie Frost in *Shopping* (1994)   178
15.2   The male gang in *Smalltime* (1996)   186

Contributors

Charlotte Brunsdon teaches in the Department of Film and Television Studies at Warwick University. She is the author of *Screen Tastes* (Routledge, 1977) and co-editor of *Feminist Television Criticism* (Oxford University Press, 1997).

Viv Chadder is a Senior Lecturer in Cultural Studies at Nottingham Trent University. She is currently researching in the area of Lacanian psychoanalysis and cultural forms, particularly the performing voice.

Steve Chibnall is co-ordinator of the British Cinema and Television Research Group at De Montfort University, Leicester. His first book, *Law and Order News* (Tavistock) was published in 1977 and he has written widely for journals, edited collections and popular magazines. Recent work includes articles on *Brighton Rock*, Basil Dearden's youth problem films, British SF movies and 'showmanship' in film exhibition. His book *Making Mischief* on the cult films of Pete Walker was published in 1998 and he is currently editing a collection on the British horror film and writing a book on J. Lee Thompson.

Andrew Clay is currently completing a PhD on the British crime film at De Montfort University and writing a book on Lewis Gilbert. He has contributed to the *Journal of Popular British Cinema* and *Moving Performance: British stage and screen, 1890s–1920s*.

John Hill is Professor of Film and Media Studies at the University of Ulster. He is the author of *Sex, Class and Realism: British Cinema 1956–63* (BFI, 1986) and *British Cinema in the 1980s* (Oxford University Press, 1999) and editor of *The Oxford Guide to Film Studies* (Oxford University Press, 1998).

Leon Hunt is a lecturer in Film and TV Studies at Brunel University. He is the author of *British Low Culture: From Safari Suits to Sexploitation* (Routledge 1998), and has also contributed to *Velvet Light Trap*, *Necronomicon* and *You Tarzan: Masculinity, Movies and Men*.

Brian McFarlane is an Associate Professor in the English Department of

Monash University, Melbourne. His latest books are *Novel to Film: An Introduction to the Theory of Adaptation* (Oxford University Press, 1996) and *An Autobiography of British Cinema* (Methuen and BFI Publishing, 1997).

Claire Monk teaches Media Studies at De Montfort University and is completing her doctorate on British heritage films at Middlesex University. She has contributed to a variety of publications including *Sight and Sound*, the *Journal of Popular British Cinema*, and the *Electronic Journal of British Cinema*; and she is currently co-editing a collection on the British historical film.

Robert Murphy is the author of *Realism and Tinsel* (Routledge, 1989), *Sixties British Cinema* (BFI, 1992) and *Smash and Grab* (Faber, 1993) and editor of *The British Cinema Book* (BFI, 1997). He is senior research fellow at De Montfort University.

Tim Pulleine is on the editorial staff of the *Guardian* and has written extensively on the cinema for that newspaper and for various publications, including *Sight and Sound*, *Monthly Film Bulletin* and *Films & Filming*.

James C. Robertson, a retired teacher, is the author of two books on British film censorship, a study of director Michael Curtis and articles on film and international affairs. He has recently completed a book on Sir Dirk Bogarde and is currently doing research on the 1984 Video Recording Act.

Jon Savage has worked in journalism since 1977 and some of his best work was collected as *Time Travel* (Chatto & Windus, 1995). His book on punk rock, *England's Dreaming* was published by Faber & Faber in 1991. He has recently written a documentary on Brian Epstein, broadcast on BBC's Arena.

Andrew Spicer has recently completed a PhD thesis on the representation of masculinity in British cinema 1943–58 at the University of Westminster. He teaches part-time in Film, Media and Cultural Studies at the University of the West of England, Bristol.

Acknowledgements

Robert Murphy would like to thank Paul Marris, Richard Dacre, Eric Hedling, Tracey Scoffield, Dave Campbell, Susanne Hartley, Pete Todd, Andrew Clay, Pius Hume, Pete Shaw, Honey Salvadori, Eileen Murphy, Sophie and Edward Noel and especially Barbara Edwards for their help and support.

Steve Chibnall would like to thank Viv Andrews, Simon Davies, Flashbacks, Jyoti Haas, Sumay Helas, Kevin Waite, friends and colleagues in the British Cinema and Television Research Group at De Montfort University, and especially Andrew Clay, Kara McKechnie and Eithne Quinn for their help and support.

We would both like to thank Harvey Fenton, and all the contributors for their patience and resilience under pressure.

Every effort has been made to obtain permission to reproduce copyright material. If any proper acknowledgement has not been made, we would invite copyright holders to inform us of the oversight.

Photo illustrations are courtesy of the British Cinema and Television Research Group's archive at De Montfort University and BFI Stills, Posters and Designs.

1 Parole overdue

Releasing the British crime film into the critical community

Steve Chibnall and Robert Murphy

Part of what's good about *The Long Good Friday*, you really did buy that these guys were villains. In our case, you didn't have any choice, because our guys *are* villains

(Guy Richie, director of *Lock, Stock & Two Smoking Barrels* (1998), interviewed by Tom Charity, *Time Out*, 12–19 August 1998)

The crime genre is likely to assume a prominence in discussion of the national cinemas of the United States, Japan and France. Why is it, then, that it plays little or no part in critics' discussions of British cinema? Denis Gifford classifies a monumental 1,336 (26 per cent) of British films released between 1930 and 1983 as crime films, but they have been relegated to an underworld beneath the critical gaze.[1] The coterie of writers who, in the 1940s, did so much to codify the values of 'quality' British cinema (Ellis 1996) largely dismissed indigenous attempts at making crime films as both imitative of American originals and in poor taste. Their views reinforced an ideology of censorship that approached any sordid subject matter with suspicion and viewed an emphasis on criminality as essentially un-British. The felonious crime genre was rigorously excluded from the canon of social realist cinema and imprisoned in the Gulag Britannia reserved for unrespectable elements of British film culture. As Charles Barr (1986: 14) has noted, this incarceration received official sanction in 1948 when Harold Wilson, as President of the Board of Trade, condemned 'gangster, sadistic and psychological films', and called for 'more films which genuinely show our way of life'. Ever since, crime films have been the British genre that 'dare not speak its name', largely ignored even in the critical literature on the social problem film (Hill 1986; Landy 1991).

While the American gangster movie and film noir have been feted by scholars, their recalcitrant British brethren have continued to languish unconsidered and unseen by all but a handful of insomniac television viewers. The films have been overlooked in the rush to liberate other British genre offerings for critical re-evaluation. The academic interest heralded by Julian Petley's (1986) call for volunteers to explore the 'lost continent' of British non-realist film may have sent cultural cartographers rushing towards Hammer horrors and Gainsborough costumers, but it passed the crime film by. Lacking the colour and exoticism of the Hammer and Gainsborough products, the black and white B-movie world of the crime drama remained lost in a limbo between half-baked realism and lukewarm melodrama. Its claims to naturalism were dismissed, on the one hand by a Marxist orthodoxy, which saw no redeeming political merit in tales of individualist adventurism, and on the other by liberal and conservative critics who preferred not to accept an interest in crime as a feature of the national character. For a sentimental student of British identity like Jeffrey Richards (1998), crime represents a hedonistic and aggressive individualism which stands in opposition to the nation's dominant values of duty, service, thrift, restraint, gentleness and concern for others. He sees the crime drama as a carrier of an 'alternative national image' and its popularity as a cause for regret, a symptom of an age of cultural decline in which 'there has come to be greater interest in, and sympathy with, criminals than victims' (ibid.: 21).

Nor have British crime films garnered much sympathy from feminist critics who tend to avoid their apparently patriarchal values, unsavoury portrayals of women and celebrations of unreconstructed masculinity. Only among the cinephiles of the 'lads' press do home-grown underworld dramas find much favour and here a few classics of the genre have been elevated to an exalted status. Mike Hodges' *Get Carter* (1971)[2] is revered as the ultimate expression of 1970s masculine cool, its hard-boiled script supplying a nostalgic litany of lines for a generation of post-feminist men. And John Mackenzie's *The Long Good Friday* (1981) is lauded, not as a diverting gangster fantasy, but as 'a frighteningly realistic film...real gangsters, real London, real violence' (*Empire*, November 1997). These films are not considered merely the pick of a second-class and derivative genre, but as great moments in British cinema. The staff at *Empire* magazine voted Mackenzie's film 'the finest British movie ever made' (ibid.). In Jack Carter's cold machismo and Harold Shand's blustering and beleaguered patriarchy, the male viewer finds co-ordinates to map the cultural upheavals created by womens' aspirations and by economic change. In an age when, as Richards (1998: 25) puts it 'a third of young men under thirty have criminal records', the crime film ceases to be vicarious escapism and becomes, instead, a means to understanding the world.

For extra-mural cinephiles, then, the British crime film has already been rehabilitated into society. It is now time that academic critics at least granted it parole. It has, after all, been doing time longer than Reggie Kray. Once it is out in the open, we will be able to explore the tensions it exhibits between realism and melodrama and see to what extent it is an important genre for investigating issues of class and gender. In exposing the flip side of working-class respectability and male gentility, it may provide crucial insights into shifting social conditions and changing masculinities since the Second World War.

Our concern in this book is not with the crime genre in its entirety, but with that part of it that we might term 'underworld films'. Although outnumbered by the murder mysteries and espionage thrillers that are such a familiar part of British popular fiction, films in which the activities of professional criminals feature significantly or which are set in an underworld milieu constitute a substantial crime sub-genre, and one with strong claims to social relevance.[3] Grouping together such films – *They Made Me a Fugitive* (Cavalcanti, 1947), *Brighton Rock* (John Boulting, 1947), *Noose* (Edmond T. Greville, 1948), *Night and the City* (Jules Dassin, 1950), *The Criminal* (Joseph Losey, 1960), *The Frightened City* (John Lemont, 1961), *The Small World of Sammy Lee* (Ken Hughes, 1963), *The Strange Affair* (David Greene, 1968) *Performance* (Donald Cammell and Nic Roeg, 1970), *Get Carter, The Long Good Friday, Stormy Monday* (Mike Figgis, 1987), *Face* (Antonia Bird, 1997) – might not produce a genre with the coherence of the Hollywood gangster film, but distinctive patterns can be traced and common characteristics discerned.

Thematically British underworld films have different emphases from their American cousins. They are rarely about the rise and fall of a gangster: *Joe Macbeth* (Ken Hughes, 1955) fits the template but it is entirely set in America.

Figure 1.1 The Strange Affair (1968): Hippy chick Susan George tempts policeman Michael York from the straight and narrow
Source: British Cinema and Television, Research Group archive, De Montfort University

Villain (Michael Tuchner, 1971), with its Ronnie Kray-like protagonist, comes close but it digresses into bungled robbery, sexual aberration and political corruption. *McVicar* (Tom Clegg, 1980) and *A Sense of Freedom* (John Mackenzie, 1981) although based around the lives of real criminals, are essentially prison dramas, and *The Krays* (Peter Medak, 1990) is more of a family melodrama than a gangster film. *The Criminal* and *He Who Rides a Tiger* (Charles Crichton, 1965) which look dispassionately at the lives of their underworld professionals and refrain from moralising are more authentic and significant. Very few films are about the police infiltrating a gang (the two interesting exceptions are *Offbeat* (Cliff Owen, 1961) and *i.d.* (Philip Davis, 1995). And only in *The Informers* (Ken Annakin, 1963) and *The Strange Affair* is police corruption an important element – though the figure of the corrupt policeman as chief villain (not uncommon in television crime series) made its cinema debut in *Face*.

From *Noose* to *The Long Good Friday*, gang bosses see their criminal empires crumble just when they seem to be at their most successful. Narcy in *They Made Me a Fugitive* and Kinnear in *Get Carter* are brought down, too, but the emphasis is less on them than on the avengers who destroy them, and these films can be seen as prime examples of revenge films where a wronged man, denied access to the law, pursues his own path of justice. John Guillermin's *Never Let Go* (1960) and Michael Apted's *The Squeeze* (1977) – where down-at-heel heroes regain their self-respect by taking on boastful, complacent gangsters – can be seen as bridges between the two types of film. Their villains – Peter Sellers in *Never Let Go*, Stephen Boyd in *The Squeeze* – are smaller-scale operators than the underworld bosses of *Noose* and *The Long Good Friday*, but they are considerably nastier.

Films that focus on actual robberies are surprisingly rare among A features. *A Prize of Arms* (Cliff Owen, 1962) and *Robbery* (Peter Yates, 1967) concentrate on the planning and execution of a robbery (as does their comic variant, *The Italian Job*, Peter Collinson, 1969). But more typical are films like *The Good Die Young* (Lewis Gilbert, 1954), *Payroll* (Sidney Hayers, 1962) and *Face*, which deal more with the tensions and conflict within the gang before and after the robbery.

Only a handful of British underworld films centre upon a tough criminal hero. Shortie Matthews in *They Drive by Night* (Arthur Woods, 1938) has just come out of gaol but he is a small-time crook and innocent of the murder he is accused of. Tom Yately in *Hell Drivers* (Cy Endfield, 1957) is more formidable but he too is determined to go straight and only resorts to violence when provoked. Of the spiv movies of the forties, only in *Brighton Rock* and *Night and the City* is the spiv the central figure and they are both pathetic, doomed figures. Deserters and disgruntled ex-serviceman, who could plausibly involve themselves in the underworld without becoming part of it, were more acceptable protagonists to British film-makers chary of showing too much sympathy for the criminal. When active criminals begin to emerge as protagonists in the early 1960s, they are shown either as men living on the edge who act with intelligence and honour in the harsh world they are trapped within – Johnny Bannion in *The Criminal* and Peter Rayston in *He Who Rides a Tiger* – or troubled gang bosses like Vic Dakin in *Villain* and Harold Shand in *The Long Good Friday* coping badly with the problems of power and responsibility. Michael Caine's Jack Carter is atypically ruthless and remorseless but like all such unreformable characters, death awaits him at the end of the film. Stacy Keach in *The Squeeze* (Michael Apted, 1977), Terence Stamp in *The Hit* (Stephen Frears, 1984), even Sean Bean in *Stormy Monday*, are little men fighting against the odds. Robert Carlyle's Ray in *Face*, with his distinguished record in the class struggle, acts like a contemporary substitute for the ex-serviceman sucked by his disillusion into the underworld.

In the 1930s, strict censorship combined with literary and theatrical traditions of melodrama to move British crime films towards the macabre and the fantastic. Films like *The Terror* (Richard Bird, 1938) and *Dark Eyes of London* (Walter Summers, 1939) borrowed visual techniques from German Expressionism, and *They Drive by Night*, with its rainy roads, glittering dance halls, dismal lodgings and degenerate murderer seems to prefigure American film noir. In the late 1940s, the threatening shadows and asymmetrical framing of *They Made Me a Fugitive*, *Brighton Rock*, *Noose* and *Night and the City* mark them as films noir, though thematically they are quite different from their American counterparts. *Noose* has a female protagonist (Carole Landis) and in *Brighton Rock*, Pinkie's adversary, the loud, blowsy, cheerful Ida, with her indelible sense of right and wrong, is the opposite of a *femme fatale*. *They Made Me a Fugitive* and *Night and the City* have the doom-laden atmosphere of film noir, but as in Carol Reed's more international *The Third Man* (1949), women are suffering victims and steadfast helpers rather than temptresses, and it is the hero's own weakness and naiveté which leads him into trouble.

'Noirish' tendencies linger on in the 1950s and are still apparent in *The Challenge* (John Gilling, 1960), *Never Let Go* (John Guillermin, 1960) and the prison sequences of *The Criminal*; but they are balanced by New Wave trends towards location shooting. With the switch to colour after 1965 a sort of dirty realism emerges in films like *The Strange Affair*, *Get Carter*, *Villain*, *The Squeeze* and the *Sweeney* spin-offs. Their location shooting and lack of stylisation adds to their feel of representing a seedy, run-down Britain. *The Long Good Friday* is much brighter and although its glossy New London is exposed as a sham, there is still a feeling of optimism and dynamism about the film. Subsequent British crime films – such as *Stormy Monday* and *Shallow Grave* (Danny Boyle, 1995) – have reverted to a more stylised, noirish look associated with contemporary cinema's fusion of genre and art film.

Gangster films grew out of the American experience of violent struggles for power among gangsters grown rich supplying the public with alcohol during the Prohibition era. Their exploits very quickly found their way into novels and films. British gangsters kept a lower profile and provided less scope for mythology. Their main source of income came from protection

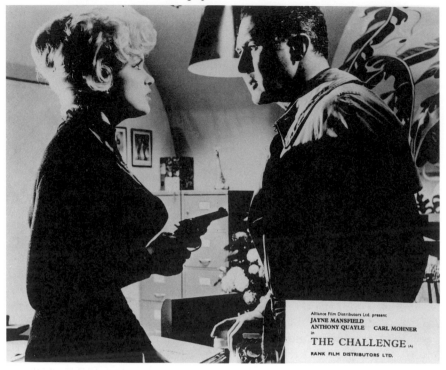

Figure 1.2 Noir tendencies: Jayne Mansfield as the femme fatale and Anthony Quayle
        as the fall guy in *The Challenge* (1960)
Source: British Cinema and Television, Research Group archive, De Montfort University

racketeering on the racecourses and the illegal street-betting industry and
they tended to be shadowy figures who kept well away from the limelight. In
contrast to the spectacular gun battles American gangsters seemed to enjoy,
internecine conflicts in Britain were settled with chivs (taped-down razors)
and broken bottles. Nemesis for a British gangster was more likely to come in
the form of a bottle smashed over his head in a pub toilet than a machine gun
attack on his luxury mansion. British gangsters operated with a casual
brutality – fifties gang leader Billy Hill (1955: 155) cheerfully admits to
torturing lesser criminals to make them reveal their secrets – and there are
hints of such cruelty in *They Made Me a Fugitive*, *Brighton Rock*, *Noose* and
Night and the City. But in terms of iconography their style and methods were
less easy to adapt for the cinema than the guns, cars and high death counts of
American gangsters.

 Ironically the underworld itself was an area particularly susceptible to
Hollywood influences. A local reporter investigating 'Islington's most notorious café' in 1933 found that: 'Nearly every girl was acting a "hard-boiled

Kate" role. Nearly every youth with a very long overcoat and a black hat on the rear of his head, was to himself a "Chicago nut" ' (quoted in Napper 1997: 39). Up and coming thirties gangsters like Jack Spot, Billy Hill and Albert Dimes looked to Hollywood films for style guidance and wore smart suits and hats rather than the mufflers and caps worn by gypsy wide boys like Arthur Skurry and older gang bosses like Alf White and Darby Sabini. Eddie Raimo, chivman for Alf White's Kings Cross mob wore black suits and white ties in imitation of George Raft.

British crime films go back to the early days of cinema (the two films about Sheffield burglar Charles Peace in 1905, for example), but British film-makers attracted to the idea of making gangster films found their task an uphill struggle. As James Robertson shows in Chapter 2, the British Board of Film Censors (BBFC)'s 'chief fear was that the American gangster dramas would spawn equivalents set in Britain' (p. 16, this volume) and the censors did everything in their power to stop it. When film-makers turned to more authentic representations of the underworld in Britain, they faced hostile objections to the use of bad language and the depiction of brutality.

The spiv cycle of the late 1940s can be seen as the first surge of an indigenous British underworld genre. In Chapter 3, Tim Pulleine cites three important influences: Neo-realism, film noir and changes within the English underworld. The influence not only of Italian Neo-realism but of a wider realism apparent in British war-time cinema and American documentary-influenced exposé films, made the serious study of contemporary society a legitimate subject for mainstream feature films. The underworld was not an aspect of British society it was thought healthy for film-makers to dwell upon, but in the 1940s, it had expanded rapidly as war-time disruption increased demand for prostitutes and gambling, and rationing (which continued long after the war was over) and fostered the growth of a black market. Spivs and racketeers entered the public consciousness and inevitably began to appear in films and novels.

Critics argued about whether Robert Hamer's ability to capture realistic detail balanced out the sordid aspects of *It Always Rains on Sunday*'s (1947) low-life milieu, and the mixture of realism and expressionism in *They Made Me a Fugitive* puzzled and alienated them. Arthur Vesselo in *Sight and Sound* (1947: 120), admitted that it was 'horrifyingly well-made' and that 'the atmosphere of London's underworld is all too plausibly conveyed'. But he criticised its director Alberto Cavalcanti – ex-head of the GPO Film Unit and architect of Ealing realism – for 'morbid burrowings' and discerned 'a parade of frustrated violence, an inversion and disordering of moral values, a groping into the grimier recesses of the mind'. Dilys Powell doubly condemned *Night and the City*: not only was it 'squalid and brutal' but Jules Dassin took liberties with London's geographic space, creating a 'never-never city which does service in the cinema for any capital' (*Sunday Times*, 18 June 1950). But sneers at *Night and the City*'s Americanisations were mild compared to the outraged reactions to *No Orchids for Miss Blandish* (St John L. Clowes, 1948), released two years earlier, which even the *Monthly Film Bulletin* considered to be 'the most sickening exhibition of brutality, perversion, sex and sadism ever to be shown on a cinema screen' (1948: 47, April). Brian McFarlane in Chapter 4, investigating the furore around the film, discerns two main reasons for critical distaste. First, the relationship between heiress Miss Blandish and her kidnapper Slim Grisson, which disturbed critics by showing a middle-class woman having a sexual affair with a gangster and enjoying it. Second, the slavishness with which *No Orchids for Miss Blandish* models itself on an American gangster film. This was seen as particularly treacherous at a time when British cinema was struggling to maintain the national identity it appeared to have established during the war.

No Orchids for Miss Blandish and *Night and the City* were treated with such hostility because they were seen as Hollywood incursions. The spiv cycle had secure roots in the particular circumstances of post-war Britain – despite the fact that *They Made Me a Fugitive* was backed by Warners' and William Hartnell and Bill Owen had been promoted as 'the British James Cagney' – and as Pulleine argues in Chapter 3, *Night and the City* could be seen as an attempt by Hollywood to reclaim its own generic property from the threat of appropriation by British cinema.

By the early 1950s, the trends that had shaped the spiv movies had run their course. From the late 1940s to the mid-1950s, the crime rate fell, the police force was built up to its pre-war strength and the underworld settled down as deserters were integrated back into society and full employment and the beginnings of affluence provided alternatives to a life of crime. No doubt the censorship scandal around *Miss Blandish* encouraged the BBFC to keep a tight rein on what was shown, but the dearth of major underworld films in the 1950s seems to have more to do with a studio-dominated insistence on family entertainment as John Davis consolidated his hold on the Rank empire, than a BBFC attempt to screw down the lid on film-makers eager to explore the world of crime.[4]

Robertson claims that, in the 1950s, 'the British film-maker's preoccupation with domestic organised racketeering all but disappeared' (p. 21, this volume). Certainly most of the best-known 1950s crime films – *The Lavender Hill Mob* (Charles Crichton, 1951), *The Ladykillers* (Alexander Mackendrick 1955), *The Long Arm* (Charles Frend, 1956) and *Gideon's Day* (John Ford, 1958) – are either whimsical comedies or celebrations of the Scotland Yard detective rather than serious explorations of the underworld. But Pulleine is not convinced, arguing that although in some ways British crime films re-embraced the status quo, tie-ups with American companies and the import of American stars made the films harder edged than their pre-war counterparts.

Andrew Clay's filmography reveals that more crime films were released in the 1950s than in the previous and subsequent decade and if most of them are B films they still hold considerable thematic interest. The opening premise of Clay's Chapter 5 on troubled masculinity in underworld films between 1946 and 1965 is that crime films used professional crime and men who became involved in it, 'to express men's contradictory experience of power' (p. 51). He sees two main problems being played out: first, the readjustment of ex-servicemen to peacetime society, explored in films ranging from morbid melodramas like *They Made Me a Fugitive* to black comedies like *The League of Gentlemen* (Basil Dearden, 1960); second, the problem of an unsureness by men about how to deal with powerful (and almost inevitably evil) women.

Clay investigates late 1940s films such as *They Made Me a Fugitive*, *Noose*, and *The Flamingo Affair* (Horace Shepherd, 1948), where ex-servicemen come up against black marketeers who have done well out of the war. But he also looks at 1950s films where ex-servicemen continue to find it difficult to come to terms with an increasingly comfortable and affluent society. *Soho Incident* (Vernon Sewell, 1956), for example, transforms Jim Bankley, the hero of *Wide Boys Never Work*, the 1930s novel, on which it is based, from a surly, lazy, criminally inclined Coventry car mechanic, into a brave-hearted Canadian airforceman with too many scruples to thrive in the underworld. He survives, chastened by his experiences, to look forward to a life on the straight and narrow with a good woman. Typically, ex-servicemen seduced into criminal activity by bad women or a sense of adventure (as in *The Flamingo Affair* and *Soho Incident*) get a second chance. Where ex-servicemen team up to use their war-learned experience to commit crime, they pay a heavy price for it. The bands of criminal ex-servicemen in *The Good Die Young* and *A Prize of Arms* all die, as does the psychopathic Jack Havoc in *Tiger in the Smoke* (Roy Baker, 1956) and even the 'League of Gentlemen' looks set for a stint in gaol.

The crime film provided an arena for different types of masculine performance. In Chapter 7, Andrew Spicer argues that one of the reasons why Britain found it difficult to emulate the American gangster film was that there was no British tradition of a tough-guy hero. Instead, British cinema had the gentleman, whose 'métier was restraint, moral authority and the preservation of the status quo' (p. 9). Spicer notes the appearance of tough guys in *Appointment With Crime* (John Harlow, 1946) and *No Way Back* (Stefan Osiecki, 1949), but he points out that the actors who starred in them – William Hartnell and Terence de Marney – became versatile character actors rather than consolidating a tough-guy persona. Trevor Howard's cynical ex-officer in *They Made Me a Fugitive* breaks the rules of society and becomes a criminal (as more innocently does Rex Harrison in *Escape* – Joseph L. Mankiewicz, 1948) but he remains a gentleman and his desire to clear his name links back to earlier struggles for redemption by fallen gentlemen played by Ivor Novello in *Downhill* (Alfred Hitchcock, 1926) and John Clements in *The Four Feathers* (Zoltan Korda, 1938).

When established stars like Trevor Howard or John Mills demonstrated an ability to be tough and ventured into the underworld (as Mills did in *The Long Memory* – Robert Hamer, 1953), they did it as a brief holiday from being

Figure 1.3 A man, a woman and money: an iconic image. Derren Nesbitt shows
        Margaret Whitting the wages of sin in *The Informers* (1963)
Source: British Cinema and Television Research Group archive, De Montfort University

an officer or a gentleman. Throughout the 1950s, the British crime film relied
on minor American stars to play tough guys until robust British actors such as
Stanley Baker emerged to take on these roles. Baker, a working-class Welsh
actor who found it difficult to fit into the middle-class mould required of
British leading men, was cast by American exiles Cy Endfield and Joseph
Losey as a sympathetic crook in *Hell Drivers* (1957) and *The Criminal*, but
Spicer sees his most significant role as that of Inspector Martineau in *Hell is a
City* (Val Guest, 1960), a hard-boiled, disrespectful policeman who can be
seen as a progenitor of John Thaw's Inspector Regan in *The Sweeney*.

   The status of post-war women and the worries this caused are also played
out in crime films, where there is often a contrast between ambitious, materialistic women, whose relations with men are predatory and pecuniary, and
loyal, altruistic women who are honest and faithful. In Chapter 6, Viv
Chadder examines four films – *Good Time Girl* (David Macdonald, 1948),
Yield to the Night (J. Lee Thompson, 1956), *The Flesh is Weak* (Don Chaffey,
1957) and *Passport to Shame* (Alvin Rakoff, 1958) – which focus on women.

Good-time girls, murderesses, prostitutes, fell outside the 'stereotype of nurturing, caring, femininity' (p. 71). When they became the subjects of films it led to interesting contradictions. In *Good Time Girl* Gwen Rawlings defies middle-class norms of femininity – putting pleasure before duty and responsibility – and she is made to suffer for it. But as she is vivacious and likeable and she is pushed along the road to self-destruction by the misguided efforts of an uncomprehending judicial and penal system, she gains our sympathy. *Yield to the Night* is ostensibly an earnest plea for the abolition of hanging but the casting of 'Britain's sex symbol', Diana Dors, and J. Lee Thompson's intrusive directorial style turn the film into a gripping melodrama. Similarly, *The Flesh is Weak* and *Passport to Shame* are fascinating because of the tension between their desire for journalistic authenticity and their temptation into melodramatic excess.

In Chapter 8, the easy dismissal of the genre as escapist melodrama supplies the motivation for Steve Chibnall's defence of the relevance of the crime film to British society in transition. The period in which English New Wave cinema emerged in a blaze of attention (1959–63) also saw the release of record numbers of crime films which quickly disappeared into obscurity. Chibnall argues that, in neglecting these films, critics and historians have overlooked fascinating representations of metropolitan society coping with its passage into the new era of the 1960s. Although most B movies remained largely derivative of American formulae and iconography, feature films like *Hell is a City* opened up new possibilities for British verisimilitude with location shooting and a fresh honesty about place and underworld politics. Films like *Offbeat*, *The Criminal*, *Never Let Go*, *Piccadilly Third Stop* (Wolf Rilla, 1960), *The Informers* and *The Frightened City* document a host of changes in crime and policing occasioned, in part by legislation such as the Street Offences Act (1959) and the Betting and Gaming Act (1960). Beyond their realistic depictions of crime, however, there is a strong sense of anxiety in which fears about 'cultural vulnerability, commercial reorganisation and moral deviation' have been 'displaced into genre cinema and refracted through its conventions' (Chibnall, Chapter 8, p. 108, this volume).

In Chapter 7, Spicer sees the use of a 'generic rather than "realistic" space' in *Hell Drivers* as important in the creation of 'a "frontier" world of gravel pits, chalk quarries, roadhouses and repair yards' (p. 11). And in Chapter 13, Charlotte Brunsdon argues that 'we can discern a fluctuating but persistent, articulation of two kinds of space in the British crime film' (p. 148, this volume). She traces the division between generic space borrowed from Hollywood with the local space of the English location in three films – *It Always Rains on Sunday*, *Night and the City* and *Stormy Monday*. In the narrative of *It Always Rains on Sunday*, the cosy East End community is threatened by the disruptive presence of convict-on-the-run Tommy Swann, but there is also a stylistic challenge to Ealing Studios' realist ethos, particularly in the last part of the film where Tommy is chased and finally trapped in a railway marshalling yard. *Night and the City*, with its American director and stars, is inevitably more Hollywood orientated and Brunsdon explores 'the way in which London is brought to the screen as both a recognisable real city and as a setting for a film noir. *Stormy Monday*, set in Newcastle during 'America Week', addresses the theme of overlapping British and American space directly. The American gangster, Cosmo (Tommy Lee Jones), is confounded in his attempt to buy up the Newcastle waterfront and the heroine played by Melanie Griffith renounces American glamour for English authenticity. But in a Newcastle 'of retro-noir with Hopper colour and a jazz sound track' (Brunsdon, Chapter 13, p. 156, this volume), with a protagonist who reads Hemingway and wants to get back to Minnesota, this is only a very limited victory.

Brunsdon shows that the British underworld film is locked into a permanent struggle with the conventions of the Hollywood gangster genre. Even the period between 1959 and 1963, which might be seen as the heyday of the indigenous British underworld film, is riddled with American influences – Joseph Losey and Sam Wanamaker's contribution to *The Criminal*, John Crawford's improbably Mancunian–American villain in *Hell is a City*, the Cassavetes-influenced improvisatory style of *The Small World of Sammy Lee*. Nevertheless, a coherent and sophisticated genre was beginning to emerge when changes in cinema-programming killed the market for B films and destroyed the genre's foundations. After 1965 it is difficult to find a black and white crime film and even a low-budget exploitation film like Pete Walker's *Man of Violence* (1970) was made in colour as a main feature. Charles Crichton's *He Who Rides a Tiger* might be seen as the last of the breed of tight, no-nonsense, black and white British crime films, though with Tom Bell's superbly edgy performance as a cat burglar, it is innovatory in its unpatronising representation of traditional underworld ethics. Peter Yates' *Robbery*, a fictionalised account of the Great Train Robbery of 1963, left its robbers only sketchily developed and focused its plot on the planning and carrying out of the crime. It was followed by a succession of internationally orientated, semi-comic caper films such as Ronald Neame's *Gambit* (1968), Bryan Forbes' *Deadfall* (1968) and Peter Collinson's *The Italian Job*. More interesting, if less typical, is David Greene's *The Strange Affair* an odd melange of swinging London (Susan George, Barry Fantoni and a flock of white-clad followers of an Indian guru), underworld brutality ('Daddy Quince' and his boys) and an unusually frank depiction of police corruption.

It was more easily dismissed than Nic Roeg and Donald Cammell's *Performance*, which combined underworld and underground more thoroughly and convincingly. Jon Savage's interview with Donald Cammell (see Chapter 9) reveals how Cammell, its scriptwriter and co-director, approached the figure of the gangster as it moved centre-stage in the London of the late 1960s. Cammell talks about the gangster's star persona and status as a champion of the dispossessed and argues for a realistic representation of his 'performance'. This concern with the gangster's masculine performativity is again evident in Michael Caine's compelling portrayal of a criminal hard man in *Get Carter* (released immediately after *Performance*). In Chapter 10, the film's director, Mike Hodges, discusses the politics of *Get Carter*, its relationship to other works in the crime genre and his own work and recalls the revelation of seeing Michael Caine in the part for the first time. Robert Murphy in Chapter 11 notes the renewed interest in *Get Carter* and considers it as an avenger's tragedy in which a wronged protagonist takes revenge on underworld elements who have violated its code of honour.

Get Carter vies with *The Long Good Friday* as the classic British gangster film. But it was not particularly well-received at the time it was released and had no successors. *Villain*, with its old-fashioned plot and irredeemably seedy gangsters is a more relevant model for the only other 1970s crime films of interest – *Sweeney!* (David Wickes, 1977), *The Squeeze* and *Sweeney 2* (Tom Clegg, 1978). These films with their anti-heroes and uncertain moralities all exhibit a cynical pessimism, not only about the administration of justice but also about the failure of Britain as a prosperous and honourable society. Leon Hunt (Chapter 12) demonstrates how the films capture something of the rundown, unreconstructed quality of pre-Thatcherite Britain, but the period between *Get Carter* and *The Long Good Friday* (made in 1979, released in 1981) is a disappointingly thin one for British underworld films and Hunt concludes that '1970s British crime films are too sparse to get much intertextual purchase on, at least without reference to television' (p. 146, this volume).

It was television series like Granada's *Big Breadwinner Hog* (1969), the BBC's *Gangsters* (1976–7) and *Law and Order* (1978), and Euston Films' *Out* (1978) that prepared the way for *The Long Good Friday* and it was only the good offices of George Harrison's HandMade Films that prevented it from being consigned – in a degutted and truncated version – to the small screen. A prescient warning of Thatcherite things to come, *The Long Good Friday*, was a critical and commercial success, but there was a considerable delay before it was followed by a clutch of films that took up its themes and concerns. Mike Hodges's *A Prayer for the Dying* (1988) re-worked the idea of combining gangland with the IRA, though Hodges works in parodic elements, and casts Bob Hoskins against type as an altruistic priest. *Mona Lisa* (Neil Jordan, 1986), *Empire State* (Ron Peck, 1987) and *The Young Americans* (Danny Cannon, 1993) contrast old-style Cockney villains with newer, more ruthless elements, though here they are represented not by the IRA but by a different sort of gangster who has thrown aside the old criminal code and moved into the despised but increasingly lucrative areas of drugs and prostitution.

John Hill in Chapter 14 points out that, with the home market for genre films no longer viable, British cinema, now virtually an adjunct of the television industry, tended to mix and fuse various elements. For the crime film, this led to self-conscious stylisation and an incursion of themes and motifs from art cinema. *The Hit* (Stephen Frears, 1984), for example, overturns conventions, making its hero a man who has turned his back on the criminal code and betrayed his colleagues in return for immunity against prosecution. *Stormy Monday* and *Mona Lisa* delve into depths associated with film noir, but

they end safely and optimistically. For Hill, the gangster film, with its stress on greed, materialism and economic self-interest, was particularly useful for commenting on a society which seemed to be advocating those very values, and non-crime films such as *My Beautiful Laundrette* (Stephen Frears, 1985) and *The Cook, the Thief, his Wife and her Lover* (Peter Greenaway, 1990) borrow elements of the gangster film in their mission to serve as allegories of the state of British society.

After the fall of Mrs Thatcher (in November 1990) and the turn towards a less abrasive style of government, such parallels were less easy to draw. Claire Monk (Chapter 15) argues that changes in business structure – down-sizing, job insecurity, de-skilling – might be expected to find some reflection in gangster films. But the British underworld film never had been strong on organised crime: the criminal empires of Sugiani in *Noose* and Harold Shand in *The Long Good Friday* are ramshackle, one-man-and-a-dog concerns with business plans that look like grandiose fantasies. What she does find is a continuation of the hybridisation of the gangster film. *Shallow Grave* is a Yuppie thriller haunted by elements of an underworld nightmare. *Shopping* (Paul Anderson, 1994) is an attempt to come to terms with contemporary crime – ram-raiding – plagued by post-modern obsessions with designer-label fashion and the need to be cool and enigmatic.

Smalltime (Shane Meadows, 1997) and *Face* – the most recent films Monk deals with – are less eager to escape the conventions of the genre. *Smalltime* is a low-budget film set in Nottingham concentrating on petty crime; *Face* returns to the well-used formula of a gang falling out after carrying out a robbery. What makes them innovatory is their treatment of women. In *Face*, Ray's mother and girlfriend hang on to their ideals and are still fighting for a better society. The ending signifies that Ray may have learnt his lesson and will henceforth work for change within the law. This use of women to represent acceptable values is less satisfactory and adventurous to Monk than the representation of femininity in *Shopping* and *Shallow Grave*, where women are not in any way weaker or less smart than the men, and in *Smalltime* where they turn out to be more resourceful and self-sufficient. In the real underworld it is difficult to imagine any dilution of the tough macho ethos, but it is encouraging to see – thirty years after *Performance* – that ethos being questioned and challenged. The English underworld is no less mean or nasty than it ever was but it continues to provide inspiration for tales of treachery, courage and troubled sexuality which enriches British cinema in at least as fruitful a way as adaptations of Jane Austen and Henry James.

Notes

1 Gifford (1986: 12) defines the crime film as a 'dramatic plot turning on any aspect of crime including mystery, murder, detection, violence'. This is admittedly, a catch-all classification which sweeps both James Bond films and adaptations of Dickens like *Oliver Twist* (David Lean, 1948) into its net.

2   There will occasionally be discrepancies between the dates ascribed to films in the main text – which are release dates – and those given in the filmography, which are their date of registration as a British film.

3   It should be noted that the crime film's relevance is overwhelmingly to English (as opposed to British) metropolitan society.

4   Duncan Webb's exposés of the Messina brothers and other Soho vice racketeers in the *People* indicates that there was still a popular fascination with the sordid underbelly of British society.

Bibliography

Barr, C. (1986) 'Introduction: amnesia and schizophrenia', in C. Barr (ed.) *All Our Yesterdays: 90 Years of British Cinema*, London: BFI.

Ellis, J. (1996) 'The quality film adventure: British critics and the cinema 1942–1948', in A. Higson (ed.) *Dissolving Views: Key Writings on British Cinema*, London: Cassell.

Gifford, D. (1986) *The British Film Catalogue 1895–1985*, London: David & Charles.

Hill, B. (1955) *Boss of Britain's Underworld*, London: Naldrett.

Hill, J. (1986) *Sex, Class and Realism: British Cinema 1956–1963*, London: BFI.

Landy, M. (1991) *British Genres: Cinema and Society 1930–1960*, Princeton N.J.: Princeton University Press.

Napper, L. (1997) 'A despicable tradition: quota quickies in the 1930s', in R. Murphy (ed.) *The British Cinema Book*, London: BFI.

Petley, J. (1986) 'The Lost Continent', in C. Barr (ed.) *All Our Yesterdays: 90 Years of British Cinema*, London: BFI.

Richards, J. (1998) *Films and British National Identity: From Dickens to Dad's Army*, Manchester: Manchester University Press.

Vesselo, A. (1947) 'Films of the quarter', *Sight and Sound* Autumn.

2 The censors and British gangland, 1913–1990

James C. Robertson

The depiction of crime on the screen was, arguably, the most important reason why, in 1913, the British film industry set up the British Board of Film Censors (BBFC). However, it was not until the American gangsterism associated with Prohibition gave rise to films like Mervyn LeRoy's *Little Caesar* (1930), William Wellman's *The Public Enemy* (1931), and Howard Hawks's *Scarface* (1932) that the BBFC was compelled to confront the issue of organised crime in Britain. During the 1930s the BBFC gradually accepted the American gangster genre, and when these films were cut – none was rejected outright – this was for either excessive violence or immorality. The BBFC's chief fear was that the American gangster dramas would spawn equivalents set in Britain, even though no large-scale British organised crime on the American model seems to have existed. The BBFC was also concerned that the British police should not be seen carrying, let alone using, firearms in a British setting. In 1932, under a pre-production system of scenario censorship designed in 1930 and lasting until mid-1949, the BBFC received a scenario entitled *When the Gangs Came to London*. It was based on an Edgar Wallace novel and centred upon London in the grip of Chicago gunmen, with the Metropolitan Police unable to cope before it calls in an American top cop who cleans up the situation. The BBFC opposed this scenario, and a similar fate befell *Soho Racket* and *Public Enemy* in 1934 and 1935, respectively. In all three cases the films were never made (BBFC scenarios 34/1932; 420/1934; 488/1935; Richards 1981: 106–7). No further such scenarios were submitted before 1939, but following a late 1938 House of Commons film censorship debate, the BBFC's previously uncompromising stance was seemingly softened, for in the following year it allowed uncut John Paddy Carstairs's *The Saint in London*, in which the suave Leslie Charteris anti-hero Simon Templar (George Sanders) outwits a London counterfeit gang. This represented a more significant BBFC shift than is immediately apparent, for the film itself was actually shot in London.

How far this new-found tolerance of organised crime in a British setting would have extended at the BBFC is impossible to know, for the gangster film in its traditional form became outdated during the Second World War. From then onwards, American hoodlums invariably worked, sooner or later, for their country's anti-Nazi or anti-Japanese cause. This made life easier for the BBFC, which was faced with few gangster films or scenarios in any setting until the very end of the war. But while the war had removed crime films as a major BBFC problem, except for a tendency towards more brutal personal violence in such films as John Huston's *The Maltese Falcon* (1941) and Stuart Heisler's *The Glass Key* (1942), the period also saw theatrical productions which would influence a revival of the genre during the immediate post-war years. The first of these was the long West End stage run, beginning in 1942, of *No Orchids for Miss Blandish*, an American crime play based upon a James Hadley Chase book, dealing with the abduction of an American heiress by the notorious Grisson gang in 1936 Kansas City. Although the actual film was not made until 1948, the BBFC received a scenario as early as 1944. However, at least here the setting remained American, whereas in 1943 *Brighton Rock*, Graham Greene's pre-war novel dealing with organised crime at the southern seaside resort, was also converted into a play. This had only a short London run, but all the same it provided a pointer to the direction in which post-1945 British crime depiction in the theatre and on screen might head.

The conclusion of the European war in May 1945 ushered in a period of British post-war austerity that did not entirely disappear until the mid-1950s. Many commodities were impossible to obtain or were very highly priced, and although food rationing was eased by stages, it was not abolished until 1954. In consequence, the flashily dressed spivs, the nickname generally applied to those suppliers of rare coveted goods like nylon stockings from dubious sources, prospered (Murphy 1993: 81–91; Chibnall 1985). Moreover, a rise in so-called juvenile delinquency and crimes of personal violence, including murder – all painted in over-sensationalist terms by the popular press – contributed to a general image of increased lawlessness by pre-1939 standards. Before 1939, the BBFC had been much concerned to see that films should demonstrate that crime did not pay, but the post-1945 social scene rendered this policy virtually untenable. The proliferation of spivery showed all too plainly that crime did indeed pay, while the knowledge of profiteering and racketeering, a legacy from the war, was too extensive for their existence to be convincingly ignored.

British film-makers naturally sought to capitalise on these developments within the immediate post-war entertainment boom, and BBFC efforts were concentrated upon keeping in check depictions of violence that were too vivid. As early as March 1945, the BBFC received a scenario entitled *Watch the Lady*, a conventional American gangster film set in London. Significantly, the theme was accepted in principle, and objection was made only to some minor dialogue and a scene in which the gang boss is shot by a British police sergeant (BBFC scenarios 113, 113a/1945). However, the film appears never to have been produced and an early 1946 scenario submitted as *999* confronted in a more head-on way the question of London's organised crime, this time led by a man masquerading as an art dealer famed for his generous philanthropy. It opens with a smash-and-grab raid in which one of the gang is trapped by his wrists in a wire spring blind and is left by two other gang members to be caught by the police, tried and convicted. After he has served his sentence, he kills those who had left him in the lurch, but is again captured by the police. The BBFC took exception to a bottle-throwing incident, a torture scene, hospital operating theatre shots, a scene in which pepper is thrown into a woman's face before her handbag is snatched as a crime capable of imitation, and shots of the police taking a dead man's fingerprints and of a police doctor extracting a bullet from a corpse's head (BBFC scenarios 2, 2a/1946). Most of this material seems to have been omitted at pre-production stage, for on 14 May 1946 the film itself, John Harlow's *Appointment With Crime*, was only slightly cut, although the precise details are no longer available at the BBFC.

Towards the end of the same year the BBFC had to consider two scenarios tackling British organised crime in a blatantly real post-war environment. The lesser one was *South East Five*, concerning a taxi driver who, with the aid of his commando ex-comrades, exposes a black marketeer gang using a dance hall as a front for their activities. Here the BBFC expressed reservations only over the brutal presentation of commando-style unarmed combat (BBFC scenarios 42, 42a/1946). The film was passed uncut as John Paddy Carstairs's *Dancing with Crime*, with Richard Attenborough as the taxi driver. However, the near simultaneous scenario for *A Convict Has Escaped* aimed at even more realism, laced with unprecedented brutality in BBFC terms. In this Clem Morgan, demobilised from the Royal Air Force and unsuccessful in civilian life, turns to a black-market racket run by Narcy (short for Narcissus) who uses a fake funeral parlour as his headquarters and coffins to transport his wares, which include nylons, drink and drugs. Morgan is kept in the dark about the full extent of the gang's activities, and when he learns about the drugs, he wishes to leave the gang. He knows too much for Narcy to allow him to go, and the spiv arranges for his arrest while carrying out one last job in which a policeman is killed. While serving his sentence, Morgan escapes and eventually kills Narcy in a tremendous fist fight among the funeral parlour coffins before being taken back into custody.

This was by far the most authentic gangland script that had ever been submitted to the BBFC. As the censor noted, 'This type of film is not to be encouraged as in my opinion it is far too sordid, but I cannot see on what grounds we can turn it down' (BBFC scenario 41/1946). The point of no return was in prospect, and for this reason the BBFC's scenario comments are worth detailed scrutiny. The recently appointed chief censor, Lieutenant-Colonel A Fleetwood-Wilson, wanted Narcy's beatings-up of two women toned down and reduced to a minimum; the deletion of the words 'bleeding' and 'cocaine' from the dialogue; the excision of the heroine hitting a gang member with a bottle; of Narcy landing a rabbit punch on Morgan's neck and kicking him in the stomach and throat; and of Morgan twisting Narcy's foot back on its pivot and Narcy screaming in agony during their final struggle. He also wanted Narcy to be seen lying in the street at the end rather than being seen all the way down from the roof until he hits the street. Madge Kitchener, the niece of the famous Lord Kitchener, echoed much of Fleetwood-Wilson's abhorrence at the violence and drug references, but she was also concerned about the bad taste entailed in a number of Biblical quotations in the dialogue, and concluded that Morgan's remark, to the effect that he only continued doing what his country had put him into uniform to do, was a disparagement of the armed forces unlikely to assist recruitment. In the event, most of the material objected to by the BBFC was removed from the final film, but the ruthlessness of Narcy was not modified, while the effects of the beatings-up of the two women – one of whom is kicked in the face – were graphically shown. None the less, when *A Convict Has Escaped* became Alberto Cavalcanti's *They Made Me a Fugitive*, the BBFC passed it uncut on 19 June 1947. It was the most vicious portrayal of British gangland yet seen, and it set the pattern for the BBFC's treatment of this genre.

Between the submission of the *A Convict Has Escaped* scenario and the passing of the final film, John and Roy Boulting submitted *Brighton Rock*. This deals with the rivalry between two Brighton racing gangs, one led by the merciless Pinkie Brown (Richard Attenborough famously recreating his 1943 stage role), and their savage methods of dealing with each other and with transgressors from within their own ranks. The BBFC reservations were confined mainly to religious dialogue references and the use of razor blades and vitriol, both of which were considered to be totally unacceptable (BBFC scenarios 55, 55a/1947) and were without precedent in BBFC policy. The Boulting brothers and Graham Greene took the religious objections seriously and altered the script accordingly. The vitriol disappeared, but Pinkie's use of a razor and the razor slash across a victim's cheek were retained. Just the same, *Brighton Rock* was allowed uncut on 23 September 1947 and was released in January 1948 when critic Reg Whitley described it as 'false, cheap, nasty sensationalism' (*Daily Mirror*, 8 January 1948).

In fact, notwithstanding Whitley's outburst, the BBFC had judged the public mood accurately, for *They Made Me a Fugitive* and *Brighton Rock* aroused little criticism from the local authorities, who possessed the legal censorship powers, from the critics or from the general public. Thus the way lay open for more of the same. In December 1947 a scenario had been submitted for *Noose*, a Richard Llewellyn play that had run in the West End for several months. Millie Sharp, one of gang leader Sugiani's night-club dancing girls, is found drowned in the River Thames. Her friend Annie Foss suspects that Sugiani is behind the murder and confides her suspicion to Linda Medbury, an American journalist, who determines to expose him in an article. During the ensuing events, the Sugiani gang is smashed and Sugiani himself is killed by one of his own mob after much activity involving beatings-up and torture.

By now a theme of unremitting gang violence scarcely raised a ripple at the BBFC. Fleetwood-Wilson was more worried that one of the female characters should not be seen in her underwear, although he also drew attention

Figure 2.1 To cut or not to cut? The razor slashing of Pinky Brown (Richard
Attenborough) by a rival gang of racecourse racketeers in *Brighton Rock*
(1948) causes a problem for the censor

Source: British Cinema and Television Research Group archive, De Montfort University

to the possibility of undue brutality, either in sound or vision, during the
beating-up and torture sequences. Madge Kitchener's remarks ran along much
the same lines, although she also did not wish for an over-emphasis on the
unsavoury details of the dead Millie or on Annie's distress when she identified
Millie's corpse (BBFC scenarios 112, 112a/1947). In the event, Edmond
Greville's completed film did not initially satisfy the BBFC, for it was
amended and then, unusually, seen by BBFC President Sir Sidney Harris and
Assistant Secretary Arthur Watkins. But the film contains more comedy and
less brutality than the play and it was passed without further cuts on 9 July
1948. This unnecessarily cautious BBFC treatment of relatively inoffensive
material compared to *They Made Me a Fugitive* and *Brighton Rock* is accounted
for by the furore that had erupted around St John L. Clowes's *No Orchids for
Miss Blandish* during the previous April, when the BBFC had conducted a
humiliating public retreat in the face of militant Watch Committees.
Significantly when *Noose* was released in October 1948, it suffered no repeti-
tion of the *No Orchids* uproar, indicating that by then the critics and public
alike had come to accept Britain's gangland as a valid screen topic.

Inside the BBFC, the *No Orchids* affair cast a long shadow, inducing an ultra-caution not far short of panic over crime films in general. Even the innocuous *Uneasy Terms*, Vernon Sewell's disastrous attempt at a private eye movie with Michael Rennie as Peter Cheyney's Slim Callaghan, had one reel overhauled before being allowed on 24 May. Such craven circumspection still prevailed at the BBFC almost a year later when Ealing Studios submitted its scenario for its celebrated homage to the Metropolitan Police, *The Blue Lamp*, directed by Basil Dearden. Fleetwood-Wilson's criticisms were centred entirely upon dialogue, eroticism and violence. Words such as 'tart' and 'bastard' were deplored; two murders with a revolver at close range, including that of the hero, PC George Dixon (Jack Warner), ought to be toned down; Tom Riley (Dirk Bogarde), the chief villain, should not be seen beating a middle-aged man into unconsciousness or slipping his hand inside girl-friend Diana's dress to feel her heartbeats or bending her over towards the bed. Diana's father should not be seen either hitting his wife with a leather belt or slapping her hard across the face. A child's question to a policeman when the revolver that was used to kill Dixon is found, 'Will you be able to hang him now?' should be deleted; and the jeweller, Jordan, should not be seen in bed with his girlfriend (BBFC scenario 55/1949). Assistant censor Frank Crofts, soon destined to be Fleetwood-Wilson's successor, commented in much the same vein and went on to remark:

> As the company is to have police co-operation, one can reasonably hope for a factual treatment, without sensationalism. It would be disastrous to treat the dangerous subject of adolescent criminals with any glamour. On the other hand, whilst it is necessary to show the criminals as mean, cowardly sneak-thieves, there should not be much emphasis on cruelty towards women: and though the background is sordid, there should not be any prostitution or eroticism.
>
> (BBFC scenario 55a/1949)

The shooting script submitted in June 1949 took account of most of the BBFC's scruples, although the two deaths by shooting were retained, as was the child's question about hanging (ibid.). In this form, the completed film was allowed through uncut on 3 November and went on to be the top British box office hit of 1950.

During the first half of the 1950s austerity slowly gave way to affluence. The figure of the spiv vanished, rationing was abolished, and ownership of television sets became more widespread. Crime continued to be a problem, especially during the 'cosh boy' panic of 1952–3, but it was a problem that society found itself more able to accept than in the immediate post-war years. One result was a reduction in the number of crime films as the British film-makers' preoccupation with domestic organised racketeering all but disappeared. At the BBFC the pre-production scenario system had been discontinued under Watkins's secretaryship. This, coupled with a clear-out of BBFC files ordered by Stephen Murphy after he became Secretary in mid-1971, has sometimes made it difficult to trace the censorship of what few crime films in a British setting there were at this time. For instance, Lewis Gilbert's *The Good Die Young* (1954), the tale of four crooks all with personal problems who set out to rob a mail van, was cut on 18 February 1954, but there is now no BBFC file to tell us what was removed and why.

However, there is some evidence of a slight relaxing of censorship in the films themselves. For example, the BBFC's dislike of the use of firearms by the police did not prevent them being seen to fire back at IRA terrorists in *The Gentle Gunman* (Basil Dearden, 1952). By the later 1950s, strip clubs were proliferating in the main British city centres, pornography became easier to obtain and prostitutes paraded in larger numbers in the so-called red-light areas such as Soho, with the result that some of these developments were mirrored in British films, desperately struggling after 1955 to fight off the competition from commercial television. In 1959 the government passed the Street Offences Act, which made it a crime for prostitutes to solicit for custom in public, and one film that exploited this new situation was John Lemont's *The Shakedown*, made before the year was out and released in January 1960. In this, Terence Morgan plays a vice king who can no longer run prostitutes on the street and turns instead to having prominent people photographed in compromising sexual situations as a means of blackmailing them. This was slightly cut in November 1959 to remove shots of girls' naked breasts, a strange event in that the BBFC had abandoned its 'no nudity' policy in the previous year after a long battle with the local authorities over Max Nozzeck's naturist film, *The Garden of Eden*. The year 1960 saw the release of Joseph Losey's *The Criminal*, up to then the most relentlessly savage depiction of both British prison and underworld life. It features Stanley Baker as an underworld figure who after one stretch in prison robs a race track, is then betrayed by his scorned ex-girlfriend and returns to prison after burying the £40,000 loot. There he comes under pressure from other criminals who arrange his escape to learn the whereabouts of the money before killing him. Apart from the unceasing grimness of the theme, there are several violent scenes, including Baker's use of a knuckle-duster on the face of another prisoner in a cell fight and of handcuffs to beat a prison warder over the head in a van during the escape sequence, yet the only BBFC cut in May 1960 was the drastic reduction of an early beating-up scene in a prison cell.

This relaxation of previous BBFC policy had come about due to the more liberal reign of Secretary John Trevelyan from 1957 to 1971 (Trevelyan 1973), but during the so-called 'Swinging Sixties' British gangland films were few and far between. However, towards the end of the decade there were stark reminders that the British underworld remained alive and well in London. These were the highly publicised trials of first the notorious Richardson mob, to whom the use of sadistic torture was almost routine, and then in 1969 of the Kray twins, protection racketeers who received 30-year sentences for murder. This development, coupled with the regularity of television crime series, revived the interest of film-makers in British gangland and gave rise to a number of 1970s movies. The best of these was Mike Hodges's *Get Carter* (1971), in which Michael Caine stars as Jack Carter, a London racketeer who travels to Newcastle to investigate the death of his brother Frank. He finds and kills the gangsters who murdered Frank but is then himself killed. Hodges's film was presented to the BBFC on 30 October 1970. Sex and violence were much in evidence, two scenes in particular arousing concern. The first was one in which Jack's mistress Anna (Britt Ekland) caresses herself and writhes on a bed while Jack talks sexily to her on the telephone. This included shots filmed from the bottom of the bed showing her with her legs open. The second scene involved the screening of a pornographic film in which Frank's girlfriend (Dorothy White) undresses and makes love to Frank's teenage daughter (Petra Markham). In both instances the BBFC pressed for reduction to an absolute minimum. Thereupon Hodges cut them, but Trevelyan and censor Ken Penry viewed the shortened versions several times before finally allowing the film through. However, so much sex and violence remained that critic Ernest Betts in *The People* (14 March 1971) was moved to wonder why the BBFC had ever passed the film at all.

The genesis of the Dick Clement/Ian La Frenais script for Michael Tuchner's *Villain* (1971) lay in the James Barlow book *The Burden of Proof*. In a clear reference to Ronnie Kray, this centred upon Vic Dakin, a homosexual East End gang boss with a mother fixation (Richard Burton), and had been presented to Trevelyan in book form as early as April 1968 in the aftermath of the Richardson gang trial. Then, Trevelyan had listed several potential areas of BBFC anxiety centring upon Dakin's psychopathic preoccupation with violence towards others and the excitement he experiences therefrom; the use of knuckle-dusters with razor blades or nails embedded in plaster of Paris; the depiction of Dakin's open homosexuality with Wolfe Lissner (Ian McShane); and the heterosexual element during a party attended by MP Gerald Draycott (Donald Sinden) and Lissner's girlfriend. The script eventually arrived in September 1970 when Trevelyan again raised many objections. These included the excessive violence of an early scene in which one of Dakin's victims is kneed in the crotch and then razor slashed; dialogue referring to the cutting off of the victim's testicles with a razor; the use of knuckle-dusters and ammonia by Dakin and his gang in a robbery sequence; the use of a rolled-up magazine as a phallic symbol in a strip-club scene; shots of Draycott and Lissner's girlfriend copulating naked inter-cut with shots of Dakin's beating-up of the strip-club owner, which too blatantly linked sex with violence; and Dakin's pumping four bullets into a sick man at the end.

Much of this material was eliminated before filming but retained were Dakin's open homosexuality with Lissner; the early kneeing in the crotch and razor slashing (unseen); subsequent vague dialogue referring to the widespread use of the razor all over that victim's body; the use of ammonia in the robbery; Dakin's beating-up of the strip-club owner with a knuckle-duster; the frequent use of clubs and truncheons by the gang; and the four bullet wounds. On 22 March 1971 the BBFC nevertheless passed the film with only

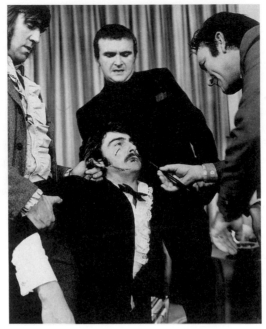

Figure 2.2 'Excessive violence':Vic Dakin (Richard Burton) threatens a croupier with
     another cut in *Villain* (1971)
Source: British Cinema and Television Research Group archive, De Montfort University

one minor cut (in Dakin's brandishing the razor before the face of his
intended victim).

In 1976, soon after Trevelyan's successor, Stephen Murphy, had been
replaced by James Ferman (Phelps 1975), British gangland reappeared with
Michael Apted's *The Squeeze*. This is the story of an alcoholic ex-policeman
(Stacy Keach) who rescues his ex-wife and her daughter by her second
husband from kidnappers led by David Hemmings. The emphasis lies upon
unpleasant detail, and as BBFC examiner Rosemary Stark noted (14 October
1976):

> There is a tough realism about the action (and the dialogue) which
> demands an 'X' classification. This certificate also covers scenes of Jim's
> (the ex-policeman) pathetic alcoholic degradation, particularly in a scene
> where he is beaten up and at the mercy of a couple of villains who pay
> him off and send him home naked, and a horrifying scene of his with-
> drawal treatment in the addiction clinic. The kidnapping scenes,
> particularly one in which the gang throw the girl's dog from a car, also
> demand an adult classification. There is a scene in which the gang force

Jill (the ex-wife) to strip for their amusement....The sex scenes are, however, mild within the 'X' category and totally non-exploitative.

Ferman and Penry, now chief censor, agreed, so that the film was passed uncut, after the production company had agreed to accept the 'X' classification rather than cuts for the less severe 'AA', on 14 October 1976.

The most striking 1980s offering in this genre was John Mackenzie's *The Long Good Friday*, in which Bob Hoskins as ruthless East End gang leader Harold Shand finds his position under threat by outside attacks while he is trying to set up a property deal with American mobsters. The source of these attacks is unknown, but they eventually turn out to be the work of the IRA. There is much vicious and bloodthirsty detail, including the tying up of rival gang leaders upside down in an abattoir and a bottle blow to the neck that produces a fountain of blood. The production company, Black Lion/Calendar, was a subsidiary of ITC, the media group headed by Lord Grade, and when the film was completed in mid-1980, it turned out to be so good that the company wished to clean up the language, tone down the violence and dilute the dubious politics so that it could be launched as a television special. The BBFC was prepared to allow it through uncut, and indeed Ferman contacted Lord Grade to persuade him that no cuts be made so that it could be shown in cinemas. Whether or not Ferman's influence in this direction was decisive is unknown, but the film was retained for the cinema and was passed uncut on 2 February 1981. It may have been no coincidence that in the same year the Kray brothers, still languishing in prison, were reportedly attempting to arrange for a film to be made based upon their lives. This project encountered various obstacles before it finally came to fruition in the form of Peter Medak's *The Krays* in 1990. Made with the brothers' co-operation, it did not shrink from graphic violence. Shown to the BBFC, now the British Board of Film Classification (since 1985), in a rough cut, the film contains a scene in which Ronnie Kray pushes a sabre into a man's mouth until it reaches an ear, a real-life Kray trademark. The sight of the slow cutting action movement and the resulting blood seen from behind the victim's head was objected to and reduced, and the shot of the same man with a slashed 'smile' on his face removed altogether, still at rough cut stage, so that in this form the BBFC allowed the film, the first to be based directly upon the 'careers' of actual living gangsters.[1]

The foregoing account does not aspire to a comprehensive analysis of British underworld movies, but it appears that this genre has mostly concerned itself with mobster rivalry, the police usually being background figures to gang warfare. In the immediate post-1945 years the interests of social realism compelled the BBFC to accept the screen existence of the British underworld. Once the principle of British gangland films had been conceded, the BBFC concentrated upon controlling the genre's depiction of sex and violence, although the frontiers of screen brutality and sexuality have themselves been steadily pushed forward.

Note

1   *McVicar* (Tom Clegg, 1980) and *A Sense of Freedom* (John Mackenzie, 1981) were slightly different in being based on the careers of reformed criminals.

Bibliography

Chibnall, S. (1985) 'Whistle and zoot: the changing meaning of a suit of clothes', *History Workshop* 20: 56–81.

Murphy, R. (1993) *Smash and Grab: Gangsters in the London Underworld 1920–60*, London: Faber and Faber.

Phelps, G. (1975) *Film Censorship*, London: Victor Gollancz.

Richards, J. (1981) 'The British Board of Film Censors and content control in the 1930s: images of Britain', *Historical Journal of Film, Radio and Television* 1, 2: 106–7.

Trevelyan, J. (1973) *What the Censor Saw*, London: Michael Joseph.

3   Spin a dark web

Tim Pulleine

The City is of Night; perchance of Death,/But certainly of Night.
(James Thomson (1834–1882), *The City of Dreadful Night*)

In the context of British cinema of the 1930s, the term thriller denotes works that, whatever their individual qualities, tend towards artificiality and operate at a considerable remove from the realities of criminal activity. The predominant influences in this cinema were the popular writers of earlier in the century, such as Edgar Wallace, whose *The Ringer* was filmed in 1931 and again, as *The Gaunt Stranger*, in 1938, and A.E.W. Mason, whose *House of the Arrow* reached the screen in both 1930 and 1940.

Espionage, or at least pseudo-espionage, also provided a recurring theme, particularly in the pre-war films of Alfred Hitchcock, and for obvious reasons such a preoccupation, with a more marked patriotic inflection, manifested itself in the thrillers of the war years. Occasionally a British film would concern itself with 'everyday' crime, a noteworthy example being *They Drive By Night* (1938), but in general, pressures of censorship served to reinforce a cultural climate that ensured that such undertakings were exceptions to prove the prevailing rule.

After the war, matters were different. In the cinema at large, Neo-realism was exerting an influence not simply in location filming, but also in subject matter, and what has subsequently come to be dubbed film noir was a pervasive presence, especially in the crime melodrama. In British society, where film-going reached an all-time high in 1946, the cries about a New Jerusalem that had greeted Labour's 1945 election victory were echoing ever more distantly amid a reality of shortages, rationing and the proliferating black market, profitably presided over by the 'spivs'. The black market, which had taken root during the war, changed the popular perception of criminality and may have served to dissipate the notion of the criminal as belonging to an obscure separate caste.

During the latter 1940s, a group of films was produced in Britain that have come to be referred to in critical shorthand as spiv movies, although the centrality of the spiv figures varies from one to another. The films discussed here – in what does not purport to be a comprehensive account of the sub-genre – were generally given a cool reception by the critical establish-ment (and in some instances an overtly hostile one), but they proved successful at the box-office. If the nocturnal half-world that they conjured up reflected the anxiety and disillusion of the post-war age of austerity, it also ambiguously embodied the urge to escape from that era's chafing restraints.

Dancing With Crime (1947, screenplay Brock Williams, director John Paddy Carstairs) is explicitly about post-war transition. 'Civvy Street seems pretty strange to some of the boys', opines an avuncular Scotland Yard man, and the film's taxi driver protagonist (Richard Attenborough) is, in a neatly assimilated touch of symbolism, seen on more than one occasion still wearing battledress (as many ex-service working men in fact did at a time when clothing and cash were in short supply). Where Attenborough is struggling to make a go of things, his war-time comrade (Bill Owen) has taken a short cut ('A bit of this and that – no coupons, no questions') and is entangled with a gang whose robbery and black market operations are run from a South London palais de danse. When Owen is shot by his double-crossing confederates, suspicion falls on Attenborough, and the rest of the story concerns the latter's efforts to clear his name by exposing the crooks.

Apart from being about transition, *Dancing With Crime* is itself a transitional movie. Aspects remain of a somewhat juvenile comedy–thriller in the 'amateur sleuth' tradition, particularly in the tongue-in-cheek sub-plot in which the hero's plucky girlfriend (Sheila Sim) gets a job at the dance hall in a quest for evidence. At the same time, the film signifies a break with the more genteel past, aptly reflected in the casting against type of Barry K. Barnes, best known as the suave hero of films like *This Man Is News* (1938), as the hard-bitten chief executive of the crime ring. A comparable effect, as a harbinger of changing times, is afforded by the brief appearance of Diana Dors as one of the hostesses, making ribald small talk as she props up the bar. More significantly, the episodes of brutality – Attenborough decoyed by thugs to an empty warehouse; the gang's despatch of an unreliable subordinate, run down by a heavy lorry; the prolonged climactic set-to – are more graphic and detailed than audiences for a British film at this time might reasonably have expected. The picture's disparate elements are held together by the skill of its realisation: the pastiche of American crime melodrama is, particularly in the exposition of the criminal enterprise's chain of command, conspicuously accomplished, and the brio of the elaborate boom shots around the palais affords the viewer a pleasurable sense of complicity.

This form of cinematic expertise is absent from *Night Beat* (1947, screen-play T. J. Morrison, Roland Pertwee and Robert Westerby, director Harold Huth), but the film touches several of the same nerves. The ex-service theme reappears – the first shot shows a lorry full of demobbed soldiers, bearing the slogan 'Civvy Street Special' – allied here to the narrative premise of long-time friends who wind up on opposite sides of the law. Hector Ross and Ronald Howard play ex-commandos who seek to recapture camaraderie and a sense of purpose by joining the police. This proves a forlorn hope for

Howard, who soon quits in favour of shadier pursuits. In a lurid but less than convincing sequence of events, he is framed by a jealous rival, emerges from jail bent on revenge, and becomes chief suspect when the rival is inopportunely murdered by his mistress. Quota quickie dialogue ('It's no use − I'm in this too deep') only serves to underscore the ramshackle construction, but the film intermittently manages to convey a whiff of authentic tawdriness. This is primarily due to the characterisation of the racketeer (Maxwell Reed), prospering on 'grog shops and swindle clubs'. Where the villains of *Dancing With Crime* − Barnes and his outwardly ultra-respectable boss (Barry Jones) − have no specific contemporaneity, Reed is unmistakably the spiv, replete with flash clothes, a lavishly decorated flat and a ready line in spiel ('Manual labour − who's he, a Spanish dancer?'). He is aptly complemented by Christine Norden, who, smothered in make-up and costume jewellery, purveys an anaconda-like sensuality as his inamorata-cum-nemesis. It is these figures who stay in the memory after the laborious plot has faded from mind.

Somewhat similar considerations apply to *Noose* (1948, screenplay Richard Llewellyn and Edward Dryhurst, director Edmond T. Gréville), which, though it boasts a more accomplished surface, contains a comparably uneasy melange of elements. An opened-out adaptation of a successful play, the film retains a theatrical tenor. The nominal leads are Carole Landis and Derek Farr as journalists cast in the smart-talking mould of Hollywood B pictures. After Landis gets vital evidence against a vice lord, the latter threatens retaliation, and in a frankly incredible sub-plot, Farr's sportswriter − again, a newly demobbed commando − raises a private army from among his boxing associates to put paid to the mobsters, with the police (led by, of all people, Stanley Holloway) bringing up the rear for a mopping-up operation.

Here, too, the distinctiveness tends to reside in the depiction of the underworld heavies. The film's approach to this is bifurcated. On the one hand, Nigel Patrick's Bar Gorman is an overtly comic characterisation: he maintains a stream of Cockney locutions of the 'Keep your 'air on' and 'Use your loaf' variety as he juggles deals in petrol coupons and counterfeit money. However, his boss, Sugiani, is far from a laughing matter. As played by Joseph Calleia, he cuts a figure somewhat evocative of the then notorious vice magnate Eugenio Messina, and it is a testament to Calleia's performance that the allusion is only slightly blunted by contemporary censorship's proscription of direct references to prostitution. Sugiani's depredations are on a sizeable scale and there is a Jacobean tinge to his dealings with the 'Barber' (Hay Petrie), his right-hand man and periodic assassin; it is at the hands of this slighted figure rather than at those of the law that he ultimately meets his fate.

Visually, *Noose* is a work of some sophistication. The upside-down effect created at the outset by a shot of a reflection in a puddle introduces a recurring motif; later a sense of disequilibrium is maintained via the inverted reflections of Landis in a cocktail-cabinet mirror and of performers at Sugiani's club in the mirror-like dance floor. Linking with this pattern of association, the figurative smashing of Sugiani's enterprises by the 'commando' team finds physical expression at the conclusion in the depiction of Gorman's arrest as seen reflected in the shattered mirrors in his office. The final scene picks up on the same notion in humorous fashion, effecting an ironic sense of closure by showing Farr and Landis picking their way through the broken glass that litters the ground in the wake of the climactic affray.

Such elaborations suggest that with a more integrated script, the Frenchman, Gréville, might have fashioned a notable British addition to the canon of film noir. In the event, that distinction fell to an even more cosmopolitan figure, the Brazilian-born Alberto Cavalcanti, who had, more paradoxically still, worked with John Grierson in the pre-war documentary movement. *They Made Me A Fugitive* (1947, screenplay Noel Langley, director Cavalcanti) is British cinema's most elaborate, as well as most expressionistic, study of post-war malaise. The film's chief heavy is Narcy (Griffith Jones), a self-professed exponent of 'free enterprise', who operates from behind the cover of a funeral parlour, at which arrive coffins stuffed with nylons and contraband cigarettes, together with packets of 'sherbet' (illegal drugs). Set briefly alongside him is Clem (Trevor Howard), an ex-RAF officer and prisoner of war ('I gave up [killing] when it went out of season'), now sunk in booze, whose upper-class accent and manner Narcy condescendingly claims will be good for business. However, Clem's aversion to drug peddling, and Narcy's coveting of Clem's current girlfriend, leads, in a plot manoeuvre reminiscent of *Night Beat*, to Narcy framing Clem for manslaughter and getting him railroaded into jail. The story's third principal figure is a chorus girl (Sally Gray), who after being jilted by Narcy, rallies to Clem's aid as part of a scheme of revenge. This leads to her being brutally beaten up by Narcy, an episode treated obliquely but at some length, and there is no mistaking the fact that Narcy (like Sugiani in *Noose*) derives satisfaction from violence against women. His victim's judgement is a telling one: 'He's not even a respectable crook, just cheap, rotten, after-the-war trash'.

The narrative concerns Clem's escape from jail and subsequent attempts to evade the law long enough to exact revenge and clear his name. The formulation of the plot, not just in terms of Clem's being pursued by both police and underworld, but in the sense of his being ensnared by a malign concatenation of events (typically, a woman who is prepared to aid his getaway wants him to kill her husband in return), is pre-eminently noir, and so is the film's stylistic apparatus. The sets might have been designed at Ufa in the 1920s; the action occurs almost entirely at night; and incidental details provide ironic counterpoint, as in the glimpse of the musical comedy in which the heroine is appearing, with its carefree couples waltzing in evening dress. Moreover, the spectator is denied the release of a happy ending: Clem catches up with Narcy, but the latter falls off a roof, subsequently swearing to the attendant police with his dying breath that Clem was guilty all the time. The conclusion does, however, hold out a longer-term prospect of justice being done. The closing exchange redoubles the film's sardonic tone by localising it in the bureaucratic realities of British life. As Clem is hustled into a police car, the

Figure 3.1 'A malign concatenation of events': The trade advertisement for
         Cavalcanti's expressionist *They Made Me A Fugitive* (1947)
Source: British Cinema and Television Research Group archive, De Montfort University

sympathetic detective (Ballard Berkeley) who has been on his track tells him
that the case may now be referred back. 'How many forms will you have to
fill in?' asks Howard, to receive the resigned reply: 'Millions'.

Narcy's expiring on a note of vengeful mendacity might summon up the
universe of Graham Greene, and the screen version of his 1938 novel *Brighton
Rock* (1947, screenplay Graham Greene and Terence Rattigan, director John
Boulting), the story of the last days in the life of Pinkie, youthful leader of a
protection gang (scarifyingly played by Richard Attenborough), also possesses
a noir coloration. With hindsight awareness of Greene's subsequent cultural
standing, the film may tend now to be viewed in the context of literary adaptation, but it does not seem to have been primarily perceived in that light at
the time, and the intention to annex it to the gangster genre was rendered
unambiguous in the American release title of *Young Scarface*. It may be that the
Catholic and metaphysical concerns of the original are simplified in the translation, though the satisfying melodrama that remains is fuelled by
crypto-religious imagery. Pinkie's symbolic fall from the pier at the conclusion is foreshadowed by the episode in which the stool pigeon is pushed to
his death from a high balustrade, descending into the basement of the lodging
house as if into hell itself. At any rate, the configuration of the drama centrally
draws upon this area of cinematic tradition, not least in the character of the
drink-sodden lawyer (Harcourt Williams) who affords Pinkie his professional

advice. It is a felicitous coincidence that this figure should be furnished with a quotation from *Doctor Faustus* – 'Why, this is hell, nor am I out of it' – which, in more extended form Greene had invoked in his 1937 review of the Hollywood gangster film *Marked Woman* (Greene 1972: 166). While locations are effectively used in the story's earlier stages, the film's increasing interiority, and the sense it communicates of being trapped within its malign protagonist's psyche, provide its motive power, and render to a large degree irrelevant (other than in public relations terms) the insistence in a prefatory caption that the action occurs in a pre-war Brighton that has long since disappeared.

A notional Brighton locale that is fixed in the post-war era is to be found in the latter stages of *Good Time Girl* (1948, screenplay Muriel and Sydney Box and Ted Willis, director David Macdonald), where Griffith Jones, as thoroughgoingly spivlike as in *They Made Me a Fugitive*, organises the peddling of black market whisky and nylons from the salons of the Silver Slipper Club. Makeshift in its production values, *Good Time Girl* is closer to the social problem genre than the crime story in its recounting of the downward progress of a disadvantaged teenager (Jean Kent). The pseudo-social conscience angle is rendered the more pronounced in that the narrative is framed as an awful warning delivered by a magistrate to a might-be delinquent (Diana Dors again: the casting, at least retrospectively, manages to nullify some of the implicit smugness). The film does, however, contain a colourful gallery of low-life types, not least Peter Glenville's incarnation of Jimmy the Waiter, vain and malevolent, and in appearance, with his striped suit, brilliantined hair and pencil moustache, the epitome of the small-time spiv. It is he who obtains for the heroine employment of a sort ('No wages, a share of the tips') as a skimpily costumed hat-check girl in a dubious West End club. The glimpses of life in this milieu, along with the later scenes of booze-fuelled hedonism in Brighton, convey the lure of escape from the drab confines of austerity Britain, and do so all the more strikingly, perhaps, for seeming not to be artistically 'placed' by the film's makers.

Since both derive from novels by Arthur La Bern, *Good Time Girl* can be bracketed with the Ealing production *It Always Rains on Sunday* (1947, screenplay Robert Hamer, Henry Cornelius and Angus Macphail, director Robert Hamer), though the latter possesses considerably more cinematic finesse. Hamer is one of British cinema's small number of auteurs, and his work in a variety of genres is characterised by a vision that is at once ironic and deterministic. These qualities manifest themselves here in the film's delineation of the situation of Rose (Googie Withers), a working-class East End housewife whose former lover, Tommy Swann (John McCallum), is an outwardly smooth but violent criminal. The flashback to their past relationship is introduced in quintessentially Hamerian fashion, using a mirror in a way that echoes the director's 'Haunted Mirror' episode in *Dead of Night* (1945), and contriving to make the gilt-and-plush pub where Rose worked as a barmaid into an expressive alternative world to that of her stifling latter-day domesticity; sociologically, the effect can be read in much the same way as the club scenes in *Good Time Girl*.

The substantive narrative treats Swann's return to home ground after breaking out of jail, and his betrayal of Rose's lingering romantic belief in him. At the climax, he assaults and robs her, before being hunted down by the police in the grimly geometric surroundings of a railway marshalling yard. The double-edged thrust of the film (escape/suppression) is enhanced by the wryly detailed observation of the scenes of Rose's life with her older husband (Edward Chapman) and his two daughters. Given that George Orwell's essay 'Decline of the English Murder' was originally published in 1946, with its subsequently oft-quoted evocation of *News of the World* culture − 'You put your feet up on the sofa…the fire is well alight.…What is it you want to read about? Naturally about a murder' − the view of Chapman settling himself on the couch with his Sunday newspaper might almost assume a self-reflexive dimension, with Swann representing (in Orwell's terms) a latter-day perversion of 'traditional' criminality (Orwell 1965: 9). As a further cross-reference, it might be noted that Orwell contrasts the 'traditional' English murder (as typified by the Crippen or Maybrick cases) with the 1944 'Cleft Chin' case, whose 'background was not domesticity but the anonymous life of the dance halls and the false values of the American film', and that it was this same case that indirectly provided the basis, albeit that the correspondence is diluted in the screen adaptation, for the novel from which *Good Time Girl* derived.

While Rose's dreams of hedonistic escape are buried at the end of *It Always Rains on Sunday*, Googie Withers was to return to a more expensive realm of bright lights and hucksterism in what is in more ways than one the culminating film of the cycle. In *Night and the City* (1950, screenplay Jo Eisinger, director Jules Dassin), Withers has a role whose trajectory more expressionistically echoes that of Rose in the previous film. Her character, Helen, plans to escape from her possessive older husband, club owner Nosseros (Francis L. Sullivan), by starting up a rival business. In ironic counterpoint, her scheme to make use of expatriate tout Fabian (Richard Widmark) to this end is balanced by his making use of her, or at least of her money, in pursuit of a bigger plan to muscle in on the fight game, which involves double-crossing the all-powerful promoter Cristo (Herbert Lom).

The reverberant title of *Night and the City* evokes the sub-genre's two predominant motifs, and the introductory images of central London by night echo the credit sequences of both *Dancing With Crime* and *They Made Me a Fugitive*. Produced in Britain by the Hollywood company 20th Century Fox, the movie has considerable technical resources, and not least through the agency of Franz Waxman's score, its intense style conjures up a frenetic universe. In Nosseros's club, the song with which the well-heeled pleasure seekers are regaled is a hymn to oblivion: 'Here's to the wine.…Drink till the daylight is dawning'. With fitting irony, it is in the grey light of dawn that the story reaches its grim conclusion, with Helen broke and defeated, and Fabian dead at the hands of Cristo's tame thug, 'the Strangler'.

The relationship between Fabian and the club's singer Mary (Gene Tierney), despairingly loyal to him even as she sees the prospect of marriage and stability recede, is introduced in a scene in which he seeks to steal the money she has set aside for their future together. In due course, he does make off with it, and at the nihilistic climax he endeavours to repay her by trying to persuade Cristo that Mary has fingered him and should be paid the price that Cristo has put on his head. In the three-cornered dealings between Nosseros, his wife, whom he refers to as 'bought and paid for,' and Fabian, she is unambiguously sexual in her efforts to enlist the tout in her scheme to throw over her husband and set herself up in business, using funds stolen from Nosseros. When the latter (to whom his wife's remarks seem in coded form to ascribe impotence) discovers the truth of the matter, his jealousy takes the form of his hatching a plot to bring Cristo's wrath down upon Fabian. And when Helen leaves her husband, he assures her that she will soon want to come back, then murmurs to himself with characteristic perversity, 'And I'll want you back'.

Beneath its graphic, fast-talking surface, *Night and the City* is borne along by a diversity of cultural allusions. Partly these are English: Nosseros (played by the actor who was Jaggers in the 1946 film of *Great Expectations*) is presented with his highly cadenced utterances as a Dickensian figure, and a mock-Shakespearean reference might be perceived in his assertion to Cristo that Fabian is 'not an honourable man'. Additionally, there is a wider debt to German theatre and cinema: if the army of beggars and thieves that Cristo mobilises to hunt for Fabian is a device reminiscent of the Brecht–Weill *Die Dreigoschenoper* (1928; filmed 1931), then the narrative ploy of the underworld combining to track down a troublesome member of its own recalls Fritz Lang's *M* (1931).

Yet more than anything, the film's dramatic sub-text is American. This is apparent not just in Fabian's distorted embrace of the success ethic – 'I just want to be somebody' – but in the popularised Freudianism that underpins the scenario as it does that of so many other contemporary American plays and films. Specifically, this attaches to the father–son relationship: Fabian's worst transgression in Cristo's eyes is to have used the latter's estranged father in his empire-building schemes and falsely to have become a surrogate son to the old man, whose death he inadvertently brings about, and this schema is extended by the avenging Cristo's becoming a grotesquely punitive 'father' *vis-à-vis* Fabian. At the climax, as Fabian speaks a soliloquy of failure, 'All my life I've been running – from welfare officers, thugs'…it seems almost inevitable that the litany concludes with '…my father'.

Ultimately this transatlantic ambience envelops the film, and it seems to carry with it a wider implication: *Night and the City* can plausibly be interpreted as an act of reclamation, as Hollywood's renewing its title on generic properties that have been at risk of partial appropriation by British producers. At any event, as the 1950s got under way, the spiv cycle petered out. The emblematically named *Wide Boy* (1952, screenplay Rex Rientis, director Ken Hughes) has the lowly status of a 67-minute B picture, with the leads taken by Sydney Tafler and Susan Shaw, minor supporting players in *It Always Rains on Sunday*, and the arm of the law upheld by Ronald Howard, as if returned to office after his fall from grace in *Night Beat*.

As the decade progressed and the 'New Elizabethan' age brought the beginnings of a new affluence, British crime movies could, from one perspective, be thought to have re-embraced the status quo, and sure enough, 1952 brought another *The Ringer* and 1953 another *House of the Arrow*. But that is, at most, only half the story. The themes absorbed during the immediate post-war years began to re-emerge, and in the wake of tie-ups with American companies, Hollywood re-exported elements of influence along with its export of the second-string stars – everyone from Gene Nelson to Wayne Morris – who populated British studios' crime movies of the time. And, intermittently at least, the movies were harder-edged than their pre-war counterparts. A typical programmer of the period might be *Soho Incident* (1956, screenplay Ian Stuart Black, director Vernon Sewell), with Hollywood's Faith Domergue as the boss of a betting gang and Lee Patterson as the opportunistic drifter who succumbs to the lure of easy money but baulks at murder and helps to call time on the crooks. The source was the novel *Wide Boys Never Work* by Robert Westerby, one of the screenwriters of *Night Beat*. For its American release, the film's title was changed to *Spin a Dark Web*.

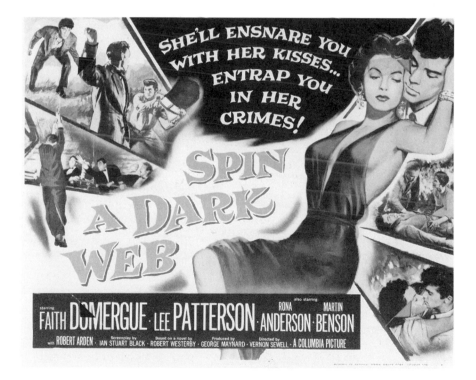

Figure 3.2 British noir: Faith Domergue plays the ensnaring temptress in *Spin a Dark Web*, the American title for Vernon Sewell's *Soho Incident* (1956)
Source: British Cinema and Television Research Group archive, De Montfort University

Bibliography

Greene, G. (1972) *The Pleasure Dome*, London: Secker & Warburg.
Orwell, G. (1965) *Decline of the English Murder and Other Essays*, Harmondsworth: Penguin.

4   Outrage: *No Orchids For Miss Blandish*[1]

Brian McFarlane

'I wanna take a gander at that baby', says a gangster early in St John Clowes'
film version of *No Orchids for Miss Blandish*. So, apparently, did large numbers
of filmgoers, however strenuously the moral watchdogs of the period warned
them against the corrupting potential of doing so. The violence of the critical
reaction to Clowes' *No Orchids for Miss Blandish* makes very suggestive
reading. Mere ineptitude could never have triggered such intemperance. It is
as though the distributors had indeed 'released' upon an unsuspecting public
some horrifying monster of the deep.

Seeing the film today, one is struck by how much more brazen about sex
and violence it is than any of the films that were earning British cinema a
new respect at home and abroad. Critics (and others in prominent positions)
greeted it with quivering distaste when not indeed with moral outrage. *Miss
Blandish* is unashamedly melodramatic, and this raised the hackles of middle-
class critics at the time of its release. It also foregrounds the issue of female
sexuality with a boldness not to be found in films of the earlier 1940s and it
was held to have 'sadistic' elements, any suggestion of which was bound to
elicit critical abuse.[2] And above all there is the threat of an Americanisation of
British cinema: the film's genre, location and idiom all aspire to transatlantic
models.

In the light of some of the questions raised above, *Miss Blandish* offers
evidence for the view that a film doesn't need to be 'good' (by the criteria of
1948 or of 1998) to be interesting and that its context may be more resonant
than the text itself. Consider one aspect of context: the proliferation of related
texts. The film's direct antecedents are James Hadley Chase's crime novel,
which was first published in 1939, and was an immediate success for Chase,
pseudonym for René Raymond, librarian and wholesale bookseller. The play
version, by Chase and Robert Nesbitt (with additional dialogue by film
director and screenwriter Val Guest), opened in London on 30 July 1942. It
had been extensively toured before settling in to a run of 203 performances at
the West End's Prince of Wales Theatre. The film's descendants include Robert
Aldrich's US film, *The Grissom Gang* (1971), another theatrical version, 'A
Play by Robert David MacDonald, based on the novel by James Hadley
Chase' (1978), and a 1983 edition of the novel 'rewritten and revised by the

author who felt the original would not be acceptable to the new generation of readers'.[3] It is, then, clearly a fiction that has gone through more transmutations than most. It seems to be one of those titles that are part of popular mythology (and descended from an older one as we shall see) widely known about even if neither read nor seen.

Before suggesting why the 1948 British film should have been so reviled, it is worth stressing that the basic events of the Chase original do not vary much from one transmutation to another. In outline, a small-time gang kidnaps the eponymous heiress, kills her boyfriend and is in turn wiped out by the more powerful Grisson gang, presided over by the formidable Ma Grisson. Her sexually repressed son Slim takes a fancy to Miss Blandish and loses interest in the terms of the kidnapping. Following the intervention of Fenner, a former newspaper reporter turned private eye, the gang is routed, Slim is shot down by police bullets and Miss Blandish throws herself from an upper-storey window (except in the Aldrich version in which she is restored to her unwelcoming father). However, though this narrative skeleton survives successive re-tellings, there are some major differences of motivation, the most crucial of which is probably that leading to the suicide of Miss Blandish: in the two versions of the novel and the two plays, she kills herself because her forced sexual liaison with Slim leaves her feeling irrevocably soiled; in the 1948 film she does so because life without him would be intolerable. This difference, to which I shall return, is almost certainly one of the key factors in the kind of response that greeted the film.

The novel is out of print and difficult to find, except in the revised edition of 1983, reprinted in 1985 in Large Print for the benefit of those with impaired vision but robust sensibilities. On the basis of this version, the only one available at the time of this study, it is a fast-moving thriller of murder, kidnapping, violence of various kinds and an element of repressed – and not-so-repressed – sexuality. Its most recent publishers claim that it has sold over four million copies. It was an immediate success when first published and was quickly translated into a dozen or more languages, and according to George Orwell 'enjoyed its greatest popularity in 1940, during the Battle of Britain' (Orwell, 1965: 68).[4] Orwell considered it 'a brilliant piece of writing, with hardly a wasted word or a jarring note anywhere' (ibid.: 69). The *New Statesman*, reviewing a later novel by Chase, wrote: 'The characters and events are all handled with the merciless precision that one may confidently expect from the author of *No Orchids*'.[5] The crime writer Colin Watson has described it as 'a semi-pornographic novel written in imitation of the American "tough" school of William Faulkner and Dashiell Hammett' (Watson 1987: 51), and the *Encyclopaedia of Mystery and Detection* records that 'This shocking blend of violence, sex, and American gangsters sold more than 1 million copies within five years of publication' (Steinbrunner and Penzler 1976: 81). Opinions on the novel's quality vary; it may have been seen as a more-or-less sensational piece in some quarters, but it certainly does not seem ever to have been a subject for scandal and concern.

The first theatrical version enjoyed a considerable success with its no doubt more limited audiences. According to Linden Travers, who starred in it and was the only cast member who also appeared in the film, 'It ran for about nine months. Robert Newton was a big movie star, so he was a draw, and Hartley Power was also a quite well-known actor'.[6] She recalled certain outrageous bits of 'business' that the charismatic but unreliable Newton would insert, but its solid though not remarkable West End run suggests neither public disdain nor wild clamouring at the box-office. Certainly, *The Times* review of the play did not register outrage, describing it as a 'good gangster play' and 'extremely well acted', and allowing that: 'Playgoers who do not happen to be squeamish will probably enjoy the impact of its brutality'.[7] Ironically, though, the reviewer also says: 'The film has a way of registering the brutalities as part of a smooth-running and exciting game: on the stage the same brutalities appear raw and are either more shocking or more boring', an interesting, at least arguable point. The later play version, written for and first performed at the Citizens' Theatre, Glasgow, is divided into two acts of, respectively, ten and eight 'chapters' (the term recalls its origins in the novel), and, while retaining the late 1930s setting (Constance Bennett and Norma Shearer are adduced as big film names), the period ambience is curiously shattered by language, especially in the use of four-letter words. One does not doubt that they were used by real gangsters in the 1930s, but they were not used in the theatre or novels of the period, and, now, the affiliations of *Miss Blandish* are with the world of fictional artefacts that produced it rather than with any actual social reality. Whatever depravities are going on in Chase's novel, they are conducted in a diction that may be 'tough' but would not of itself attract charges of obscenity.

Robert Aldrich's film version, *The Grissom Gang*, appears to have taken advantage of the relaxed censorship codes of the early 1970s in its representation of sexuality and violence, but without drawing attention to itself particularly in either respect.[8] Its Slim (Scott Wilson) is much nearer Chase's concept of the sexually retarded oaf, and its Miss Blandish (Kim Darby) is both sexually alert and remarkably unattractive, never (as Linden Travers does effortlessly) justifying the term 'classy'. *Films and Filming* noted that it was 'a remake of *No Orchids for Miss Blandish*, an eyebrow-raiser of several decades ago' (Gow 1972: 52), without any suggestion that contemporary eyebrows need be raised. The *Monthly Film Bulletin* reviewer didn't much like it, dismissing it as 'a piece of manufactured gloss as dubiously sensationalist as anything since *The Dirty Dozen* [an earlier box-office hit from the same director]' (Wilson 1971: 240). *Sight and Sound*, in its quarterly round-up, was predictably sniffy, finding it 'a fashionable blend of camp, violence and synthetic dialogue' ('Film Guide', *Sight and Sound*, Winter 1971/72, p. 60). Significantly, none of these versions provoked anything like the storm of protest that greeted the 1948 British film. Nothing could have been less 'fashionable' than that.

Not until Michael Powell's *Peeping Tom* a dozen years later was the British critical fraternity of the time stirred to such a frenzy of disapproval by a film. The film's script had gone through various versions since it was first submitted to the British Board of Film Censors in 1942 until it was finally approved in early 1948 when 'a more liberal policy had emerged towards gangster films and violence as crime flourished in immediate post-war Britain' (Robertson 1989: 94). In the event the BBFC was taken aback by the ferocity of the response, considering it a 'normal gangster film, no more brutal than many made in Hollywood' (*News Chronicle*, 25 April 1948). A sample of the critical reactions: Arthur Vesselo (1948: 99), writing in *Sight and Sound* saw it as 'the latter-day offspring of those unhealthy peepshows that were once commonly met with in funfairs'. The normally sedate *Monthly Film Bulletin* (April 1948: 47) believed it to be 'the most sickening exhibition of brutality, perversion, sex and sadism ever to be shown on a cinema screen'. That doyenne of middle-class reviewing, C.A. Lejeune of the *Observer* (18 April 1948), felt that 'This film has all the morals of an alley-cat and all the sweetness of a sewer', and her sister-in-dudgeon, the usually more flexible Dilys Powell, wrote her review in the form of a letter to the censor, claiming:

> I was surprised that you, with your well-known caution in these matters, should have found the piece fit for public exhibition. I was more than surprised; I was stunned; I was momentarily so incapable of movement that I sat, unseeing, through the newsreel.
>
> (*Sunday Times*, 18 April 1948)

Leonard Mosley, of the *Daily Express*, believed the film 'sets out to appeal to the prurient-minded, the twisted, the unbalanced' (16 April 1948), who proved to be legion; and Milton Shulman, of the *Evening Standard* dismissed it as 'a disgrace to the British film industry' (13 April 1948).

The reactions did not stop with the critics. Dr Edith Summerskill, Parliamentary Secretary to the Ministry of Food, in the Labour Government, deplored 'the fact that this film was produced by a British company for commercial profit only' and warned the Annual Meeting of the Association of Married Women that the film 'will, in my opinion, pervert the minds of the British people'.[9] Parliamentarians asked questions in the House about 'standards of decency and morality in films shown in public cinemas' (*News Chronicle*, 23 April 1948); the London County Council ruled that the film 'MUST BE CUT OR BANNED' (headline in *Daily Telegraph*, 24 April 1948), while some other local authorities banned the film altogether.

It is not the function of this piece to chart in detail the processes by which this film sought censorship approval or how the official bodies acted in response to indignant outcries, though two points might be made here. First, the BFFC's later apology for its failure to deal more severely with the film set back post-war liberal reform, so that *Miss Blandish* may be said to have had an influence out of proportion to its intrinsic qualities. Second, where the film *was* shown it was a considerable box-office success, especially at London's

JACK LA RUE
HUGH McDERMOTT
LINDEN TRAVERS

RENOWN PICTURES
PRESENTS
THE ST JOHN LEGH LLOWES PRODUCTION
OF
JAMES HADLEY CHASES
"NO ORCHIDS FOR MISS BLANDISH"
WITH
CHARLES GOLDNER · FRANCES MARSDEN AND MACDONALD PARKE

FEATURING
WALTER CRISHAM
AND
LESLIE BRADLEY
AND INTRODUCING
ZOE GAIL AND JACK DURANT

Figure 4.1 'The most sickening exhibition of brutality, perversion, sex and sadism ever
to be shown on a cinema screen'
Source: British Cinema and Television Research Group archive, De Montfort University

Plaza Cinema in the West End, scarcely suggesting that the film was as offensive to widely held moralities as critics and other commentators claimed. What is most interesting to me is to consider the possible sources of the hysteria that greeted the film's release, why it seemed so threatening to the middle-class sensibilities of critics and other moral guardians. Mrs Whitehouse, thou shouldst have been living at this hour!

The film famously failed to fit either of the categories that were winning critical plaudits for British film-makers in the mid-to-late 1940s. Although it was derived from a novel, it was not the kind of literary or theatrical adaptation that was bringing such prestige to British cinema of the period. It had little in common with, say, David Lean's Dickens films, *Great Expectations* (1946) and *Oliver Twist* (1948), or his Coward films (most notably, of course, *Brief Encounter*, 1945), or Carol Reed's collaborations with Graham Greene – *The Fallen Idol* (1948) and *The Third Man* (1949) – or Anthony Asquith's with Terence Rattigan. It was not just that these films were derived from writers of high cultural status; the *kind* of adaptation strategies they exhibited indicated a strong respect for the precursor text, and there was about them a degree of sophistication in the writing and filming that marked them out as fare for discriminating audiences. They were not essentially genre pieces and they were not based on popular genre fictions. The other key element in the post-war prestige of British cinema was the realist strain that first made itself felt in such war-time films as *Millions Like Us* (1943) and *San Demetrio, London* (1943). In these, the documentary-style interest in people and place and activity made an impact on fictional features as it never had before the war, and it persisted in such post-war films as *It Always Rains on Sunday* (1947) or *Holiday Camp* (1947).

It is clear that the two critically privileged strands are entwined in such films as *Brief Encounter*, whereas neither is at stake in *Miss Blandish*. Its literary antecedent had won mere popularity (always suspect with the middle-class reviewers of the time as though it were easier to please many people than few), and it has no pretensions to realism.[10] It is wholly studio-set and looks it, and its generic affiliations are with the gangster thriller and the sex melodrama, neither of which was likely to find favour with the critics, who must often have been piqued to find, as in this case, how little effect they had on cinema-going habits, except perhaps counter-productively. The most charitable construction one might place on the critical reaction to *Miss Blandish* is that, at this time, to those who cared about the international reputation of British films, it seemed inimical to hard-won prestige to lavish money and attention on so 'unBritish' and, in their view, insalubrious an enterprise.

Merely not fitting either of the favoured categories would not alone have set off such hysteria. Another major source of offence seems to have been the film's American ambience and its appropriation of what was seen largely as an American genre and its characteristics. One can easily fault it from this point of view: its dialogue, for instance, is often a ludicrous pastiche of Hollywood gangster melodramas ('I wanna take a gander at that baby', 'Shut ya trap' on several occasions, 'Quit beefin'. You ain't done so bad', and so on); and the attempt to replicate the character types of the genre (e.g., the drunken, deregistered doctor with a florid turn of phrase, played by MacDonald Parke, or the ill-used moll, played by Frances Marsden) is not always convincing. In some other respects, though, it is no better or worse than any number of Hollywood counterparts. The action is for the most part well-paced, and some of the beatings and murders can still look quite shocking in the 1990s when one might have supposed viewers to have become anaesthetised to screen violence. The brutal murder of Miss Blandish's fiancé Harvey (John McLaren), or the breaking of a decanter over the head of barman Ted (Sidney James) has a raw power that belongs to the genre; 'belongs' in the sense that to omit all such evidence would be to soften the edges of the genre's world and its preoccupations. Further, the production values ensure that such key sets as the Grissons' night-club are appropriately and vulgarly luxurious, and the acts staged there for the amusement of the customers are well-managed (even if one rather foolhardily invokes such magisterial shades of the genre as Sydney Greenstreet and Peter Lorre). It must be said that the log cabin in which Slim and Miss Blandish share an idyll hardly suggests the American woods, but the other settings (the Blandish house, assorted bars, restaurants, hide-outs and gas stations) are more than equal to their generic functions.[11] One does in fact get a sense of a squalid underworld in settings like Johnny's hide-out, where Slim's gang wipes out the small-time crooks who have kidnapped Miss Blandish, and the *mise en scène* of the Grisson Club makes clear that we are moving into a more plush, if no less ugly, quarter of the underworld. The acknowledgement of an underside to life in such films as *Brighton Rock* or *They Made Me a Fugitive*, unless it were accompanied by a morally improving rhetoric, as in *The Blue Lamp* (1950), was apt to unsettle the critics, though the phenomenon of post-war crime was well-known and substantiated. To most of them, *Miss Blandish* seemed to be rubbing their noses in the malodorous, the more so because of its 'American' setting. Only Jympson Harman praised it as 'more honest in showing gangster types in a thoroughly nauseating light' (*Evening News*, 15 April 1948).[12]

The fact that British film-makers were imitating what was seen as an

Figure 4.2 Gunman and bottle blonde: Hugh McDermott confronts Zoe Gail in the notorious *No Orchids for Miss Blandish* (1948)
Source: British Cinema and Television Research Group archive, De Montfort University

American genre, (as indeed Chase had in the novel), seems to have angered the critics. There is a persistent stream of negative references to the American/Hollywood influence in the reviews, partly deriving from a sense that this is unbecoming for British film-makers, partly disguising such distaste with the suggestion that the British can only make poor copies of the American prototype. For instance: the *Manchester Guardian* saw it as 'an attempt to make a British copy of the kind of tough brutal American film which, whether or not we are fond of the genre, we have to admit the Americans make well', but defines the 'appeal' of the film as 'thoroughly un-British' (17 April 1948). *The Times* derides it as 'an English film misguided enough to put on a knuckle-duster and an American accent' (19 April 1948). The *Monthly Film Bulletin* drew attention to its 'pseudo-American accents' (April 1948: 47). C.A. Lejeune felt it must have 'scraped up all the droppings of the nastier type of Hollywood movie' (*Observer*, 18 April 1948). The *Mirror* found it a 'very inferior imitation of an old-time Hollywood gangster film' (16 April 1948) and *Picturegoer's* review read: 'About eight murders, two or three beatings-up comprise the total of this American-style gangster melodrama. And with all that it is dull. No flowers by request' (Collier 1948: 13). Against these and others like them, the perception of the *Macclesfield Times* that: 'It is a British film depicting American life better than American films depict British life' or the remark of James G. Minter, governing director of Renown Pictures, the distributor whose first essay in production it was, that 'I regard it as an English "Scarface" and that film has been running successfully for over ten years', were not likely to cut much ice.[13] There is interest, however, in the mere attempt at a British-made film set wholly in America, and its studio-based representation of city apartments and night clubs is no more nor less false than all those MGM versions of English villages in such films as *Random Harvest* (1942) and *The Uninvited* (1944). An article in *Picturegoer* noted that it was 'probably the first film made in England with a purely American setting' (Hollis 1948: 10). Only the film-going public seems to have enjoyed itself. The critical distaste for ersatz American film fodder may, again, be partially explained on the grounds that, at this time, British cinema was nearer to establishing a reputation as a *national* cinema than at any time in its history – before or since – and a film like *Miss Blandish* must have appeared to have nothing to do with such an enterprise, to have been in fact irrelevant at best, counter-productive at worst. It is the most blatant example of the period of the attempt to make a British version of an American genre film, though there are others – *Mine Own Executioner* (1947), for example, replicates the then–popular American 'psychological drama' genre – they were in genres less likely to cause critical offence.

When one looks more closely at the actual content of the film, other explanations for the critical outrage suggest themselves. Its central plot depicts an upper-class woman, Miss Blandish (Linden Travers), falling in love with the gangster Slim Grisson (Jack La Rue) who has kidnapped her. This is perhaps one of the film's key sources of offence: not only does it acknowledge a woman's sexuality as being a drive as important to her as a man's to him, but it dares to show her engaging in a sexual affair with a gangster, and actually enjoying it. (This recalls the Gainsborough films, especially *The Wicked Lady*, in which Margaret Lockwood, bored by her aristocratic marriage, seeks solace in the arms of a highwayman – and audiences, unlike critics, adored that too.) Miss Blandish is played by Linden Travers with a sensual acceptance of the role's requirements that makes one wish British films had made more and better use of her beauty and vividness and reminds one that Graham Greene, as reviewer for *Night and Day*, had noted a decade earlier, her capacity to render a human being 'under the ugly drive of undifferentiated desire' (Greene 1972: 167). It is pretty remarkable in a British film of this (or any?) period for a woman to behave in the *amour fou* manner of Miss Blandish, and the love scene in a log cabin has some real passion, even without the cut to the metaphoric flames in the fireplace.

At least two mythic impulses appear to be at work here – the Beauty and the Beast archetype, in which the Beast is softened into love, and the myth of Persephone, unfitted by her time in the underworld to return whole-heartedly to the life she knew before her abduction to Hades. The latter myth is less explicitly at work in the film than in the novel, where, at the end Miss Blandish, tainted by the psychotic Slim Grisson's rape of her while she is in a drugged stupor, kills herself rather than return besmirched to her old life. Her father, in fact, wishes she were dead. When she is rescued by the investigator, Fenner, she wants to die, fearing that 'she would soon be free, and the real misery and hell of her experience would begin' (Chase 1985: 304), saying: 'I'm ashamed of myself. I'm a person without any background, any character or any faith' (ibid.: 317). There is also a feeling that the experience of Slim will always be with her: on the most literal level, she may be pregnant as D. Streatfield, in a major study of the novel in relation to ancient mythologies, has suggested.[14] Streatfield has claimed of *Miss Blandish* that 'its popular success demonstrates that its subject-matter has made an immediate appeal to the contemporary collective unconscious' (Streatfield 1959: 223–4). She has become a symbol of divided sensibilities and loyalties and impulses. Of her role in the novel, Streatfield writes: 'Her mission is to descend into the underworld and to stay there, despite all opposition and the suffering entailed, until she has redeemed her bewitched and degraded lover: she must transform the Beast into Prince Charming' (Streatfield 1959: 179). In the film, she returns jewellery to her enraged father with a letter saying that she doesn't want to 'return to a restricted life [she] hated', and we recall how her fiancé wanted to 'melt the ice in [her] veins'. Surrounded by luxury and servants, she has known no serious emotional response except boredom. The film's Slim is more Beast gentled by love than corrupting lord of the underworld, though that is how he is introduced. The love scenes are, on occasion, not very well written, with some descents into boy-and-girl-against-the-world sentimentality, as if we were dealing with Nicholas Ray's teenagers in *They Live By Night* (also 1948). There is elsewhere, though, a convincing breath of sensuality. The long shot of their double bed and their ease with each other as they sit around in bathrobes clearly indicates that she has become his mistress; in one passionate moment he seems to put his hand down the front of her gown. It is rare in British cinema of the period, except for melodramas such as Marc Allegret's *Blanche Fury* or Lewis Allen's *So Evil My Love* (both 1948), to get a whiff of real sexuality, and both those other films focus on women brought to sensual life by, if not Beasts, men beyond the pale of respectability. Slim's former girlfriend, Margo (Zoe Gail), chanteuse at the Grissons' night-club, sings a witty song, 'When he got it, did he want it?' which provides a parodic comment on the progress of Slim's affair with Miss Blandish and on the Beauty-and-the-Beast motif.[15]

> From the beginning of time dames have been carried off by rough men.
> Song and story and rhyme tell of these take-no-rebuff men.

As she sings of how 'His mad obsession for possession/Could only end one way', the camera cuts to Slim looking reflective, as Margo moves suggestively through the audience and to the song's climax: 'If you take by force you must keep it/You can't even give it away'. (Margo's other song, 'Still Waters', under-lines the course of her own affair with Slim, ending on the awareness that 'My chances are through'.)

And there is too a blocked Oedipal drama in Slim Grisson's dealing with his mother (Lily Molnar). There is a striking anticipation of Raoul Walsh's *White Heat* (1949) in the idea of a gangster with a dominant mother who angrily objects to Miss Blandish: 'I never did like women around the place. They make trouble'. In the novel and in the more recent play version, Slim is represented as a psycho-sexual cripple, ruled by his mother, who simultane-ously promotes and retards his sexual blooding. He doesn't appear for fifty pages (or, indeed, for the first thirty minutes of the film). When he does appear, he is described as 'tall, reedy and pasty-faced. His loose, half-open mouth, his vacant, glassy eyes made him look idiotic' (Chase 1985: 52), and this is followed by an account of how his mother, 'determined he should become a gang leader' (ibid.: 1985: 53), has masterminded his career. There are frequent references to his sexual inexperience, and, Eddie, one of Ma's henchmen, objects to the idea of 'Slim relieving his repression on that girl' (ibid.: 113), when it has become apparent that Ma will – unwillingly – let Slim have his way with Miss Blandish. In the later play version, the mother–son drama is still more explicitly dealt with. Slim begs his mother to 'Come upstairs with me. Come upstairs and make her. Hold her for me, Ma, so she don't…you know. I can't do it on my own' (MacDonald 1978: 29), and just before the Act 1 curtain, we have this exchange in Miss Blandish's pres-ence:

Ma   *(Whispering)* Go on, son.
         (She unbuttons him, pulls his trousers down)

Slim	Can I Ma? Can I?
Ma	Sure, son.
	(Slim shuffles over to the bed)

Even a film that seemed so sensationalist to many commentators at the time could scarcely have contemplated such a situation in 1948, and in fact the whole character of Slim has undergone some major changes. Ma is still the gang leader, but is allowed to be no more than equivocal about Slim's keeping Miss Blandish upstairs, and Slim challenges her leadership: 'From now on you're gonna do what you're told, like the rest of them', adding 'OK Ma?', perhaps as a serious question, to which she replies carefully, 'All right Slim', as a guarded relinquishment of power. The protagonist of a 1948 movie was clearly not going to be able to duplicate Chase's descriptions (as Scott Wilson did twenty-three years later). Jack La Rue, in 'a fine, restrained performance of repressed violence' as Robert Murphy has accurately noted (Murphy 1989: 188), brings suggestions of Bogart in a minor key: a charismatic toughness concealing an unexercised capacity for tenderness, though the role is under-written and the motivation remains sketchy.[16] Such a hero, acceptable in an American film, may well have been seen as unBritish: if men were to be brutes, they needed an aristocratic background, like James Mason's in *The Man in Grey* or *Fanny by Gaslight*, and they were villains rather than heroes. Even then, ladylike reviewers were inclined to be sniffy. Slim is certainly not aristocratic and he is American to boot. And the idea of a well-born heroine (her father is played by the very gentlemanly Percy Marmont and receives the police in his library) succumbing with pleasure to the advances of one who is a thug by profession must have seemed very shocking in the context of post-war British cinema.[17]

Murphy is right to say that '*No Orchids* is not a film that stands up to close critical scrutiny' (Murphy 1989:188). St John Clowes' screenplay shows that he has not absorbed the American idiom as thoroughly as Chase had, and, apart from La Rue and Travers, the acting is not distinguished, though the critical nagging about 'phoney American accents' seems captious. The original aim was for a big-budget production with major Hollywood stars, but in the event it became a modestly budgeted film for its first-time production company, with only La Rue, who had a long career playing minor gangsters, from Hollywood. (He had acted in a British film before the war.) Of the others, Walter Crisham (as Ma's henchman, Eddie) was born in Massachusetts; Hugh McDermott (Fenner), who almost invariably played Americans or Canadians in British films, was actually a Scot; and MacDonald Parke played so many pompous Americans (as in David Lean's *Summertime*) that one could be forgiven for supposing him to be American, but I cannot establish his birthplace. They suggest the 'Americanness' of their characters at least as well as a Canadian like Walter Pidgeon suggests the Home Counties in *Mrs Miniver*. It is part of the snobbery of British film reviewing of the period to regard an American influence as inimical to a film's quality but this film, for the most part, preserves adequately the illusion of an American big-city setting.[18] As noted earlier, its production values are mostly equal to the task, and George Melachrino's music is rather more than that.

According to the *British Film Yearbook 1949–50*, producer–director–writer Clowes 'wrote, produced and directed his first film in 1928, and subsequently made a series of "quota" pictures' (Noble 1949: 505). Unlike the subversive art of, say, Ibsen in the 1880s and 1890s or the Pasolini of *Salo* a century later, where the artists took a calculated risk with public opinion and excited widespread obloquy as a result, there is nothing in Clowes' background that points to an urge to *épater le bourgeois*.[19] Mr James G. Minter, Governing Director of Renown Pictures, stressed the idea of films as 'a commercial art'.[20] And the inclusion of 'sensational' elements that middle-class film-makers and reviewers deplored were more likely to be present for their prurient appeal than for any subversive artistic reasons.

The 'suggestive' nature of the dialogue (and the film *is* more outspoken in sexual matters than most British films of its time) comes in for a good deal of notice, yet it is no racier than many of the drawing-room comedies (from Noel Coward and others) of the period. One suspects that the film reviewers are applying a different standard to the cinema audience from that which their colleagues would apply to a middle-class stage audience, which would be assumed to be more sophisticated and therefore less likely to be corrupted – or 'perverted', as Dr Summerskill feared. Maybe the film's largely middle-class reviewers were outraged at being made to confront their own inner drives, even their 'perversions'. Maybe the invasion of the upper-middle-class purlieus of the Blandish home by the Grisson low-lifes raised the spectre of such a threat to middle-class life – and to middle-class critics – in the real world. Whether or not it is a 'good' film, the critical response to it and other crime melodramas such as *Noose*, *They Made Me a Fugitive* and *Good Time Girl* can instruct us about the period's mores. These are films that parade what the national psyche preferred to repress, and which the more prestigious arms of the British film industry usually treated with a decent reserve. Sexual and other impulses, especially of a violently disruptive kind, will lie buried for another decade when the Hammer Studios at Bray will make a fortune by giving them an airing in the generic guise.

Notes

1 See *No Orchids for Miss Blandish*, London: British Film Institute Microfiche File (quotations from newspapers are taken from here unless otherwise noted); *No Orchids for Miss Blandish*, London: Theatre Museum File on 1942 play; 'No Orchids for Miss Blandish', unsigned review in *Monthly Film Bulletin* (April 1948, no. 172, vol. 15).

2 Fifty years later, the Canadian film *Crash* has been embroiled in controversy for 'sadistic' content, and one recalls similar recoil from *Straw Dogs* and *A Clockwork Orange*.

3 Producer's note, introducing Magna Print Books edn, Long Preston, North Yorkshire, 1985, p. 8.
4 Orwell compared it with E. W. Hornung's *Raffles*, as two examples of 'glamorised crime' (p. 63).
5 As reported in the blurb of *A Lotus for Miss Quorn* (London: Hale, 1960).
6 Interview with Linden Travers, London, 1992 (published in B. McFarlane *An Autobiography of British Cinema*, London: Methuen and BFI, 1997).
7 This review, *The Times*, 31 July 1942, is unsigned, as was the paper's convention then.
8 Grisson has been changed to Grissom in this version alone.
9 It is not clear from the report given in the *Evening Standard* (17 April 1948) whether she had actually seen the film.
10 George Orwell's praise for the quality of the writing is interesting in this respect; he so often seems the archetypal, austere, leftist middle-class voice of his generation.
11 Reigate, as Linden Travers recalled (interview with Linden Travers, 1992).
12 Not that Harman wanted British studios to persevere in the genre, ending his review with 'Leave it to Hollywood, chums!'
13 Both quoted in a 'Supplement to "The Other Side": *No Orchids for Miss Blandish*', published by Renown Pictures Corporation Ltd, undated but probably early June 1948.
14 Streatfield's book-length study draws substantially on *Miss Blandish* in relation to the Persephone myth and to the Jungian concepts of archetypes and the 'anima'.
15 Written by George Melachrino (composer of the film's music) and James Dyrenforth.
16 As Linden Travers has pointed out, to be the leading man and a criminal was unusual at the time: 'it was only John Garfield and one or two others who were allowed to be the hero *and* a baddie' (interview 1992).
17 There are grounds for further – psychoanalytic – study in a comparison of Miss Blandish's rejection of her father's world and Slim's coming to terms with his mother's domination.
18 Robert Baker, producer of many of Tempean Films' co-features in the 1950s, said quite frankly that his aim was to emulate American thrillers as closely as possible, in such matters as plot, speed and setting, and often used minor American stars to boost US distribution (interview with Robert Baker, 1995).
19 In fact, C.A. Lejeune's response to the film employs a diction similar to Clement Scott's critiques of Ibsen in the *Daily Telegraph* and a range of periodicals in the 1890s: *Ghosts* was both 'loathsome' and 'deplorably dull', thus covering the double critical ground of the *Blandish* banshees, cloaking squeamishness with apparent aesthetic discrimination.
20 See note 13.

Bibliography

Chase, J. H. (1985) *No Orchids for Miss Blandish* (first published 1939), Long Preston: Magna Print Books.
Collier, L. (1948) '*No Orchids for Miss Blandish*', in *Picturegoer*, London, 3 July.
Gow, G. (1972) '*The Grisson Gang*', in *Films and Filming*, January.
Greene, G. (1972) *The Pleasure Dome*, London: Secker & Warburg (review of *Brief Ecstasy* first published in *Night and Day*, 16 September 1937).
Hollis, G. (1948) 'Jack La Rue has the secret of happiness', in *Picturegoer*, 27 March.
Mathews, T.D. (1994) *Censored*, London: Chatto & Windus.

MacDonald, R. (1978) *No Orchids for Miss Blandish* (based on the novel by James Hadley Chase), Birmingham: Oberon Books.

McFarlane, B. (1997) ' "Linden Travers" and "Robert Baker" ', in *An Autobiography of British Cinema, as Told by the Actors and Filmmakers Who Made It*, London: Methuen and British Film Institute.

Murphy, R. (1989) *Realism and Tinsel: Cinema and Society in Britain 1939–49*, London: Routledge.

Noble, P. (ed.) (1949) *British Film Yearbook 1949–50*, London: Skelton Robinson.

Orwell, G. (1965) 'Raffles and Miss Blandish' (1944), in *Decline of the English Murder and other Essays*, Harmondsworth: Penguin, in association with Secker & Warburg.

Palmer, J. (1978) *Thrillers: Genesis and Structure of a Popular Genre*, London: Edward Arnold.

Robertson, J.C. (1989) *The Hidden Cinema: British Film Censorship in Action, 1913–1972*, London: Routledge.

Steinbrunner, C. and Penzler, O. (eds) (1976) *Encyclopaedia of Mystery and Detection*, New York: McGraw-Hill Book Company.

Streatfield, D. (1959) *Persephone: A Study of Two Worlds*, London: Routledge and Kegan Paul.

Vesselo, A. (1948) 'British Films of the Quarter', in *Sight and Sound*, Summer.

Watson, C. (1987) *Snobbery with Violence: English Crime Stories and Their Audience*, London: Methuen (first published 1971).

Wilson, D. (1971) '*The Grissom Gang*', in *Monthly Film Bulletin*, London: British Film Institute, December.

5   Men, women and money

Masculinity in crisis in the British professional crime film 1946–1965

Andrew Clay

> *Joe Macbeth:*   For crying out loud, what do you want? We got the
> house, we got money, we're sitting pretty. Isn't that
> enough?
> *Lily Macbeth:*   No Joe, it isn't.
>
> (*Joe Macbeth*, Ken Hughes, 1955)

One characteristic of films featuring professional criminality in the post-war years is that they are only ostensibly about professional crime. More accurately they should be seen as films that use crime to express men's contradictory experience of power. Under patriarchy, men may be dominant but they can also feel a sense of powerlessness (Coltrane 1994; Kaufman 1994). From the evidence offered in British crime films, this contradiction seems to have been particularly acute in the two decades after 1945.

Two separate themes were prominent in constructing a sense of masculine crisis through narratives about professional crime in this period. First, attention was paid to the problems of readjustment of returning ex-servicemen. A contrast in fortune was often drawn in crime films of the late 1940s between the unrewarded demobilised servicemen and the 'spivs' who had unfairly prospered in their absence. However, the contrasting of a satisfying masculine performance in war-time with an unsatisfactory post-war experience of peace and prosperity, continued to influence the crime film in the 1950s and 1960s. The unifying theme of these influences was a loss of masculine status. As the actor George Baker has recalled, 'There was an awful lot of people wandering about who were unable to find their place again' (McFarlane 1997: 38).

Second, there were those films that dealt in various ways with the ideological impact on men of the rising importance of women in post-war society brought about by the opportunities provided during war time for women to experience non-traditional roles and through their centrality to consumerism (Hill 1986: 25). Elizabeth Wilson (1980) argues that women were central in the attempt to build a consensual notion of citizenship, but that the apparent victory of feminist advancement was largely won mythically and ideologically. Nevertheless, the ideological construction of equality must have contributed to a worry amongst men about their place in this post-war world and a nostalgia for the war-time society in which they were privileged. Thus, the crisis in masculinity that emerged in crime films at this time consisted of both a feeling of a loss of war-time agency and an anxiety about the status of post-war women. In many crime films these themes are evident in relationships between men, women and money.

Men

The dramatisation of masculine crisis is a characteristic of British post-war cinema that is shared by a number of genres and styles of film-making at a time when films based on women's experiences declined and male problems were a predominant focus (Street 1997: 61–91). The crime genre in the first two post-war decades was a bastion of male protagonism. In the late 1940s crime films often feature ex-servicemen who are returning to a socially disrupted world where their sacrifice is unrewarded and their status is in stark contrast to that of the black marketeers who have exploited scarcity. This problem was shown to affect both officers and ranks, although officers were more prominent as individuals, whereas 'squaddies' appeared as a group. For example, *Dancing with Crime* (John Paddy Carstairs, 1947) and *Night Beat* (Harold Huth, 1948) featured pairs of ex-servicemen from the ranks, whereas *They Made Me a Fugitive* (Cavalcanti, 1947), *The Flamingo Affair* (Horace Shepherd, 1948) and *Noose* (Edmond T. Greville, 1948) had individual officers.

The device of pairing ex-servicemen together was used to tell moral tales of contrasting fortunes for the male protagonists in the threatening post-war world. In *Dancing with Crime*, Ted (Richard Attenborough) and Dave (Bill Owen) are veterans of Tobruk now living in London. Clearly bonded by their war-time friendship, they have taken different directions on Civvy Street. As a cab driver, Ted is burdened with low status and little money, but is working hard to try and get married to his sweetheart, Joy (Sheila Sim). Dave has opted for easier money (obtained through theft), which he spends on a hedonistic bachelor lifestyle with girlfriends in clubs and dance halls. Dave's transgression is punished when he is murdered by the real villains, a gang who are working behind a dance-hall front. Thus, the film presents a threatening low-life milieu where organised crime and the 'Palais de Danse' are as inextricably linked as in other films at this time such as *Appointment With Crime* (John Harlow, 1946). As in most of these late 1940s films, black marketeering and other forms of professional crime constitute a perversion of the war because their replication of the conditions of war-time conflict and excitement are in the interests of financial gain rather than patriotism.

In *Night Beat*, two recently demobbed commandos, Don (Hector Ross) and Andy (Ronald Howard), return to London where they reluctantly become police recruits. Don, because he is more stable and responsible, settles down to a life of low pay, low status, high danger and unsocial hours. Andy, however, drifts towards what he sees as an easier and more rewarding job with black marketeer and 'swindle club' owner, Felix (Maxwell Reed). This places him in a position of danger where he becomes vulnerable to arrest and then falsely suspected of murdering Felix.

The male protagonists in *They Made Me a Fugitive* and *The Flamingo Affair*, however, are ex-officers who are tempted into the dangerous world of black marketeering. For ex-RAF officer Clem (Trevor Howard), in *Fugitive*, this proves to be a nightmarish experience. Clem is neither straightforwardly innocent nor heroic, although as an audience we would tend to identify with his battle with the real villain, black marketeer and dope peddler Narcissus (Griffith Jones). Clem is experiencing a peacetime malaise. His middle-class girlfriend observes that 'He needs another war'. He confounds this hangover from the war with drink and seeks some consolation in women. So alienated is he from any sense of purpose that he allows his fate to be decided by the toss of a coin. This propels him into the clutches of the 'spiv', and results in Clem being falsely accused and imprisoned for the murder of a policeman.

Ex-Army Captain Dick Tarleton (Denis Webb) in *The Flamingo Affair* also attempts to cure his malaise with women and drink. Dick lives in a topsy-turvy world where he has been reduced in status from commander to menial. In voice-over he describes himself at the beginning of the film as 'now plain Dick'. He works as a garage mechanic and in the evening he sits on a bar stool buying drinks for his old drill sergeant. In his own words, he has fallen from a 'noble profession' to a 'ruddy injustice'. In contrast to the satisfying meritocracy of war-time, peacetime seems to Dick an unfairly egalitarian society of nationalisation and popular education, where 'people forget too easily' about soldiers like himself. His own sorry situation is compared with the luxury afforded by criminality when he starts a relationship with black marketeer Paula (Colette Melville). To keep this relationship intact he has to live up to her lifestyle and so his corruption into crime seems to offer a possible compensation for his war-time loss.

In *Noose*, however, the relationship between the ex-commando officer Jumbo Hoyle (Derek Farr) and the corrupt black market society is quite different. He is not corrupted into a life of crime, but rather, becomes one of the primary agents of its destruction. Unlike the other ex-servicemen in these late 1940s films, Jumbo appears comfortably readjusted to civilian life as a sports writer. He reasserts himself as a natural commander of men by leading a group of motley working-class vigilantes, including several ex-servicemen, into action against the racketeers who are preying on obedient society.

Far from being merely a feature of a temporary period of post-war adjustment the theme of corrupted servicemen continued into the 1950s and 1960s. It became an ideal vehicle to express film-makers' sense of disappointment, loss and betrayal amidst increasing comfort and affluence. For example, Ginger Edwards (Michael Medwin), a former tank trooper, in *The Intruder* (Guy Hamilton, 1953), is denied a successful readjustment to peacetime life by a chain of unfortunate circumstances that reduces him to a desperate fugitive. Other films present ex-soldiers who are more willingly corrupted into crime.

In *Soho Incident* (Vernon Sewell, 1956), for instance, Jim Bankley (Lee Patterson), an ex-Canadian airforceman looking for better paid work, offers to use his war-time engineering skills to help a gang involved in gambling racketeering. Ex-Army officer Turpin (Stanley Baker) in *A Prize of Arms* (Cliff Owen, 1962), however, is driven by revenge. Frustrated and embittered by a charge for black marketeering offences that has abruptly ended his career, he recruits two other ex-servicemen to help him steal a payroll from an Army camp.

Thus, not only were ex-servicemen shown to become individually criminalised, but they were also depicted as groups of men bonded together in crime. Disbanded war-time outfits were resurrected as criminal gangs in two films directed by Basil Dearden, *The Ship That Died of Shame* (1955) and *The League of Gentlemen* (1960). In the former, an ex-war-time motor boat crew begin to use their old ship for smuggling and, in the latter, a group of ex-Army officers are recruited for a bank robbery. In *The Good Die Young* (Lewis Gilbert, 1954) another group of men come together to rob a Post Office van. Told in flashback, the film seeks to explain what has brought together four men from 'different walks of life' in a stolen car. They are a clerk, Joe (Richard Basehart), an airman, Eddie (John Ireland), a boxer, Mike (Stanley Baker) and a 'gentleman of leisure', Rave (Laurence Harvey). Their empathy for one another is possible because they are all war veterans experiencing a loss of role. As Joe remarks, they are all 'chartered members of the lame dog club'. Crucially, this 'disability' is largely represented by problematic financial and emotional relationships with women.

Women

In the black marketeering films of the late 1940s, where ex-servicemen are drawn into organised crime or else attempt to overcome it, women generally were either presented as 'good' women who help the hero, or 'bad' women who impede or threaten his safety. In *Dancing with Crime*, for example, Joy helps Ted to track down Dave's killers by going undercover as a dance hostess, perversely adopting the disguise of the transgressive 'good time girls' whose relationships with men are reduced to monetary exchanges.

Sally (Sally Gray), Narcy's rejected girlfriend in *Fugitive*, supports and nurtures Clem in his quest to clear his name. In *Night Beat*, Julie (Anne Crawford), widow of the murdered spiv Felix, helps her erstwhile boyfriend, Don, to trap the murderess and clear her brother's name. Jumbo is aided in *Noose* by his fiancée, Linda (Carole Landis), who, driven by a strong sense of injustice, convinces her boyfriend of the need for action against the Soho racketeers and pursues them through her newspaper articles.

However, these films also contain corrupt women who threaten the hero's safety or draw him into the criminal world. In this sense, these films invite a comparison with American film noir and provide further evidence for a British noir cycle (Miller 1994). Clem's situation in *Fugitive* is worsened when, after refusing to help a woman kill her husband, she frames him for the murder she subsequently commits herself. The ex-servicemen who are criminalised in *Night Beat* and *The Flamingo Affair* are corrupted by 'good time girls'. Andy in *Night Beat*, falls for Jackie (Christine Norden), a singer prepared to use her sexuality for material gain. A present he buys for her is stolen property and he is thrown out of the police. He then begins to work for Felix with the hope that this will provide easy money to woo Jackie. Jackie's ambitions, however, are for the more wealthy Felix and her true nature is revealed. Her love of men is not romantic, but sexual and materialistic. 'Money', as 'good woman' Julie remarks, 'is the one sacred thing in her life'. Rejected by Felix, who only wants her for sex, Jackie stabs him with Andy's commando knife. Andy's war-time souvenir and symbol of his more satisfying masculine role, is treacherously used to implicate him. Paula, in *The Flamingo Affair*, conforms to the 'spider woman' stereotype of film noir (see Place 1980). She is identified symbolically in the *mise en scène* by her association with the spider-and-web lighting decoration that hangs in the Flamingo Club where Dick narrates his story of entrapment. When Dick meets Paula at the garage where he works, it is clear from her furs that she has prospered from the war and post-war scarcity. Dick is quickly subject to her sexual power but finds that he can only pursue his obsession if he can keep her in the luxury she privileges. 'Love's all very well', she tells him, 'but it won't pay for the ride'. Her black marketeering provides her with money and thrills. She removes his moral constraints and encourages him to join in her transgression. In a post-coital moment of plenitude, he agrees to her suggestion that he should rob his employer.

Some of the films of the 1950s and 1960s also misogynistically presented ex-servicemen's post-war malaise in terms of problematic relationships with women. In *The Good Die Young*, for example, Joe, an American, has lost his job and needs money to take his pregnant wife back to the USA. However, his plans are frustrated by an oppressive, hypochondriac mother-in-law. Mike has been forced to quit boxing because of an injury that led to an amputated hand. His nest egg of £1,000, however, has been squandered by his wife. Eddie, another American, is ignored by his actress wife in favour of her latest co-star. Rave's role is one reversed in relation to the patriarchal norm. He is a 'kept man', relying on handouts from his aristocratic father and a rich wife who ceases to support his gambling debts. These problematic relationships constitute the motivational circumstances that lead the men to commit crime. Similar circumstances motivate the ex-servicemen in *The League of Gentlemen*. Porthill (Bryan Forbes) is kept by an older and richer woman. Weaver (Norman Bird) is trapped in an oppressive suburban household with his wife, father-in-law and the television. The leader of the gang himself, Hyde (Jack Hawkins), has been made redundant and is separated from his wife.

In *The Intruder*, Wolf Merton (Jack Hawkins), ex-tank commander, returns home to find that his home is being burgled by Ginger, his war-time crew member. From then on, he attempts to find out 'what turned a good soldier into a thief'. Merton discovers that Ginger's misfortune started from the moment he returned home to find that his girlfriend, Tina, had not waited for him and had taken up with an exempted civilian. Ginger had wanted to marry so that he could take his younger brother away from their abusive uncle. The brother had been accidentally killed running away and, after taking revenge, Ginger is sentenced to ten years for the manslaughter of his uncle and becomes a fugitive and a thief.

Not every ex-servicemen's post-war crisis is presented as a breakdown in relationships with women. In *A Prize of Arms*, for example, women play no part in Turpin's drive for recompense. Also, *The Ship That Died of Shame* differs markedly from *The League of Gentlemen*, in the way that it genders the moral force for good as feminine. The motor boat *1087*, for example, is gendered as female and, although it is a machine, it ('she') exercises a moral conscience against the men who are using 'her' for crime, by, for instance, failing 'her' engines. Moreover, Helen (Virginia McKenna), the wife of the film's hero, Bill Randall (George Baker), functions as his moral purpose for fighting the war (O'Sullivan 1997: 179). In *The League of Gentlemen*, therefore, women are presented as one of the causes of male post-war disillusionment, whereas in *The Ship That Died of Shame* they signify war-time moral virtues that have been lost or are under threat in peacetime.

'Good' and 'bad' women are crucial to Jim's readjustment to post-war society in *Soho Incident*. He is assisted into crime by one woman, but helped out of it by the love of another. Jim, recently arrived from Canada, is looking for opportunities for easy money. He contacts an old war-time comrade who is working for a gambling racketeer, Rico Francesi (Martin Benson). Jim is taken on by Rico, largely because Rico's sister, Bella (Faith Domergue), is attracted to him. Her transgressive femininity resides in her desire to control Jim. He is attracted to her, but she wants to dominate their relationship by buying him clothes and being the seducer. Supported by Bella, Jim rises in the gang, but once he realises the violent nature of the criminals, and especially of Bella herself, he tries to leave. This is something she cannot tolerate. 'Nobody leaves me', she rails at him. 'I walk out when I'm ready. And you don't go until I tell you to'. Jim is a man manipulated by a money-conscious, controlling woman, but his relationship with a 'good' woman, Betty (Rona Anderson), however, is based on love not lust, on support not control and on middle-class restraint rather than showy materialism. She represents the decent world that he had temporarily abandoned for the sake of 'a fast buck', aided by a 'fast woman'. At the end of the film we see Betty, dutifully sitting in court with her father, awaiting the return of the repentant sinner, Jim, to whom they have offered succour.

Money – imaginary solutions and dominant resolutions

In the professional crime films of the late 1940s, both society as a whole and war veterans in particular, were shown to be vulnerable to the temptations of black market racketeering and victimised by its conspiracy. Ex-servicemen were also shown to recover their war-time heroism by defending society against the exploitation of scarcity and the corrupt abuse of money and power by villainous black marketeers. This, perhaps, would have provided the male audience with a satisfying representation of traditional masculinity. Alternatively, it may also have reminded them of what they had lost in peace-time, for these films reproduced the problematic of low status and readjustment of ex-servicemen in the austerity of the first post-war years, but offered few solutions. Crime was imagined as one way in which ex-servicemen might seek to solve their problems. The hero's vulnerability to criminal corruption was presented with a degree of liberal empathy, but it was not condoned as a solution. Instead, these films advocated hard work, self-restraint and sacrifice and conformity to traditional class structures of power.

For example, in *Dancing with Crime*, Dave is a sympathetic character full of warm and generous affection for his war-time comrade, Ted and his girlfriend. His murder serves, on one level, as a punishment for pursuit of easy money. In contrast to his hard-working friend, Dave may be morally weak, but he hardly deserves to be murdered. When Ted helps to bring the villains to justice, he temporarily regains his combat status by using physical action, first to over-come Dave's killer (Barry K. Barnes), and second, to rescue the heroine from the gang's leader (Barry Jones). When Ted phones the police after his fight with the killer, we see that he is still wearing his army tunic, complete with medal ribbons and that his face is streaked with blood. Previously, the costume functioned naturalistically in terms of the poverty of his situation and symbolically to remind us of his loss of war-time status. Now it works to support a fleeting image of the recovery of war-time heroism. Ted's brief and successful foray into crime-fighting together with his hard work and self-restraint confirms his moral superiority over his war-time friend, Dave, whose indulgent 'dance with crime' is fatal.

Night Beat offered a similar resolution. Don perseveres in the police force and prospers. By the end of the film he is wearing a smart suit, rather than battle dress. It is a sign of his successful return to civilian life and reward for his application and probity. Reunited with his 'girl', Julie, they link arms with Andy, Don's morally-fallen comrade, and lead him out of the criminal world. This world, as personified by the spiv Felix and the acquisitive Jackie, is again associated with materialism and hedonism. It self-destructs under the moral force of middle-class authority. First, Jackie kills Felix. Then, when confronted by authority, she hysterically throws herself out of a window and out of the bourgeois world that she covets, but in which she has no legitimate place.

The ex-officer films contain middle-class heroes who stand in a different relationship to the dominant ideology from their comrades from the ranks. Jumbo, in *Noose*, is a natural-born leader who has few problems of readjust-ment and provides an edifying fantasy of middle-class social control. However, the readjustment of the other two ex-officers to the post-war world is more problematic and indicative of a society gone wrong. Clem, in *Fugitive*, manages to cause the death of the black marketeer in a rooftop fight finale. However, the dying man does not clear Clem's name. No imaginary solution is offered to his malaise. The ending of *The Flamingo Affair* is less bleak, but still offers no solution to Dick's loss of war-time status. He is able to temporarily recover some heroism by fighting crime, in a reversal of his earlier intentions, when he had named his plan to rob his employer 'Operation Solo'. When real villains arrive with the same intent, he uses the military tactics that he remembers from the war, relayed to the audience in a subjective voice-over, to repel the raiders. The recovery of his war-time status brings about a revelatory conversion. He severs his last link with the criminal life by rejecting Paula. He gives back her cigarette case, realising that, like the case, which is plated and not solid gold, she is a sham. His release from her influence is confirmed when the spider-and-web lighting decoration collapses as he leaves the club at the end. However, he is unable to escape the predicament that Paula had exploited. Like Ted in *Dancing With Crime*, Dick temporarily recovers a heroic masculine role by opposing crime. Unlike Ted, however, Dick has no 'natural' social role to return to.

The problems for the officer-class heroes in post-black market films like *The Ship That Died of Shame*, *The League of Gentlemen* and *A Prize of Arms* are that they are experiencing a loss of the power that they possessed in war-time. Bill Randall, for example, the former commander of the torpedo boat in *The Ship That Died of Shame*, fails in business and is unable to get his old pre-war job back. In this film, and particularly in *The League of Gentleman*, war-time camaraderie and officer-class authority is restored through crime. However, the films conform to the conventional morality of the time and these illegal solutions end in failure. Randall's 'rebirth' as a smuggler of post-war luxuries degenerates, without his knowledge, into providing an escape route for a child murderer. This fall can be taken as a cruel metaphor for the decline of post-war Britain itself. Randall and the ship's 'conscience' combine to end this sordid conspiracy and the final flashback images of the film remind us of post-war loss as the motor boat is shown speeding across the waves at the height of its war-time glory. Similarly, Hyde in *The League of Gentlemen*, experiences a brief renewal of purpose, before his nostalgic caper is defeated by misfortune and a vigilant police force.

Turpin's criminal 'mission' also fails, but *A Prize of Arms* provides quite a contrast to the Dearden films. A mood of noir fatalism replaces one of nostalgia. Instead of the authority of George Baker's and Jack Hawkins's middle-class professionalism, there is the ambiguity of an ex-officer represented by Stanley Baker's more lower-class tough-guy persona. Turpin and his two fellow ex-servicemen (Helmut Schmid, Tom Bell) use their Army skills, not as a way of recovering war-time purpose, but for financial gain. Only Turpin's personal motivation for the robbery is elaborated in any detail. In the early scenes on the night before their assault on the army camp payroll, Turpin's conversation reveals how at the end of the war in Hamburg, he was given an immediate dishonourable discharge for being involved in a minor black market coffee racket. Left with 'just three holes on each shoulder where the pips used to be', he is driven by a sense of injustice and an inability to relax and forget who he was. This obsession/determination, combined with a sense of fatalism and dark visual style is what gives the film a noir sensibility. Turpin's doomed robbery unfolds against a background of an uncertain post-war Britain, where bureaucrats with briefcases interfere in minor law breaking, where British troops are mobilised for controversial post-colonial conflicts abroad, and where an Army without bullets pursues those who have robbed from their own.

Officer-class subjectivity is again privileged in *The Intruder*. Ex-officer Wolf Merton's quest to uncover the truth behind Ginger's criminality is at the centre of the narrative. This quest places him in a position where, out of a sense of war-time loyalty, he is forced to compromise his respect for the law and authority by aiding Ginger's escape from the police. Merton's integrity, however, is not compromised, because Ginger faces up to his responsibility and turns himself in. Only under the paternalistic authority of his old commander can Ginger confront his problems and seek a successful adjustment to his changed circumstances.

The masculine crisis of the ex-servicemen in *The Good Die Young* forms the main part of this melodrama. The heist and its aftermath constitutes only the very end of the film. The robbery becomes one imaginary solution to the men's problems, but it is Rave who corrupts the others into crime. He exploits their vulnerability by reminding them of their plight. He argues that they all fought in the war and deserve something better. However, again within the conventional morality, their attempts to solve their relationship problems end in failure. The gang self-destructs through guilty conscience and double-cross. Rave is particularly at fault as a villainous, aristocratic wastrel, whose attempts to take all the money for himself results in the death of them all. The film closes with an image of the cemetery where the money is hidden (money = death) and on the soundtrack, the Voice-of-God narrator draws a moral conclusion about the money being an illusion that would not have helped them. Thus, denied this resolution, there is no solution to the men's problems other than through death.

Jim's corruption into crime in *Soho Incident* is presented with a degree of liberal sympathy similar to that accorded to Dave in *Dancing with Crime*. Jim's war-time background is again presented as a positive attribute, but moral weakness leads him to misapply his talents for material reward and it nearly costs him his life.

Men, women and money

Crises of masculinity were not confined to ex-servicemen in the post-war British crime film. Professional criminals and assorted amateurs who become criminalised were also shown to be experiencing 'female trouble'. Men and women were often inextricably linked in a nexus of criminal motivations in a number of films that stand as symbolic responses by men attempting to deal with the changing status of women.

'The picture hints that the wise- and the tough-guy are equally susceptible to feminine wiles, but it's too muscle-bound to make the proposition stick' (*Kinematograph Weekly*, 21 July, 1949). 'The picture' was *No Way Back* (Stefan Osiecki, 1949) and, as indicated by the nihilistic title, it was one of the darkest films made at that time. Terence de Marney stars as a boxer, 'The Croucher'. Like the ex-servicemen who become civilians, he loses a secure masculine role when he is forced to retire after losing the sight in one eye. He is further damaged when his materialistic wife, Sally (Shirley Quentin) deserts him when money runs short. 'I want better things from life. If I can't have them with you, well, it's just too bad', she informs him. She is a glamorous showgirl and the implication is that the relationship has always been based on money.

The Croucher becomes a drunken has-been until he is swept up from the pub by an old girlfriend, Beryl (Eleanor Summerfield), a 'good' woman whose love for him shakes him out of his self pity. However, Beryl is a 'kept woman', the girlfriend of Joe Sleat (Jack Raine), the leader of a gang of dockland low-lifes. Joe crows, 'I've got success and money and the girl's love me now'. He tries to keep The Croucher down by giving him menial jobs, but eventually his jealousy drives him to set up a raid on a jeweller's as a trap to deliver The Croucher to the police. Beryl foils the plot and the three of them end up being chased by the police to a siege at a warehouse.

The Croucher's crisis of masculinity is more than a subtext. This film is a crime melodrama that centres around the boxer's change in circumstances and his consequent confusion about his role. The power of men is measured in this film through their ability to obtain women through money. Joe's villainy is that he achieves his masculine role through crime. Sally is also corrupt because she values the money more than the man. The Croucher measures his own worth in terms of being a champion with a beautiful wife. He clings to an ambitiously potent, heightened masculinity. In the warehouse, thinking about his past and looking at Beryl's photograph of him in his boxing prime, he confesses that 'A man wants to feel like that again', to be a 'real man' and a 'big shot'. After Beryl has killed Joe, The Croucher receives reassurance when she tells him that 'she loved him then, she loves him now'. However, this does not seem enough. His loss seems unbearable. Accompanied by a loud speaker that blasts out a radio broadcast of his past glories to the assembled crowd, he leads Beryl to their off-screen deaths at the hands of police gunmen.

It is significant that Shakespeare's tragedy, *Macbeth*, was remade in this period as a gangster melodrama, *Joe Macbeth* (Ken Hughes, 1955). This film sets 'the Scottish play' in New York's underworld. Joe Macbeth (Paul Douglas) is a gunman who gets promoted to second in command in the gang. This fails to satisfy his wife, Lily (Ruth Roman), who wants more than the nice house and money that Joe's crimes have already provided. Her demands, therefore, go beyond conventional materialism, to the exercise of power through her dominated husband. She pushes him into killing the boss and taking his place at the head of the mob. Lily's scheming villainy is more heinous than Joe's profession of violence, since it leads to the destruction of the male world of the gang. This destructive reversal of traditional power structures is wonderfully captured in a photomontaged advertisement (*Kinematograph Weekly*, 27 October 1955), which shows a large close-up of the face of wide-eyed Joe looking up at a castratingly terrifying full-length image of Lily in slacks. The copy asks rhetorically, 'who wore the trousers and who did the KILLINGS?'.

The corrupt machinations of 'material girls' are again evident in *The Gentle Trap* (Charles Saunders, 1960). Johnny Ryan (Spencer Teakle) is a locksmith who helps an old professional thief in a diamond robbery. Double-crossed by a gang who try to snatch the gems, Johnny goes on the run. He is befriended by a 'good' woman, Jean (Felicity Young), who wants to know what got him into his situation. He blames Sylvia (Dawn Brooks), who has sold him to the gang. According to Johnny, she is 'A girl in love...with money. The kind of money a locksmith doesn't cart home'. Once the gang have been apprehended by the police, Johnny is free to build his new life with romantic Jean.

Tread Softly Stranger (Gordon Parry, 1958) is a noirish story that revolves

Figure 5.1 The problems of the patriarch weigh heavy on Joe Macbeth (Paul Douglas) in Ken Hughes' film (1955)
Source: British Cinema and Television Research Group archive, De Montfort University

around two brothers, Johnny (George Baker) and Dave (Terence Morgan), who are sexually attracted to Calico (Diana Dors). Their problems stem from work and money. Calico's job at a dance club is low-paid. Johnny shirks from work and prefers to earn easier money from gambling. It provides him with a bachelor lifestyle in London, but recent gambling debts have forced him back home to lie low with his brother in a northern industrial town. Dave works as a wages clerk at a factory and is motivated to steal from the firm to buy love from Calico. Dave begins to panic when the auditors are due and will discover the missing money. Once the idea of robbing the safe to hide the shortfall is jokingly raised by Johnny, it strikes Dave and Calico that it is the solution to all their monetary and sexual problems. Calico then takes the lead in persuading the men to go through with the plan, taunting Johnny as a coward and encouraging the nervous Dave. Although misfortune contributes to their fate, it is largely Calico's predatory and selfish manipulation of the men that is to blame for their downfall. She pushes Dave into the robbery, forcing a gun upon him for courage, the gun that delivers the men to the police for the murder of the night-watchman.

As his more confident and assertive brother observes, Calico has one hand on Dave's knee and the other in his pocket, she has got him 'by the short hairs'. In a potent image Johnny burns the stolen cash because it will incriminate them, but it also releases them from the matriarchal grip of the acquisitive Calico. The brothers' abuse of money is contrasted with the normative relationship of the factory worker, Paddy Ryan (Patrick Allen), who is engaged to another employee, Sylvia (Jane Griffiths). Unlike Johnny, Paddy is trying to make money the 'hard way', working night shifts and staying in to save up to get married. Sylvia agrees with what she calls his 'old-fashioned idea' that he doesn't want her to work once they are married. Paddy is also the son of the murdered night-watchman and in defence of his disrupted family and the dominant social order it represents, he has the narrative function of pursuing the two men until their capture. Thus, a traditional male 'breadwinner' successfully asserts himself over two men corrupted by a disruptive, empowered woman.

A *femme fatale* is also to blame for the corruption of another professional male in *Payroll* (Sidney Hayers, 1961). In this film, Katie (Francoise Prevost) drives her husband, Dennis (William Lucas), into crime by emasculating him with complaints about his stalled career and their consequent lowly status. He is an accountant who becomes the inside man for a gang of robbers. After the robbery, Katie abandons her husband, who has crumbled with guilt, and seduces the gang's leader, Johnny Mellors (Michael Craig), before finally failing in an attempt to double-cross him over the stolen money.

Blame was not always attached to women implicated in men's entry into professional crime. In *The Frightened Man* (John Gilling, 1952) and *The Man in the Back Seat* (Vernon Sewell, 1961), for example, men from different classes commit crime in a desire to please women, but they are experiencing a confusion of role more than a crisis directly attributable to the fault of

Figure 5.2 Katie, the emasculating woman (Francoise Prevost) and Dennis, the
desperate post-war man (William Lucas) in *Payroll* (1961)
Source: British Cinema and Television Research Group archive, De Montfort University

women. In *The Frightened Man* it is revealed that an antique dealer has
become a fence for a gang of robbers to pay for an Oxford University
education for his son[1]. Rosselli senior (Charles Victor) is bound into a life of
crime by a promise he made to his dying wife to look after his son, a wife
who 'always wanted good things' for their child. The son, Julius (Dermot
Walsh), unaware of the source of his father's income, rejects the privileged
start he has been given and attempts to become 'his own man'. His incentive
is that he has found a woman, Amanda (Barbara Murray), to marry. 'You're
going to be proud of me Amanda', he explains. 'I'm going to make money.
I'm going to make it fast'. He becomes the getaway driver for the gang on a
warehouse robbery and then sets up a diamond robbery with the gang's
leader, Alec Stone (Martin Benson). Tragically, the father unknowingly
delivers his son into a police trap because he is being double-crossed by
Stone. In attempting to escape, the son falls to his death from a roof.
Everything has gone wrong because relationships have been reduced to
financial transactions. The two men had made money too important. During
one conversation, Julius reassures Amanda that money is important because

'it gets you everything you want'. Unconvinced, Amanda responds by saying 'Except love'.

Similarly, Frankie (Keith Faulkner) in *The Man in the Back Seat* is experiencing a crisis in his relationship with his wife which he thinks he can solve with money. He mugs a bookie with the more experienced Tony (Derren Nesbitt), but the robbery goes wrong. Having driven away from the crime scene in the bookie's car, the drama of the film centres around the robbers' attempts to separate the money bag that is chained to the heavily coshed bookie and then to decide what to do with the unconscious victim. Frankie becomes involved mainly to help his 'mate', however, more detailed motivational characterisation emerges in the scenes at Frankie's house. In argumentative exchanges between Frankie and his wife Jean (Carol White), he explains that he committed the robbery for her. He thought that the money would improve their relationship. Frankie tells her that 'You could have given up work and we could have got out of this stinking basement'. While Jean is content to stay as they are, Frankie is desperate to provide for her and it destroys him. Tormented by guilty visions of the ghost of the dead bookie, 'the man in the back seat', he causes a car crash in which Tony is killed.

Conclusion – treading softly and dancing with crime

Apart from *Joe Macbeth*, the films used here to explore the gender relationships in the crime film between 1946 and 1965 do not centre around men for whom crime is an established career. Instead they can be described as films in which troubled men take up crime in an attempt to solve problems that generally involve relationships with women. The films of the late 1940s, in particular those featuring working-class ex-servicemen, are morality tales of good and evil, where the heroes encounter the villainy of 'spivs', racketeers, vice kings and the corrupt women who join them in their hedonistic activities. If the heroes are corrupted into professional crime, such as Dave in *Dancing With Crime*, it is presented with a degree of empathy with the vulnerability of their condition and the problematic experience of loss of power, agency and collective purpose.

The post-black-marketeering films also centre around the creation of a criminal identity. Men are shown to become criminalised as part of the problems of post-war readjustment (*The Intruder*), or because it gives them a chance of redress against their unfortunate circumstances (*Soho Incident, A Prize of Arms, The Ship That Died of Shame, The League of Gentlemen, The Good Die Young*) or through the influence of materialistic women (*Soho Incident* again, *The Gentle Trap, Tread Softly Stranger, Payroll*), or simply through a confusion over their roles (*The Frightened Man, The Man in the Back Seat*). Men transgress from a position where masculinity is felt to be under strain. They want to repair a sense of loss, chaos, fragmentation and perceived decline in power.

These films, then, which are otherwise quite varied and disparate, are all crime melodramas of masculine crisis, across which the themes of war-time loss and post-war women are significant. In a society that was perceived by older, middle-class men to have deteriorated since the war, and where the growth of consumerist culture had raised the status of women at their expense, men had to tread softly, or they would get caught in gentle traps and dark webs. They were forced, one might say, to dance with crime and became fugitives, intruders in a post-war society that wouldn't accommodate them.

Note

1 In this respect it closely resembles both *No Road Back* (Montgomery Tully, 1957), in which a mother fences to enable her son to be educated as a doctor in America, and *Assassin For Hire* (Michael McCarthy, 1951) in which a man uses the money from his contract killings to help his brother become a professional musician.

Bibliography

Coltrane, S. (1994) 'Theorising masculinities in contemporary social science', in H. Brod and M. Kaufman (eds) *Theorising Masculinities*, Thousand Oaks, California: Sage.

Hill, J. (1986) *Sex, Class and Realism: British Cinema 1956–63*, London: British Film Institute.

Hopkins, H. (1964) *The New Look*, London: Secker & Warburg.

Kaufman, M. (1994) 'Men, feminism, and men's contradictory experience of power', in H. Brod and M. Kaufman (eds) *Theorising Masculinities*, Thousand Oaks, California: Sage.

McFarlane, B. (1997) *An Autobiography of British Cinema*, London: Methuen.

Miller, L. (1994) 'Evidence for a British film noir cycle', in W.W. Dixon (ed.) *Re-Viewing British Cinema, 1900–1992*, New York: SUNY.

O'Sullivan, T. (1997) 'Not quite fit for heroes: cautionary tales of men at work – *The Ship That Died of Shame* and *The League of Gentlemen*', in A. Burton, T. O'Sullivan and P. Wells (eds) *Liberal Directions, Basil Dearden and Post-war British Film Culture*, Trowbridge: Flicks Books.

Place, J. (1980) 'Women in film noir', in A. E. Kaplan (ed.) *Women in Film Noir*, London: British Film Institute.

Street, S. (1997) *British National Cinema*, London, New York: Routledge.

Wilson, E. (1980) *Only Halfway to Paradise*, London: Tavistock.

6   The higher heel

Women and the post–war British crime film

Viv Chadder

> Was not the body so mutilated that it appeared as if an army of stiletto-heeled furies had gouged…
>
> (Public Prosecutor *A Question of Silence*)

Cinema would have to wait until 1981 for Marlene Gorris's film *A Question of Silence* to realise explicitly the male castration anxieties attached to the stiletto. This seemingly innocuous item of ladies' fashion was elongated and refined from the modest 'court' to the ultimate pinnacle of design achievement between 1947 and 1962. In this period, this shoe condenses a nucleus of meanings: it speaks of the relaxation of post-war austerity, modernity, female consumption, feminine aspiration and desire, but also the dangerous association of gangland weapon, the Italian 'other', and the troublesome eruption of the unknowable element of female sexuality. The stiletto recurs like a leitmotif in crime films of the period. It will do so in this chapter, for while it cannot drive and control meaning, it is nevertheless a site/sight of ambivalence: resistance *and* recuperation, the pointed heel of deviance, delinquency and the modern woman.[1]

The masquerade of feminine crime

The post-war British crime film offers up for public entertainment and enlightenment the revelation of an underworld, a dark mirror that mimics the paternalistic structures of the welfare state. The underworld, after all, has its own equally paternalistic systems of 'welfare' (protection, education/initiation), and offers its own routes to an affluent *embourgeoisement*. A framing device frequently guarantees the authenticity and urgency of the criminal threat to the safety of the social order, while the crime film as a whole eschews documentary realism in favour of melodrama to engage the popular imagination in its project. Most often, the focus is on the masculine structures of organised crime, armed robbery, racketeering, fraud, inter-gang violence, or on its juvenile equivalent the 'cosh boys'. Sometimes the cinema digs deeper and the 'problem' of criminality in women takes centre stage. Criminal women are not of course, exclusive to the British crime film. The image of the *femme fatale* in film noir, for instance, is often enhanced by criminal acts.[2] The significance of films that represent the criminal woman as part of an endemic social problem in this period should not, however, be underestimated.

It was not until the 1970s, that feminist work in social studies claimed that criminality in women had been subjected to statistical suppression, ignored alike by criminological theory as by policy-making institutions as of little account in the social process. Carol Smart attributes this neglect to 'orthodox, control-oriented criminology' with 'its traditionally narrow concerns with only those topics officially designated as social problems' (Smart 1976: 3). Criminology, however, is not confined to the realms of theory. It impacts directly on policy-makers, the penal code and popular belief. How far, then, do the agendas of criminology and the crime film concur in their construction of the criminal woman?

It is salutary to reconstruct the history of classical thought on the subject of women and crime, and to remember that its orthodoxy remained largely unchallenged until the 1970s. On the subject of female delinquency, W.I. Thomas writes in 1923:

> The beginning of delinquency in girls is usually an impulse to get amusement, adventure, pretty clothes, favourable notice, distinction, freedom in the larger world....The girls have usually become 'wild' before the development of sexual desire, and their casual sex relations do not usually awaken sex feeling. Their sex is used as a condition of the realisation of other wishes. It is their capital.
>
> (Thomas 1923: 109)

For Thomas, the woman 'craves' stimulus, a psychical destiny that puts her in breach of her social role irrespective of economic or any other predisposing factors. A criminal career is the inevitable outcome of a girl's resistance to a regulated role of subordination and unfulfilment. Her sexuality becomes a commodity for exchange on the open market, the tacit assumption being that men are always ready to take up their side of the bargain, though they are not, in this respect, considered to be the same threat to social stability. That responsibility lies with the delinquent girl and the unattached woman.

Otto Pollak in 1950, offered some subtle refinements on these existing themes. Beginning from a physiological 'truth', that women can deceive over sexual response whereas men can not, Pollak derives the whole nature of womanhood. The capacity to lie is fundamental to women's psychical makeup. The opportunity to exploit this innate skill is built in to the social role women are required to play. Thus female crime is 'masked' and sexualised in much the same way as Victorian medicine found a correlation between the reproductive phases of women and feminine forms of insanity, Pollak systematises female crime: 'Particularly because of the social meaning attached to them in our culture, the generative phases of women are bound to present many stumbling blocks for the law-abiding behaviour of women' (Pollak 1950: 43). The 'feminine' crime of shoplifting is the combined effect of the 'uncanny ingenuity' of 'modern sales techniques' and women's primary role as shoppers. In a wave of paranoia, Pollak records that :

> Each of the social roles which women perform in our culture furnishes such opportunities. Marriage in itself delivers a whole array of possible objects of attack for crimes against the person, practically defenceless, into the hands of the potential woman offender. Compared with the ease with which the preparer of meals, the child-rearer, and the nurse of the sick can direct an attack against physical well-being or life, the task of the male killer in our society is difficult indeed....In short, the criminality of women reflects their biological nature in a given cultural setting.
>
> (Pollak 1950: 43)

Pollak recognises that the post-war emphasis on women's domestic role will be attended by frustration and 'irritability' and acknowledges the existence of a sexual double standard that punishes women more harshly for breaches in sexual morality than men. However, he sees the consequences of women's sexual and social repression as a predisposition towards criminal behaviour. Women's 'natural' desire to redress these inequalities only masks deeper, and darker, unconscious desires. Behind every devoted wife and mother nurtured by the cult of domesticity in the period, there may lurk a secret and successful poisoner. The dedicated female consumer targeted by the burgeoning post-war economy may conceal a seasoned shoplifter. A woman who makes accusations of a sexual content may be deploying her innate skills in perjury.

Pollak's aim in 1950 was to raise the profile of female crime, developing ideas inherited from earlier commentators. We should not underestimate their influence. In 1976 Carol Smart can still claim that 'much of his argument has become common currency today and may even be shared by policy-makers and others who become involved with female offenders' (Smart 1976: 46). It may be argued, that female desire, in the form of sexual immorality and rebelliousness against the social roles expected of women, is itself criminalised. If the pleasures of consumption and the deep satisfaction of the pivotal role of domesticity did not suffice to reconcile women to these social roles, then the structures of reform and reprimand could coerce into conformity.

Down at heel

In 1949, Gainsborough Studios released *Good Time Girl*, produced by Sydney Box and directed by David MacDonald. This film afforded Jean Kent a rare opportunity to escape from lightweight roles into the serious dramatic part of 'good time girl', Gwen Rawlings. The film requires her to transmute from naive girl, to delinquent, to 'sophisticate' perpetrator of criminal acts. The narrative is framed by an opening scene where Lyla Lawrence (the young

Diana Dors) is marched into the awesome chambers of the juvenile court to be addressed by the magistrate (Flora Robson). Gwen Rawlings' story so alarms her that she is reconciled to family life, subsidising a drunken and abusive father and curtailing her desire for 'distinction, freedom in the larger world'. Tradition appears to prevail over modernity. The Hogarthian style 'progress' of Gwen from innocent to accomplice in murder should run uninterruptedly, but there are awkward breaks, inconsistencies, ellipses, sites/sights of ambivalence where female desire may install itself, albeit in a criminalised form.

Gwen's own appearance in the juvenile court in a scene early on in the film condenses and displaces the locus of criminality. On top of the feminine offences of incorrigibility and running away, she is found guilty, but not convicted, of petty larceny. The evidence on hearsay of the pawnbroker to the effect that she stole (borrowed) a brooch for which he sacked her, compounds her guilt. That he offers to conceal the 'theft' in exchange for sexual favours is not even raised. The character reference supplied by Red, the middle-class club pianist is impaired by the impropriety of him having sheltered a minor in the absence of his wife, and the court places an unlikely confidence in the testimony of Jimmy the spiv that she stole the landlady's jewels and subjected him to violent attack. Both the pawnbroker and Jimmy seek revenge for Gwen's rejection of their advances, her refusal to realise her capital asset in the sexual economy. Jewels stand in for the disruptive allure of female sexuality, for which Gwen is multiply punished. The juvenile court can clearly decipher this substitution. She is given the maximum sentence of three years in an approved school.[3] The correctness of judgement, if not of justice, is supported by the ensuing scene, where Red and Gwen exchange a passionate, open-mouthed kiss before the fascinated gaze of the female court-room attendant. The 'official' narrative cannot support this manifestation of unregulated female desire and claims its price finally when Gwen is the link, the cause and the unknowing accomplice to Red's murder at the conclusion of the film's action.

The Approved School fails in its project to regulate, train and reform. This should be accountable to Gwen's excessive rebelliousness or some other predisposing factor. But there is a clear attribution of institutional failure that is shown to accelerate rather than restrain her descent into 'depravity'. These schools were seen as a solution to the problem of delinquency. Training proceeded strictly along the lines of prescribed gender roles. *Good Time Girl* affords some glimpses into this regime, and also some account of the power relations that sustain its survival. The girls are shown dutifully at work on that most fulfilling of female activities – mopping; they are compulsorily dressed in the most functional, unfeminine utility dress; inflammatory literature (such as Red's love letters to Gwen) is carefully censored. Gwen's initial rebelliousness against middle-class authority figures marks her out for the attention of Roberta (Jill Balcon).[4] A violent and intimate struggle on the floor ensues. Roberta undertakes the true training process of the school, showing that the pretence of conformity pays dividends. The teachers may preserve their liberal reformist stance, training through kindness, firmness and example but their support is an underground power structure where 'senior' girls use the younger ones as 'fags' to procure cigarettes and alcohol, demanding absolute loyalty to their leadership and where deviance is punishable by ear-twisting. Lip service alone is paid by the film to the liberal intentions of these institutions – the staff meeting, for instance, where the headmistress deplores staff shortages – and a structural contradiction emerges between middle-class interests and beliefs and the real condition on which their philanthropy is predicated. The official narrative of the film favours the headmistress's philanthropic aspirations but the spectator is positioned ambivalently in regard to Gwen's determination to escape from the institution: to identify with her desire for freedom in the world is to become complicit with her rejection of middle-class idealism and norms of femininity.

In her return to the world of underworld drinking clubs, Gwen's descent into criminality is confirmed. It can be argued that the underworld in this period functions as a distorting mirror to the welfare state and we might expect to see its structures doubled or perverted. There is indeed an interesting doubling of father figures in this film: Gwen's 'real' father, drunken and abusive and her underworld father, the rather more 'genteel' club owner, Max (Herbert Lom). The doubling testifies to a weakness of the paternal signifier. Both fathers fail to regulate Gwen's 'wildness', which takes the form of a demand for self-determination and its underworld perversion, sexual assertiveness. In this respect, *Good Time Girl* reproduces post-war anxieties and instability and searches for official solutions. Women may not reconcile themselves to the domestic role after the 'freedoms' of war-time. Men may not regain their authority within the home or may be unwilling or unable to resume it. Civil society may not afford the same potential for heroic action as in war-time, or its capacity to absorb masculine energies. Gwen's final role as stooge for a pair of army deserters that leads to murder, represents a lethal condensation of the destabilisation of masculine structures and unregulated female sexuality.

It is in this context that we should understand the visibility of the 'good time girl' as an urgent social problem in this film. Cinema managers were advised to launch their publicity campaign for the film on two fronts. First, a challenge is offered to a potentially male audience, to shoulder responsibility for this unavoidable fact of modern life, to face up to the shocking truth of her existence. As the trailer puts it:

> Whether you Like it or Not, YOU are
> Responsible for the 'GOOD TIME GIRL!'

The content of this appeal is not, however, to accept blame for Gwen's criminal career but to take up the paternal role in earnest. It is, after all, the woman who is the problem.

The second recommendation for 'first rate publicity' for *Good Time Girl* offers interesting possibilities: Jean Kent's shoes. These shoes are the condition of pleasure in an otherwise moralising narrative. The star appeal of Jean Kent has already led, it would appear, to a 'solidly established range of extremely smart and attractive ladies' footwear, created by the well-known firm of S.A. Squirrel and Co. Ltd., of Leicester'. While contemporary reformists constantly insist on the lumpen gracelessness of the delinquent girl, Gwen's progress through the film is marked by constant costume changes, from the modest 'utility' dress of the pawnbroker's assistant, reduced to a severe and improving minimalism in the approved school, to a simulation of the Dior 'New Look': graceful, elegant, risky, designed to display the lines of the 'best possible' feminine figure, supported by the light and refined 'court' shoe with Louis heel. Here, is where the traces of female desire are inscribed.

The higher heel

Murder is still a statistical rarity among the crimes committed by women. The cyclical outbursts of popular revulsion against Myra Hindley testify to a persistent and profound belief in the natural antipathy of women and violence. The woman who transgresses against this is indeed evil. When the woman kills, she does so either in Pollak's image of secret and undiscovered poisoner within the domestic environment, or in calculated self-defence against domestic abuse deploying feminine weapons such as the kitchen knife, the rolling pin, the pillow. In either instance the crime tends to be sexualised. Feminine means to a feminine end. Men are presumed to be the typical victims of women's murderous attentions. Of course, women murderers populate the cinema, but J. Lee Thompson's film *Yield to the Night* (1956) locks itself in to a contemporary debate on crime and punishment.

This is only one year after the hanging of Ruth Ellis for the murder of her lover, a *crime passionel*. In a fascinating journalistic reconstruction, Laurence Marks and Toby Van Den Bergh (1977) evoke the milieu of the drinking clubs where Ruth Ellis held the position of club hostess. Here is an alternative topos to the Persil homes and Babycham world of 1950s advertising. These clubs are a parody of *embourgoisement* with their intermingling of tarts, film stars, sports celebrities, politicians, racketeers and aristocrats.

Ruth Ellis's hanging fired public debate on the issue of capital punishment. The opposition lobby implicitly depended on the stereotype of nurturing, caring, femininity to display the brutality of a masculinised criminal justice system. Marks and Van Den Bergh describe the consequences of Ruth Ellis's fatal request for the services of a hairdresser before her trial:

> Instead of a dejected young woman, tired-looking, sombre, and about to stand trial for her life, she looked like she was attending the première of a West End show. She was dressed in a two-piece suit with an astrakhan collar, and a white blouse. Her hair was immaculate and dazzling blonde....All eyes focused upon her as she calmly, calculatedly walked

across from the dock to the witness box. The courtroom was silent. Her stiletto-heeled shoes clicked in time to her heartbeat.

(Marks and Van Den Bergh 1977: 134)

In reality, it would seem, Ruth Ellis was hanged as much for her transgressive image as for the failure of her lawyers to bring a case of diminished responsibility.

In British cinema one earlier attempt to deal with the sensitive subject of capital punishment, *Daybreak* (1949) had suffered two years of delay over struggles with the censors. In 1956, in the context of a growing lobby against capital punishment, *Yield to the Night* confronts its theme with confidence. From the death cell, Mary Hilton (Diana Dors) recalls, in spasmodic flashback, the events leading up to her crime, and simultaneously confronts her impending execution. The dual unfolding of the narrative accommodates Diana Dors' reputation as Britain's glamour queen and her new role as serious dramatic actress. The distributors, Associated British Pathé, clearly intended the film to draw on and generate discussion on a national issue. Publicity material asked 'Would YOU hang Mary Hilton?'

Figure 6.1 Female transgression and the dilemmas of its punishment: Diana Dors
poses some difficult questions in J. Lee Thompson's harrowing film (1956)
Source: British Cinema and Television Research Group archive, De Montfort University

There are certain restraints however. The social milieu inhabited by Ruth Ellis seems to be exorcised from the film (except that we might expect that what is excised may always return in another register). Mary Hilton, prior to her crime, pursues one of the few legitimate and glamorous career opportunities open to women in the 1950s – the beauty business. She is a model of social mobility, the product of a working-class family dedicated to 'improvement' (working-class mother on a prison visit refers to dead father's sacrifices on account of his now erring daughter). Class issues announce themselves implicitly. Flashbacks reveal Mary to be estranged from her husband. Prison visits confirm Fred to be caring, affectionate, solid, reliable and ultimately 'boring'. By contrast, Jim, the club pianist Mary falls passionately in love with, has a cultural capital that attracts her. She picks up the copy of *A Shropshire Lad* in his bedsit and lingers over the lines 'Loveliest of trees the cherry now/ Is hung with bloom along the bough'. But as with *Good Time Girl*, the social world of this film is beset with the failure of masculine structures. A more expert reader than Mary might have been alerted by this poetry that tells of suicide, murder, death in the prime of life, infidelity, unrequited love, post-war malaise. The lines return, internalised, in deadly form, to haunt her on prison exercise.[5]

After Jim's suicide, the narrative economy allows for only one possible victim. Mary's crime is to kill the 'other woman' out of jealous revenge on the level of the narrative, but in cold blood (no possible case of diminished responsibility here). The film allows for no uncertainties concerning Mary's guilt. She does not repent and there is no concern with the niceties of motivation. The case is simple, reduced to a brief debate between two death-cell wardresses. Is there anything to be gained from taking another life? With this project, *Yield to the Night* can afford to be even-handed. The death-cell routine even has its apologist in the form of Miss Bly, the benevolent prison reformer. Mary is assured that her body will obey the rituals she has been 'taught', while her mind will be 'in a dream'.

Yield to the Night uses the resources of cinema to dramatise fear rather than to berate institutions or individuals. Dors is faced with a difficult acting task that puzzled some critics. Denied histrionics, de-glamourised in the death cell, she is left with nothing to do but to gaze blankly at the camera as the voice-over, deprived of narrative content, murmurs on. As the time of execution approaches, the camera peers at Mary's face from every angle, staring in close-up at the wide-open unblinking eyes, the beads of sweat. In as much as the camera demands knowledge, meaning is evacuated. The body is impenetrable. The imposition of the murmuring voice-over promises intimacy, but death does not yield up its secrets.

In 1956 Gollancz published Koestler's *Reflections on Hanging*. Surveys had shown that women were less inclined to pardon Ruth Ellis than men and Koestler suggests that this severity conceals an unconscious identification. Women would really like to be in the position to punish infidelity in husbands and lovers (though this film punishes the woman). How, one wonders, did the female members of the audience for *Yield to the Night* respond to the advance publicity appeal to judge Mary Hilton? Did they put on the 'cloak of moral righteousness', as Koestler suggests, to clothe over jealousy and envy for her crime of striking out against the seductive other woman? Or were they lured by the possibility of purchasing Dors' belted, camel hair coat, her 'chunky' bracelets or her 'heeled toe-less leather shoes'?

Tie-up publicity stills for *Yield to the Night* picture Dors parading a 'toe-less' sandal with high fine heel and elegant ankle-strap. By 1956 the stiletto was a coveted object of popular demand. The pre-credits sequence opens with the clicking of a pair of similarly heeled shoes with rounded toe advancing through the streets and squares of the metropolis. The camera intercuts warningly to a pair of iron gates secured with a heavy padlock and chain, to the naked masculine foot of a public sculpture, to the booted foot of a man kick-starting a motorcycle and comes to rest on danger as a nylon-clad feminine foot slides seductively into a stiletto discarded beside the throttle of an expensive car.[6] Mary Hilton clearly knows what's at stake as she stares down from the security of her own stilettos and throws her lover's revolver contemptuously to land between the crumpled legs of her victim. Cut to Mary Hilton in the death cell She complains 'my foot hurts me'. Cut to the beauty parlour in flashback. A note of longing creeps into Mary's confident narrating voice-over, 'the first thing I noticed about Lucy was her very high heels.'…This woman, Lucy Carpenter, is pure masquerade. She is the cruel dominatrix of Jim's fantasy that intervenes between him and Mary.[7] She is a collection of female body parts, a hand dripping with 'chunky' bracelets, a luxurious fur coat, an immaculate pair of seamed nylons, a purring voice on the telephone, stilettos straight from the pages of *Vogue*. We know that in 1956 the construction of this shoe was impractical, demanding skill from the wearer, to balance and to cling to, especially in the toe-less version. It was precarious (the wooden heel could snap). This competition of the heel in *Yield to the Night* is the point where meaning slides metonymically from permissible feminine enhancement to deviant dangerous excess.

In the death cell, Mary Hilton experiences a heightening of sensory awareness. She is alert to the steady beat of the prison governess's footsteps as she approaches to confirm the time of execution. The camera focuses in close-up on the smart 'court' shoe, denoting a modern outlook, progressiveness. Mary's own foot has been forced into prison-issue, leather lace-up, hobbled, swollen and reduced to the flat shuffle of the carpet slipper. An oedipal castration. The sole of a wardress's shoe fills the frame as the last murmur of Mary's voice-over directs us to the 'sensible' wooden heel protected against wear by iron studs, a model of conformity, economy and tradition. The primacy of this rare instance of a female voice-over in 1950s British cinema must be attended to. Mary's voice-over drives the narrative, records the history of her crime. Alternatively, it sinks to the faltering tones of desire. Her last murmur, in retroactive enchainment of the signifier (Zizek 1992: 69) animates the absence of metal knives in the death cell (Mary complains at having to cut her food with wooden spoons), the recollection of her foot blistered and swollen by a skating boot (another shoe supported by metal blade). We may include also the metal keys that are always in Mary's control, the key to the drawer in which she locks and unlocks the revolver, the key that she fits in the lock to Lucy Carpenter's house, a redundant act on the level of narrative as she doesn't need to enter. This signals possession of the power to unlock a peculiarly feminine space. On the level of the narrative, Mary Hilton's story is the vehicle of a liberal reforming project. On the level of the image and the sound track, something is recuperated.

The highest heel

In September 1957, after three years of consideration, the Wolfendon Committee presented its report on criminal offences relating to prostitution (and homosexuality). It recognised the impossibility, if not the desirability, of eliminating this oldest of all professions by criminalising prostitution as such. It focused on the visible nuisance of street walking and the improvements necessary in criminal law to clean up the streets. It is commonplace to observe that the recommendations of the committee leave the male client of the almost exclusively female prostitute beyond the reach of the law. The parade of the prostitute was deemed to be more offensive than the male footfall of the customer. A simple economic model of supply and demand is applied. If women were not street walking, then male demand would diminish. Increased fines and terms of imprisonment were to be the deterrent. The report is unconcerned that this will drive the trade underground where it will become an 'organised vice' and increase the exploitation of women by middlemen. The existing evidence was not seen to support this outcome and the rigorous application of existing laws against exploitation was believed to suffice. The sight of the prostitute was the real point of danger.

The enslavement of women as passive victims of vast criminal organisations is dismissed as a 'popular impression'. The report reassures itself that: 'today, either through the effectiveness of the law or through changes which have removed some of the economic and social factors likely to result in a life of prostitution, she is in less danger of coercion or exploitation against her will' (Wolfendon 1957: 100). 'Protection' is viewed as a mutual arrangement from which the woman profits, a commercial and emotional transaction (ibid.). Here, the Wolfendon Report approaches a problem to which, in a Freudian manner it continually returns, the unknowable element of female sexuality. What *is* the aetiology of female prostitution if the stimulus of economic need, childhood abuse and coercion have been discounted? 'We still do not know at all precisely what element it is in the total personality of a woman which results in her adopting a life of prostitution' (ibid.: 98).

Popular cinema of the period as one might suspect, responds to the melodramatic potential of 'popular impression'. The narrative trajectory of *The Flesh is Weak* (Don Chaffey, 1957) and *Passport to Shame* (Alvin Rakoff, 1959) positions the woman as unwilling victim of organised crime, to be rescued from the unspeakable fate of prostitution notably *not* by the institutional forces of law and order, but by middle-class philanthropists or salt-of-the-earth community-spirited London taxi drivers. *Kine Weekly* describes *The Flesh is Weak* as a 'sex melodrama', 'compounded of fact and fiction', 'ruthlessly (exposing) the white slave traffickers', while *Passport to Shame* (scripted by a Fleet Street investigative journalist) 'vividly reveals the tricks of London's white slave traffic' (quoted in Hill 1986: 187, 192). However, the *Monthly Film Bulletin* condemns *The Flesh is Weak* as 'crudely melodramatic' while *Passport to Shame* gains the accolade of 'wildly incredible' and 'wholeheartedly absurd' (quoted in Hill, ibid.). As certainly, though, both films lay claim to a level of authenticity and topicality. We could try to balance the account between the evidence of the Wolfendon Report, which denies the existence of extensive trafficking in women on an international scale and vast vice rings of organised prostitution, with its thematic persistence in popular cinema. But we might also address the evident rupture in these X-certificated narratives between authenticity and melodramatic excess.

Publicity material for *The Flesh is Weak* puts a premium on exposing the 'truth' about London's vice kings. The screenwriter Leigh Vance supposedly frequented their haunts for accurate detail and he is given fictional representation in the film as Buxton, the middle-class philanthropist who makes notes, studies the methods of the Giani brothers' racket and poses as a client in the interest of eliminating vice. Raymond Stross the producer 'insured himself for £20,000 against personal injury' and stressed that: 'he well realises that many of London's vice bosses will not like what he has to say about them on the screen'! This promise of an enticing insight into the 'real' activities of the criminal underworld is compounded by the appearance of the glamorous Italian actress Milly Vitale as Marissa, the innocent visitor to London who becomes the victim of an elaborate plot to trap her into prostitution. A feminine weakness for luxury and excitement makes her easy prey for the romantic attentions of Tony Giani (John Derek) who throws aside her predecessor (Shirley Ann Field) to seduce her and initiate the 'breakdown' process that will persuade her into walking the streets on his behalf. In the course of this she incurs the statutory £2.00 fine for soliciting (and the title 'common prostitute') and a spell in Holloway on a faked-up charge for defying the Giani brothers. She is quite unable to extricate herself from the tangle and is rescued by Buxton who persuades her to testify against Tony. The narrative puts forward its case for cleaning up the streets by destroying the vice rings, while Marissa is offered the prospect of a decent future.

In an apparent contradiction, the official forces of law and order seem more than adequate to the task of dealing with the Mafia-style gang warfare that arises during the course of the narrative. The police inspector treats the elder milk-drinking Giani brother and the opposing gang leader, Santi, like a pair of naughty schoolboys in an almost comic scene, though the police generally appear powerless to curtail the Giani's organisation of street-walking activities that originate from a down-at-heel café and an unassuming terrace house. Once again, it would seem it is the woman that is the problem. In two crucial scenes, masculine anxieties come to the fore. As Tony Giani initiates Marissa in the bedroom of the Brighton flat, he pushes her head suggestively down his naked upper body. A telephone call interrupts, but the camera swings round to show him in self-contemplation, the woman dismissed, smoothing his hand over his body in displaced auto-eroticism. Later as Marissa resists his plans, he breaks out into a diatribe on the subject of frailty in women of pathological proportions. Female desire is either criminalised, subjected to vicious retribution or anaesthetised in this narrative. Quietly, it reasserts itself in another register. As Marissa's career advances towards prostitution, she acquires a wardrobe to die for! The sensible clothes of her arrival in London and the flat walking shoes are exchanged for elegant, sophisticated day–evening wear: a striking over-checked shirt with peplum, patent leather belt and pencil skirt; an array of furs; and of course, stilettos. In a risky moment, Marissa asserts her freedom to walk the streets outside male control, dressed in figure-displaying draped jersey, stiletto heels and assertive, square-shouldered fur cape. This clearly is the image that must be recuperated. In the same dress she walks from the gates of Holloway prison. The camera drops to the level of the stiletto, met by two pairs of arresting male feet. Buxton 'rescues' her from the Giani brothers and bundles her into a taxi. But, for a brief moment in this film, the woman marks a point of resistance to both order, decency and criminal underworld alike, an excess beyond documentation and the boundaries of melodramatic convention.

In 1959 British Lion released *Passport to Shame*, hoping to profit from the visibility of the still controversial Wolfendon Report, and equally as happy to flout some of its wisdom. It offers up to the popular imagination an 'exposure' of a tangled web of organised vice on an international scale presided over by Herbert Lom as the Italianate East Ender Nick Biagi. The style is wildly eclectic, breaking at one point into a modern dance fantasy where the innocent Malou (Odile Versois) in drug-induced state is dragged down into a cauldron of predatory young men with nude torsos and outstretched arms. The plot is perfectly symmetric and wholly absurd. Pretty Parisian waitress, Malou, is framed for theft from the till and offered the 'protection' of genteel English lady Aggie (Brenda de Banzie). A *mariage blanc* is arranged between Malou and taxi driver Johnny (Eddie Constantine), for Malou to acquire the necessary passport. Malou is horrified to discover its true purpose. Nick and Aggie have marked her out as a 'special' and promise her a rewarding career in high-class prostitution. Resisting, she is forced out onto the streets to ply her trade as common prostitute. Johnny, guilt-ridden, sets out to rescue her. Meanwhile, Malou attracts the sympathy of the experienced Vicki (Diana Dors), who is already installed in the 'bad' house adjoining Aggie's respectable mansion. The film rushes to a feel-good conclusion. As Johnny leads a raid of London cabbies on the bad house, Vicki traps Nick in a box room at the top of the building and sets it on fire in hatred and revenge for the mutilation of her sister (this offers Diana Dors the opportunity for a fine range of facial contortions!). As his friend Mike leads Malou and Vicki to safety, Johnny heroically stays to rescue Nick who despite the liberal scattering of bank notes on the crowd and firemen below, falls to his death from the building. In a final shot, Aggie lovingly arranges the tie and handkerchief on Nick's dead body, while Johnny and Malou embrace and Vicki walks off on Mike's arm to the sound of a romantic theme tune. All of this, needless to say, met with the scorn of serious film critics.

Almost as a by-product, the film joins in with a discussion on femininity in late 1950s Britain. Publicity stills display 'Britain's Sex Symbol', Diana Dors, and 'the enchanting French star' Odile Versois standing together, an unlikely alliance of modest decency and sexual assertiveness. Odile Versois dressed in shirt blouse with full skirt, restrained blonde curls and moderate-heeled shoe strikes a refined pose, while Diana Dors' hourglass figure is emphasised by close-fitting belted jersey, starched blonde hair, thrusting bosom, hands on hips to accentuate pelvis, legs apart on six-inch-high white stilettos with cutaway pointed toe. The film itself is quick to compare the two women on the level of style. After Fabian of the Yard's introduction, the credits sequence

Figure 6.2 'An unlikely alliance of modest decency and sexual assertiveness': Odile
        Versois and Diana Dors display clean and dirty pairs of heels in the trade
        advertisement for Alvin Rackoff's prostitution melodrama (1959)
Source: British Cinema and Television Research Group archive, De Montfort University

enlists the audience in a playful guessing game. With the camera held at street level, feet come and go, swing, run or creep, a woman's foot in down-at-heel sandal and beat girl's pumps cross the frame, brothel creepers silently approach a woman's basket to pilfer a choice tin, street cleaner's broom sweeps up muddied newspaper with the crumpled headline 'Police Swoop on London Vice Ring', male voice calls out a warning as a stunning pair of stilettos is about to step off the kerb onto the street. The camera travels appreciatively upwards to reveal Vicki, uplift bra risen to shelf-like proportions, tethered to the neck by a single diagonal halter strap. The camera cuts to Johnny, window-shopping for a new cab, and cuts again to the window of a Parisian boutique, where the price of the taxi translates into francs as the tag for a pretty, confectionery-style Easter bonnet, which Malou's reflection tries on approvingly.

This stylistic separation between the two women is sustained throughout the film, which complicates normal narrative procedures. Malou's initiation into prostitution begins as Aggy throws open the wardrobe door and picks out a glamorous cocktail dress. Her resistance is registered in a persistent pref-erence for the shirtwaister. Malou stands for the preferred model of 1950s femininity in her respect for romance and domesticity, her maternal instinct confirmed by cuddling of the cat. Vicki is her underworld reflection: sexually assertive, independent but recuperable through her 'strong sense of values' on the level of the narrative. This neat model is played out in the theme of two houses: the respectable mansion and its criminal underworld mirror, the bad house where the tarts drape themselves over the balcony. And of course there is the sliding door between them, the suggestive interface between the crim-inal world and the social order. While Malou's version of femininity is wholly alien to the bad house, the more transgressive Vicki is equally at home in either space. She alone is entirely free to come and go without visible adapta-tion, through the connecting door between the two houses.

I propose that the modern woman becomes the troublesome symptom of criminality in British crime films of this period. From the flower-filled diamanté-studded stiletto table decoration that sits between Johnny and Nick in *Passport to Shame* can be deduced the extent to which the shoe carries the woman. We know that by 1959 the stiletto heel had risen to maximum height and refinement of point, enabled by the new technology of the steel core. As the street-walking scenes from these two crime films of the late 1950s demonstrate, this shoe demanded from its wearer the skills of the fashion model on the catwalk. A weapon indeed!

Notes

1 This chapter is generally indebted to Lee Wright's essay 'Objectifying gender: the stiletto heel' (1995) and also to discussions with Sue Harper, Reader in Film History at the University of Portsmouth.

2 Raymond Durgnat's inclusive definition of the British crime film in the age of austerity as any film in which crime is committed, reveals more than one criminal

woman. See R. Durgnat (1997) 'Some lines of inquiry into post-war British crimes', in R. Murphy (ed.) *The British Cinema Book*, London: BFI.

3 'It has been my experience…that when a girl's behaviour is such that she needs training in an approved school at all, she needs it for considerably longer than the short-term school provides' (J. Watson (1942) *The Child and the Magistrate*, London: Jonathan Cape, 151.

4 An earlier version of the script had been quite explicit about the sexual content of Roberta's interest in Gwen, including a scene where Roberta strokes Gwen's hair, for instance.

5 Laurence Marks and Tony Van Den Bergh (1977) offer an interesting account of the spiralling descent of Ruth Ellis's father, admittedly from a starting point in the mid-1920s, from classical cellist to Palm Court musician to cinema orchestral player to hall porter.

6 'In films of the fifties and sixties…(the) removal of stilettos was often used to imply a sexual encounter' (Wright 1995: 16).

7 The sexual arrangements in this film are perfectly Lacanian: there is no sexual relation.

Bibliography

Hill, J. (1986) *Sex, Class and Realism: British Cinema 1956–1963*, London: British Film Institute.

Marks, L. and Van Den Bergh, T. (1977) *Ruth Ellis: A Case of Diminished Responsibility*, London: Penguin.

Pollak, O. (1950) 'The masked character of female crime' in F. Adler and J. Simon *The Criminality of Deviant Women*, New York: University of Pennsylvania Press.

Smart, C. (1976) *Women, Crime and Criminology: A Feminist Critique*, London: Routledge.

Thomas, W.I. (1923) *The Unadjusted Girl*, Boston: Little, Brown.

Wolfendon Report (1957) *Report of the Committee on Homosexual Offences and Prostitution*, London: HMSO.

Wright, Lee (1995) 'Objectifying gender: the stiletto heel', in J. Atfield and P. Kirkham (eds) *A View From the Interior: Women and Design*, London: Women's Press.

Zizek, S. (1992) *Looking Awry*, MIT Press, p. 69.

7 The emergence of the British tough guy
Stanley Baker, masculinity and the crime thriller

Andrew Spicer

The urban tough guy or 'city boy' has been identified as the central masculine type in American popular culture (Sklar 1992). The city boy is tough, energetic, unburdened by illusions; a man from a deprived background surviving and succeeding through his own efforts, including crime, in a competitive world. He often dares to challenge the status quo. By contrast, British culture's central type has been the gentleman, a product not of modernity and the city, but of tradition, Home Counties' pastoralism and the London club. The gentleman did not need to be tough, though as Bulldog Drummond he might aim a well-directed punch to some unsporting foreign miscreant. The gentleman did not need to compete since he was already successful; his privileged background gave him access to whatever he needed. His *metier* was restraint, moral authority and the preservation of the status quo.[1]

However, the social and cultural changes caused by the war and shifts in British film production and consumption gradually allowed a specifically British working-class tough guy to emerge in the late 1950s, dependent on American models but also transforming them. After a brief overview of these changes, I shall analyse the ideological work the British tough guy could perform and the kind of masculinity he represented through a discussion of several films starring Stanley Baker.

The dislocations of the war and the problems of readjustment were refracted in a spate of crime films produced in the immediate post-war period, particularly a cycle of 'spiv' films, urban thrillers with London settings (Murphy 1989: 146–67). However, the majority of these were second features, which lacked cultural status. William Hartnell as 'Britain's Cagney' in *Appointment With Crime* (1946) or Terence de Marney's sub-John Garfield role as an East End city boy, The Croucher, in *No Way Back* (1949), had a limited impact and both actors went into character roles.[2] It was only through American finance that crime thrillers were made as first features: Warner Bros' *They Made Me A Fugitive* (1947), directed by Cavalcanti, and Twentieth Century Fox's *Night and the City* (1950) directed by Jules Dassin. Both were adapted from British crime novels and used a noir visual style to portray a brutal, lawless and violent society in which the police are a marginal presence and the criminal a thrilling and challenging figure.

They Made Me a Fugitive was the more topical and its characters unmistakably British. It paired a new social type, the maladjusted veteran – bored, cynical and hard drinking ex-RAF officer Clem Morgan (Trevor Howard), who has become addicted to exciting action – with the underworld dandy, Narcy (Griffith Jones). Narcy, handsome, sophisticated, street-wise, immaculately dressed and puffing on a cigarette-holder, is both a glamorised contemporary East End gangster and a Gothic villain, an updating of the cruel, sexy aristocrats of the Gainsborough costume melodramas. Narcy has also been state trained, 'I learnt just as many parlour tricks in the war as you did'. Clem is soon out of his depth, his scruples about handling drugs cause Narcy to frame him for the murder of a policeman. The central scenes show Clem, unshaven and with a back full of buckshot, on the run after escaping from Dartmoor, a man brutalised by his war experiences and his contact with the underworld. Laconic, mistrustful and hard-bitten, no longer a hero 'because I went on doing what the country put me in uniform to do after they'd taken it back', Clem struggles to clear his name in a hostile and unforgiving world where even a respectable middle-class woman propositions him to kill her husband. In the final struggle, Narcy falls to his death but refuses Clem any death-bed reprieve and he returns to prison. This bleak conclusion is only softened by the loyalty of Narcy's ex-girlfriend Sally, alienated by her lover's brutality and attracted by the battling courage of Clem.

They Made Me a Fugitive provoked critical outrage. One influential commentator suggested that such representations were, 'socially dangerous in a world suffering from the severe after-effects of the moral distortions of war' (Manvell 1946: 62). The film's capacity to unsettle was precisely related to its ability to threaten a consensual and co-operative model of post-war society by plunging its middle-class anti-hero into a nightmarish, predatory Hobbesian world where only the most ruthless have a chance of survival. But it obviously spoke to powerful anxieties and desires in post-war audiences: *They Made Me a Fugitive* performed well at the box-office.[3]

Despite this success, Warner Bros, like other American majors, shifted its British production into historical adventures such as *Captain Horatio Hornblower RN* (1951), which proved a successful strategy and discouraged any further production of crime thrillers. The lack of interest in the battling tough guy on the part of British film-makers stemmed from their essentially middle-class commitment to a law-and-order paradigm in which society and the state were beneficent. Hence, their use of the 'delinquent', pathologised, from *Black Memory* (1947) through to *Serious Charge* (1959), as unstable and vicious, rather than tough and exciting. The society the delinquents disrupted was orderly and paternalistic, embodied in kindly policemen, caring probation officers and progressive clergymen. Only the adaptations of Graham Greene – *Brighton Rock* (1948) and *The Third Man* (1949) – showed the subversive potential of the criminal. But both were carefully distanced: a pre-war Brighton 'now happily no more' and the vertiginous ambiguities of a war-torn and divided Vienna.

In the first half of the 1950s the British crime thriller became marooned as the lower half of the ubiquitous double bill, supplied by small companies with an eye to the American market. Hammer Films switched from adaptations of the well-bred adventures of BBC radio sleuths to tough thrillers because it 'could supply at reasonable cost the kind of modest B-picture that was fast dying out in Hollywood due to rising costs and a shrinking market' (Eyles *et al.* 1994: 29). A similar policy was pursued by Anglo-Amalgamated, Tempean and the Danziger brothers (from 1954). This explains the plethora of low-budget British crime thrillers in the 1950s made with tough and laconic American male leads. *The Gambler and the Lady* (1952) starred Dane Clark as Jim Forster, a two-fisted fortune hunter who has stayed on after the war to become one of the major controllers of Soho's 'spielers'. His success is blighted by his obsession with gaining entry to the British aristocracy, becoming a gentleman, not a gangster. His minder is repeatedly told to call him 'sir' not 'boss' and he takes lessons in etiquette and horse riding. The film contains some sharp criticisms of upper-class snobbery and presents Forster as an attractive city boy ultimately out of his depth socially and in his struggle with the Colonna mob. As a second feature, its popularity is impossible to judge, but it was one of the more interesting Anglo-American crime thrillers that dominated the B market.

Because of their use of American leads, the second-feature crime thrillers allowed British actors few opportunities to build up a persona that could gather interest, strength and complexity from repeated performances. Although Sydney Tafler starred as an overreaching spiv in *Wide Boy* (1952), this was a 67-minute 'programmer', not the kind of film that could establish him as an important star and he went back into bit parts. The film's director, Ken Hughes, went on to make several subsequent tough-guy crime thrillers, but with American stars and financed by Columbia Studios.[4] Because crime films lacked status, important stars were reluctant to appear in them except during lean periods in their careers. John Mills gave an admired performance as 'the Old Country's Jimmy Cagney' in *The Long Memory* (1953), but regarded that as a 'rent and tax job', not a major role, and swiftly went back into uniform (Mills 1981: 321). Dirk Bogarde appeared in a number of man-on-the-run films after his success in *The Blue Lamp* as a gun-wielding delinquent.[5] *Films and Filming* thought that Bogarde's good looks had 'made out of the spiv, the deserter and the petty thug creatures of mystery and fascination' (*Films and Filming*, 1955: 3, August). But most reviewers urged that he should be given different roles and his career as the 'man in a dirty raincoat' was ended by his success in *Doctor in the House* (1954).

The fortunes of the tough-guy crime thriller were bound up with the social and cinema-going changes that were taking place in the 1950s. In an important survey of English society at this time Geoffrey Gorer identified two 'anxious classes': the lower-middle-class, which approved of the authority of the state that carried out its ideals and the upper-working-class, which was self-reliant, self-confident and opposed to state authority (Gorer 1955: 298).

The complex changes associated with affluence increased the economic power and confidence of the upper-working-class at the same time as it eroded the status and strength of the lower middle class (Lockwood 1959: 48–53, 100–205). And it was the upper-working-class that came to dominate cinema audiences as age, class and gender patterns of film consumption changed significantly in the 1950s. The most important single element became the young working-class male.[6]

Working-class males enjoyed urban crime thrillers and preferred American culture to British culture (Worpole 1983: 29–48). Herbert Gans, basing his judgements on one of the rare preference surveys of British audiences undertaken at this time, suggested that American male heroes offered working-class young men 'models of mobility aspiration': an 'attractive, virile and ambitious hero, pursuing a combination of personal and social aspirations against a hostile environment....The hero is a young person seeking to establish his role and status in the adult world'.[7] These heroes allowed fantasies of empowerment and success for male cinema-goers estranged by the middle-aged, middle-class orientation of British film producers.

It was companies with an American orientation that were best placed to respond to the aspirations and fantasises of a younger male audience and the modest budgets required by the crime thriller made it the handiest vehicle. George Minter's small company, Renown, which had scored a *succès de scandale* with the Americanised gangster film *No Orchids for Miss Blandish* in 1948, produced *Tread Softly Stranger* in 1958, centring on the city boy Johnny Mansell (George Baker). Mansell, a handsome spiv, who has failed to make a go of it in London, returns to the place of his birth, Rawborough, after ten years away. His efforts to go straight are frustrated as he becomes enmeshed in his brother's bungled theft.

Tread Softly Stranger was symptomatic of new directions in the British crime film in several ways. First, the location is not the studio-bound Soho milieu of earlier British crime thrillers but a composite northern industrial town, with its connotations of virile working-class masculinity. This iconography is established through numerous shots of the blast furnaces and belching chimneys of a huge steel works. As in many of the New Wave films, the North is imbued with tough, masculine traits, as opposed to the middle-class effeminacy of the South (Storey 1963: 161). *Violent Playground* (1958), *The Long Haul* (1958), *In the Wake of a Stranger* (1959) and *Beyond This Place* (1959) all used Liverpool as their setting. *Hell is a City* (1960) was set in Manchester, *Payroll* (1961), in Newcastle. Second, the cinematography employed a bleak, harsh style for exterior scenes, coupled with sultry, claustrophobic interiors. The late and untypical Ealing thriller *Nowhere to Go* (1958) was another example of this visual style. Third, it portrayed a sexually attractive, ambivalent anti-hero who is confused about his role in the world, but who embodies the toughness, energy and aggression of his environment. In *Tread Softly Stranger* Mansell is a big, powerful man whose body is prominently displayed in several scenes to the admiring gaze of the *femme fatale* Calico (Diana Dors). Finally, its leading actor, George Baker, was British. The film did well at the box-office (*Kinematograph Weekly* 18 December 1958: 7).[8]

But for George Baker the film was a one-off. Like most British leading men he had been used to playing officers and gentlemen. The actor who was a potentially viable British tough guy was Stanley Baker. His working-class South Wales physicality had never allowed him to play gentlemanly leads and his success had come from playing brutes. His first major role in *The Cruel Sea* (1953) was as a working-class first lieutenant, an alien presence amongst the gentrified officers. In *A Hill In Korea* (1956), he played a rough-neck bullying sergeant against George Baker's gentlemanly lieutenant. Rank used him as a menacing villain in *Checkpoint* (1956) and in *Campbell's Kingdom* (1957), in which he played against Anthony Steel and Dirk Bogarde, respectively. By then reviewers had started to comment on his presence in these films, his 'boxer's body', 'falcon eyes' and 'juggernaut jaw' and to speculate on his future roles.[9]

His transformation from villain to tough guy hero was not made by unimaginative Rank executives, but by McCarthyite exiles C. Raker Endfield and Joseph Losey, both trying to rebuild their career in Britain after being blacklisted in Hollywood.[10] Both saw the potential of Baker's powerful, complex and ambivalent presence. For Losey, Baker's admirable drive to succeed, to make his mark in a society that offered his class very little, brought with it a narrow, arrogant and aggressive sexuality that was puritanical and intolerant (Ciment 1985: 174–78). But the corollary to this was a vulnerability caused by an insecurity about his role in the world, an instability and depth that could also be exploited.

Endfield's *Hell Drivers* (1957) was the first film to use this potential. Although produced on a limited budget from Rank, *Hell Drivers* was a year in script preparation, indicative of the seriousness with which the writer–director viewed the project (Pfeiffer and Lisa 1993: 33). Baker plays Tom Yately, a handsome, virile and resourceful city boy, an ex-convict whose term inside has equipped him for survival. As a gaolbird his prospects are limited and he takes a job as a short-distance ballast haulage driver. The bleak black-and-white visual style creates a harsh, ugly and exploitative world with a brutality of the everyday that sets it apart from Rank's other thrillers in exotic settings.[11] *Hell Drivers* reworks popular Hollywood genres, the western and tough crime thrillers like Raoul Walsh's *They Drive By Night*, to create a 'frontier' world of gravel pits, chalk quarries, roadhouses and repair yards. This creation of a generic rather than 'realistic' space allows the primitive male culture of the drivers to unfold unimpeded. For aficionados of British acting, the film has rich pickings – cameo roles from Wilfrid Lawson, Sid James, Alfie Bass, Gordon Jackson and Sean Connery – but the central drama is a three-way contest between the saintly Gino (Herbert Lom), the psychotic and brutal team leader, Red (Patrick McGoohan) and Tom.

Tom is not simply tough. He is haunted by the knowledge of his responsibility for crippling his younger brother Jimmy (David McCallum) in the

Figure 7.1 Tough guy in generic space. Stanley Baker (pictured here with Herbert
Lom and Peggy Cummings) stands tall in a 'frontier' world of roadhouses
and repair yards.

Source: British Cinema and Television Research Group archive, De Montfort University

robbery that led to his imprisonment. The brief scene between them is delicately handled. Baker's body language – the half-completed gestures,
downward glances, restless movement – betray his insecurity and still
unformed sense of purpose and identity. It is this sensitivity that allows him to
befriend Gino, whose Catholicism he respects, unlike the other drivers who
simply find it incomprehensible. But this thoughtful, caring side becomes
eclipsed by his drive, literal and metaphorical, to succeed, his obsessive need to
take Red's place in truck No. 1, which he believes will give him the certainty
he craves. This intense, unrelenting competitiveness escalates from a brutal fist-
fight to full-scale revenge after Gino is killed in Tom's place and the
corruption of boss Cartley (William Hartnell in an interesting extension to
his 'tough' career) and Red is exposed. After the final showdown, truck to
truck, Tom is left, bruised, battered and bleeding, his lorry nearly overbal-
ancing into the deep quarry where Red and Cartley have just perished. Lucy
(Peggy Cummings), the western 'gal' in tight jeans, who left Gino for Tom,
drives up to lead her warrior home. He has succeeded, made his way in the

world, worked through his obsessive drives and now occupies a symbolic middle ground between weakness and corrupt brutality.

Hell Drivers has its *longeurs* – repeated low-angle shots of trucks hurtling towards the camera – but pounds with a raw energy and violence that sets it apart from the typical British film. Most reviewers dismissed it as pastiche Hollywood, but some noted new directions and forces: 'at last Rank is trying to inject some blood into its pictures...Stanley Baker, looking like our version of Jack Palance, gives a good tough performance' (*Daily Herald* 26 July 1957). In Endfield's *Sea Fury* (1958), one of Rank's 'mid-Atlantic' action–adventure melodramas, Baker plays another ambivalent hero, Abel Hewson, who, because of some undisclosed disagreement with a shipping magnate, has to get work aboard deep-sea rescue tugs. A drifter, whose father was a miner who died from alcoholism, Hewson proves himself by his skill, guts and toughness.

Baker's persona was extended by three roles as ambivalent professionals whose loyalty to the state is not absolute and whose values are working class. As Inspector Morgan in Losey's *Blind Date* (1959), Baker plays the upwardly mobile son of a chauffeur, only too clearly aware of the ways in which the police force, and British society as a whole, are riddled with class privilege and corruption. It is this sense of establishment duplicity that forces him into an alliance with the falsely accused Dutch artist Jan Van Rooyen (Hardy Kruger), another outsider. In Hammer's *Yesterday's Enemy* (1959), directed by Val Guest, Baker plays Captain Langford whose brutal toughness is justified by the need to fight as ruthlessly as his Japanese adversaries. For Langford, the two-fisted professional not the gentleman, 'There's only one way to fight a war: with gloves off'.

Baker's third role was the most richly complex: Inspector Harry Martineau in Hammer's *Hell is a City* (1960), written and directed by Val Guest. *Hell is a City* was an A feature, indicative of the increased status of the crime thriller and of Hammer's enhanced role within British film production. Its visual style is characteristically grim. Guest strove for a harsh, brutal realism. 'I wanted to give it a newsreel quality. I tried desperately to get the quality of realism about the streets, houses and crowds' (McFarlane 1992: 108). The bleak Lancashire settings give a raw, edgy quality to the *mise-en-scène*, which is mirrored in the tense edginess of Baker's performance as the tough city boy. The film begins and ends with him framed against the night-time Manchester streets. Martineau's working-class roots mean that he is happiest on the streets or in the pub, enjoying the company of other men or chatting to his long-time admirer, the warm-hearted barmaid Lucky Lusk (Vanda Godsell). The tenderness of their scenes together contrasts strongly with his fraught relationship with his wife Julia (Maxine Audley). The film loads the dice heavily against Julia. Her middle-class pretensions are unattractive and she refuses to have the children that Martineau craves. For most of the film he cannot bear to be with her in their spacious semi-detached home.

Martineau has a pent-up energy and capacity for violence, a lust for pursuit and capture, that makes him the ideal opponent for Don Starling (John

Crawford), the jewel thief, rapist and now murderer who has returned to the city. Martineau can succeed in running his quarry to ground because they are *Doppelgängers*: 'I know how his mind works. I grew up with him. We went to the same school together, fought in the same war'. The raw competitive ener-gies of working-class men, trained in uniform, have bifurcated into policeman and villain, separated by what is clearly a thin divide. Each has the same over-powering need to be number one. The film moves relentlessly towards their final confrontation on a roof-top, each wounded by the other's bullet. But even with Starling's death, it is clear the bond is unbroken. Pacing around his living room at the moment of execution, Martineau shouts, 'I'm on the edge Julia. Can't you see I'm on the edge?' When she tells him that Starling deserves to die, he replies, 'None of us are perfect'. It is an extraordinary moment, a point at which any happy restitution of the family unit is fore-stalled as Martineau recognises his bond to that 'other self' that will always haunt him. He must go back onto the streets, lonely, impersonal, the only place where he can comfortably inhabit his tough masculine role.

Although the film is modelled on the Hollywood crime thriller, Martineau is not an American-style private eye. He is a British copper, but in a new mould, a radical revision of the burdened but noble inspectors played by Jack Hawkins in *The Long Arm* (1956) and *Gideon's Day* (1958), who are home-loving, middle-class suburbanites. Critics lavished praise on the tense ambivalence of Baker's performance and recognised him as a distinctive pres-ence within British cinema. One reviewer referred to:

> his violent, modern, unheroic personality....This man intrigues me because he is so utterly against the run of leading men. His big boxer's body, crag of a chin, his flat voice and assertive masculinity – all make him the odd man out of British films.
>
> (Anthony Carthew, *Daily Herald* 30 April 1960)

Films and Filming's profile of Baker as the 'the new breed of British actor', stressed the ambivalence of his roles. 'His success in films has been due to a flow of parts in which he has played hard, tough characters, neither particu-larly sympathetic, nor particularly villainous.'[12] Though the 'odd man out' of the 1950s, Baker's Inspector Martineau – mobile, street-wise, often brutal, constantly bending the rules, prepared to go to almost any lengths – is a progenitor of John Thaw's Inspector Regan in *The Sweeney*.[13]

Hell is a City succeeds through an intelligent and adroit reworking of generic conventions. Losey's *The Criminal* (1960), which explored the contra-dictions of the tough guy even further, is more the product of a gifted *auteur* working in inauspicious circumstances. Losey's approach was Brechtian, looking for an underlying, causal realism rather than a surface naturalism or set of familiar genre codes.[14] He asked television screenwriter Alun Owen, who had a reputation for regional working-class realism, to completely rewrite the original script by Hammer screenwriter Jimmy Sangster, which Losey

thought a mere pastiche of Hollywood prison films.[15] Losey's greatest asset
was Robert Krasker's superb cinematography that creates a harsh, bleak visual
style very different from the romantic expressionism of his work for Carol
Reed on *Odd Man Out* or *The Third Man*.

The central character, Johnny Bannion, was based not on American models
or the British stereotype of the foreign mobster, but on the notorious Soho
gangster Albert Dimes.[16] Losey thought that Dimes possessed 'violence of
unbelievable brutality but mixed with humour and a certain kind of compassion'. Dimes was talented and strikingly handsome, but his creativity was
shackled by a rigid and inexorable set of gangland codes (Ciment 1985: 186).
The role offered Baker the opportunity to work through these contradictions
that in some ways mirrored his own. *The Criminal* is part celebration, part
critique of the hard man; an attempt to understand underworld and prison
culture and the kind of men it breeds. In the self-contained and brutal world
of prison, Bannion seems untouchable, aloof, glisteningly attractive. Much of
the power of Baker's performance, here as elsewhere, comes from this sense of
contained energy, of withheld strength and violence – shown by how he
holds his body or a look or a half smile – that, when unleashed, enables him
to best even the two tough thugs placed in his cell by the malevolent head
warden Barrows (Patrick Magee). Bannion's raw toughness and secure sense
of himself contrasts with Barrows' smooth but neurotic sadism, which is
colluded with by the *New Statesman*-reading governor (Noel Willman), whose
paternalism is now emptied of all moral authority.

Losey's desire to set the film entirely in prison was overruled by his
producer, Jack Greenwood, used to churning out episodes of the *Scotland Yard*
policiers, and acting on behalf of Anglo-Amalgamated, whose reputation was
built on fast-paced thrillers.[17] But this compromise becomes a virtue as the
scenes outside prison display Bannion's insecurities. He is clearly ill at ease in
the modish luxury of his West End flat, with its pre-Swinging Sixties decoration and sleazy portraits of nude women. But in his unexpected relationship
with Suzanne (Margit Saad), who, for all the obvious sex-kitten characteristics
of her role is more than a dumb blonde, he discovers a different way of living.
Her intelligence and mocking humour releases a tender, romantic side to his
nature symbolised by his carelessness over the money for a ring, which leads
to his re-arrest. Revealingly, when she visits him in prison and declares how
much she misses and loves him, Bannion is tongue-tied, awkward at showing
emotion in front of the 'screws'.

The Criminal is imbued with a romantic pessimism, a sense of *fin-de-siècle*.
Bannion represents individualised villainy at a moment when it is being
superseded by anonymous and ruthless organisations. Both the prison godfather Frank Saffron (Gregoire Aslan), and the underworld dandy Mike Carter
(Sam Wanamaker), are unattractive organisation men, against whom Bannion
appears admirable. They ensure that inside and outside prison Bannion can no
longer control his own destiny. His attempt to break free leads only to his
death in the bleak field where he hid the proceeds of the robbery. His demise

Figure 7.2 'Contained energy and withheld strength and violence': Stanley Baker as
        Johnny Bannion is the centre of attention in Joseph Losey's examination of
        the hard man, *The Criminal* (1960)
Source: British Cinema and Television Research Group archive, De Montfort University

is ambivalent. There is a fearful grandeur as he screams at Suzanne to let him
die alone and desperately babbles about damnation. But this is coupled with a
sense of insignificance, displayed in the final extreme high-angle shot where
Carter, who has been cradling Bannion tenderly in his arms, dumps him
unceremoniously on the frozen ground when he fails to reveal the money's
location.

The *Criminal*'s complexities, its critique of individualism and the cult of the
tough guy, gained the approval of the left-wing critical elite; it won a
Diploma of Merit at the Edinburgh Festival, where it was premiered in
August 1960. But its general release came the day after *Saturday Night and
Sunday Morning*, which dominated the attention of reviewers and the public.
More than Stanley Baker, Albert Finney came to symbolise a new generation
of tough, aggressive non-gentlemanly British actors. Subsequently, it has been
the New Wave films that have been enshrined as marking a decisive break
with the authoritarian paternalism of British culture.

However, in the gradual change from a culture that had little space for the socially mobile and preferred the working class to be 'steady' and biddable to one in which working-class characters had the right to be truculent and aggressive, the tough crime thrillers played an important role. Their use of Northern settings, a bleak visual style and ambivalent working-class heroes struggling to succeed in a competitive world, all contested the dominant middle-class paradigms of British culture in the 1950s. As Baker's roles show, the clear moral lines between policemen and criminals have become blurred, both are individualised outsiders in a world increasingly conceived as corrupt and brutal. In *A Prize of Arms* (1962), Turpin (Stanley Baker) wants to rob the army payroll because he was arrested for black-market activities in Hamburg after the war while more senior officers got away with it. He knows now that, 'You're on your own. Get no help from anyone. You're a mug if you expect it. If you want anything in this world you just have to go out and take it'. The tough guy's sense of an unfair, lawless and competitive world justifies his ruthlessness. Baker led the way for the dominant anti-heroes of the 1960s, particularly James Bond.[18]

Richard Dyer has commented valuably that the tough guy 'work[s] through contradictions in the male role, which are disguised in more traditional types (cowboys, swashbucklers, war heroes)' (Dyer 1979: 56). His role can be, at certain historical moments, a socially progressive one. In the 1950s he could function as an empowering figure for working-class males to symbolically dispute the moral and cultural authority of the state and its masculine ideal, 'that paralysed and paralysing hegemony of gentlemanliness'.[19] But the tough guy's version of masculinity, exclusively realised through prowess and potency, can be limited and reactionary. As David Glover has argued, the tough guy's need for action, speed, pursuit and violent combat, 'an ecology of male power', narrows the repertoire of masculinity to one that can only recognise itself through testing and conflict (Glover 1989: 73–77). It is one that demands a subordination of women and of various forms of solidarity and mutuality. The real form of mutuality in these films, as I have shown, is the overpowering need for a male opponent on whom to release all the tough guy's pent-up energies, a homosocial bonding that is deeper than any other satisfaction he can enjoy. In the more intelligent post-war British crime thrillers these contradictions are played out in ways that still have the power to involve and challenge audiences.

Notes

1 The best brief discussion of gentlemanliness is Harold Laski's essay 'The danger of being a gentleman', in *The Danger of Being a Gentleman and Other Essays*, London, Allen & Unwin, 1939, pp. 13–31.

2 For details of Hartnell's career see Jessica Carney, *Who Goes There?*, London, Virgin Books, 1996.

3 See *Kinematograph Weekly*'s yearly round-up of box-office successes, 18 December 1947. Howard's subsequent stardom was based on playing different kinds of

misfits; Jones played another menacing spiv in *Good Time Girl* (1948), but had no further opportunities to build on these roles.

4   For an assessment of Hughes's career and a filmography see Allen Eyles, 'A passion for cinema – Ken Hughes', *Films and Filming*, Spring 1971, pp. 42–51.

5   The films were *Blackmailed* (1951), *Hunted* (1952), *The Gentle Gunman* (1952) and *Desperate Moment* (1953).

6   These changes can be appreciated by examining the tables and graphs in *The Cinema Audience: A National Survey*, London, Screen Advertising Association, 1961. See also John Spraos, *The Decline of the Cinema*, London, Allen & Unwin, 1962.

7   Herbert Gans, *American Films and Television Programs on British Screens: A Study of the Functions of American Popular Culture Abroad*, Pittsburgh, University of Pennsylvania Institute for Urban Studies, 1959, pp. 60–8. Gans was given access to the Cinema Audience Survey undertaken by Research Services Ltd. for the Rank organisation in December 1955, under the direction of Mark Abrams, which was not published.

8   I would not wish my comments here to suggest that all crime thrillers exhibited these tendencies. More conservative British film-makers clung to the old paradigms. Basil Dearden and Michael Relph set *Violent Playground* in Liverpool, but it was a law-and-order film that valorised the efforts of the caring professional, juvenile liaison officer Sergeant Truman (Stanley Baker), and condemned the delinquent Johnny Murphy (David McCallum). But the film shows signs of severe strains and tensions, partly registered in Baker's performance.

9   Baker has yet to receive the attention he deserves. Anthony Storey's *Stanley Baker – Portrait of an Actor*, London, W.H. Allen, 1977, is preoccupied with his fight against cancer rather than his acting roles, though the filmography compiled by Allen Eyles is helpful. The BFI library microfiche on Baker contains many useful early reviews from which I plucked those descriptive phrases. For an overview of Baker's place in relation to other male stars of this period see my 'Male stars, masculinity and British cinema', in Robert Murphy (ed.) *The British Cinema Book*, London, BFI, 1997.

10 For an informative analysis of both directors see Brian Neve, *Film and Politics in America*, London, Routledge, 1992, pp. 122–6, 176–81 and *passim*.

11 For example, *Checkpoint* was set in Italy and *Campbell's Kingdom* in the Canadian Rockies.

12 Derek Conrad, 'Stanley Baker: tough at the top', *Films and Filming*, November 1959, p. 5. This profile has a photograph of Baker in military uniform but he is smoking a cigarette rather than the customary officer's pipe. Baker's expression is knowing and somewhat aggressive, not the usual stiff upper lip. Conrad argues that Baker's performances show that 'ordinary men can be exciting and often are'. He notes that his 'hero with the sadistic streak in *Hell Drivers* showed an enormous increase in his fan mail from girls between the ages of 17 and 20'.

13 For a study of shifts in representations of the police see Clive Emsley, 'The English bobby: an indulgent tradition', in Roy Porter (ed.) *Myths of the English*, London, Polity Press, 1993.

14 See his comments in an interview for *Oxford Opinion*, 1960.

15 For Owen, see Stuart Laing, *Representations of Working-Class Life 1957–1964*, London, Macmillan, 1986, pp. 150–2. For Losey's opinions about the screenplay see Ciment 1985: 184 and Tom Milne (ed.) *Losey on Losey*, London, Secker and Warburg, 1967, p. 46.

16 For details of Dimes' career see Robert Murphy, *Smash and Grab*, London, Faber and Faber, 1993, pp. 120–4.

17 The film's budget was a mere £60,000 and its running time cut from 130 to 95 minutes by the distribution company prior to release. See David Caute, *Joseph Losey: A Revenge on Life,* London, Faber and Faber, 1994, pp. 139–41.

18 With Sean Connery's James Bond, the tough guy changed from outsider to insider. This new Bulldog Drummond was a radical refashioning of the debonair gentleman so that it absorbed the tough guy's laconic, aggressive, Americanised machismo. The Establishment needs Bond's ruthless, controlled brutality to win the Cold War.

19 Martin Green, *A Mirror for Anglo-Saxons*, London, Chatto and Windus, 1960, p. 120. Compare Dennis Potter's sense of 'the genteel traditionalism that was once again stifling English life', *The Glittering Coffin*, London, Gollancz, 1960, p. 129.

Bibliography

Ciment, M. (1985) *Conversations With Losey*, London: Methuen.

Dyer, R. (1979) *Stars*, London: BFI.

Eyles, A., Adkinson, R. and Fry, N. (eds) (1994) *House of Horror. The Complete Hammer Films Story*, London: Creation Books.

Glover, D. (1989) 'The stuff that dreams are made of: masculinity, femininity and the thriller', in D. Longhurst (ed.) *Gender, Genre and Narrative Pleasure*, London: Unwin Hyman, pp. 67–83.

Gorer, G. (1955) *Exploring English Character*, London: Cresset Press.

Lockwood, D. (1959) *The Blackcoated Worker. A Study in Class Consciousness*, London: Allen & Unwin.

McFarlane, B. (ed.) (1992) *Sixty Voices. Celebrities Recall the Golden Age of British Cinema*, London: BFI.

Manvell, R. (1946) 'The gangster comes home', *Sight and Sound*, 15, 58: 61–2.

Mills, J. (1981) *Up in the Clouds Gentlemen, Please*, Harmondsworth: Penguin.

Murphy, R. (1989) *Realism and Tinsel: Cinema and Society in Britain 1939–49*, London: Routledge.

Pfeiffer, L. and Lisa, P. (1993) *The Films of Sean Connery*, New York: Citadel Press.

Sklar, R. (1992) *City Boys: Cagney, Bogart, Garfield*, New Jersey: Princeton University Press.

Storey, D. (1963) 'Journey through a tunnel', *The Listener*, pp. 160–3, August.

Worpole, K. (1983) *Dockers and Detectives*, London: Verso.

8 Ordinary people
'New Wave' realism and the British crime film 1959–1963

Steve Chibnall

Johnny Remick:	Crime, that's all you get these days. I wouldn't mind [watching television] if they showed the under-world as it really was.
Ruth Lombard:	But then they would have to show criminals as ordinary people trying to make a living. The public would never stand for that.

(Offbeat, Cliff Owen, 1961)

An American actor (Sydney Chaplin) drops a coin in the slot of a Seeberg jukebox and, to the sound of a sleazy saxophone, shuffles back to the bar of a roadhouse. 'Hey, Mister, do we have to have the same record over and over?', complains the barman. We might be watching almost any Hollywood film noir, but in fact this is the beginning of a British crime film: Ken Hughes' *Confession* (1955). Of course, English barmen rarely address their customers as 'Mister', but the line perfectly encapsulates some essential truths about British cinema's attempts to move beyond the played-out pre-war formulae of the white-glove detective mystery and to fashion crime narratives with a different ambience, sensitivity and class disposition.

Early attempts to develop an indigenous cinema of the picaresque by bringing the novels of James Curtis to the screen (*They Drive by Night*, Arthur Woods, 1938; *There Ain't No Justice*, Pen Tennyson, 1939) had been largely eclipsed in popularity by the James Hadley Chase and Peter Cheyney pastiches of Yankee pulp fiction such as *No Orchids for Miss Blandish* (St John L. Clowes, 1948) and *Uneasy Terms* (Vernon Sewell, 1948). Proletarian or 'classless' hard-boiled fiction became indelibly typed as American, just as the style of its filmic realisation, the expressionist inspired noir aesthetic, became identified with Hollywood. The post-war spiv cycle (Murphy 1986) may have given the style a British gloss, but it is telling that one of the last and most celebrated of the spiv films, *Night and the City* (1950), balanced its use of London locations with an American director (Jules Dassin) and stars (Gene Tierney and Richard Widmark). An American star presence gave the British crime film of the 1950s not only an aura of genre authenticity, but also a better chance at the US box office.

The complaint of 'the same record over and over' might be levelled at the repetitive and formulaic nature of Britain's crime cinema of the 1950s. Although the crime movie was one of the more abrasive elements in the stifling conservatism of the period, it was almost as reluctant to take risks with form, challenge the prevailing censorship rules or alienate transatlantic distributors as other genre productions. Ken Hughes' own attempt to make a gangster movie in Britain, *Joe Macbeth* (released in 1955, the same year as *Confession*), had played safe by locating the action in an American city and basing the script (by Philip Jordan) on the most respectable of literary sources, the Shakespearean tragedy. However, things were about to change.

By 1962 Hughes, returning to criminous subject matter after a gap of five years to make *The Small World of Sammy Lee* (1963), was able to adapt his television play about a Soho wide-boy with few concessions to Hollywood aesthetics or American audiences. Sammy's anglocentric orientations failed to prevent the TV play winning an Emmy award or the film opening to enthusiastic reviews from US critics (*Kine Weekly*, 22 August 1963). The nature of authenticity in the crime film had broadened to embrace location shooting and what *Kine Weekly* (18 April 1963) called 'a vivid kaleidoscopic impression of London's seamy side.'

What had occurred in the space between Hughes' films was the upheaval brought by the New Wave directors' collaboration with Britain's 'Angry Young Man' school of writing. From *Room at the Top* (Jack Clayton, 1959) to *This Sporting Life* (Lindsay Anderson, 1963), the New Wave films brought a revived interest in depicting the lives of ordinary people and a valorisation of the Northern working-class community not seen since the heyday of Gracie Fields. For twenty years, the critical orthodoxy hailed the 'kitchen sink' films of Richardson, Reisz, Schlesinger and Anderson as a progressive flowering of British cinema's tradition of social realism, its finest post-war hour.[1] More recently, however, commentators such as Andrew Higson (1984), John Hill (1986) and Terry Lovell (1990) have questioned the films' commitment to collectivist politics, criticised their misogynist features and identified their perspectives on working-class culture as often elevated and external. What the 'kitchen sinkers' offer, it is argued, is not so much a social realism unmediated by narrative convention and authorial voice, but a literary 'poetic' realism that manages the demands of authenticity and those of melodramatic narrative by paying particular attention to the depiction of the urban landscape. This new cinema of plebeian realism may have its shortcomings, but most critics have continued to place it in opposition to an old cinema of escapist studio-bound genre productions that is held to include the crime film. Roger Manvell, for example, in *New Cinema in Britain* (1968: 52) fails to recognise the crime film as having much to do with 'working class people in working class environment'. Alexander Walker's *Hollywood England* (1974) devotes the best part of seven chapters to a handful of New Wave pictures and (aside from *The League of Gentlemen*) less than a page to the films concerned with professional crime made between 1959 and 1963. Predictably, Roy Armes' *A Critical History of*

British Cinema (1978: 287) finds only one crime film from the period worthy of any discussion: Joseph Losey's *The Criminal* (1960), an auteurist work that is praised by most commentators for its character's ability to transcend the 'banal material' of the crime genre (Perry 1974: 198). Surprisingly, most of these movies manage to find the blind spot in Raymond Durgnat's wide-angled vision, and hardly feature in his study of post-war British film (Durgnat 1970). We might have expected that John Hill would acknowledge a cinematic discourse on crime in *Sex, Class and Realism* (1986), but his lengthy discussion of the 'social problem' film contains barely a mention of pimping or protection rackets. Like the New Wave film-makers themselves, he colludes with the idea that criminality has no place in realist representations of working-class culture. We have to wait until Robert Murphy's *Sixties British Cinema* (1992) for that idea to be challenged and for the most prolific period in the history of the British crime film to be given any sustained consideration.

Reading between the lines of Hill's account of Basil Dearden and Michael Relph's social problem films, it is clear that, throughout the 1950s, they used the generic structures of the crime film to explore wider social concerns. *The Blue Lamp* (1950), *Pool of London* (1951), *Violent Playground* (1958), *Sapphire* (1959), *The League of Gentlemen* (1960) and *Victim* (1961) all adapt this technique to elevate subtextual social issues, thus revealing 'the dominant ideological assumptions and attitudes of the period' (Hill 1986: 67). We can see the same method employed in Losey's early British films *Blind Date* (1959) and *The Criminal*. The usual interpretations of these films is that genre conventions compromise any commitment to realism and impede the free development of radical ideas and messages.[2] A directorial giant like Losey is obliged to transcend the restrictions of a genre, which subordinates character development to narrative drive (Murphy 1992: 204; Caute 1994: 131–2). But the dismissal of genre as a hindrance to 'serious' film-making elides its ability to provide the exploration of social issues with a dramatic structure which may, as in the cases of *Sapphire* and *Blind Date*, parallel the films' aim of investigating attitudes and exposing prejudice. As James Leahy (1967: 83) argues, the mystery is the 'ideal genre' for the investigation undertaken in *Blind Date*. 'The movie is essentially about the processes of deception and revelation, about "seeing" and "seeming", about illusion and reality.' There may be a tension between conventional generic demands and unconventional ideas (Sobchak 1977; Hess 1977) but, in the best crime films, this is a creative rather than a stifling tension. The crime genre lends itself to the deployment of sub-textual meditations on social and philosophical issues at least as well as any other. Moreover, in its overt interest in offences against the person and property, and in the legal regulation of morality, the genre addresses key concerns and, most likely, experiences of its audience. Thus, the failure to include the crime film in discussions of social realism and the cinema during any period is misguided and it is a particularly significant omission when the New Wave realism of the late 1950s and early 1960s is being considered.

Anyone familiar with writing on Britain's New Wave will probably also be aware of the important social, economic and political transformations that supply the context of its emergence at the close of the 1950s. Jeffrey Richards (1992), for instance, summarised these changes as the disappearance of the British Empire, the growth of a distinctive youth culture, the rise of working-class affluence and the revival (in the face of massive electoral success for the Conservatives) of an intellectual Left. These transformations give the New Wave texts their contradictory characteristics of nostalgia for a disappearing culture and sympathy for discontented and desiring young proletarian males. We can see these same contradictions present in the crime films of the same period, but they are given a genre specificity by the parallel transformations in Britain's criminal underworld and in the organisation of policing.

The principal legacy of the commodity shortages of the 1940s had been the penetration of the economic system by an illicit alternative economy created by the activities of increasingly sophisticated criminal organisations. During the 1950s there was a scaling-up of illegality and a shift of locus from the race track to clubland. Unarmed and small-scale safecracking and 'smash and grab' raiding were largely replaced as the crimes of choice by lorry hijacking, payroll snatching and, in the early 1960s, by armed bank robberies (Morton 1993; Campbell 1994). The individuals and small groupings left over from an earlier stage of craft-based criminal organisation were recruited into shifting teams to carry out more elaborate robbery projects (MacIntosh 1976). At the same time, gangland came to be run increasingly along corporate lines by paternalistic family 'firms' engaged in protection and fraudulent commercial operations but investing their profits in legitimate businesses. Syndication, or the forging of loose alliances between firms, was becoming a growing attraction as a means of maximising profits (Morton 1993: 74–5). The most successful syndicate of the 1960s (which controlled vice in London's West End) ensured its survival by paying regular taxes' to Metropolitan Police detectives (Morton 1993: 204–24; Cox *et al.* 1977: 140–210). As an enlarging proportion of London's CID became enmeshed in the profitable regulation of crime rather than its elimination, there were moves to limit and formalise police fraternisation with the underworld, but they would be mainly cosmetic until Commissioner Robert Mark's reforms of the early 1970s. Crucially, the transformations in the relationship between the underworld and the police were not only facilitated but positively accelerated by legislative attempts to regulate vice and leisure in Macmillan's 'never-had-it-so-good' society.

By 1959 the frigidity of the 1950s sexual culture was already thawing with a growing availability of 'girlie' magazines, and the arrival of short 8 mm 'glamour' films for home projection. In London's Soho the brazen clip joints and brash new striptease clubs announced a fresh confidence in the corporate commodification of sex. The Street-Offences Act (1959) largely cleared prostitutes from city thoroughfares but swept them into the thriving clubs controlled by the underworld. The clubs (as well as betting shops) were further boosted by the Betting and Gaming Act (1960), which relaxed the law on gambling and supplied gangland with legitimate sources of finance (Kelland 1987: 31–8). Finally, the Licensing Act (1961) designed to regulate 'members' clubs aided the extension of syndication and of police corruption by allowing the consolidation of large-scale operations, the closure of smaller drinking clubs and the conversion of some into striptease emporia (ibid.: 109–12).

These developments framed the everyday experience of urban (and particularly metropolitan) life in the early 1960s. Their consequences were every bit as real as the charred chimneys and terraced streets of New Wave cinema and their representation in the crime films of the period cannot be easily dismissed as exotic or fanciful escapism. It is the capacity of the crime film of the period to incorporate and illuminate the changes in underworld organisation and practice, as much as its naturalism of dialogue and location, that constitute its claim to social realism.

Between 1959 and 1963, the peak period of British film production, more than one film in every three was a crime movie. Gifford (1986) lists 218 of which 81 featured underworld activity. Of these, more than three-quarters were B movies. The period proved the swan song of second-feature factories such as Independent Artists, Butcher's, Danzinger's and Merton Park, whose output varied enormously in quality (Murphy 1992: 211–15). Programmers like Butcher's *Gaolbreak* (Frances Searle, 1962) or *Impact* (Peter Maxwell, 1963) are simply as bad as the crime film gets. The presence of a young Carol White in *Gaolbreak* cannot compensate for the film's flat and sluggish direction, a script that would be embarrassingly simplistic in a children's matinée and two of the least-threatening villains in screen history (a newsagent and his mum). *Impact* has all the force of a feather hitting a cushion. Its dreary narrative and languid pacing suggests a generic form that is winding down and the only elements that mark it as contemporary are references to a mail train robbery and the use of a gambling club as a legal front for criminality. But among the tarted-up *Boy's Own* yarns like these, one can find films that, like rather more of their American counterparts, combine pace, imaginative cinematography and realistic dialogue to create a stylish and economic thriller. *The Man in the Back Seat* (Vernon Sewell, 1961) and *Naked Fury* (Charles Saunders, 1960) with their criminal-centred narratives are, as Murphy (1992: 211–12) notes, among the most distinguished, but even the better films made little more than a perfunctory attempt to situate themselves in the changing reality of the underworld. The major exception to this rule is Cliff Owen's directorial debut *Offbeat*, an offering remarkable for its moral ambiguity and political critique. Like a number of other crime films with higher budgets, it manages to convey a strong sense of a society in transition with less of the nostalgic baggage carried by many of its more illustrious New Wave contemporaries.

In *Offbeat*, the cosy-but-constraining mores of a class-bound culture have largely passed away and in their place are the uncertainties of a new order in which everything seems to be up for grabs. Crime is no longer confined to its enclaves within an urban underclass because criminality is being stitched into the fabric of social and economic life. The old underworld is modernising according to the same logic of corporate rationality and monopoly capitalism as the legitimate economy. The prediction is that they will soon be indistinguishable. This aspiration to the embourgeoisement of criminality is perfectly expressed in the film by Dawson (Anthony Dawson), one of the crime syndicate's senior executives: 'The only way to make crime really pay is to get it organised like the big business cartels. After all, there's not much difference'. Dawson's office looks like that of any successful businessman, lined with books and managed by an efficient secretary (an ex-pickpocket forced into retirement by arthritis). He considers his importing business 'quite legitimate'. 'New staff' are carefully screened and paid a retainer, and Dawson even has ambitions to provide them with a company pension ('I always think people work a lot better when they feel secure.').

The new scientific management is no respecter of morality. The protocols of the deal – the balance sheet, percentages, start and finish dates – apply to anyone in a business suit, whatever the legitimacy of their trade. The syndicate's patriarch, J.B. Wykeham (Ronald Adam), laments the trend towards

Figure 8.1 The criminal fraternity looks after its own in *Offbeat*, Cliff Owen's challenging account of New Wave crime

Source: British Cinema and Television Research Group archive, De Montfort University

'paperwork, mergers, liquidations, take-over bids', and is nostalgic for the days 'when problems were simple and could be solved with a gun'. Crime has lost its moral prohibition in a cynical world of hypocrisy, fakery and self-interest. In this 'age of betrayal' the symbols of a past society, like the 'Imperial Jewellers', which the syndicate target for robbery, are ripe for plunder. The spread of affluence mocks the old values of sacrifice, abstinence and fidelity. Why do an honest day's work when, as a neon sign reminds us, you can 'Win a Fortune – with Paul's Pools'? Paradoxically, the criminal organisation with its promise of 'equal shares, team ethos and mutual dependency' offers a moral high ground, a last refuge for those seeking the security of brotherhood and community. Undercover investigator Steve Ross (William Sylvester) is drawn towards the friendship and trust he finds in the underworld, defending the honour of his new colleagues when his police controller accuses them of being motivated only by greed. 'I found them different – just people, maybe a little mixed up, trying to make a living – dishonestly. Why pick on crooks? That'll be the day when you can trust anyone.' In the end, the faith that the syndicate place in Steve is their undoing and it is the police's philosophy of 'trust no one' that triumphs. In a cynical denouement Steve is an unwitting traitor to his friends in the underworld. 'Nowadays there's always someone waiting to be betrayed', he complains as he is told of the 'thirty pieces of silver' that he may receive from an insurance company as a reward for his undercover efforts.

Offbeat is an unusual movie, not only in the quality of Peter Barnes' script and in the care of its direction, but also in its refusal to advocate a conventional morality. Its perspective of moral equivalence is rare even in first features but its impression of a society in transition is also given by the more upbeat and optimistic *Bomb in the High Street* (Terence Bishop and Peter Bezencenet, 1963), a tense little tale of bank robbery that inflects its narrative with cultural anomie. It combines a story of disillusioned ex-servicemen using the skills the army has taught them in the pursuit of private profit with a micro-examination of the dissolution of class barriers.

Using the cover of a bomb scare, the band of military and colonial discards ('one minute you're saving the empire, the next you're on the scrapheap') evacuate a sleepy home-counties town so that they can rob the bank. The town is cleared of everyone except a young couple from different sides of the class divide whose relationship is threatened by disapproving parents. For a few halcyon hours, the town's deserted hotel provides them with a liminal space free from censorial prejudice before they are caught up in the robbers' vengeful struggle for money. Although the film's carefully developed suspense is squandered in a melodramatic and conventional closure, *Bomb in the High Street* remains notable for its critique of prevailing social attitudes and values. Memorably, the freedom of the hotel and access to the bank vault become metaphors of utopian aspiration, while the accelerating pace of social change towards a more desired state is neatly conveyed by the speeding-up of the bank's clock to activate the vault's time-release opening mechanism.

In the main, however, the B thrillers are more interested in recycling the standard ingredients of an American-led crime genre than in engaging with contemporary British developments. Formulaic characterisations and plot structures remain operational even when, as in Butcher's *The Hi-Jackers* (Jim O'Connolly, 1963), new trends in criminality are depicted. The one change that is evident in these second features, and particularly marked in the A films of the period is the willingness to shoot quite extensively on location. This means that the real topography of Britain is increasingly glimpsed. However, rather than the vistas of working-class housing and factory-filled Lowryland characteristic of New Wave Northern realism, the crime film is more likely to contrast a neon-drenched Soho with a wasteland of decaying dockland warehouses or a Legoland of standard-build suburban shopping parades. Both cinemas inevitably recognise a distinction between urban and rural spaces but British crime films imbue the dichotomy with less moral significance than their New Wave contemporaries (Higson 1984) or, for that matter, their American counterparts.

One would expect to find the contrast between the sinfulness of the city and the purity of the natural landscape at its most dramatic in the extravagant location filming of Val Guest's powerful *Hell is a City* (1960). What we discover, however, is that the toughness and pessimism with which the mean streets of Manchester are evoked transfer themselves to the film's bleak moorland locations, which seem less an idyllic refuge from urban squalor than an unpoliced wilderness where wrongdoing might escape detection. Lacking the wide-open spaces of the United States, the countryside in this overcrowded isle cannot offer a successful *cordon sanitaire* around the city. Instead, the contagion of crime spreads out beyond the sprawling conurbations and ribbon developments until it finds some place where robbers can hide, bodies can be dumped, gambling can flourish or lorries can be hi-jacked with impunity. In *Hell is a City* the country is barely less dangerous ground than the urban street; and in *The Criminal, Nowhere to Go* (Seth Holt, 1958) and *Rag Doll* (Lance Comfort, 1961) agricultural land provides an alien graveyard for the urban criminal − a corner of a farmer's field that is forever gangland. Even in *A Place to Go* (1963), Dearden and Relph's over-sentimental attempt to introduce a criminous dimension into New Wave urban realism, the dream of rural plenitude has been displaced to the high-rise new-town living of the working-class diaspora.

The *Monthly Film Bulletin* (May 1960) rightly pointed to the way in which *Hell is a City* maintains 'a perpetual feeling of barely suppressed savagery' and although this is principally a function of the pace and assurance of Guest's direction, it is also related to the way in which tension and threat are maintained across a variety of *mise-en-scène*. Arthur Grant's panoramic cinematography maintains tension by immersing his moorland locations in the same climate of menace as his cityscapes. Guest, a former journalist, approached the project 'almost as a semi-documentary, as if we were a newsreel team following the story' (Jezard 1995), using 'real people' rather than

Figure 8.2 Crime and apprehension on the streets and rooftops of Manchester: Don
Starling (John Crawford) finally meets his nemesis in the form of Inspector
Martineau (Stanley Baker) in Val Guest's underrated *Hell is a City* (1960)
Source: British Cinema and Television Research Group archive, De Montfort University

actors as extras and bit-part players, in a style inspired by Elia Kazan's *Panic in
the Streets* (1950). But the veneer of verisimilitude conceals the truth that, by
the film's release in 1960, its *Brighton Rock* world of small-time hoodlums led
by a ruthless psychopath and preying on bookmakers was almost as anachro-
nistic as the street soliciting it also depicts. Ex-policeman Maurice Proctor's
(1954) source novel provides a convincing portrait of Manchester's underworld, but he is writing about the early 1950s rather than the early 1960s.
From 1960, the Betting and Gaming Act would allow the replacement of
moorland 'tossing' rings featured so evocatively in *Hell is a City* with the
street-corner betting shop seen in *Get Carter* (1971). Generically, too, the
anomaly created by casting policies of an apparently American gangster (John
Crawford) bossing a bunch of British heavies would shortly be consigned to
history.

Whereas Guest's film constructs a disappearing world, Losey's *The Criminal*,
like *Offbeat*, situates its narrative in a zone of transition where the old patterns
of both criminality and masculinity are being challenged by a nascent mood
of sexual permissiveness, fresh opportunities for consumption and a new
corporatism in criminal organisation.

Billed as the 'the toughest picture ever made in Britain', *The Criminal* lives up to its press book's boast that it 'lifts the lid off Britain's underworld', offering an uncompromising view of prison and the criminal milieu. Beyond Losey's Brechtian devises and bravura flourishes there is a story that is saturated in contemporary cultural developments. The film tells the story of a London 'face', Johnny Bannion and his doomed struggles to maintain independence and freedom in the face of the twin threats of prison and syndicated criminality.

Prison, the fixed point in a continuous cycle to which career criminals like Bannion must return, reproduces criminal workers just as the class system reproduces industrial workers. For the criminal, it is his essential environment, a theatrical space to practice and perfect the masculine performativity that is so important to successful role playing in the underworld. Life outside the prison gates is a holiday experience, a Hugh Hefner fantasy of penthouse hedonism in which both the penitentiary and the class system can be temporarily transcended. Losey contrasts the two worlds by exchanging the expressionistic sets and camera work of the prison scenes for more lyrical and naturalistic locations filming. But Bannion's freewheeling style of criminality is being obliged to give way to a more organised and regulated structure of crime which, like the prison, will eventually become independent of its temporary functionaries. Thus the film plays the unchanging criminal justice system against the changing pattern of criminality, and the rigidities of class society against the destabilising effects of proletarian affluence.

Stanley Baker is ideally cast as Bannion. Baker had a number of underworld friends (Frazer 1995: 200, 203, 217) and his performance was inspired by the flamboyant race track gangster Albert Dimes, who acted as a consultant on the film. Losey described Dimes as 'a huge, staggeringly handsome man [who] drove around in a smashing, big white convertible with black upholstery' (Caute 1994: 139) and Baker perfectly captures his professionalism and sense of cool while Scott Macgregor's production design suggests the seductively subversive potential of the American bachelor lifestyle.[3] Bannion's narcissistic world accepts women only as occasional playthings, otherwise they are 'a bad risk' and their ability to stir desire is a threat to masculine selves that are mutually sustaining. There are strong suggestions of latent homosexuality in the prison scenes, but it might be useful to think of the prison itself as a metaphor for the type of infantile masculinity in which Bannion is trapped. 'You must play with your playfellows, Johnny', Barrows, the sadistic warder (Patrick Magee) advises him at one point and, in many ways, Bannion is refusing to grow up, not least in his commitment to old-fashioned modes of criminal practice (racetrack robbery) and his refusal to accept the syndication of crime. At the end of the film he is told by his nemesis, Carter, his former partner, that his ways are too maverick for the new criminality: 'We belong to a proper set up. We're important, yes, but things would go on without us. With us it's a team – it's business. But your sort doesn't fit into an organisation.' Alun Owen's script displays the same feeling of moral ambiguity as *Hell is a*

City and *Offbeat* and links the two films in tracking the movement of crime towards corporatism. Its sense of a society in transition, though, is present in other crime films of the period. *Never Let Go* (John Guillermin, 1960), for example, associates crime with the trend towards a consumer economy and a heightening of business rationality.

John Cummings (Richard Todd) is an old-fashioned shampoo salesman living in a new-fangled tower block and working for a 'conservative' company in the throes of modernisation ('we can't stand still, we've got to do better, move faster, even to keep up'). Comfortable in his woollen cardigan and uncomfortable with new 'scientific' selling techniques, Cummings is plunged into anomic despair when his new Ford Anglia car – the possession that symbolises his attempts at keeping pace with the speed of change – is stolen by crooked garage owner, Lionel Meadows (a performance of frightening intensity by Peter Sellers). The bullying Meadows represents the anti-social reality behind the facade of the new economic order. His 'legitimate business' is barely more ruthless than Cummings' own employer. Both suggest an evilness inherent in the spirit of advanced capitalism and the world it is shaping. In this new Jerusalem of post-war reconstruction, the young hang out in the ironically titled 'Victory Cafe'. Here the Americanised ton-up boys and sweater girls listen to rock 'n' roll on the jukebox and wait to be corrupted by an older generation, which has lost its way. For their Fagin they have Meadows, a violent spiv whose ambitions are as overblown as the American car he drives.[4] His motto is 'Keep *moving, get organised*', which is exactly what poor Cummings is unable to do without his Anglia. But Cummings will 'never let go' and, in a sort of *High Noon* in suburbia, overcomes his diffidence and fear to confront his criminal persecutor, and rescue the young (Adam Faith and Carol White) from bondage. The *Monthly Film Bulletin* (July 1960) revealed its prejudices about social realist cinema when it criticised the sadism of this 'unlovely' exercise 'from the new traumatic school' of independent British film-making: 'Obtrusive shock cutting, exaggerated camera angles and a self-consciously strident use of "adult" language all serve to accentuate the essential falsity of the characterisations.' Even in straight-laced 1960, stolen-car racketeers were known to utter the odd expletive and, although the characters exhibit some stereotypical traits, and Alun Falconer's melodramatic script pays homage to Fred Zimmermann's classic Western, there is a toughness and energy about this film that gives an authenticity to its narrative and undercuts its reactionary attitudes to change.

The management of change is also the theme of the same writer's *The Informers* (Ken Annakin, 1963), but here Falconer exhibits more ambivalence towards the Metropolitan Police's efforts to modernise their detective force in the wake of a Royal Commission, in the teeth of public criticism and in response to new methodologies of crime.

> 'From now on we're going to work together *scientifically* as a team', one
> senior policeman tells his detectives: 'No-one's going to be able to point

the finger of suspicion at *us*. The old methods are out. No more frater-nising with crooks. No more snouts.'

But the film's protagonist, Chief Inspector Johnnoe (Nigel Patrick) is uncon-vinced that the tried-and-tested informant system can be replaced by detective science. 'You can't catch the bad boys with a lot of transistorised Mechano sets', he complains, voicing the fears of the film's technical consul-tant, ex-Detective Superintendent John Gosling. *The Informers* may have doubts about the new methods, but it is far from sentimental in its depiction of the police and their relationships with criminals. In this it takes its lead from *Hell is a City* and its idea of the crook as a dark reflection of the detec-tive.[5] As with *Offbeat*, Annakin takes further this questioning of the moral superiority, if not of the law, then at least of its enforcers. 'I used to think a snout was the lowest kind of vermin', Johnnoe's reluctant informant complains, 'but now I know there is one thing lower, and that's the copper that keeps him at it'. Nor does the film shirk from implying, like the other-wise avuncular *Gideon's Day* (John Ford, 1958) before it, that some policemen can be bought. 'You know what I'd really like?' the oily villain Bertie Hoyle (Derren Nesbitt) asks Johnnoe, 'I'd like a policeman, you know, one that I could call my very own.' Johnnoe rejects the suggestion, but we are left in little doubt that other detectives might have fewer scruples.

Interviewed during the film's extensive location shooting, producer William MacQuitty had promised sharp realism 'in the new wave style' (*Kine Weekly* 27 December 1962) and veracity is evident not only in the police characters, but also in the way the underworld is represented. Annakin and MacQuitty had deliberately cast little-known actors who could play working-class parts convincingly and seem at home in a multi-ethnic criminal milieu and, if Frank Finlay as Hoyle's manipulative partner Leon Sale is now hard to accept, he still offers a dramatic contrast to Nigel Patrick's patrician policeman. Underworld vernacular – 'drum', 'bogey', 'manor', 'stir', 'ponce' – is now familiar from hundreds of episodes of *Minder* and *The Sweeney*, but provided a fresh authenticity in 1963. Nesbitt's cocky and unstable Hoyle is another in the line of socially aspiring spivs that included Peter Seller's Meadows, but there is an emphasis on his *nouveau riche* lifestyle that recalls Stanley Baker's Bannion. Two years on, however, Hoyle's tastes are less Americanised than Bannion's, and reflect, instead, that developing *rapproche-ment* between London's gangster fraternity and the well-heeled thrill seekers of the 'Chelsea Set', which Colin McCabe (1998) has identified as so impor-tant to the underground-meets-the-underworld masterpiece, *Performance* (Donald Cammell and Nicolas Roeg, 1970).

In contrast to the style-blind ex-cons of a contemporary film like *Calculated Risk* (Norman Harrison, 1963) Hoyle apes the English gentleman with chauffeured Bentley, bowler, Crombie and silk dressing gown but his shrewder partner, Leon, is the more interesting figure. As a commando turned crook, he links to a tradition of seeing criminality as an adaptation to demobilisation, but he also looks towards a new era of professionalism that will transform both crime and policing. 'I'm not a criminal', he assures Johnnoe, 'I'm just in business…buying and selling things, moving things about.' The film's distrust of such 'modern economics' is perfectly expressed by the gun Leon keeps hidden in the 'bible' he never travels without: G.K. Galbraith's *The Affluent Society*. Although its claims to naturalism are undermined by some histrionic roughs and tumbles, *The Informers* demonstrates how far the British cinema had itself travelled towards rehabilitating organised crime as a component of modernity. Like *Offbeat* it questioned the moral dichotomy between crime and control, realigning the debate around the new imperatives of professionalism, corporatism, and scientific rationality versus informality, mutuality and pragmatism.

This trajectory of the British crime films, its aspirations to realism and its relevance to the emergent society of the 1960s is most clearly traceable in a trilogy of films scripted by the journalist Leigh Vance. The first, *The Shakedown* (John Lemont, 1960) was rushed out to exploit interest in the Street Offences Act. Like a number of films released at this time – *Beat Girl* (Edmond T. Greville, 1960), *The Challenge* (John Gilling, 1960), *Too Hot to Handle* (Terence Young, 1960), *Jungle Street* (Charles Saunders, 1961), *Strip Tease Murder* (Ernest Morris, 1961) – it draws on a public preoccupation with vice in London's West End which had been intensified by the striptease craze of the late 1950s. *The Shakedown* deals with prostitution and the 'dirty picture' racket, but that is about as far as its claims to contemporaneity will stretch. In other respects it is a sluggish, largely studio-bound exercise in standard B-film making extended to feature length.

Vance's attempts to offer an authentic depiction of the Soho underworld are bedevilled by Lemont's unimaginative direction and some dubious casting decisions, which have Harry H. Corbett playing a Maltese gang boss and well-spoken Terence Morgan trying to convince us he is an Italian pimp. The narrative is criminal-centred but its resolution is conventionally moral with avenging bourgeois blackmail victim shooting foreign vice baron. Ultimately, *The Shakedown*'s most endearing feature is a knowingness about its own exploitative relationship with its audience, which is revealed in its title. It delivers as much as contemporary censorship would allow, but its marketing encourages expectations of a good deal more.

Vance's second collaboration with producer Norman Williams, *Piccadilly Third Stop* (Wolf Rilla, 1960) moves its criminal milieu out of the vice haunts of Soho and into the illegal gaming parties and decadent socialising of Mayfair and Chelsea to paint a picture of (to use Derek Raymonde's phrase) 'the crust on its uppers'. A well-bred wastrel who supports himself by crime was not a new figure – Rave in *The Good Die Young* (Lewis Gilbert, 1954) is the model but Vance and Rilla use the character of Dominic (a more appropriate casting for Terence Morgan) to represent the terminal decline of a social class.

Dominic is a sculptor who supports himself by petty theft and supplying gambling clubs with naive punters. On the margins of high society, he is a playboy crook with a casually exploitative attitude to the women he charms and a contempt for the 'chinless wonders' and 'society jackasses' with whom he mixes. He and his criminal associate, the tough smuggler Joe Preedy, are 'sick of being lectured to by people who have had it handed to them on a plate', telling one to 'run back to mater and pater and live on charity like the rest of your useless mob'. The more ruthless and resourceful face of the officer class is presented by Dennis Price as Edward, a supercilious swine who organises roulette parties. At the turn of the decade the underworld is becoming a melting pot for gentlemen rogues, who are obliged to find increasingly dubious ways to maintain their customary position, and rogues who would like to be gentlemen. The two co-exist in an environment where ready cash is more eloquent than manners and where an expensive accent too 'often covers up for the absence of both' (Press Book).

Piccadilly Third Stop's concerns with class decadence and moral dissolution would have been at home in a Losey movie and anticipate a film like *Nothing But the Best* (Clive Donner, 1964), but they are grafted uneasily onto a heist thriller, which is clearly inspired by *The Asphalt Jungle* and even has a character (a safecracker played by William Hartnell) who is based directly on Doc Reidenschneider. Rilla handles the robbery scenes with pace and some panache but, like *The Shakedown*, they end conventionally although this time there is an ironic suggestion that money may be no substitute for status but it is a great leveller. The final tableau shows the car crash that has killed Dominic and his girlfriend and we see their loot strewn under a No Entry sign.

The trilogy of films written by Leigh Vance and dealing with changes in contemporary crime is completed by *The Frightened City* (John Lemont, 1961). From its genre-definitive title sequence, shot from a car driving through London by night as The Shadows twang out the theme tune, this is a movie with a finger on the pulse of the underworld. It evidences diligent research by Vance to get the 'genuine "low down" on the rackets' (Press Book) and invaluable consultancy from its technical advisor ex-Detective Inspector Sidney Careless of the Flying Squad. Careless would certainly have approved of the film's message that the law and the traditional organisation of policing must be adapted to deal with the syndication of crime on the American model or, as the film's old-fashioned copper–hero (John Gregson) puts it hopefully: 'Justice is slowly catching up with the twentieth century'. The plot is based on the loose territorial agreements then being forged between London's regional 'firms' (Morton 1993: 74–5).[6] But it is the film's eye and ear for detail of both underworld and police argot and practice, and its cynical tone that really support its press book's boast of authenticity and toughness.

The Frightened City gives us the first glimpse of the protection racketeers who would eventually figure so prominently in the cast list of 1960s London. It is clear that they are already poised to take their business from small-time clubs and bars to the heartlands of the new consumer capitalism: 'We won't be bothering with single units any more. We'll go for chain stores, brewers with hundreds of pubs, dry cleaning organisations, cinemas; dealing always with head office direct.' To 'play in the first division' they will need the backing of friends in high places. Against this Mafia vision of systemic corruption, old-school crook Paddy Damion (Sean Connery), a cat burglar drawn into racketeering to support his disabled partner-in-crime, provides some reassurance that there is still honour among thieves.

The films written by Vance are significant, less for their cinematic quality than because they document a key moment of transition in both legal and illegal business culture. As British society moved from relative stability based on well-understood class modes, sexual customs and economic practices into the *déclassé*, permissive and commercially rapacious 1960s, so criminal culture began to reject the shared expectations that circumscribed the underworld, and to aspire to a place above ground. While critical attention has been focused on a handful of contemporary New Wave films that show the ripples of change spreading to the working-class communities of the Northern provinces, there clearly are movies that deal with the social earthquake at its metropolitan epicentre. These films may be thought to lie outside the privileged category of social realist cinema, but they offer invaluable insights to cultural historians interested in the ambivalent responses to the social and economic transformations of the early 1960s. The anxieties about cultural vulnerability, commercial reorganisation and moral deviation that they index may be displaced into genre cinema and refracted through its conventions, but they remain near to the surface even in these underworld dramas.

Notes

1 Of course, the critical consensus was not absolute. Some contemporary commentators such as V.F. Perkins (1962) and Peter Graham (1963) remained unconvinced by an aesthetic awareness compromised, as they saw it, by a commitment to social issues.

2 See, for example, the review of *The Criminal* in the *Monthly Film Bulletin*, November 1960. Losey's approach to realism was to reject 'naturalism' in favour of a Brechtian technique that heightened elements of truth: 'the only way to approach reality is to break down the thing, clean it out…then select the reality symbols that you want and place them back in the scene…in a heightened way' (*Oxford Opinion*, 18 February 1961).

3 Losey would have preferred Bannion's apartment to be less glossy and more 'tatty' (Caute 1994: 492).

4 Meadows strongly resembles Albert Spica (Michael Gambon) in Peter Greenaway's *The Cook, the Thief, his Wife and her Lover* (1990).

5 As Guest remarked:

> I tried to show the fact that police officers are people who have moments when they flare and moments when they are quite ordinary people…they should have light and shade, not just go around shooting people and being shot at, nor being a gentle Sherlock Holmes.
>
> (Jezard 1995)

6 Although the alliances were real, full syndication remained a gangster's dream, as Pearson (1973: 129) reports: 'Ronnie was planning an alliance of gangsters to control London…a warlike federation using violence to get power'.

Bibliography

Armes, R. (1978) *A Critical History of British Cinema*, London: Secker & Warburg.

Campbell, D. (1994) *The Underworld*, London: BBC.

Caute, D. (1994) *Joseph Losey: A Revenge on Life*, London: Faber.

Cox, B., Shirley, J. and Short, M. (1977) *The Fall of Scotland Yard*, Harmondsworth: Penguin.

Durgnat, R. (1970) *A Mirror for England*, London: Faber.

Frazer, F. (1995) *Mad Frank: Memoirs of a Life of Crime*, London: Warner.

Gifford, D. (1986) *The British Film Catalogue 1895–1985*, London: David & Charles.

Graham, P. (1963) *The Abortive Renaissance: Why Are Good British Films So Bad?* London: Axle.

Hess, J. (1977) 'Genre film and the status quo' in B.K. Grant (ed.) (1977) *Film Genre: Theory and Criticism*, Metuchen N.J.: Scarecrow: 53–61.

Higson, A. (1984) 'Space, place, spectacle: landscape and townscape in the "Kitchen Sink Film" ', *Screen* 25: 2–21.

Hill J. (1986) *Sex, Class and Realism: British Cinema 1956–1963*, London: BFI.

Jezard, A. (1995) '*Hell is a City*', *Hammer Horror*, 5 July.

Kelland, G. (1987) *Crime in London*, London: Grafton.

Leahy, J. (1967) *The Cinema of Joseph Losey*, London: Zwemmer.

Lovell, T. (1990) 'Landscapes and stories in 1960s British realism', *Screen* 31: 4.

McCabe, C. (1998) *Performance*, London: BFI.

MacIntosh, M. (1976) *The Organisation of Crime*, London: Macmillan.

Manvell, R. (1968) *New Cinema in Britain*, London: Studio Vista.

Morton, J. (1993) *Gangland: London's Underworld*, London: Warner.

Murphy, R. (1986), 'Riff-raff: British cinema and the underworld', in C. Barr (ed.) *All Our Yesterdays: 90 Years of British Cinema*, London: BFI, 4–5: 286–305.

—— (1992) *Sixties British Cinema*, London: BFI.

Pearson, J. (1973) *The Profession of Violence: The Rise and Fall of the Kray Twins*, St Albans: Granada.

Perkins, V. (1962) 'The British Cinema', *Movie* 1.

Perry, G. (1974) *The Great British Picture Show*, London: Hart-Davis, MacGibbon.

Richards, J. (1992) 'New waves and old myths: British cinema in the 1960s', in B. Moore-Gilbert and J. Seed (eds) *Cultural Revolution? The Challenge of the Arts in the 1960s*, London: Routledge.

Sobchack, T. (1977) 'Genre film: a classical experience', in B.K. Grant (ed.) (1977) *Film Genre: Theory and Criticism*, Metuchen N.J.: Scarecrow: 39–52.

Walker, A. (1974) *Hollywood England: The British Film Industry in the Sixties*, London: Michael Joseph.

9 Performance

Interview with Donald Cammell[1]

Jon Savage

This interview was undertaken in the summer of 1984: it was organised by Tim Bevan and Sarah Radclyffe of Aldabra Productions (now Working Title) to promote Donald Cammell's then current script, *The Last Video*, which was never filmed. It was a hot night in Chelsea: Cammell was staying in Don Boyd's second-floor flat in Cadogan Street. There were a few people when I arrived, but they were soon dispelled, after which we got stoned and talked about many things.

The main reason I wanted to talk to Cammell was *Performance*, which then was still under-researched and ill-understood. It had had a huge impact on me when I first saw it – on psychedelics at a private club – in autumn 1972. Because it was so dense and so disruptive, I kept on returning to the film as it was rebroadcast on TV and made available on video. The more I watched, the better it got: even now, each viewing brings a fresh surprise.

Don't forget that 1984 was the moment when the New Right rhetoric against the 1960s was moving into top gear: Cammell was an unreconstructed 'High Sixties' man, who had helped to alchemise the changes that occurred during those much maligned few years (1965–1969). As we talked, I could feel the sense of possibility that had fuelled *Performance* and which makes it the ultimate sixties film – not least because it's so darkside.

JOHN SAVAGE: Was *Performance* your first film?

DONALD CAMMELL: It was. It wasn't the first script. I wrote a script and sold it to an American company and it was made into a film – I thought it might have been done a little better. I should never criticise other people's movies actually, because I know how hard it is to be faithful to a story, and you can actually transform a story making a film and make it much better. So anybody who tries that, I'm all for it. I don't believe in being specifically faithful to any scripts.

JS: What was the film?

DC: When I wrote it, it was called *Avec Avec* and when it finally emerged, it was re-written, and called *Duffy*. I met James Fox when I was working on that. I was an artist at the time, a retired artist that is, I'd given up painting. And writing that script was the end result of becoming interested in movies and meeting James and seeing a really great actor work. And working with him at that time, I learned a great deal I think quite quickly. The next thing I wrote was *Performance* and that was put together quite speedily.

JS: Can I just check something – are you English? Were you born and brought up in England?

DC: Scots. Yeah. Born in Edinburgh. Brought up mostly in London, South of England, Devon, Westminster.

JS: The thing that interests me, what I'm leading to, is had you lived in England pretty much most of the time when you wrote *Performance*?

DC: No. I went to live in America when I was in my early twenties and then I was living in France after that. I was living in France when I made *Performance*. Just came here. I wrote the story in France.

JS: Because it seems to me very much as though various aspects of English life are seen in that film with the clarity that maybe somebody here, who'd been living here all the time wouldn't have got?

DC: Well, Maybe. Maybe you're right. I hope so. I don't know if I'm any good at observing reality but I think that is probably quite important in trying to make the sort of movies that interest me, that I think I would be best at. Accurate observation has to be the start of it. Before you fuck around with it. And I have a good ear for dialogue, because I could write London dialogue as if it was a foreign language. And I write American dialogue in the same way and I know that in fact their veracity is quite high. Not their quality necessarily. But it's a different thing, isn't it? Truthful dialogue which accurately mirrors human speech is a beginning, it's a tool, in movies you've got to have that. Then you make it terse.

JS: I watched *Performance* again recently and it seemed you somehow instinctively got it right, because it still has enormous resonance as an historical piece, also as a film it's still very relevant and has lots of interesting ideas. And the thing that struck me was how much a reflection now it seems of the various sixties obsessions – like the criminal. You had the two pinnacle sixties obsessions: the criminal and the pop star together. From the time when criminals were pop stars.

DC: They still are. In America they always have been, and everywhere in the world the bandit has been the star of the poor working stiff. And the poor, period, have always seen him as both a revolutionary figure and a star, they both are seen in a political sense. I don't think I can theorise about a view of the social world because I don't think I have a coherent one. I think it can emerge in a piece like *Performance*, or something else I might attempt, but I do see highly anti-social figures as being part of reality – I'm a little bit of a Neo-Darwinist. And that one has to respect them and deal with them as a part of reality you can't wish them away.

JS: You were mentioned in a recent book about the Rolling Stones, as being one of the people who was around when the Stones suddenly became taken up by high society, in about 64/65. Is that the case?

DC: I suppose I was. Just about around then. But I was living a very sort of marginal existence to society at the time, because I was living in Paris and I was not involved with the pop society at all. I was involved with some artists and people, and I was also pursuing a girl a lot at the time, going through a very romantic period in 64 and 65, I remember. And I met the Stones, not in a pop society, I met them by accident. Brian Jones, through…because he fell in love with a girlfriend of mine called Anita Pallenberg.…A marvellous girl. He showed up in Paris and spent a lot of time at a little studio I had over there in Montparnasse. But then we went to Morocco – Brian and me. And Brion Gysin was there and Bill Burroughs, people whom I'd met. And as you know Brian became completely lost in that world for a while and brought it back into the music. He was a very instinctive musician you know. Even when he was just, you know, a sort of very pale, perpetually fatigued kid, always seemed to be living on the edge of his own adventure. He used to dress up in the most extraordinary way, he'd a great deal of visual imagination. The way he saw himself was extremely original in those days. He was totally unconfined by any rock 'n' roll rules. And he would be very much outside any formal norms today in music if he was around. But it may have hurt him as a rock 'n' roller.

JS: I think he was probably ahead of his time and paid the price. Was in any way the character of Turner based on Brian? Did you think of him when you were writing that character?

DC: Yes.

JS: Certainly Mick Jagger seemed to take on some of the persona.

DC: Well, he did because it was necessary to the role and the point came where Mick really tried to become that character, partly because I helped him or bullied him and partly, well let me put it this way, he certainly was a little unenthusiastic about the essential part of that character. He was a little scared of it because it was about a guy who had gone over the top and taken a great fall. And Mick, you know, emotionally likes to take a very dominant view of things and it was a bit risky. I think the fact he did it made for it being a very good performance.

JS: Anita Pallenberg seems pretty much to be playing herself in a lot of ways – I don't know whether that's true or not?

DC: I think probably more than any of the other characters.

JS: Yes. But the other two seemed to be grappling with the roles, which involved them in fundamental personalities. In other words, the roles that they are forced to play…because of what they are as people, actually there's an incredible tension because they're finding it hard to come to terms with those roles. Which gave it a real edge.

DC: It was hard for James because he was going through a sort of, I guess you would call it, a spiritual crisis at the time. And dealing with the role of playing somebody who is an inexorably villainous character, almost a sort of emblem of everything that is glamorous about wickedness and the art forms of violence, was both very exciting and very frightening. He's a gifted actor. He still is I'm sure. He told me quite recently that he didn't want to grapple with that kind of role again. And in fact would never try and do it again.

JS: But that in a way is what is exciting about that particular film. It is very much a film on the edge. The first time I ever saw it I could not understand it, I was very stoned I must admit. But I could not understand the first 20 minutes because of the form, because of the fast cutting and because of the compression. I mean, it's only now that I've seen it on video that I really understand it.

DC: I told you about that didn't I? I had to re-edit it before they would release it, and I re-edited it two or three times and I was on my own in Los Angeles and I'd been more or less instructed…ordered to remove a good 15 minutes of the first 40 minutes of the picture. Or nearly half.

JS: What did that contain?

DC: It contained some of the most, maybe some of the most interesting scenes between the villains,…but re-editing it made it more of a movie

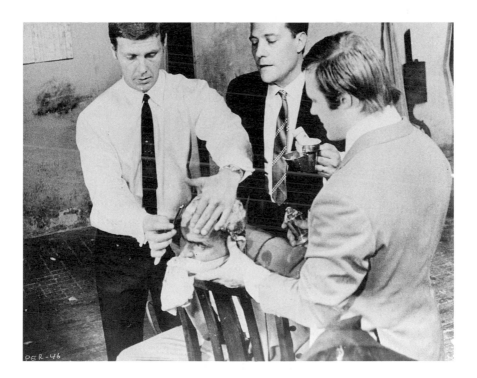

Figure 9.1 An 'emblem of everything that is glamorous about wickedness and the art forms of violence': Chas Devlin (James Fox) plays Sweeney Todd in Donald Cammell's *Performance* (1971)

Source: BFI stills, posters and designs

to me. I became engrossed in getting the main point across as, I guess, what movie-makers call a montage. My original interest in the film was visual – because I'd been a painter and given up painting – that became my favourite part of the film.

JS: The actual editing?

DC: Well, what remains after the editing. After the editing, the restructuring of it. I would not attempt to make a commercial film at this time that is so non-linear as that first two or three reels of *Performance*. But having done it, I think I was very pleased that it happened. But of course Nic Roeg hated it like that, and there's an argument that in its original form it may or may not have been better. Certainly Mick preferred it as a straight-forward story at the beginning. Later on that non-linear form became…you see it now being used…certain techniques.

JS: Being compressed though….

DC: You can see that being used – certain compression styles are now becoming part of the promo vernacular.

JS: And also mainstream commercial movies. Instead of 20 minutes, it's 2. Do you know what I mean?

DC: Well, Eisenstein was doing some pretty hot cutting many years ago, and I wouldn't claim to have originated anything, but it certainly developed it to a point. I know I developed it to quite a sharp point in 1970–1.

JS: The thing with *Performance* now is that people tend to think of it, because of his subsequent career, as Nic Roeg's film. A lot of people I've talked to, I've said I'm going to talk to Don Cammell and they say, 'Oh, didn't he write *Performance*?' People don't realise that you co-directed it, because everybody thinks it's one of Nic Roeg's *oeuvre*.

DC: I'm sure that's understandable. Because I think it formed Nic's style, to a certain extent, that he has repeated – whether consciously or not – certain movie manoeuvres that were originated in *Performance*. Of course, I would say that they were part of the original plan for *Performance* and I can certainly understand that the fact that I haven't made any movies and that Nic has made a number, that have stylistic resemblance to parts of *Performance*, might give rise to that misapprehension that you mention.

JS: I mean, thinking about what those stylistic things are, one of the things I noticed very much in *Performance* was sudden close-ups, but very specific close-ups. There's a wonderful bit where the eel pops out of the tank or there's a bit where there's a close-up on, just very short but very strong close-ups on say, Anita Pallenberg putting some mushrooms in very delicately or taking some mushrooms out and short, very short but very acute close-ups.

DC: Well, they're little moving pictures. If I'd been able to do it painting I would have, but I couldn't. So there they are – very pleased you noticed it. Actually the film in a larger sense is also a collection of pictures that are very disparate and were often criticised as being incoherent both in style and in form, but I think people looking at it now would see that it is coherent.

JS: There are connections that you now make, like the criminal as pop star, which is actually quite illuminating – because after I saw *Performance* again recently I read the Kray brothers' book and just suddenly realised how much they were show business. What was it? Richard Burton went to see Ronnie Kray in Broadmoor. He wears silk monogrammed shirts and all this sort of shit. The guy is a superstar. There are lots of things in *Performance* like that – there's a whole resonance about the Rolling Stones....I thought it got that feeling of Chelsea and Rolling Stones and whatever in 67, not 70...but it was at that time when all of that was fresh, it hadn't turned sour. It was still very utopian...and all that looking at pictures of Persia and stuff was wonderful.

DC: Yes, that's another little moving picture. I'm a bit of a lateral thinker. *Performance*, as I wrote it, was I think a good story. I've already assumed for your purposes the blame for its demands, the circularity of the story – it became not just too lateral but too introverted. I'd like to criticise it rather than say that I think it's okay. I'm very proud of it of course. I mean, I'm not going to knock it. But I look back on it and see how I could develop from that. The original story of *Performance*, and the dialogue, we were very faithful to it when Nic and I shot it. Anita Pallenberg, had a lot of influence on the way that I saw *Performance*. And she's not often credited with it. I became fascinated by some things that she was already deeply involved in, like Artaud theatre, 'Theatre of Cruelty', like she'd worked before with Schlondorff on her first picture. So I give her full credit. And I was a great enthusiast then and now for South American literature, then I was into...there were various translations coming out then. I put a little snapshot of Borges in...inside....

JS: Mick's brain? Is that it? When the bullet....

DC: He never knew it....

JS: After *Performance* was it difficult to get further commissions to do scripts and to direct?

DC: It probably would have been if I'd been looking for work like that, but I was writing my own stuff and trying to make another picture, that started off on the premise that if it was possible to make *Performance*, then it was possible to continue with that line of film entertainment. And so I wasn't in the least discouraged until the time came when I put together another cast, another script and I had quite a commercial looking package. And then I came up against a sort of prejudice against maybe the style of *Performance*. So in that sense I did – it took about three years before I faced up to the fact. It's got to be a sort of game you play with the audience, where you must involve literally millions of people in a story that involves their emotions and their passions. Good movie making involves the passions of the audience, not the detached contemplation of the audience. It's a very visceral thing.

Note

1 A longer version of this interview was published in *Vague* (1991), 23.

10 Mike Hodges discusses *Get Carter* with the NFT audience, 23 September 1997

Q: Did you have Michael Caine in view for the part of Carter from the beginning?

MH: Well, it's quite curious. I read the script and then had discussions about who should play the role. I must be truthful and say that I'd always seen Ian Hendry in the role. I'd always seen him as even seedier than he is. And I must be honest that when I shot the very first scene in the bar with Michael Caine – I'd done two television films prior to that and for television in those days you didn't have to have stars at all – I was looking through the camera, and he walked up to the bar and filled the screen and ordered a beer in a straight glass, and I looked through the camera and I realised that I was in a completely different ball game. It wasn't to do with reality any longer, it was something else that I had no idea of. I mean, I was always a film buff, but as a director I had never really understood, I think, until I first saw Caine's face fill the screen and that changed my whole conception of film-making.

Q: What was it like working with John Osborne?

MH: He was extraordinary, actually. He was an actor before he was a playwright. He was weird to work with because he was very quiet – the sound man was always complaining – and I didn't realise the guile of some people. The guile was to speak incredibly quietly so that you really did listen. John used to disappear during the day. I never saw him socially during the film. He wore Chekhov glasses in those days and he would just come on, do the scenes, and nobody saw him. But certain actors just do that, they don't socialise. But I became a friend afterwards.

Q: Why did you choose Roy Budd for the score?

MH: It was my first film and the producer suggested Roy. The experience of working with him was quite odd. He was always known as 'Sparky', he was the magic pianist. He was a jazz pianist and quite a flash guy, an extraordinary young man and incredibly talented and it was weird because he wrote a lot more music than I put into the film. I have this reputation of using as little music as possible – I find in the contemporary cinema it's used as an aid to make the films slide down a little easier. So in the original theme music at the beginning, he had this very simple theme tune and I just like simple music, I like simple things, I like shooting films simply. The way to do everything is to make them as simple as possible. So I said to Roy, 'I really like the theme embedded in your opening music'. In the scene when Carter goes in to see his dead brother, he just played it on vibes, that's all. Music can be wonderfully evocative but, for my money, it has to be very simple and maybe quite repetitive too.

Q: Why did you decide to kill off Jack Carter at the end of your film when there are two other Carter books by Ted Lewis?

MH: They were written after I made the film. At the end of Ted Lewis's book, *Jack's Return Home* we are never quite sure whether Carter's died or not. But I insisted that he died — they tried to convince me otherwise, needless to say, but I'm afraid I refused.

Q: I have seen the film a few times and I have not noticed that the hit man is on the train with Carter from the beginning. Why did you do that so subtly? You could easily miss that.

MH: Well I don't think anything should be stated obviously. I mean if you look at any of my films they are filled with all sorts of things like that. I have always been obsessed by the detail in pictures. You know, he's [Carter's] reading *Farewell, My Lovely*, which was basically saying 'You're going to die. The titles are going to run over you at the end of the film, and the killer is sitting there in the corner' — if you see, the newspaper he is reading is about the Mafia or something.

Q: In the scene where Carter drives up to the crematorium there are funeral cars coming out. Are these meant to represent the people who are going to die before the end of the film?

MH: Oh I like that idea! The hearses going out represent the number of people who are going to be killed by the end — sadly, I'm a moderately honest man, and I have to say that did not cross my mind.

Q: *Get Carter* is a very bleak and violent film. What is it like filming such a downbeat story? Are you worried about the way you have depicted violence?

MH: The two films that I made before *Carter* — one was an extremely personal film about my family, I mean it's a fiction story which I wrote, but it was personal; but it was still about murder. The story was called *Suspect*, and it was about the murder of a young child and, running parallel was the story of a middle-class family (which I came from) and the murder within the marriage because they never laid hands on each other. So I ran the two things parallel. The second film was called *Rumour*, which was about the freedom of the press and the abuse of the freedom of the press. And then *Carter* was offered to me as a result of these two films and I had also worked on *World in Action* and so I had seen a certain element of truth which Britain was trying to keep hidden. It was as corrupt as every other country. It was as bleak as every other country — and it was worse, in a sense, because it pretended it was some-

Figure 10.1 Mike Hodges on the set of *Get Carter* (1971)
Source: BFI stills, posters and designs

thing else. So then I was offered *Get Carter* and I had some trepidation, but having decided to do it, I then decided also that I would make it as honestly as I possibly could. I had seen villains. I had mixed with, or observed, people of the kind that were in the film; but *Carter's* not all that different from what actually transpired to be true in Newcastle. I mean, *Our Friends in the North*, which I was offered to direct, is about a corrupt city, and I began to smell the corruption in the city. The story that I added on to Ted Lewis's novel was based on a true story. I come from *World in Action*, I come from that sort of background where I wanted to investigate what actually was going on in Newcastle, where I had chosen to shoot it, and I came across this story of the murder of a man outside a nightclub called La Dolce Vita, and I began to investigate what had happened. It was remarkable how far that sort of thing went on in reality, let alone what I was doing in a piece of fiction. So, having decided to do that, I went for it. I've made far more unsettling films for myself. *The Terminal Man* was a deeply unsettling film, and indeed *Croupier*, the one I've just finished, is. So there are films I find hard to live with in life, but cinema sometimes shows people facing the sort of reality we all face in our personal lives, its not just film-makers. So it is hard when you are making a sad or depressing film, but I don't feel that with *Carter*. Maybe its because it was my first film and I was exhilarated by it, and also the odd thing about making a film is that you do it in bits and pieces. I mean, I was completely taken aback by the audience's reaction, I never thought I would ever make a feature film for a start. I made television films which people watch in their own homes, but when you sit with an audience and see how they react it's quite frightening I can tell you. I was terrified. I ran. And I made a comedy next, I tell you.

Q: Did you see yourself as working within any tradition of British crime films? Did you see *Get Carter* as something different from what had gone before?

MH: Obviously, if you make any film you hopefully want it to be different from films you've seen, but, I mean it's impossible not to be influenced, although there wasn't a great tradition. The films that I really had liked among British crime films were *Brighton Rock* particularly, I really loved that film, and there was another film that seems to have got slightly lost down the line, *The Small World of Sammy Lee* with Anthony Newley. I've only seen it once but I remembered it and I remember being impressed by it and, indeed, when I was asked to make *Carter*, I sought out the cameraman, Wolfgang Suschitsky who had shot that film in black and white and I thought he was the only person I would want for my film. American films I certainly have been influenced by. They were seemingly the best films in that genre, without a doubt.

Q: Did you have any trouble with the censor?

MH: The most trouble was the knifing. Luckily I covered it so you never see the knife actually go in – the knifing of Albert. So there was that, and there were some words. I've still got probably somewhere these amazing lists the censor used to send you of all the words and they used to read, I swear to God, like the poem 'Howl' by Alan Ginsberg – fuck, bloody, page so-and-so. That was the only trouble I can think of.

Q: How much did *Get Carter* cost to make in those days?

MH: It was £750,000.

Q: How was the film received in America?

MH: It was odd, actually. I never got to go there, but the producer kept ringing me and saying, 'Michael, they don't understand the opening dialogue, right. Do you mind if I revoice it?' So he revoiced the entire opening scene, and when I heard it back here in England, there was this unbelievable LA cockney and, I cannot tell you, I just went insane. But as a result of all this no one was seeing the film and MGM was in trouble – every time I make a film, the company I make it for seems to get immediately into trouble – and MGM was in trouble so they just shoved it straight out into the drive-ins, and then within a year they make a black version of it.[1] It was like running the negative! It was extraordinary. So that was the end of that really. But it's sort of gathered momentum over the years, but it was never a big hit in the cinemas. Within a certain small

Figure 10.2 Wilfred Brambell and Anthony Newley in Ken Hughes' *The Small World of Sammy Lee* (1963), one of Mike Hodges' inspirations for *Get Carter*
Source: British Cinema and Television Research Group archive, De Montfort University

group of people it has a prestigious reputation and was watched quite a lot, but it was never a commercial success.

Q: When *Get Carter* was first released it didn't cause much of a stir but now it has come to be regarded as something of a classic. Why do you think it has now developed this reputation?

MH: My career seems so odd, really. I don't know, I come to regard making films as putting a message in a bottle. If you manage to get whatever you are talking about into the bottle at least it's out there on the ocean somewhere and it may float in and hit the shore at some point or other. And I'm just glad that *Get Carter* patently is becoming interesting, and it seems that maybe young people have rediscovered it. I knew it was probably on its way back when they turned it into a strip cartoon in *Loaded*, actually.

Q: Have you thought about doing another Carter film?

MH: I did write a synopsis, but not based on the Ted Lewis novels. Jack Carter was dead, but I did suggest there was quite an interesting idea that Carter had a son with the Britt Ekland character and with all the knowledge since I made *Get Carter* of DNA and genetics, I thought it was quite an interesting thing for a young lad to be finding out that Carter was his father. That was, needless to say, rejected. I think they are also talking about a remake of *Get Carter* – I don't know – there are a lot of rumours flying around.

Q: Do you regard *Get Carter* as your best film?

MH: They have all been so totally different. I certainly abandoned trying to make serious films for a period of time. I did *Carter* and then I did *Pulp*. I must say that the most seductive thing about *Carter* was hearing an audience laugh – I love hearing laughter. I did *Pulp*, which was kind of political satire, and then I did *The Terminal Man* which was a really sad and despairing film, and then I just couldn't get a film made for four or five years. And then I was offered *Flash Gordon*, so I did *Flash Gordon* and then I did the second of my sort of facetious period because I thought they would give me more elbow room if I had some box office successes, so I did the much-maligned *Morons from Outer Space*, which was my dedication to the twentieth century, the latter part of the twentieth century, and contemporary culture...I couldn't get Mel Smith and Griff Rhys Jones to take it seriously but I thought the idea was brilliant. I really thought the idea was absolutely brilliant. It was anti-Spielbergian, which I am, anti Spielbergian. So then I was able to get back to doing serious films. I managed to get *Black Rainbow* made and *Prayer for the Dying*, and now I've finished a film called *Croupier* with a wonderful script written by Paul Mayersberg who wrote *Eureka!* and *The Man Who Fell to Earth* and, yet again, I'm in trouble I think with this one – they don't see it yet as a theatrical release.

Note

1 *Hit Man* (George Armitage, 1972) starred Bernie Casey in Michael Caine's role.

11 A revenger's tragedy – *Get Carter*

Robert Murphy

I've come to regard making films as putting a message in a bottle. If you manage to get whatever you are talking about into the bottle at least it's out there on the ocean somewhere and it may float in and hit the shore at some point or other.

(Hodges 1997a)

Since it was released early in 1971, *Get Carter* has progressed from modest commercial success to major cult status – shown uncut in Alex Cox's *Moviedrome*, cover featured in *Crime Time*, serialised as a strip cartoon in *Loaded*, given a top scoring of five hammers for hardness in *Men Only*. Such recognition is welcome but there is a tendency to see *Get Carter* as an isolated masterpiece, an inexplicable eruption of genius out of a sea of dross. Neil Spencer in an otherwise enthusiastic and well-informed celebration of *Get Carter* in *Uncut* magazine, asserts that: 'with the honourable exception of 1947's *Brighton Rock* (with Dickie Attenborough as a 16-year-old Scarface) British crime movies meant dozy crooks having their collar felt by coppers after a chase in the Wolseley down the Great West Road' (Spencer 1998: 31).[1]

Attenborough's Pinkie wasn't the only cold-blooded killer from the 1940s – Dirk Bogarde's Riley in *The Blue Lamp* (Basil Dearden, 1950) and Griffith Jones's Narcy in *They Made Me a Fugitive* (Cavalcanti, 1947) are equally effective; and there had been interesting, if not wholly convincing explorations of the underworld in films such as Edmond T. Greville's *Noose* (1948), Jules Dassin's *Night and the City* (1950), Joseph Losey's *The Criminal* (1960) and John Lemont's *The Frightened City* (1961). But Spencer is right that *Get Carter* is different, marking a turn from the optimism of the 1960s: 'part of the wake-up call for the new decade, a discomforting reflection of Britain as it entered a sourer, more cynical age' (Spencer 1998: 32). Director Mike Hodges cites *Brighton Rock* (John Boulting, 1947) and Ken Hughes' rarely seen *The Small World of Sammy Lee* (1963) as influences and there are a number of films made around the same time as *Get Carter* with an equally bleak, violent view of the world.[2] John Boorman's *Point Blank* (1967) is set in Los Angeles and Don Siegel's *Dirty Harry* (1971) in San Francisco, but in both films tough men plough a lone, violent furrow through a treacherous world. Closer to home,

David Greene's *The Strange Affair* (1968), Nic Roeg and Donald Cammell's *Performance* (1970), Jack Gold's *The Reckoning* (1970) and Michael Tuchner's *Villain* (1971) share *Get Carter*'s view of a post-swinging Britain where permissiveness has curdled into pornography and violence.

Mike Hodges had served his film-making apprenticeship in television, experimenting with documentaries on 'The Information Explosion', 'Leisure', and 'Stimulants' (banned because of its treatment of LSD) for Kenneth Tynan's arts programme, *Tempo*, and moving on to investigative journalism on Granada's *World in Action*. In 1969 he directed *Suspect* for Thames Television, a 76-minute play/film paralleling the break-up of a marriage with the investigation into the disappearance of a child. It was closely followed by *Rumour* (1970), the first television film made by the Thames subsidiary Euston Films (which five years later was to launch *The Sweeney*). Just as *Get Carter* catches something of the Poulson/T. Dan Smith scandal that enveloped Newcastle in the early 1970s, *Rumour*, where a journalist's attempt to investigate political scandal invokes dark forces that destroy him, hints at the high-level corruption that was to hover like a miasma over the death of Pope John Paul 1 and the Italian banker Roberto Calvi.

Producer Michael Klinger had entered the entertainment business, running striptease clubs in Soho, but the Tekli-Compton film company he set up with Tony Tenser in the early 1960s had been responsible for Roman Polanski's *Repulsion* (1965) and *Cul de Sac* (1966) as well as more standard exploitation films like *The Yellow Teddy Bears* (Robert Hartford-Davis, 1963). In 1969 Klinger was approached by Nat Cohen (another producer whose career spanned the art/exploitation frontier) to help make a couple of films for MGM, who were in the process of closing down their Borehamwood studios but didn't want to be seen to be deserting Britain completely. Klinger had already decided to exploit the recent upsurge of interest in the English underworld aroused by the trial of the Richardson and Kray gangs to make a hard-hitting, realistic British gangster film and he had bought the film rights to an as yet unpublished crime novel, Ted Lewis's *Jack's Return Home*.[3]

Lewis, brought up in Barton on Humber in north Lincolnshire, was of the post-Angry Young Men generation – not quite old enough to remember the war, coming of age just as National Service was abolished and the affluent society of the sixties was emerging. His first novel, *All the Night and All the Way Home* (1965) made little impression but Lewis was an accomplished draughtsman and he was able to find work on animation films. In 1968 he completed *Jack's Return Home*. It was rejected by his publisher (Hutchinson) but picked up by Peter Day at Michael Joseph, despite a reader's report that took Lewis's colloquialisms as evidence of illiteracy, and seized upon by Klinger as the sort of hard-hitting gangster subject he was looking for.

Characters in the stories of Alan Sillitoe (such as *Saturday Night and Sunday Morning* and *The Loneliness of the Long Distance Runner*) and Bill Naughton (*Alfie* and short stories such as *Spiv in Love* and *The Little Welsh Girl*) moved

easily between the core of hard-working, respectable, working-class communities and the semi-criminal penumbra that surrounded them. But in *Jack's
Return Home*, Lewis shifted the emphasis from the working-class milieu to the
criminals moving through it. British gangsters, spivs, wide boys had dominated the novels of James Curtis and Robert Westerby in the 1930s and
Gerald Kersh and Arthur La Bern in the 1940s, but in the 1950s, the crime
novel turned away from sordid low-life concerns and concentrated on crime
in the world of debutantes and ex-officers.[4] Those seeking less anaemic fare
had to rely on pseudo-American sensationalists like Hank Janson, Peter
Cheyney and James Hadley Chase. Curtis and Westerby's socially concerned
explorations of Britain's lower depths found an echo in the work of Ken
Loach and other left-wing contributors to the BBC's *Wednesday Play*, but as a
literary tradition, the British gangster novel appeared to have died an early
death. Lewis's attachment to his own provincial authenticity coupled with the
need for commercial success (Lewis had given up his animation work to
devote himself to writing) broke through the blockage and *Jack's Return Home*
launched a new wave of British regional crime fiction.[5]

In Lewis's novel, Jack Carter, a gangster based in London, returns to his
home town somewhere not far from Doncaster, to investigate his brother
Frank's death. He discovers that Frank was murdered by local villains because
he threatened to expose them to the police after finding out that they used
his 16-year-old daughter in a pornographic film. Jack takes his revenge, but is
himself badly injured.

Lewis was eager to help out with the script but Hodges wanted to write
his own adaptation. He claims that his script 'ultimately bore very little relation to the book' despite the fact that all the major characters and most of the
dialogue comes from Lewis's novel (Hodges 1972: 2). The main casualty was
the complicated back story about Jack and his brother. In the novel, Frank is
an important character and his childhood relationship with Jack is explored
extensively. In the film we see him lying in his coffin and there is no attempt
to bring him back to life in explanatory flashbacks. Similar economies are
made with other characters. Albert Swift, the catalyst who splits the teenage
Jack and Frank apart and the centre of the pornography ring that traps Frank's
daughter is glimpsed briefly a third of the way into the film, appears mute in a
blue movie and only gets one chance to speak before Jack silences him for
ever. Jack's love affair with his boss's wife, Audrey (Anna in the film) is cut to a
minimum and the incident that explains why Eric Paice has such a grievance
against Jack, is left out.

Other changes came about because of casting decisions. In Lewis's novel,
Kinnear, the local godfather, is a typical Chandler/Hammett fat-man villain:

> Cyril Kinnear was very, very fat. He was the kind of man that fat men
> like to stand next to. He had no hair and a handlebar moustache that
> made his face look a foot long on each side. In one way it was a very
> pleasant face, the face of a wealthy farmer or an ex-Indian army officer in

the used car business but the trouble was he had eyes like a ferret's. They had black pupils an eighth of an inch in diameter surrounded by whites the colour of the fish part of fish fingers. He was also only five foot two inches tall.

(Lewis 1971: 72)

Hodges persuaded Klinger to cast John Osborne, the Angry Young Man whose play *Look Back in Anger* had rudely shattered the conservative consensus in 1956. He was tall, thin and bearded.

For Jack Carter, Hodges envisaged Ian Hendry who had effectively played roguish, good/bad characters in *Live Now Pay Later* (Jay Lewis, 1961) and *The Beauty Jungle* (Val Guest, 1964). But Klinger was already determined that Michael Caine should play the part. Caine had become internationally famous as the womanising hero of *Alfie* (Lewis Gilbert, 1966) and as Harry Palmer, the cash-starved, bureaucratically cramped secret agent of *The Ipcress File* (Sidney J. Furie, 1965), *Funeral in Berlin* (Guy Hamilton, 1966) and *Billion Dollar Brain* (Ken Russell, 1967). Caine was keen to extend his range beyond the light comedy roles he had been asked to play since *Alfie* (in *The Wrong Box* and *The Italian Job*, for example). But he was not prepared to cast aside his distinctive South London accent. Hodges was quickly convinced that Caine's star persona made this an irrelevance:

> I was looking through the camera and he walked up to the bar and filled the screen and ordered a beer in a straight glass, and I looked through the camera and I realised that I was in a completely different ball game. It wasn't to do with reality any longer, it was something else which I had no idea of.

(Hodges 1997a)

The other major change is the shift in location, though it is not, as one might have expected, southwards to London to suit Caine, but further north, to Newcastle. In the novel, Jack gets off the London train at Doncaster and changes on to a local train for his un-named destination. Paul Duncan, in his useful piece on Ted Lewis, claims that this is Barton on Humber, where Lewis lived from the age of six (Duncan 1997: 24). But to anyone familiar with the Goole, Grimsby, Gainsborough triangle it is obvious that Lewis's setting is not the Humber port, Barton, but the steel town, Scunthorpe.

Scunthorpe isn't an obvious first choice for the setting of a crime novel, but Lewis acutely picks up on three factors in its favour. It is big enough to support a criminal subculture but small enough for everyone to know – indirectly at least – everybody else. Its landscape of fiery furnaces and smouldering slag heaps has an element of exoticism. And in the sixties it was a boom town, growing rapidly as the steel industry flourished. High wages for hard, dangerous work bred a tough, macho ethos where money was spent lavishly on entertainment and conspicuous consumption rather than invested as a means of climbing up the social hierarchy.

> As a kid it had always struck me that it was like some western boom town. There was just the main street where there was everything you needed and everything else just dribbled off towards the ragged edges of the town. Council houses started immediately behind Woolworth's. Victorian terraces butted up to the side of Marks and Spencer's. The gasworks overshadowed the Kardomah. The swimming baths and the football ground faced each other only yards away from the corporation allotments.
>
> (Lewis 1971: 9)

It is a good setting for Lewis's story, which is more about small-town nastiness than high-level crime (a remake – rumours of which circulate constantly – might resurrect the *Blue Velvet*-like strangeness beneath the banal surface quality of the novel). But it didn't appeal to Mike Hodges. Travelling north in Michael Klinger's Cadillac, he found that sixties town planning had imposed a depressing modernist uniformity on northern towns: 'Lowestoft, Grimsby, Hull. Each had been decimated by developers. The pubs, cafes and dodgy boarding houses gone' (Hodges 1997b: 20).

Remembering docking in North Shields when doing his National Service in the Royal Navy, Hodges continued further north and found what he was looking for in Newcastle. Though the city was being rapidly re-developed, it was still visually interesting and Hodges was able to relocate scenes at the racetrack, on the ferry between North and South Shields, on two of the bridges, and he moved the final conflict between Carter and Eric Paice from a deserted brick-works to the sea-coal shoreline. He also picked up on the aura of corruption and gangsterism that permeated the city and introduced it into the film in place of the parochial realism of Lewis's novel.

Get Carter was released in March 1971. Mike Hodges claims 'it was never a big hit in the cinema' (Hodges 1997a) and at a cost of £750,000 it was a sufficiently high-budget film to need some success in the international market. Unfortunately, MGM mishandled its release in America, delaying to redub some of the more difficult-to-understand Cockney dialogue in the pre-credits sequence and then rushing it straight into the drive-ins. A year later they remade it with a black cast as *Hit Man*. Director George Armitage inventively relocates sequences to a brothel, a dog fight, a private zoo, and makes Tyrone (Bernie Casey), the black gangster who stands in for Carter, a more sympathetic character. But he misses out on the depth and intensity of the original.

Critical reception of *Get Carter* in Britain ranged from dismissive disgust to grudging respect for its pace and professionalism. Nigel Andrews considered that:

no amount of picturesque violence (bodies splayed across car windscreens or hurtling from high buildings) can redeem *Get Carter*'s perfunctory plot, its mechanical manipulation of characters or a vision of the British underworld that relies totally on cliché (homosexual chauffeur, bloated tycoon, glamorous mistress).

(*Monthly Film Bulletin*, March 1971)

Thomas Elsaesser, in a general attack on British films for 'seeking realism on the level of location and atmosphere' and 'exploiting a social milieu simply for its spurious exoticism', declared that in *Get Carter*: 'the sordid has become unashamedly decorative' (Elsaesser 1972: 5). Alexander Walker worried about its 'merciless view of life as a state of impending menace and grievous bodily harm', but conceded that it was a well-directed and effective thriller (*Evening Standard*, 11 March 1971). George Melly admitted to 'complete and shameless enjoyment' but warned that: 'if *Love Story* is like a loaf of sliced bread, this is a bottle of neat gin swallowed before breakfast. It's intoxicating all right, but it'll do you no good' (*Observer*, 14 March 1971).

Criticism of the film centred on its plot – which was considered incomprehensible and mechanical – and its violence. According to Michael Caine,

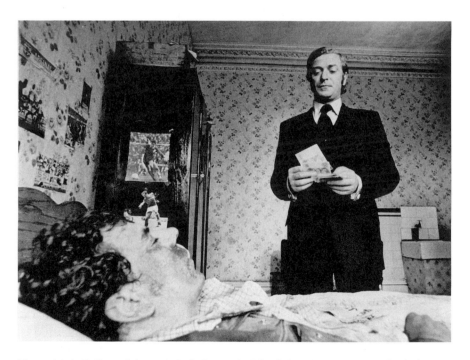

Figure 11.1 Collateral damage: Jack Carter (Michael Caine) compensates his helper (Alun Armstrong) for the beating he has taken on Carter's behalf

Source: British Cinema and Television Research Group archive, De Montfort University

he and Hodges were determined to show violence as it really was: 'In real life, every single punch in the face tears skin and cartilage and often breaks bones' (Caine 1992: 323). Ironically then, much of the violence occurs off screen. We don't see Frank murdered. We don't see Keith being beaten up. We don't see Anna paying for her affair with Carter by having her face destroyed. We don't see broken bones. Mike Hodges explains that '*Get Carter* is about a violent man, but there isn't a lot of blood everywhere or anything, there's more of a sense of violence' (Hodges 1972: 2). It is the implacability with which Carter drags Glenda from her bath, despatches Albert and abducts Margaret that chills. Hodges claims that 'I am personally terrified of meeting some guy I couldn't talk to to stop him killing me or doing me over' (Hodges 1972: 2). And it is this relentless, unstoppable quality that makes Carter both frightening and fascinating. Caine carries it off convincingly because of what Michael Bracewell calls 'his manipulation of ordinariness' ('The man on the screen', *Guardian Weekend*, 8 February 1997: 12–16). His nuanced, realist acting is central to the film's achievement in combining the mythological and the mundane. Anne Billson describes Carter as 'an implacable avenging angel in a black raincoat' but this is only half the picture (Billson 1991: 102). From his fussy concern with nose drops, vitamin pills and the cleanliness of British Railways' cutlery to his inability to discern that Thorpey would give him the wrong name or that Margaret would bring Con and Peter to their rendezvous, he is riddled with human frailty.

Concern about *Get Carter*'s violence is understandable, criticism of the plot seems less justifiable. What Thomas Elsaesser calls 'a plot so complicated as to become unimportant' (Elsaesser 1972: 6) is precisely organised and thoroughly consistent – which is not to deny that it is extremely convoluted. One of the reasons for *Get Carter*'s popularity on video is that it rewards detailed scrutiny. Repeated viewings reveal nuances of the plot – the crucial importance of Anna Fletcher and Albert Swift, for example – which are difficult to grasp on a single viewing. And clues such as the appearance of the contract killer on the train during the title sequence are so deeply embedded as to be virtually impossible to pick up without prior knowledge. This is a very rich text then, but unusually, *Get Carter*'s plot is completely linear, with no flashbacks and no sub-plots.

In most films, sub-plots serve as vehicles for developing psychological depth to the main characters and for exploring thematic material. In *Dirty Harry* the relationship between Harry and Chico, his university educated Mexican–American partner is used to show Harry's prejudice and invulnerability as a mask concealing his compassion and loneliness. In *Taxi Driver* (Martin Scorsese, 1976) the relationship between Travis and Betsy charts the trajectory of Travis's character from likeable loner to violent psychopath. *Get Carter* doesn't work like this. For a time Carter has a helper, Keith (Alun Armstrong who twenty-five years later was to play the T. Dan Smith-like Austin Donahue in the BBC serial *Our Friends in the North*), but when he is carried off by Thorpey's gang, Carter shrugs his shoulders and goes to bed with his landlady.

Hodges claims that *Get Carter* is about a man 'incapable of forming relationships' (Hodges 1972: 2) and though Carter has sexual relationships with three women – Anna, the wife of his gangster boss, Gerald Fletcher, Edna Barfoot, the landlady and Glenda, the goodtime girl who seems to link up all the local villains – none of them progress far enough to allow a sub-plot carrying thematic material to be developed. Anna (Britt Ekland), a substantial character in the novel, doesn't get beyond pouting and purring: exchanging significant glances with Carter in the pre-credits sequence, caressing herself as Carter talks to her on the phone about how they will make love. Her main function is as the catalyst for conflict between Carter and Fletcher, the reason why there can be no going back for him.

Edna at least has a voice and an initial resistance to Carter, but she has no illusions about her place in the order of things and is sulkily aware that Carter will use her and discard her. Glenda seems to be more independent. At Kinnear's she is drunk and silly but potentially subversive – a degenerate variation on Gloria Grahame's Debbie Marsh in *The Big Heat* (Fritz Lang, 1953) – and she reappears as Carter's fairy godmother, whisking him away in her

Figure 11.2 Telephone sex: Gangster's moll Anna (Britt Ekland) listens excitedly to Carter's erotic phone call, suitable reading matter at the ready
Source: British Cinema and Television Research Group archive, De Montfort University

Talbot Sunbeam from the clutches of his enemies. But having rescued Carter and inadvertently given him the information that enables him to unravel the plot, she is allowed to die.

Elsaesser complains that 'the tough, brutal act or the sadistic gesture has to cover Mike Hodges' tracks whenever the plot motivation becomes too threadbare not to be conspicuous by its absence' (Elsaesser 1972: 5). This is facile, in that none of the brutality is superfluous or gratuitous, but perceptive in picking up on the sadism that permeates the film. There is a grubby looking-up-womens'-skirts quality to Lewis's novel but his misogyny allows his female characters some power and independence. Hodges is harsher and crueller in the way in which he subordinates his characters to the needs of the plot. He reduces Anna from a tough gangster's moll to a doll-like sex object, casually pawed by Gerald as he watches pornographic films, humiliated and embarrassed by him when he discovers her masturbating. Edna Barfoot goes willingly to Carter's bed in the novel; in the film Carter overcomes her resistance by ripping her blouse open. Glenda is knocked around and dunked in the bath in the novel, but she survives her encounter with Carter. In the film she is dragged wet and bedraggled to her car, dumped in the boot and drowned when it is pushed into the Tyne. Lewis has Carter shoot Margaret full of heroin, but we assume she survives. Hodges has Carter make her strip before injecting her and lowering her comatose body into Kinnear's ornamental lake. The same escalation of cruelty applies to the male characters in the film: Brumby (who survives in the novel) tipped over the edge of his multi-storey car park; Albert desperately sucking on his last fag before being slaughtered like a pig; Eric gagging on whisky before being beaten to death and dumped in the sea with the coal slag. But there is more of a sense that the men deserve their fates; the women are highly sexualised victims of male violence. Elsaesser's judgement of the film as 'a protracted sado-masochistic fantasy' (Elsaesser 1972: 5) is an uncomfortable reminder that nostalgia for unacceptable pre-feminist representations of women accounts for *Get Carter's* current popularity as much as an appreciation of the film's quality as a gangland thriller.

In his essay on revenge, Francis Bacon argues that:

> Revenge is a kind of Wild Justice, which the more Man's Nature runs to, the more ought Law to weed it out. For as for the first wrong, it doth but offend the Law, but the Revenge of that wrong, putteth the Law out of office.
>
> (Quoted by Foulkes 1996: 4)

But in *Get Carter* the Law doesn't really come into it. We don't see any policemen until the end of the film when they are summoned by Carter to take away Kinnear and his doped and dazed party-goers. The tone is set in the pre-credits sequence when Carter, before setting out on his quest for vengeance, contemptuously rebuts Syd Fletcher's assurance that the police seem satisfied about the circumstances surrounding Frank's death with 'Since when has that been good enough for us?' Anne Billson asserts that: 'Revenge is never taken on behalf of the victim, it is always for the benefit of the revenger' (Billson 1991: 81). This might be the case in films like *Taxi Driver*, *Dirty Harry* and *Death Wish* (Michael Winner, 1974) but it doesn't apply to *Shane* (George Stevens, 1953) or *Pale Rider* (Clint Eastwood, 1984) where the revenger is not motivated by personal desires but reluctantly drawn into defending a community against a cruel oppressor. As R.A. Foulkes explains: 'Revenge tragedies exploit the moral tension between the desire for justice and the urge to revenge by placing their protagonists in a situation in which they cannot obtain legal redress' (Foulkes 1996: 6). Jack Carter is neither an upholder of justice nor a saviour of the weak and humble, but he operates by a strict code that he expects his colleagues and enemies to share. Like Harry Callaghan in *Dirty Harry* and Travis Bickle in *Taxi Driver*, Carter is confronted by a society afflicted by pornographic malaise. But his righteous anger is less about sleaze itself than about how it has leaked out of its proper underworld milieu to engulf his niece and destroy his brother. Carter is not so self-consciously evil as Flamineo in Webster's *The White Devil* or as morbidly obsessed as Vindice in Middleton's *The Revenger's Tragedy* but he does share some of the characteristics of the Jacobean revenge tragedy protagonist. A wrong has been done – less to Carter himself than to his family – which must be righted at whatever cost. Elsaesser complains of 'a sentimentality difficult to bear (Caine sobbing as he watches his niece being seduced in a blue movie) let alone take seriously' (Elsaesser 1972: 5). But until he sees Doreen in the blue film, Carter's emotions are as carefully controlled as the stiff upper lips of the naval officers in fifties British war films. What for Elsaesser indicates *Get Carter*'s essentially trivial view of the world can be seen as the melancholy of the revenge tragedy hero at the corruption of innocence.

For the film to succeed as a tragedy it is necessary for Carter to die. At the end of the novel, Carter's attempt to exact vengeance on Eric goes wrong and we are left wondering whether Con McCartey, one of the men sent by Fletcher to bring him back to London, will rescue the wounded Carter or leave him to die.[6] In the film we see the contract killer on the train at the beginning, and there is a shift in point-of-view towards the end, when Kinnear phones him to arrange the killing. This is the only scene in the film where Carter isn't in some way present and it prepares us for his death. This is less a matter of satisfying the demands of censorship morality codes than of completing the structure of a revenge tragedy. Having fulfilled his task of vengeance, Carter must die.[7]

Notes

1 The Britt Ekland Fan Club has probably already taken out a contract on Spencer for confusing her with Geraldine Moffat. Britt was the pretty blonde one who wasn't shoved into her car boot and drowned, Neil.

2 Ken Hughes was responsible for some of the best of Anglo-Amalgamated's *Scotland Yard* films and for *Joe Macbeth* (1955), but he obviously didn't want to be confined to unprestigious crime films and squandered his reputation on the interesting but ponderous *Cromwell* (1967).

3 After viewing a rough cut of Pete Walker's *Man of Violence*, Michael Klinger told him: 'This is a load of old crap, son…I'm going to make a gangster film but it's going to cost a lot more than this and it's going to be better' (Chibnall 1998: 66).

4 Two of the most interesting are Marjorie Allingham's *Tiger in the Smoke* (1952) and James Curtis's *Look Long Upon a Monkey* (1956), both of which have seedy underworld elements threatening and unsettling the respectable, privileged middle-class world.

5 Lewis's first editor described him as 'one of the most incredibly arrogant people I've ever met.…He really did think he was the best author that ever lived' (Giles Gordon, quoted in Duncan 1997: 23). The robustness of the British provincial crime novel was attested by BBC Radio 4's series *Crimescapes*, broadcast in March /April 1998 with episodes devoted to David Craig, Nicola Williams, Alison Taylor, William McIlvanney, Ian Rankin and Colin Bateman.

6 Lewis wrote two more Carter books *Jack Carter's Law* (1974) and *Jack Carter and the Mafia Pigeon* (1977) but these could be considered prequels rather than sequels and the purpose of the open ending has more to do with Lewis's desire to maintain Carter's first-person narration to the end than to keep him alive.

7 *Hit Man* has a happier end: the corrupt policeman assigned to kill Tyrone refrains when his car radio informs him that his criminal paymaster is dead.

Bibliography

Billson, A. (1991) *My Name is Michael Caine*, London: Muller.

Caine, M. (1992) *What's it All About?* London: Arrow.

Chibnall, S. (1998) *Making Mischief: The Cult Films of Pete Walker*, London: Fab Press.

Duncan, P. (1997) 'All the way home: Ted Lewis', *Crimetime* 9: 22–5.

Elsaesser, T. (1972), 'Between style and ideology', *Monogram* 3: 2–11.

Foulkes R.A. (1996) Introduction to *The Revenger's Tragedy*, Thomas Middleton/Cyril Tourneur, Manchester: Manchester University Press.

Hall, W. (1981) *Raising Caine*, London: Sidgwick and Jackson.

Hodges, M. (1972) 'Interview', *Cinema Rising* 3: 2.

—— (1997a) Interviewed at the National Film Theatre, 23 September, transcribed by Steve Chibnall.

—— (1997b) 'Getting Carter', *Crimetime* 9: 20–1.

Lewis, T. (1971) *Carter* (originally published as *Jack's Return Home*), London: Pan.

Spencer, N. (1998) 'The Caine mutiny', *Uncut*: 31–3, June.

12 Dog eat dog

The Squeeze and the *Sweeney* films

Leon Hunt

Links between film and television crime dramas can be traced back to *The Blue Lamp* (Basil Dearden, 1950), but it is not until the 1970s that these links become significant for the genre. The crossover between film and television is evident in their use of the same writers (Dick Clement and Ian La Frenais, Leon Griffiths, John Hopkins) and directors (Mike Hodges, Michael Apted), and in a declining national cinema's dependence on adaptations of popular TV series. The decade sees a well-documented shift in TV cop series from the 'cosy paternal parochialism' (Whannel 1994: 184) of *Dixon of Dock Green* (BBC 1955–76) and the 'realism' of *Z Cars* (BBC 1962–78) to the screeching tyres, demotic cockney lad-speak and in-your-face violence of *The Sweeney* (Thames 1974–8). Above all, this series about Scotland Yard's 'Flying Squad',[1] like the crime films of the period, carves a characteristic generic landscape – 'an anomic urban-wasteland world' (Dennington and Tulloch 1976: 37) – out of a larger set of anxieties about the policing of a 'violent' state seemingly sliding into chaos.

The 1970s are book-ended by notable gangster movies: *Get Carter, Villain* and, belatedly, *Performance* (all released in 1971) and *The Long Good Friday* (John Mackenzie, 1981), made for television in 1979 but rejected as too violent by Lew Grade (Walker 1985: 252.) But the 1970s crime film is already anticipated by *The Strange Affair* (David Greene, 1968) with its emphasis on police corruption and the rule-bending loner cop who 'defies his superiors and mingles with the flotsam and jetsam of the underworld' (Murphy 1992: 234). The maverick cop can slide all too easily into psychosis, like Sean Connery's Johnson in *The Offence* (Sidney Lumet, 1972) who kills a suspected child molester during interrogation; Johnson is a casualty of 'the job', irreparably damaged by all the things he's witnessed.

On television, the maverick blossoms into a more populist figure with some similarities to the American 'rogue cop' films. Even so, *The Sweeney* has as much in common with *Get Carter* and *Villain* as it does with *Dirty Harry* (Don Siegel, 1971) or *The French Connection* (William Friedkin, 1971), not only in its evocation of a violent urban 'jungle' but in some of the sensibilities of its anti-hero.[2] What is immediately striking about the two British gangland films, in striking contrast with the two American ones, is the virtual absence or marginalisation of the police. In *Get Carter*, there are simply two kinds of people – competing gangsters and the unfortunates who get in the way (the police only appear at all as instruments of Carter's revenge). *Villain* gives centre stage to Richard Burton's Vic Dakin, both Kray Twins rolled into one. Nigel Davenport and Colin Welland play low-key, *Z Cars* coppers, mocked for their low pay and low status, 'keeping Britain clean on thirty quid a week.' We first meet Davenport's Inspector Matthews as he's digging his garden, and while he's prepared to bend the rules a little, he's hardly a charismatic or visionary policeman – 'The last thing I want is a fertile imagination…we're a very narrow-minded lot, us coppers'. Vic's downfall is due less to brilliant policing than the sense that there's a change in the air, perhaps associated with the incoming Heath government's stress on law and order. In the final scene, Matthews invokes a shift in consensus – 'You can't put the frighteners on all of them, not all the time.…You call 'em punters, we call 'em witnesses'. Vic is having none of this – 'If I looked at one of them, they'd piss in their pants', he bellows with the sort of red-faced bellicosity Burton specialised in by this stage in his career. But he's wrong, dead wrong – the camera adopts his paranoid viewpoint, sweeping wildly from side to side as everyone, police and punters alike, seems to close in on him. The film ends with his hoarse cry, 'Who are you looking at?' and a device that resurfaces in both of the *Sweeney* films – a monochrome freeze-frame, isolating the powerless protagonist.

The names of *The Sweeney's* Detective Inspector *Jack* Regan (John Thaw) and Detective Sergeant George *Carter* (Dennis Waterman) seem to reference Michael Caine's Jack Carter, an important prototype for the avenging, unstoppable maverick. According to Dennington and Tulloch:

> If 'normal' society is a building, then Regan is the maintenance man that must go down into the basement of society and 'do what must be done' to fight the infection that festers there and that threatens constantly to pollute the totality.
>
> (Dennington and Tulloch 1976: 39)

This involves getting 'dirty', being a bit of a bastard, but the show insists that the police are 'necessary bastards' – 'it's a corrupt world, there are some nasty people about, and you won't stop them by sticking to the rules' (ibid.: 39). Regan has a 'mandate for his "entrepreneurial" violence and rule-breaking…the price the "good" society pays for its protection from chaos' (Tulloch 1990: 69). Otherwise, he is simply an inverted gangster. In *Regan*, the 1974 pilot, the Sweeney operate like a rival gang – 'When you murder one of us, there are no rules at all', he tells one bad lad by way of intimidation. The series tended to tone this down, but his 'criminality' periodically resurfaced in intriguing ways. In *Queen's Pawn* (1975), an ambitious commissioner humiliated in court takes Regan off the leash to settle accounts with a known villain – 'There's nothing wrong with revenge harnessed to justice', he comments.

What follows is like a British *Red Harvest* as villains are played off against each other, the Flying Squad engage in some impromptu kidnapping and the bodies pile up. But somewhere between the maverick cop and the gangster is the hard-boiled detective – Dennington and Tulloch (1976: 46) cite Spillane's Mike Hammer, who justifies his almost pathological violence as 'the evil that opposed other evil, leaving the good and the meek in the middle to live and inherit the earth'. Regan must perform or countenance similar ruthlessness, but sometimes the 'good and the meek' get caught in the crossfire. In *Sweeney 2*, a hostage is fatally injured during a collision with a police roadblock. 'Why did you have to do it', her father asks Regan later, 'when you knew they had my daughter aboard?' 'To stop them', Regan answers, with blunt self-loathing.

Although the 'bookend' gangster films of the 1970s all have established or growing reputations, the other British crime movies of the decade have been comparatively neglected. I want to focus on three modest but enjoyably resonant films: *Sweeney!* (David Wickes, 1977), *Sweeney 2* (Tom Clegg, 1978) and *The Squeeze* (Michael Apted, 1977). The *Sweeney* films are interesting attempts to open out or (in the case of the first film) even partially re-think the TV series on which they were based. Their neglect is not difficult to pinpoint – British films based on TV shows tend either to be dismissed outright (all of the sitcom films) or, as seems to be the case here, offered modest praise but left unexamined. Sarah Street (1997: 101) exempts them from the alleged weaknesses of the sitcom films – overstretched narratives, lack of character development – a judgement shared by several contemporaneous reviews.

David Robinson found *Sweeney!* 'certainly livelier than most television spin-offs' (*The Times*, 14 January 1977), while Margaret Hinxman insisted that to 'describe this rattling good thriller as a TV spin-off would be an insult…the film stands on its own as probably the best British crime movie since Peter Yates' *Robbery*' (*Daily Mail*, 15 January 1977). But critical attention has been reserved mainly for the television series, with the films treated only as footnotes. *The Squeeze*, meanwhile, seems to have been forgotten about altogether, despite its reviews making it sound like a film few critics would forget – 'a savagely depressing…British thriller that seems determined to stamp on everything we boasted of in the sixties' (Russell Davies, *Observer*, 27 February 1977), a 'bestial thriller' (Margaret Hinxman, *Daily Mail*, 25 February 1977), 'a package tour of thuggery' (Arthur Thirkell, *Daily Mirror*, 25 February 1977), 'a British gangland movie determined to be quite as tough, bloody, violent, squalid and ugly as any Hollywood model it succeeds' (Alexander Walker, *Evening Standard*, 24 February 1977).

The Squeeze's 'anomic urban wasteland' is very much that of *The Sweeney* – its alcoholic hero, ex-cop Jim Naboth (Stacy Keach), is even more of a bedraggled underdog than Regan (but without his redeeming charm and humour), and the film's villains are more charismatic and ruthless incarnations of all those blaggers and hard-cases. The sense of a TV model inflated with added violence and menace is reinforced by its hand-held camera 'realism', perhaps indebted to the TV origins of director Michael Apted and the fact

Figure 12.1 Policing the 'anomic urban wasteland': The poster art for *Sweeney!* (1976) emphasises the toughness of the task

Source: British Cinema and Television Research Group archive, De Montfort University

that writer Leon Griffiths was two years away from creating *Minder* for Euston films.

The feeling in the 1970s that Britain was becoming a scarier place to live in is discernible in the press, in political discourses, in youth cult pulp novels like *Skinhead* (Richard Allen, 1970) and even sexploitation/horror–thrillers such as *House of Whipcord* (Pete Walker, 1974). The fear that Britain was becoming 'ungovernable' was seemingly confirmed by such diverse phenomena as student and trade union militancy, the trials of the Kray, Richardson and Tibbs gangs, terrorism and 'mugging'. *Policing the Crisis* (Hall *et al.* 1978) provides the most detailed account of how this fear of impending anarchy, where 'themes of protest, conflict, permissiveness and crime begin to run together into one great, undifferentiate "threat"' (ibid.: 247, 278), was used to legitimise 'the recourse to the law, to constraint and statutory power' as the means of preserving the consensus and existing power structures. This took the form of newly restrictive legislation against picketing, terrorism and immigration, and a more visible use of the police to impose 'order'. The notion of the battle against crime and disorder as all-out war is reflected in at least one reading of *The Sweeney*:

Society is a state of war.
There is no society without law.
The war is to defend the law.

(Hurd 1976: 49)

Running parallel to this, however, were growing revelations about what *Sweeney 2* calls 'the big C' – there were five police corruption trials during the decade. The fall of Scotland Yard's Obscene Publications Squad, in particular, captured the popular imagination, tapping as it did into another quintessential 1970s narrative, the unstoppable spread of Soho and the rise of the pornocrats. But if coppers-on-the-take were politically embarrassing, and Metropolitan Police Commissioner Robert Mark was the new broom cleaning a fairly grubby house, there was a lurking glamour, too, in the adjacency of policemen and seedy vice-ridden criminality – 'Now will you and your sergeant go back to your strip club', sneers a rival policeman to Regan in *Sweeney!*, 'or wherever it is you masquerade as policemen'.

If *The Sweeney* made the transition from TV to feature film more smoothly than other 1970s series, it may have been partly because it began life as a feature-length narrative. Ian Kennedy Martin's *Regan* was screened on 4 June 1974 as part of Thames'/Euston's *Armchair Cinema* series. In some respects, Regan was a hero with an uncertain future – 'Twenty years ago, he would have been a perfect cop in the days of the individualists – now he's out on a limb'. Kennedy Martin's aim was to explore Commissioner Mark's impact on an old-style loner cop, based partly on the experiences of a friend in the Flying Squad:

> (he) was now being told by Commissioner Mark that he had to work in a different way – that he was not to go to pubs in Fulham and talk to villains, that he must not make those contacts. It could all be done from a desk in an office on the third floor of Scotland Yard.
>
> (Donald 1985: 120)

The final scene implies that Regan's days are numbered, but this would be translated into an ongoing battle with authority, a central dynamic of the show, which ran for fifty-three episodes and two feature films between 1974 and 1978.

Sweeney! has two other advantages as a feature film. First, the series had been conceived as a tough action show, but it was subject to the IBA's rules concerning sex, violence and 'bad language'. The film certainly exploits the greater license granted by its 'X' certificate, with slow-motion violence and exploding blood 'squibs', and its sequel is scarcely less violent, despite receiving the more lenient 'AA' classification. Second, the series requirements of the TV show had, by necessity, squeezed out Kennedy Martin's more ambivalent feelings about the police and turned it into a more politically conservative text than was originally intended. In 'opening out' the show,

Sweeney! also tackles more complex and less reassuring themes and ideas than the series was usually able to, drawing, in particular, on elements of the political conspiracy thriller. Interestingly, this seems to have been partly a matter of expediency, a combination of product differentiation and international markets, as producer Ted Childs' comments suggest:

> the purists will argue that the first Sweeney film was very unreal because it was not within the genre that had become established, and that was true because we were under pressure to make a film that people would pay to see not only in the UK but elsewhere.
>
> (Alvarado and Stewart 1985: 67)

Sweeney! gets its 'familiar' pleasures out of the way fairly quickly. As we first meet Regan and Carter, they're engaging in some competitive but good-natured banter; they've been out on the pull the night before and George has ended up sleeping on his own couch – 'You pulled rank to get that bed!' he grumbles. Soon, they're leading the squad against a wage van 'blag', in a sequence that is so quintessential it verges on self-parody – lots of anorak-pulling and dirty punches end with delivering the (very literal) punchline to the toughest villain, 'Alright, Tinkerbell – *you're nicked*!'

The film then changes gear, moving into a world of international corruption and an exaggerated version of the oil crisis. Regan progressively uncovers a conspiracy to raise oil prices and humiliate the British government, as the Energy Minister (Ian Bannen) falls under the malign influence of his 'press agent', McQueen (Barry Foster) through a combination of blackmail and astutely deployed call girls. McQueen's methods grow increasingly direct, drawing on the services of a kind of assassination bureau, Johnson and Johnson, to despatch magazine editors and police informers with bombs and sub-machine guns or to force-feed Regan with whisky before putting him in a moving car. We never learn conclusively who McQueen is working for – 'Multinational oil companies?' Regan asks the parliamentary private secretary and receives a (confirmatory?) 'No comment' in reply. While McQueen is the 'face' of this villainy, he is also, in the final scene, its victim – Johnson and Johnson shoot him as he is about to be arrested. The real villain, in other words, is 'bad' capitalism, something more amorphous, irreducible to individuals who can be satisfyingly 'nicked'. If crime was bottom-up in the series, here it is unambiguously top-down.

In *Sweeney!* Regan loses his 'mandate' to preserve the consensus – he literally loses his badge and can be roughed up or eliminated like anyone else who interferes with bigger interests. If anyone operates as 'maintenance men', it's Johnson and Johnson, posing as policemen in one scene, window cleaners and road sweepers in others, much more efficient than Regan ever was and not hampered by having to work for the 'people'. All that Regan is left with is a kind of underdog populism, a quality discerned in the series by Ed Buscombe:

Unfortunately, support for the underdog within the police is support for the illiberal wing, for a kind of populist anti-intellectualism, suspicious of reformers or crusading newspapermen. *The Sweeney* follows the traditional lines of populist thought; its genuinely anti-authoritarian feelings find no constructive outlet and become a mere cry of frustrated rage. The desire to actually do something is channelled into action against scapegoats or those most easily singled out as personally responsible for what is wrong with society.

(Buscombe 1976: 68)

I think Buscombe is correct here, and yet it's instructive to compare this passage with a speech made by Regan in *Sweeney!* The consensus is starting to unravel and Jack's anti-authoritarian instincts are starting to grope towards some more interesting targets:

Why do you think we get such a free hand on the Sweeney? I'll tell you....They need us death or glory boys to take on the violent criminals – the blaggers, Big Tiny, that wages truck. All over the papers – 'The forces of Law and Order continue to combat major crime.' *Major crime!* How much was on that wagetruck? Twenty grand. A good accountant can make that – what? – in half an hour, fiddling some sod's income tax. It's all out of proportion....We must have scapegoats. As long as we've got them, and silly bleeders like us to chase after them, no one's going to notice the real villains out there busy skinning us all alive.

This (admittedly pretty unspecific) revelation brings swift retribution. In the next scene, he's intercepted by Johnson and Johnson, in police uniform, who kick in the tail lights on his car and 'arrest' him for drunken driving. Like most conspiracy thrillers, the film can only offer paranoia and powerlessness as an alternative – 'What's the matter with everybody?' he rants to his sceptical superiors, 'is the whole country asleep? Are you deaf as well as stupid?' Yet Regan is determined to displace this onto someone, to have a tangible target in the form of McQueen. On learning that arrest will seal the press agent's fate, he arranges precisely that, the emptiest of gestures and emphasised as such by the film. 'They didn't kill him – *you did!*' shouts Carter accusingly in the film's final line, a condemnation that allies Regan with Johnson and Johnson, acting in the interests of the 'real villains' in spite of everything. The final shot is of Regan in frozen monochrome, just as we saw Vic Dakin at the end of *Villain*, equally impotent and defeated.

Sweeney 2, disappointingly, largely proceeds as though the first film hadn't happened, its final scene underlining this process of retreat and recuperation. The same freeze to black and white this time catches Regan in a rare moment of triumph, dancing with his mates in the pub, having just pulled the telephone switchboard girl he's been after since mid-film. It's a less ambitious film than its predecessor, the narrative more like a 'padded' version of a TV episode, but also more eager to be 'topical'. Different scenes play like a ticking off of contemporaneous issues around police corruption (Regan's boss is about to go down because he's 'so bent, it's been impossible to hang his picture straight on the office wall for the past twelve months', and two sergeants pocket some of the money left at a crime scene) or the heavy-handed methods of the Special Patrol Group ('think they own the bloody city'). Several reviews spelled out why this was less than startling by 1978. The BBC's *Law and Order*, written by Gordon Newman and produced by Tony Garnett, was broadcast shortly before the film's release. The four-part drama marked a radical rupturing of the British police series which paralleled a larger split in attitudes to policing – 'The New Right were calling for tougher policing, heavier sentences and a return of capital punishment, whilst the left called for greater controls on the police' (Whannel 1994: 185.) If the paramilitary SAS-fetishism of *The Professionals* (LWT 1977–83) and films like *Who Dares Wins* (Ian Sharp, 1982) seemed to respond to the former, *Law and Order* opened up a larger fictional space for the latter, taking it as a matter of course that the police were corrupt, that they faked evidence, brutalised suspects and were indistinguishable from criminals. 'If you want the low-down on police, villainy, and those in between…you should stay at home and watch the box', advised Derek Malcolm in *The Guardian* (20 April 1978). There's some truth in this, and yet an important distinction needs to be made. *Law and Order* wasn't exactly generic – its aim was not to entertain. *Sweeney 2's* willingness to juxtapose these issues with more familiar heroics is at least worth noting as an acknowledgement of its own crisis of confidence.

There's certainly a more interesting film struggling to get out of *Sweeney 2*. If the series could be (and was) accused of displacing more complex issues onto vicarious 'action', the opening of the film actually seems to do the opposite, cutting between the preparations for a robbery anticipated in the Richmond area and Regan's refusal to testify for his crooked boss, Jupp (Denholm Elliott.) The two strands are not unconnected – Jupp has fitted up another villain for earlier robberies performed by the same team and (in an awkward flashback) gives Regan his final order 'to nail this team'. These scenes are substituted for the actual robbery and getaway – we only see the aftermath of a singularly violent shootout – 'I've never seen so many dead people', Regan observes.

This gang of upwardly mobile blaggers is the most interesting feature of the film, a 'highly motivated group' who, depending on the exchange rate, only ever take the equivalent of 100,000 dollars. These jobs are carried out with appropriately ostentatious weaponry: a gold-plated sawn-off Purdey shotgun. The robbers live with their wives and children in an elaborate complex in Malta 'like a posse of tax-exiled pop stars', as Alan O'Brien put it (*Sunday Times*, 28 April 1978.) In its depiction of the gang's *nouveau riche* lifestyle, the film invites some comparisons to be made between crime and pop as spectacular routes to rapid wealth – the Purdeys were 'nicked from that pop star in Scotland' (Rod Stewart?). One robbery is carried out to repair

Figure 12.2 A fast woman and a sawn-off shotgun, icons of the British underworld
           drama, Shirley Hicks (Anna Nygh) looks down both barrels in *Sweeney 2*
           (1978)

Source: British Cinema and Television Research Group archive, De Montfort University

their swimming pool, but to steal more than the requisite amount is still
tantamount to 'selling out': 'We've done seventeen blags, we've gained 1.7
million dollars, now that is our way. Now if we stop thinking like that, and
start pursuing short-term objectives then we may as well pack it in'. The
fantasy of a survivalist gang enduring as Britain succumbs to chaos, or simply
decadence, is an enduring and politically ambiguous one in the 1970s. It's
there in LPs like Thin Lizzy's *Jailbreak* (1976) and pulp novels like Mick
Norman' *Angels from Hell* series (1973–4), which projects the crisis of the
1970s into a 1990s dystopia of social control, fascistic policing and a
subservient, defeated populace. In both cases, all that's left in this apocalyptic
futurescape is the 'Last (male) Gang in Town' (Hunt 1998: 85–9). *Sweeney 2's*
blaggers are driven by a similar 'vision' of a hard male unit as an alternative to
a 'soft', defeated nation, as their final will and testament asserts:

> England as a nation is finished, its course is run and…the order of the day
> must be to save what you can. We have built up by our own determina-

tion and where necessary, at the point of a gun, the structure on this island which will survive.

In Norman's books, this fantasy is a left-populist one, and the *Evening News* describes the blaggers as 'a bunch of anarchist heavies' (20 April, 1978). But if the film situates them at all, it is in relation to fascism. The wife of one of the gang's drivers (killed during the opening robbery) lives with a police informer in a house full of Nazi regalia. 'I think he gives her one dressed as Adolf Hitler', quips Regan, but by the end of the film, she is sleeping with the gang's leader, Hill, and her Hitler-besotted friend is their new driver. Lurking fascism – especially linked to private armies – is a poignant 1970s scenario and there's some potential here for reviving Regan's underdog populism, but the narrative never joins these dots.

In certain respects, *The Squeeze* is a better *Sweeney!* sequel than *Sweeney 2*. Its strengths are the 1978 film's failings – its superbly drawn and vividly played villains and its willingness to utterly humiliate and disempower its ex-cop hero. It also generates a much more specific sense of place than either *Sweeney* film, in spite of its American star. *The Sweeney* – series and films – took place in a very white Britain, as though to tread carefully around the fact that race was one of the most volatile issues in 1970s policing. *The Squeeze* offers little more in its narrative – the main characters are all white – but by locating its hero in a predominantly black neighbourhood in Notting Hill, there are at least glimpses of a multiracial Britain. This was a resonant location in the late 1970s – Notting Hill Carnival had ended in a riot the previous year after the police provocatively increased their presence from 200 (in 1975) to 1600 – and an interesting, if thematically undeveloped, home for a white underdog alienated from the law. It would be nice to imagine Stacy Keach's Jim Naboth as Regan after *Sweeney!*, unemployed, bitter and permanently drunk, 'running around like a fucking boy scout' but acting in the name of no one. If the film has a major weakness, however, it's that Naboth is actually pretty dull – his alcoholism is his only defining feature and one has to take his former greatness as a policeman on trust. What Naboth lacks, through no fault of Keach's, is precisely the resonance of a series character whose more glorious past is familiar to the audience – it's tempting to suggest that *The Squeeze* would be a better film if it *was* based on a TV series.

This is a smaller, more localised narrative than either *Sweeney* film. Pornocrat gangster Vic's (Stephen Boyd) belief in coincidence ('Arthur Koestler wrote a book about it…you want to read a bit more') manifests itself in the close network of relations between the main characters. Naboth is an ex-Scotland Yard detective superintendent, thrown off the force for his drinking and divorced from his wife, Jill (Carol White). Jill and her step-daughter from a second marriage are kidnapped to pressure her wealthy husband (Edward Fox) into helping steal from one of his own security vans. Vic is the organising force here, but his right-hand man, Keith (David Hemmings), a 'vicious bastard', has been put away by Naboth on a previous occasion. Watched over by his adoring and protective shoplifter sidekick Teddy (Freddie Starr), Naboth gets on the case and finally confronts the blaggers, holding a gun to Vic's daughter's head. The gang are all killed except Vic, who has to endure a cathartic and humiliating kicking in front of his daughter. Naboth's 'dignity' seems to be restored, and a coda suggests that he's overcome the bottle to reinforce the point.

Actual functioning policemen are as absent here as in *Get Carter*, so this family melodrama boils down to dog eat dog – my hostage is bigger than your hostage. Naboth's lowest point comes during an earlier episode at Vic's house. Unwashed, stinking and sick to his stomach on cheap dry sherry, he's beaten, stripped, given a potentially lethal 'lying bastard cocktail' concocted from Boyd's drinks' cabinet and deposited naked outside his house. 'Trespassers will get their bollocks shot off', Vic advises him, suggesting that this is where real authority has shifted to – he's the underworld 'double' of Fox's 'mean nasty businessman'.[3] Even after the purge of the 'dirty' squad, pornography was Britain's major growth industry and the porn baron the seventies equivalent of the sixties gangster. Both could imagine themselves as 'businessmen', but the pornocrats not only had capitalism on their side, they had the law, too – the Obscene Publications Act and the Cinematograph Act were full of enough loopholes to allow porn to flourish until the legislation of the early 1980s. Naboth initially escapes Vic's wrath by posing as an investigator working for the Inland Revenue, looking into his clubs and other property – it's the only time a flicker of uncertainty crosses the Irish gangster's face. Vic is the film's most resonant creation, an opportunity seized with tangible relish by Boyd in his final role. He sets great store by his daughter's gymkhanas and 'meeting decent people' at Rotarian dinners. A bit of a philosopher, a bit of a family man, more than a bit of a sociopath, his creed comes unexpectedly into focus during a chat about reincarnation:

> My strength is I don't care what happens to *me*. That's what scares them. Look after your own, that's what it's all about, beat them, give them everything, die for them – sod all the other punters! We'll all meet up sooner or later.

The maverick cop is generally alienated from a 'feminine' domestic world by 'the job', but Naboth's drinking alienates him from both. Wives are a 'Bad Thing' for 1970s cops. In *The Offence*, Vivien Merchant begs Connery to tell her about the job but vomits when he does so. Regan is divorced, Carter's wife is dead. *The Squeeze* reproduces this distrust of women in the rather thankless role played by Carol White. In the film's grimmest scene, she's forced by the gang to strip to The Stylistics' 'You Make Me Feel Brand New'. What makes the scene harder to read in retrospect is the tension between its conformity to a distinctly 1970s brand of casual misogyny and the genuine discomfort White brings to an otherwise unsympathetic role (it now plays more as though it's about the star's humiliation). But White is playing against a stacked narrative deck. Naboth describes Jill as 'a mean nasty wife (who) ran out on me the first time I got so drunk I pissed the bed', an image that combines the impression of disloyalty with a non-maternal disposition. Jill, after all, has left her children (generic shorthand for a pretty callous woman) and abandoned her unlucky ex-husband for a wealthier one – Fox is such a stiff that one infers that his wealth was the main attraction. Not only is she not allowed to counter this – was Naboth violent or abusive? (evidently not if he gained custody) – it isn't even qualified, given that most of her dialogue consists of pleading for her life. Jill is redeemed by her willingness to 'debase' herself to protect her stepdaughter – stripping, sleeping with Keith (who is overcome by impotence) – but this still allows Naboth a degree of moral superiority after he rescues her, reminding her to visit their sons, a job she's neglected. In this respect, Keith functions as Naboth's criminal 'double', colluding in bringing her down a peg or two – he both wants and despises her, is found similarly inadequate in bed and finally dismisses her as a 'scrubber'. Restoring Naboth's pride seems to hinge on humiliating Jill as much as beating Vic.

In *The Squeeze*, we are much closer to the world of the hardboiled, where one 'evil' (counter-kidnapping) opposes another one. Although Naboth functions as a private eye, and Teddy speaks longingly of them setting up an office together, he doesn't even achieve that intermediary status and is still on the dole. What does happen is that he finds the 'shadow' of a job and a wife in the 'underworld'. The former is most evident as his detective skills start to return – he teaches Teddy the 'bloody boring system' for effectively tailing a car. But it's Teddy himself who becomes Naboth's spouse – he even introduces him as 'the wife' to some winos. To characterise this as a homoerotic subtext is to rather understate the case. Naboth is given a token girlfriend by way of disavowal and she's the one who gets to deliver the verdict on this relationship; 'Know what? I think he bloody well fancies you.' Twice Teddy walks in on them having sex, performing as a kind of nagging rival – 'Did the kids go to school?…Would you like a nice cup of tea?' – and departing with the bitchy observation that 'you've got a blackhead on yer arse'. He steals clothes for him, makes sure he eats properly and, in the biggest displaced love scene of all, pays for him to have a massage in a Soho parlour. This sheds new light on the otherwise unproductive alcoholism back story. Whereas Naboth's drinking has driven Jill away, it constantly binds him to Teddy, intensifying his dependence on his sidekick's 'maternal' instincts – it's certainly the only relationship the film accords any value. His girlfriend – a nurse, a rival carer – is less visible as the film goes on. She sits watching television, 'fed up being wet nurse to a grown drunk', while Naboth goes off on his worst binge – it's Teddy who takes better care of him and who enjoys the final scene with him. Such emotionally charged 'buddy' relationships in mainstream movies tend to emerge from heterosexual masculinity's unconscious, but *The Squeeze* is more knowing – Russell Davies, in the *Observer* (27 February 1977), saw Starr as 'an oddly bisexual presence' in the film. Nevertheless, these homosocial dynamics aren't so very far from *The Sweeney*, where close male relationships are made possible by 'work' and given greater value than emasculating, domestic ones with women. Teddy is the detective's 'partner' as well as a more lasting 'wife' – he is a loyal and adoring Carter to Naboth's Regan, as well as an idealised version of Jill (he won't mind him wetting the bed).

If these are scattered readings, that's partly because these are scattered films. 1970s British crime films are too sparse to get much intertextual purchase on, at least without reference to television. These films are fragments of a genre in transition, but largely in transition *elsewhere* (the British TV cop show). But among these fragments, there is much to value – their populist equation of villainy with big business, their loss of confidence in the loner hero and their ability to wring pleasurable frissons out of such relentless bleakness. These were not happy times and these are not happy films.

Notes

1 For the uninitiated, 'Sweeney Todd' is Cockney rhyming slang for Flying Squad, thus the title.
2 Clarke (1992: 235) describes Regan as 'a British Eastwood without the hats,' while *The Sun*'s review of *Sweeney!* complained that the film had turned him into 'a kind of English Dirty Harry' (15 January 1977).
3 There are at least three such doublings in the film – Naboth/Keith, Vic/Foreman, Jill/Teddy.

Bibliography

Alvarado, M. and Stewart, J. (eds) (1985) *Made for Television: Euston Films Limited*, London: BFI/Thames Methuen.
Buscombe, E. (1976) '*The Sweeney* – better than nothing', *Screen Education* 20: 66–9.
Clarke, A. (1986) 'This is not the boy scouts: television police series and definitions of law and order', in T. Bennett, C. Mercer, and J. Woollacott (eds) *Popular Culture and Social Relations*, Milton Keynes: Open University Press.
—— (1992) 'You're nicked! television police series and the fictional representation of law and order', in D. Strinati and S. Wagg (eds) (1992) *Come on Down? Popular Media Culture in Post-war Britain*, London: Routledge.
Dennington, J. and Tulloch, J. (1976) 'Cops, consensus and ideology', *Screen Education* 20: 37–46.
Donald, J. (1985) 'Anxious moments: *The Sweeney* in 1975', in M. Alvarado and J. Stewart (eds) *Made for Television: Euston Films Limited*, London: BFI/Thames Methuen.
Hall, S., Critcher, C., Jefferson, T., Clarke, J. and Roberts, B. (1978) *Policing the Crisis: Mugging, the State and Law and Order*, London: Macmillan.
Hunt, L. (1998) *British Low Culture: From Safari Suits to Sexploitation*, London: Routledge.
Hurd, G. (1976) '*The Sweeney* – contradiction and coherence', *Screen Education* 20: 47–53.

—— (1981) 'The television presentation of the police', in T. Bennett, S. Boyd-Bowman and C. Mercer (eds) (1981) *Popular Television and Film*, London: Open University/BFI.

Murphy, R. (1992) *Sixties British Cinema*, London: BFI.

Street, S. (1997) *British National Cinema*, London: Routledge.

Tulloch, J. (1990) *Television Drama: Agency, Audience and Myth*, London: Routledge.

Walker, A. (1985) *National Heroes: British Cinema in the Seventies and Eighties*, London: Harrap.

Whannel, G. (1994) 'Boxed in: television in the 1970s', in B. Moore-Gilbert (ed.) *The Arts in the 1970s: Cultural Closure?* London: Routledge.

13 Space in the British crime film

Charlotte Brunsdon

It is a commonplace of the study of British cinema that it is a cinema haunted by Hollywood. The writerly, theatrical, etiolated British film is repeatedly compared to its lusty American cousin. In the case of the crime film, this involuntary comparison has led even champions of the British cinema, such as Robert Murphy, to apprehend the British cinema through its relation to Hollywood. Thus of the 1959 film, *Beyond This Place* (Jack Cardiff, Renown), he observes that it 'looks like an American *film noir* with its low key lighting and doom laden plot' (Murphy 1992: 202). However, he then continues: 'but its use of Liverpool locations and the presence of Bernard Lee…root it solidly in English society'. Together, these two comments on *Beyond This Place* offer us a juxtaposition that I would like to explore as one of the more interesting features of the British crime film. My suggestion is that we can move beyond the implicit and explicit comparisons of British cinema with Hollywood that shape the literature, and look at the way in which this British/American comparison is inscribed in the films themselves. This could be traced through an investigation of the production processes of Anglo-American films such as *They Made Me a Fugitive* (1947), shot at the Riverside Studio at Hammersmith for Alliance, which brought together Rank and RKO, or the earlier *They Drive by Night* (1938) made in the Warner Bros' Teddington studios. It can also be explored through the use of Hollywood stars in British crime films, and I wish here to discuss two examples of this: the use of Gene Tierney and Richard Widmark in *Night and the City* (Jules Dassin, 1950), and the much later case of the use of Tommy Lee Jones and Melanie Griffith in *Stormy Monday* (Mike Figgis, 1987). Initially, however, I want to address the issue of this British/Hollywood relation primarily through the construction of space in the British crime film; to argue that this is one of the ways in which this difficult relationship is inscribed in the film texts. I suggest that we can discern a fluctuating, but persistent, articulation of two kinds of space in the British crime film. These are the two kinds of space that Murphy refers to above in relation to *Beyond This Place*. First, there is the generic space of Hollywood, 'American *film noir* with its low key lighting and doom laden plot', and second, there is the rather more literal space of the English location, in this instance, the 'use of Liverpool locations'.

I want to explore the articulation of these two different kinds of space in three British crime films, which offer us a very literal embodiment of the difficulties, contradictions and surprising felicities of the production of genre fiction in the same medium and language as Hollywood but in a different national culture. My argument is not about the existence of an indigenous noir tradition in Britain[1], nor a denial of the well-attested European origins of film noir, recalled to us by Ginette Vincendeau's (1992) reminder that '*Noir* is also a French word'.[2] Instead, I want to suggest that the international dominance of Hollywood in the 1940s over-determines the reading of certain textual features such as low-key lighting, expressive use of shadow and urban anomie as signifiers of Hollywood, and specifically of the generic space of noir.

As a preliminary, it is important to remember how various generic space is within US film noir. For example, two key films, *The Big Heat* (1953) and *Mildred Pierce* (1945) are partly structured through the comparison between noir space and melodramatic space. In *The Big Heat*, Dave Bannion (Glenn Ford) initially possesses all the trappings of the American dream – a modern house with checked kitchen curtains, a blonde wife who cooks him steak and shares both his beer and his cigarette, and a daughter who loves her daddy. All this is presented with extremely bright, high-tone lighting, creating a familiar, but, we know, generically fragile, domestic space. When Bannion's wife and daughter are killed by a car bomb meant to scare him off an investigation, his resolve is strengthened and augmented by the desire to revenge their deaths. His grief, and his commitment to this mission, is signalled by his leaving of this bright light space of the home, a space never found again in the shadowy world he then enters, but one that haunts it as motive. Likewise, in *Mildred Pierce*, Mildred's narrative reveals her origins in a very similar house where she lived with Bert when first married, a light, melodramatic space, which contrasts strongly with the shadowy mansions, bars and beach houses that dominate the present of her story. The noir space of these films is constructed within each film in contrast to a brighter, less morally duplicitous, domestic space. And the tendency of this noir space, in this contrast, but also in its European origins, is towards abstraction, an expressive rather than a realist space. But these films are also part of an internationally hegemonic audiovisual economy. And so this space along with all the other noir spaces of 1940s and early 1950s, exceeds the particular texts in which it is constructed to inform the international space of Hollywood cinema, to produce what is instantly recognised, in its very abstraction, as a generic, cinematic and American space. It is this recognition that informs any critical judgement about a British crime film being nearly as exciting as an American one.

It Always Rains On Sunday (1947, Robert Hamer) offers a clear example of the different types of space that I suggest can be found in the British crime film. This Ealing film, in which the normal Sunday of a Bethnal Green housewife, Rose Sandigate (Googie Withers) is disrupted by the sudden appearance of her former lover Tommy Swann (John McCallum), on the run after escaping from Dartmoor, was discussed mainly in terms of its realism on first release. The East End setting, and particularly the use of Petticoat Lane, was seen to offer a distinctive authenticity, with critics suggesting, for example, that 'the film could be subtitled "A Day in the Life of an East-End Street" ' (Fred Majdalany, *Daily Mail* 28 November 1947), or that Robert Hamer 'has handled this Cockney mosaic with all the skill of a first-class documentary' (Harold Conway, *Evening Standard* 28 November 1947). More recently, the film has been of interest to critics for its representation of a disturbance in the sphere of sexuality, with Tommy Swann's eruption into the Sandigate house- hold a reminder of the sexual passion that the characteristic Ealing making-do and making the best of things must repress[3]. For our purposes, what is of interest is how Tommy Swann erupts into the texture of the realist narrative of the day in the life of an East End street. Tommy is first introduced as a fugi- tive, crossing railway cuttings, running through the rainy streets and sheltering in a church porch. His progress is inter-cut with the day beginning for other characters, most particularly the Sandigates. We are properly introduced to Tommy through Rose's romantic memories of him, which are sparked by her middle-aged husband reading the news of his escape from the newspaper. Dreamily brushing her dark hair in the dressing-table mirror, Rose is trans- ported through a dissolve back to another mirror, that of the pub where she worked when her hair was blonde. This sequence is clearly marked as Rose's memory as Tommy appears in the pub, framed in his spivvy splendour by the doorway and the mirror in which she is watching him, wearing a jacket with wide lapels and a noticeably waisted cut, a flamboyant tie and handkerchief, a cigarette in his mouth and a hat knocked slightly back on his head. The detail of his appearance and the self-assurance with which he buys her a drink and proposes that they might, on her day off, 'do nothing together', both grounds him in the realist discourse of the film and shows him to be a romantic and exciting, if dangerous, prospect.

This remembered encounter shows Tommy in local – if romanticised space – a point confirmed by the *mise-en-scène* of their day 'doing nothing together', when the symmetrically framed studio countryside emphasises the fantasy of Rose's desire that there was 'no such place as Bethnal Green'. Rose's under- standing of Tommy is informed by romantic fiction and film. But she has got the genre wrong, as we see from the lighting as soon as Tommy reappears in the present day, hiding in the bomb shelter in the garden, catching Rose by surprise as she goes in there to find some old blackout material to mend a broken door pane.

In the Anderson shelter, Rose and Tommy are lit and shot quite differently. Rose is always framed with the oblong of daylight from the shelter doorway behind her. Through this doorway lies her everyday life, her family, her husband and the Sunday joint. The framing reminds us of Rose's obligations and commitments, it shows us a character grounded in an East London space. In contrast, Tommy is shot against a dark, featureless background. In realist terms, this is the dark interior of the Anderson shelter where he has been hiding. But in its very featurelessness it is also abstracted from the East London milieu. Tommy, his grimy, sweaty face shining in the dark, is in some ways in a generic, rather than a realist space. He is the con on the run, but also the insistent, demanding, physical representation of another way of making movies. This contrast is further explored in the bedroom where Rose is hiding Tommy later in the day.

This scene of Rose and Tommy together balances her earlier memory. Then, she remembered the detail of his appearance on his first entry to *The Compasses*. In the bedroom, Tommy is stripped of his finery, wearing only a shapeless jacket and trousers, his bare chest both vulnerable and shocking. Tommy's almost abstract physicality, accentuated by framing which makes him appear naked, is balanced by the naturalistic detail of the room, with Rose framed against floral curtains wearing a patterned pinny. These two spaces are then brought together with Tommy lying in the marital bed, the shiny eiderdown pulled up to his naked chest and grimy jacket. In the last part of the film, however, when Tommy is on the run, these details diminish in significance, and he is chased through a recognisably noirish space, under bridges

Figure 13.1 The violation of domestic space: Rose (Googie Withers) hides her fugitive ex-lover (John McCallum) in the marital bed in *It Always Rains on Sunday* (1947)

Source: BFI stills, posters and designs

and over the rail tracks. Suddenly, the movie is not 'the day in the life of an East End street', but something much more internationally generic, evoking other meaner streets, and certainly severing all connections with floral curtains, eiderdowns and 'haddock for breakfast'.

Another London film of the same period offers us a different articulation of these spaces. *Night and the City* (1950, Twentieth Century-Fox) had an American director, Jules Dassin – who had recently had considerable success with the location shot *The Naked City* (1948) in the USA – as well as US stars, Richard Widmark and Gene Tierney. Murphy suggests that Twentieth Century-Fox was encouraged to produce this 'spiv' film set in London's underworld following the success of *The Third Man*, but they were to be disappointed with contemporary critical reaction. He quotes Dilys Powell suggesting that the film 'will presumably pass for a British film. It is about as British as Sing-Sing; and it will do the British cinema nothing but harm' (Powell quoted in Murphy 1989: 164), but then argues that the film brought more of London to the screen than any other before the 'Swinging London' films of the 1960s. I want to discuss the way in which London is here brought to the screen, and particularly the articulation of the clearly recognisable, if geographically tricky, city, with the penumbra of the Hollywood cinema that surrounds Harry Fabian, the Richard Widmark character. It is this 'American in London' casting and theme that I think underlies Powell's discomfort, but which also, as Harry Fabian runs, throughout the film, from one racket to another, permits the display and revelation of the city.

There are two Londons in this film, and the way in which they are mapped over each other is particularly interesting in that by the end of the film it is impossible to see the first London, a public, tourist, landmark London, without understanding the way in which it is subtended by another London, one of graft, pay-offs and the hierarchies of the underworld. The film opens with 'landmark' shots of the Palace of Westminster and Big Ben from over the river as the narrator tells us that 'the night is tonight, tomorrow, any night, while the city is London' as the view changes to Piccadilly Circus and then to a high shot of Ludgate Circus, with its hero, Harry Fabian, running pursued across the screen. Although Harry runs through Ludgate Circus to a carefully framed view of St Paul's, this repertoire of public 'London-ness' is made strange, through the shooting of the dark, deserted streets and bombed wasteland through which he is chased. Harry, too, is an unusual figure for this public London, running, and dressed in a loud checked jacket, which, with the correspondents' shoes that he wears throughout, signify his professional Americanism. Here though, in the opening sequence, the key indicator of Harry's character is the way in which – while being chased – he stoops to retrieve a carnation that has fallen from his buttonhole.

Harry Fabian is a club tout who repeatedly loses money – generally other people's and particularly his girlfriend Mary's – through investing in dead certs such as a football pool or a dog track in Birmingham because he is ambitious to make it big and 'just want[s] to be somebody'. Throughout the film Harry's ambitious, irresponsible, untrustworthy, American criminality is contrasted with honest British graft (in both senses). Harry is all dreams and schemes, an American fly-by-night, willing, at both the beginning and end of the film to steal from his girlfriend, while British criminality is shown to be a skilled trade across a range of swindles.

Harry's appearance is important because his mode of operation as a tout is to exploit his nationality to befriend visiting American businessmen in London. Through deals with taxi drivers, barmen and the doorman of The American Bar in the West End, Harry works a routine round the finding of a money-filled wallet, which allows him to impress his honesty on his naive, but suspicious, touring compatriots. Honest Harry, as a man of the world, appears to be taking pity on some anxious mid-Westerners when, about to leave, he remembers that he does 'know of a place – a bit naughty, but great fun'. This sequence, which is shown in great detail up to the moment when Harry leaves The American Bar, paying off the doorman as he leaves, shortly to be followed by his three dupes on their way to The Silver Fox, establishes American-ness as either gullible or a confidence trick. Harry's game is a masquerade of national bonhomie, and he is playing for whatever he can get, always in pursuit of the big one.

This contrasts thoroughly with the mores of the British underworld, which is consistently shown to work harder and to know its place. If anything, British criminality is shown almost as necessity – certainly as requiring dedication and labour. The first scene in The Silver Fox shows Helen (Googie Withers), the proprietor's wife, instructing the girls who work there in the rules of fleecing clients. She is very strict and clear: 'No stealing from the gentlemen while you're in the club – what you do outside is none of his [her husband's] business', 'Whatever he gives you, take it, and then look disappointed'. This detailed and closely observed code is matched in Harry's tour to raise money for his new wrestling scheme by the careful limits of each member of the underworld he meets in their obscurely lit lairs. First, he visits the Fiddler, who runs a *Beggar's Opera/Threepenny Opera*-type operation, and whom we meet while he arranges the disabilities of those he is sending out to beg, 'Strap this on you, you look a good type for a stump', 'Don't forget to tuck your trousers in or you'll give the game away'. Fiddler refuses Harry money, but observes to Fabian, 'I like you Harry, why don't you settle down, get yourself a few good beggars'. He even offers to set Harry up, offering him all the supplies he would need, 'legs, eyes, stumps'. Harry, lit more brightly, in disbelief, responds, 'I bring you a fortune and you offer me beggars'. He encounters the same judicious self-limiting generosity with the forger, Googan (Gibb McLaughlin), who offers passports, birth certificates and medical licences, but observes, of the issue of giving Harry money, that 'if you ain't got socks, you can't pull them up'. Anna O'Leary (Maureen Delany), a riverwoman whose cargoes include nylons and cigarettes, also resists Harry's suggestion that she must be tired of 'living like this, shady deals, a life on the river', claiming that she is a 'hard-working, hard-headed business woman'. By the time we get to Harry's final putative backer, the owner of a drinking dive, Harry's own pitch has been eliminated by the film, and we hear only the refusal of the industrious and realistic British criminal, 'No, I don't want a life of ease and plenty, take your drink and drink it quietly and don't mess about with my customers'.

With scenes in Trafalgar Square, Piccadilly Circus, Regent Street and the Embankment, the film repeatedly grounds itself in landmark London but most of the action takes place in back alleys, glistening wet flights of stairs and sordid interiors. The imbrication of these two Londons, public London with its underworld, is made plain towards the end of the film when word is put out by Mr Kristo (who runs the wrestling racket) that he will offer a reward of £1,000 for Harry Fabian, whom he blames for his father's death. A henchman of Kristo's leaves the gym to spread the word and goes first to Piccadilly Circus to tell a newspaper vendor. Driving round the lights of the West End, his first set of messengers are all already on the streets plying legiti-

Figure 13.2 A tale of two cities: In *Night and the City* (1950), Harry Fabian (Richard Widmark) inhabits both the generic space of London's underworld and the physical space of public, tourist, landmark London'

Source: BFI stills, posters and designs

mate trades in tourist London. As more than one character has already told Harry, he is a dead man, and we the audience understand this because we see that there is no part of London that is not part of the underworld. This vision of a doubled London is embodied in the central shot of this sequence, the most flamboyant of the film, when the camera seems to pan through 180 degrees, while actually being driven round Piccadilly Circus, offering, dizzyingly, both the familiar lights of tourist London and the ubiquity of the underworld. While other characters, without ambition, have been content to remain within their particular milieu, the Fiddler in his den, Helen hoping only for another night club, Anna on her barge, with only Nosseros, who outwits Harry, venturing into Trafalgar Square and public London, Harry has wanted to make it big, to be recognised in the West End as well as the underworld. It is his ambition – and refusal of honest toil – that both articulates these two Londons together, and makes of them an inescapable trap for himself. Kristo's word is spread from Piccadilly Circus to the docks, the dogs and the drinking dives.

In the final section of the film (as with Tommy Swann in *It Always Rains on Sunday*) Harry moves out of located London into a more abstract, expressionist space. Although he dies by the river in Hammersmith, the pursuit to this final resting place takes him through a noir city, one that is intermittently recognisable, but which is more strongly figured as a hostile space, one that Dilys Powell could deny is British, but which comes not from Sing-Sing, but Hollywood.

If *Night and the City* figured its relations of production, perhaps inadvertently, in the contrast of an unscrupulous American hustler with mundane and local British criminality, nearly forty years later, we find a similarly self-conscious concern with these issues in *Stormy Monday* (Mike Figgis, 1987). Set in Newcastle, rather than London, this film directly addresses the issue of the relationship between British and American space at a thematic level. The film covers a couple of days within Newcastle's 'America Week' when one of its founders, US business man Frank Cosmo arrives to finalise a series of property deals on the Quayside. A brief early scene shows police called to a disturbance outside a record shop on the Quayside, when the distraught owner smashes his own shop windows in protest at his inability to resist the takeover. The action in *Stormy Monday* focuses on Finney's Key Club, the remaining property on the block against a backdrop – and soundtrack – of America Week. Caught up in this story, and initially on opposite sides, are, the romantic leads of the film, Kate (Melanie Griffith), paid by Cosmo as an escort for himself and others, and the newly arrived Brendan (Sean Bean), still keeping his clothes in a suitcase when he is given a job by Finney.

This theme, with its governing narrative question, 'will Cosmo succeed in his (obviously corrupt) attempt to buy up the Quayside?' poses the simple issue of who owns space and how it is used. The implication, as 'a deal with the housing committee' is involved, is a change of use from public space (shops, the Key Club, Jim's Gym) to private (luxury apartments?). However, while this narrative structures the film, offering an opposition between the two hard men, Cosmo (Tommy Lee Jones) and Finney (Sting), the most interesting aspects of the relationship between American and British space occur elsewhere. This we find particularly at the level of *mise-en-scène* and music track, for notwithstanding America Week and the simple association of the corrupt Cosmo with Ronald Reagan and Margaret Thatcher, whose portraits he orders to augment the hotel decor, the film is, as it were, already in love with the look and sound of the US. This is a Newcastle of retro–noir, noir with Hopper colour and a jazz sound track. As Brendan says to Kate when they discuss her Minnesota origins, 'It's a great place, if I had the money I'd go back tomorrow'. It is the interplay of different national and generic spaces that I want to explore in this film by looking particularly at the opening of the film and the journey of the hero.

The film opens on the road. A long shot of two white men buying petrol. We are not told, nor do we need to know, where the petrol station of this opening, pre-credit shot is located. We are offered merely the collocation of an expensive red car and two men who don't look like gin–and–jag belt professionals. Physically ill-assorted, one tall with red hair, the other short with a shock of black hair, these men are not driving a car packed full of family luggage. Within the iconography of the crime film – and this image is a British image, with petrol prices and signs in British English – these men are clearly recognisable as villains on their way to a job. After their purchase, they get back in the car and continue up the motorway to their unknown destination. Their criminal intent is confirmed as later in the sequence we see a close-up of a hand concealing a gun in the glove compartment. This is the first of the four elements that make up the opening of the film, which will progressively become intertwined with each other as the film continues.

If the first element offered us men in public space, the second, in a very traditional distinction, offers us the image of a woman in a private space. The camera dwells on a series of shots of Kate (Melanie Griffith) asleep between white rumpled, but not creased, sheets, wearing orangey satin pyjamas. Kate tosses and turns and the camera echoes and anticipates her movements, repeatedly framing her, through 180 degrees, from above, so that we do not see the edges of the bed. We know only that she is in bed, not even whether the bed is in a room. We are offered a series of medium close-ups, from different angles, of a beautiful sleeping woman framed by an abstract textured background like a series of glamour publicity stills. It is towards this unlocated image that the two villains appear to be driving, and this editing thus sets up, at the very beginning of the film, the notion that it is the Melanie Griffith character who is in some ways the prize.

But, as well as being inter-cut with the motorway drivers, Griffith is also inter-cut with the third element, the other, or ostensible, prize of the film, Newcastle. This is figured initially as a model of part of the city, showing the Iron Bridge, the Quayside and part of the Tyne. The model is in pastel colours and appears obviously unreal. Proportions are not clear, nor is its location. In this opening sequence, we don't yet understand the significance of this model of Newcastle. Is it located in space and time – we later learn that it is in the office Cosmo uses – or is it, like Melanie Griffith and the two villains, simply in movieland?

The final thread in the opening of the film is the introduction of the male lead, Brendan (Sean Bean). He, unlike all the other elements introduced so far, is located in time and space. We see him wake up to his clock radio, survey his bedroom – in which we glimpse a letter by his open suitcase signed 'love Jane (and Kevin)' – get dressed and then stand, looking out of his window at what, from the soundtrack of seagulls, we assume is the Tyne. Brendan is the only one of the main characters who exists in what we might call 'local' space, which is established in two crucial shots. The first of these is taken from outside the house as Brendan looks out of the window. We see him framed by the window, and we can see, very clearly, at the bottom of the frame, that the window sill is rotting. This bit of rotting wood, with the paint coming off, is one of the few intrusions of British naturalist space in this film (one of the others being a character, the piano tuner, who appears in more than one location). Brendan, our hero, starts off here, and is also shown to move through this space as he sets out on what will become his adventure. After leaving the house, he is framed walking through a long shot, which shows back gardens, cobbled pathways and, in the background over the hill, the great looming cranes of the shipyards. Brendan is *in* Newcastle.

However, Newcastle is in America Week, and so the radio disc-jockey that Brendan wakes to, with his cheery 'If you've just arrived in town,…' provides a soundtrack that transforms this early morning space into a speakeasy. For Brendan, too, clearly has fantasies of being elsewhere: his bedroom walls display posters of the Manhattan skyline, while his bedside table shows that he is reading Hemingway.

Brendan's early morning is inter-cut with Kate's, and, briefly, sunrise over the Tyne. The located Britishness of his surroundings is contrasted with the peachy coloured space in which Kate, the Hollywood star, has breakfast, a space of chrome and glass with toaster and coffee percolator and a huge bunch of pink peonies on the table. This inter-cutting of the two romantic leads is continued as each goes to the Metro Centre, a space that is shown quite differently for each character until they literally crash into each other. For Kate, whom we have heard being instructed to buy new outfits, the Metro Centre is a space of consumption, again a rather abstract space, peopled only by unseen shop assistants, offering not views but mirrors in which Kate parades the dresses she is considering buying. She is once again produced as image. Brendan, on the other hand, moves through a realism, which is also fantastic in its display of social heterogeneity, offering both Native Americans and punks performing for idling passers-by.

The narrative of the film can be understood through the articulation of these different kinds of space as Brendan moves through them. Brendan, after crashing into Kate, walks into a gangster movie after accepting employment from Finney and overhearing the Jaguar-driving hard men of the opening discussing whether they are meant to persuade Finney of Cosmo's offer by killing him 'or just hurt him'. This conversation takes place in a 'diner' called Weegee's where Kate works, and from where Brendan later takes her to a Polish club, where there is a reception for the Krakow Jazz Ensemble whom Finney has hired as his contribution to America Week. At this reception, which combines elements of that favoured figure of post-*Deerhunter* Hollywood cinema, the ethnicised celebration, with a Newcastle location, Kate is reminded of her Polish grandparents and renounces her past with Cosmo. On their way back, they are attacked by Cosmo's men. Thus, Brendan's loyalty to his new employer, and his attraction to Kate, move him very quickly from the naturalistic *mise-en-scène* of the opening, in which his only career opportunity is as a cleaner at the Key Club, to a series of encounters with employees of Cosmo's, which end in his committing murder in a scene in a much more generic space, in the dark, pouring rain, by the side of a motorway, filmed in slow motion. She, on the other hand, moves from Cosmo's space, movie space, with her peachy apartment and her credit cards to more hybrid, naturalistic spaces. Her job at Weegee's is a transitional space, with its *homage* to the American photographer, but its Geordie manager and poor clam chowder, while the Newcastle Polish club, with a reception for a band that plays *Polish* not American free jazz, offers an epiphany. At the end of the film, Kate's apartment has been cleaned out – there is no trace of her ever having lived there.

At the end of the film, Finney tears up his recently signed contract with Cosmo, and suggests that Mr Cosmo will be going home as 'things haven't worked out here'. Now while this may, in one sense, be true of the narrative of *Stormy Monday*, as it was, in a different way, for both Tommy Swann and Harry Fabian, the very texture of the film undermines this judgement. This is partly because of the use of Hollywood stars. Although Kate may refuse a lift with Cosmo, and thus leaves his space at the end of the film, she is not really integrated into local space – Melanie Griffith is, in her stardom, somehow implausible as mate for local boy Brendan. Similarly, Tommy Lee Jones (Cosmo), with a performance of controlled energy, is much more plausible as a villain than Sting (Finney). And there are narrative troubles too. Even though Finney, the nominal victor here, chose to celebrate Newcastle's America Week with Polish Free Jazz, Andrej, the band leader has been killed, while Brendan, the good guy, has an unacknowledged murder on his hands. Unlike *It Always Rains on Sunday*, where there is still 'haddock for breakfast', the street and a long shot of a sheet of newspaper blowing at the gated entrance to the tube to return to, or *Night and the City*, where Harry finally sees the error of his ways and begs not to be indulged, telling Mary, 'Don't be kind to me', before trying finally to provide for her through his death, there is nowhere to return to at the end of *Stormy Monday*. Although Cosmo, despite his recognition that it is not appropriate to 'go round acting like Al Capone', may be too American a villain to be permitted to actually buy the quayside, in a sense, in a movie in thrall to the Hollywood cinema and the Blues, it is already his.

Notes

1 See, for example, Miller (1994), who argues for a British noir cycle, and Murphy (1986: 304) who argues that a cycle of 'morbid' films are more likely British contenders than the 'spiv' films with which he has been concerned.
2 See, for example, the issue of *Iris* devoted to 'European precursors of *Film Noir*' (no. 21, Spring 1996), particularly, in this context, the essays by Andrew, Elsaesser and Naremore.
3 The classic account is Barr (1977), but see also Harper's brief mention of the film (1992: 222–3).

Bibliography

Andrew, D. (1996) '*Film noir*: death and double cross over the Atlantic', *Iris* 21: 21–30.
Barr, C. (1977) *Ealing Studios*, London and Newton Abbot: Cameron & Tayleur in association with David & Charles.
—— (ed.) (1986) *All Our Yesterdays*, London: British Film Institute.
Elsaesser, T. (1996) 'A German ancestry to *film noir*? – Film history and its imaginary', *Iris* 21: 129–44.
Erikson, G. (1996) 'Expressionist doom in *Night in the City*', in A. Silver and J. Ursini (eds) *Film Noir Reader*, New York: Limelight.
Harper, S. (1992) 'The representation of women in British feature film, 1945–1950', *Historical Journal of Film, Radio and Television*, 12, 3: 217–30.
Miller, L. (1994) 'Evidence for a British *film noir* cycle', in W.W. Dixon (ed.) *Re-Viewing British Cinema 1900–1992*, Albany: State University of New York Press.
Murphy, R. (1986) 'Riff-raff: British cinema and the underworld', in C. Barr (ed.) *All Our Yesterdays*, London: British Film Institute.
—— (1989) *Realism and Tinsel: Cinema and Society in Britain 1939–49*, London: Routledge.
—— (1992) *Sixties British Cinema*, London: British Film Institute.
Naremore, J. (1996) 'High modernism and blood melodrama: the case of Graham Greene', *Iris* 21: 99–116.
Vincendeau, G. (1992) '*Noir* is also a French word: the French antecedents of *film noir*', in I. Cameron (ed.) *The Movie Book of Film Noir*, London: Studio Vista.

14 Allegorising the nation
British gangster films of the 1980s

John Hill

British genre cinema has historically depended upon a home market of suffi-
cient size to allow profitability. As a result of falling audiences, this kind of
cinema became increasingly difficult to sustain from the 1970s onwards and,
during the 1980s, British film-making began (under the influence of television) to move in the direction of art cinema. The common identification of
art cinema in terms of specific formal conventions – the loosening of narrative
structures, cinematic self-consciousness, and textual ambiguity – captures only
some aspects of the art cinema of the 1980s, which was characterised by an
increasing generic hybridity and blurring of aesthetic boundaries. The 1980s
could be said to have witnessed a transition from modern to post-modern art
cinema and a dissolution of the boundaries between art and genre cinema.

In the case of the British gangster film this was manifest in a fusion of
thriller formats with the stylistic and thematic preoccupations of traditional
art cinema. Stephen Frears' *The Hit* (1984), for example, combines a gangland
story-line (the revenge killing of a supergrass) with the existential themes and
stylistic self-awareness of a European art film. More generally, British gangster
films of the 1980s display a determination to be more than 'just thrillers' by
combining gangster story-lines with a degree of social and political commen-
tary. In this respect they share a concern with other films of the period to say
something about the 'state of the nation', though through a form that departs
from the norms of social realism. Thus, gangster films of the 1980s, such as
Mona Lisa (Neil Jordan, 1986) and *Stormy Monday* (Mike Figgis, 1987), show a
strong movement away from surface verisimilitude towards stylisation, transforming real locations into expressionist milieus and investing the city with
something of the mythic dimension that it has traditionally possessed in
Hollywood thrillers.

The gangster film as allegory

However, if a tendency to use the gangster format as a means of commenting
on national preoccupations is discernible in British films of the 1980s, then
this is not so much an alien importation into the genre as a specific – national
– inflection of the allegorical impulses already evident in the Hollywood

gangster film. The gangster film has always occupied an ambivalent relationship to dominant American ideologies. The gangster shares the 'official' American ideals of individual wealth and success but, lacking conventional social advantages, sets out to achieve them illegitimately, particularly through the use of violence. It is in this sense that Robert Warshow (1975: 137) describes the classic gangster film in terms of 'a nightmare inversion of the values of ambition and opportunity' while Andrew Sarris (1977: 7) calls it 'a depraved version of the American Dream'. For Warshow (1974: 136), it is also an unceasing 'commitment to enterprise' that defines the gangster character and it is common in the gangster film for the boundaries between criminal and business 'enterprise' to become blurred.

In the case of the classic gangster film of the early 1930s (such as *Little Caesar, Public Enemy* and *Scarface*), it was the striving for success of the individual that was of primary concern. However, as the genre developed, the association of gangsterism with big business and corporate capitalism began to take shape in films such as *Force of Evil* in the 1940s, the 'syndicate' films of the 1950s and, above all, the *Godfather* films of the early 1970s in which the links between organised crime and US capitalism are most clearly drawn. This is particularly evident in *The Godfather, Part II* (1974) in which Michael Corleone (Al Pacino) is keen to legitimise the 'family' business and invest in Cuba along with 'a distinguished group of American industrialists'. John Hess notes the irony of this:

> Michael had hoped to become completely legitimate, believing somehow that would make a difference in his life and that of his family. But the dealings with…the American businessmen and politicians on Cuba show what Al Capone always knew – the legitimate businessmen are worse crooks than the gangsters.
>
> (Hess 1975: 11)

Thus, the gangster film genre already carried with it an association of crime and business that was picked up on by a number of British films in the 1980s. In the *Godfather* films, the parallel between gangsters and businessmen that is drawn is linked to an expansion of transnational corporations characterised by growing impersonality and sacrifice of humane values. But in the British movies of the 1980s, the gangster's 'commitment to enterprise' is directly linked to the 'enterprise culture' encouraged by Thatcherism and to a valorisation of small business that stands at odds with the logic of international capital.

Thatcherite enterprise and gangsterism

The Conservative government, led by Mrs Thatcher from 1979 until 1990, is associated with the encouragement of economic enterprise and efficiency through the strengthening of market forces and the 'rolling back' of the frontiers of the state through policies of deregulation and privatisation. Opening up the British economy (especially the financial and service sectors) to international capital, and restructuring the economy along post-Fordist lines, led to the encouragement of self-reliant entrepreneurs who could 'get things done', and the legitimisation of economic self-interest as the most important of values. It is not surprising, then, that a number of British films should have drawn on the figure of the gangster in order to question the ethics of such aggressive entrepreneurialism.

This was true of otherwise quite different films. Stephen Frears and Hanif Kureishi's social satire *My Beautiful Laundrette* (1985), for example, suggests how fine the line between enterprise and criminality can be. A number of the film's main characters are Asian businessmen who are apparently at ease with the Thatcherite culture of entrepreneurship ('there's no race question in the new enterprise culture', proclaims one). The spirit of enterprise in this film, however, does not recognise legal limits. Kureishi originally envisaged the film as a kind of Asian *Godfather* and the gangster element survives in the plot-line concerning the drug-dealing of Salim (Derrick Branche), and his 'double-crossing' by Omar (Gordon Warnecke) who sells the drugs he has stolen to finance the laundrette of the film's title. In this respect, criminal activity is seen as a logical extension of entrepreneurial values (taking the initiative, self-help, ambition) and also provides the means for the (legitimate) economic regeneration of the laundrette ('Churchills'). Thus, unlike the classic gangster, whose adoption of illegitimate means in the pursuit of legitimate ends precipitates his downfall, the criminal acts in *My Beautiful Laundrette* are seen to lay the basis for economic success.

The association of Thatcherism with gangsterism is also apparent in Peter Greenaway's *The Cook, The Thief, His Wife and Her Lover* (1989), which is itself a good example of the way in which elements of popular cinema were integrated with the self-conscious formal concerns of art cinema in the 1980s. Albert Spica (Michael Gambon) is a gangster whose 'business' is 'money' and 'pleasure' is 'eating'. While the film clearly uses the character of the gangster to highlight the ruthlessness of 'business' in the Thatcher era, the film's critique of the 'state of the nation' relies less on an association of Thatcherism with crime than with consumerism and cultural vulgarity. As with the classic gangster, Spica represents the upwardly mobile, self-made man whose rising social status may be measured in terms of outward display. Most of the film's actions take place in the French restaurant where he dines nightly with his (higher-class) wife and assorted henchmen and hangers on. However, the good food, the elegance of his surroundings, and his sophisticated wife reflect his wealth and power rather than genuinely good taste and cultural refinement. He is counterposed to 'the lover', a bibliophile whom he taunts for reading while he eats ('Does this stuff make money?' he demands), and 'the cook' whose 'good food' and artistry is valued less for its taste than its cost. As such, the rise in social standing that typifies the gangster's climb to the top is here associated with the emergence of the newly moneyed classes who have achieved economic success under Thatcherism but are seen to lack the 'cultural capital' to go with it. Accordingly, it is as much the 'cultural barbarianism' of the gangster/entrepreneur that the film indicts as the apparent amorality (or criminality) of unregulated capitalist enterprise.

The ethics of violence: *The Long Good Friday*

If the gangster is used in such films as *My Beautiful Laundrette* and *The Cook, The Thief, His Wife and Her Lover* to pass comment on the character of the era, the more conventional gangster films of the period display a similar allegorising impulse. One of the clearest, and most influential, examples of this is *The Long Good Friday* (1981). Made at the end of the 1970s, and finally released in cinemas in 1981, the film is in some ways a prescient piece, anticipating the growing internationalisation of the UK economy and the economic redevelopment of Docklands. Bob Hoskins plays East End gangster Harold Shand, the godfather of London gangland, who is on the verge of securing a deal with the American Mafia to invest in a major Thames-side development ('No other city has got...such an opportunity for profitable progress', he tells the guests at the reception for the visiting Mafia boss Charlie – played by gangster icon Eddie Constantine). As in the *Godfather* films, his criminal empire – 'the corporation' – overlaps with legitimate business activity (Shand describes himself as 'a businessman with a sense of history') and, in a distorted reflection of the operations of state power, commands the support of both politicians (the corrupt local councillor Harris) and police (the equally corrupt Parky).

What, however, disturbs the implementation of Shand's vision for the new London (and the profits that it will bring) is the eruption of uncontrollable violence against him and his gang – the murder of his sidekick Colin (Paul Freeman), the blowing-up of his mother's chauffeur, and the bombing of one of his pubs. Much of the film is concerned with Shand's attempts to uncover who is 'having a go' at him and it is the film's scenes of violence, such as the rounding up of other London gang bosses and hanging them by meathooks, that have assured the film a cult status. When Shand does finally learn who is responsible for the attacks upon him – the IRA – he determines upon a course of 'annihilation' despite the warnings of his second-in-command, Jeff (Derek Thompson), whose disloyalty is partly responsible for Shand's predicament, that he won't succeed (they'll 'pour back like an army of ants', he proclaims). Through Harris, Shand sets up a meeting with two local IRA men whom his men then murder in a set-piece killing. However, as Jeff predicted, his victory is only temporary and, as he leaves the Savoy after learning that Charlie is returning to America, he is seized by another two IRA men. The film then ends with the famous, lengthily-held shots of Shand's bemused reactions as he is driven away at gun point.

The film counterposes the violence of the IRA to the economically self-interested, quasi-capitalist gangsterism of Shand. In doing so, the film not only

Figure 14.1 'Bent lawmen can be tolerated only for so long as they are lubricating and you have become decidedly parched.' Harold Shand (Bob Hoskins) shows corrupt policeman Parky (Dave King) who is boss in *The Long Good Friday* (1981)

Source: BFI stills, posters and designs. Courtesy of Handmade Films.

has echoes of the clash of value systems found in *Performance* (1970) but also *The Godfather, Part II*. In this latter film, Michael Corleone is caught up in a road block at which Cuban soldiers are rounding up anti-Batista rebels. From his car, he observes the arrest of a man who, in a spirit of reckless defiance, blows himself up along with his captor. Discussing this event later with Miami gang boss Hyman Roth (Lee Strasberg), Michael notes that the rebels aren't paid to fight and, therefore, that 'they can win' – a prediction that proves justified and puts an end to his plans for investment in Cuba. Significantly, when Mafia boss Charlie in *The Long Good Friday* tells Harold that he pulling out of the deal as a result of the violence, he complains that Britain's 'a worse risk than Cuba was'. Thus, just as Castro's revolutionaries undermine Mafia business interests in Cuba, so the IRA are responsible for the upset to Shand's.

In this way, *The Long Good Friday* picks up on a perception, common in the 1970s, of the IRA as a particularly ruthless group of gangsters. As Luke Gibbons explains:

The fact that the implementation of a criminalisation policy towards republican prisoners in the North in the mid-1970s coincided with the vogue enjoyed by the *Godfather* films handed the British authorities a valuable rhetorical weapon....From then on, the leaders of Sinn Fein could be denigrated simply as 'Godfathers' and political violence similarly dismissed as 'organised crime', perpetrated by the mindless thugs of the republican mafia produced by the nationalist ghettos.

(Gibbons 1997: 51)

It is this vocabulary of the IRA as 'godfathers' of crime that the film both invokes and distances itself from. On the one hand, the IRA are indeed seen to be 'better' gangsters than the gangsters themselves, ultimately outsmarting gangland boss Shand (and presumably wiping him out). On the other hand, the source of their invincibility is seen to derive from the fact that they are 'not just gangsters' (as Parky puts it) but motivated by a form of political belief that amounts to more than just economic self-interest. As the film's director John Mackenzie puts it:

The gangster comes up against a kind of violence he doesn't understand...this other violence is being carried out with quite different motives...and their motives may be purer than his, because his motives are just for gain, for power.

(Hugh Hebert, 'Definitely Not a Kissing Phase', *The Guardian*, 16 February 1981, p. 11)

Thus, for all the clinical efficiency of Shand's violence, he is unable to eliminate his opponents just as, in line with the film's allegorical drift, the British state has been unable to impose a military, rather than a political, solution to the Northern Irish conflicts with which it has been confronted.

However, while the film was unusual (and, at the time of its release, controversial) in its identification of IRA violence as 'political', it is also fair to say that the film is also peculiarly reticent about the 'content' of the politics it identifies. Much of the film's suspense depends upon the withholding of information about the precise nature of Shand's adversaries and for much of the film we are invited to share his incredulity and confusion concerning the attacks visited on him. The film, in this respect, inhibits sympathetic identification with the IRA characters (even if the casting of a twinkling-eyed Pierce Brosnan invests them with a degree of youthful glamour) and an understanding of their motives outside of 'revenge'. Thus, while the allegorising impulse of the film apparently subverts the image of the IRA as no more than gangsters, it simultaneously reproduces a stereotype of Republican violence as largely unintelligible (Hill 1988: 174–5).

Gangsters as pastiche: *A Prayer for the Dying*

The richness of *The Long Good Friday* is testified to, however, by the way in which so many of its themes are returned to in subsequent gangster films of the 1980s. The confrontation between gangland and politically motivated violence is inherited by Mike Hodges' *A Prayer for the Dying* (1988), the clash between the old and new London reappears in Neil Jordan's *Mona Lisa* and Ron Peck's *Empire State* (1987), while the theme of US 'investment' in Britain is taken up by both *Empire State* and Mike Figgis's *Stormy Monday*. In the case of *A Prayer for the Dying*, the IRA man on the run, Martin Fallon (Mickey Rourke) is pitched against East End gangsters, Jack (Alan Bates) and Billy Meehan (Christopher Fulford) (compared to Al Capone in the original novel but clearly modelled in the film on the Krays). Like *The Long Good Friday*, Fallon's violence is associated with a superior morality to that of the Meehans whose business consists of 'murder, drugs, whores…[and] extortion'. Thus, when Kristou (Ian Bartholomew) attempts to hire Fallon for a gangland killing, Fallon tells him that he has 'never killed for money or favours' and that 'there was always a reason'. Forced into the killing (in return for a passport), Fallon nevertheless continues to be distinguished from the brothers by his commitment to a different ethical system: refusing to kill the priest, Father Da Costa (Bob Hoskins), and defending the prostitute, Jenny (Camille Coduri) from the sadistic attacks of Billy. As such, he is destined to become the brothers' nemesis, outwitting their attempts to kill him and ultimately prepared, like *The Godfather*'s Cuban revolutionary, to sacrifice himself, along with an incredulous Jack Meehan, in a final act of redemption (befitting the film's somewhat belaboured religious symbolism).

However, if the themes of the film overlap with those of *The Long Good Friday*, the tone of the film is significantly different. *A Prayer for the Dying* is characterised by a self-conscious irreverence that effectively crosses the metaphysical pretensions of IRA films such as *The Informer* (1935) and *Odd Man Out* (1947) with the black comedy of Joe Orton's *Loot* (indeed, one of the film's characters, unnamed in the original novel, is actually called Mrs Orton). This is particularly evident in the exaggerated playing of the roles of Jack and Billy Meehan, the gang bosses who hide their activities behind the facade of a funeral parlour (itself a darkly comic metaphor for the business in which the brothers are engaged). Alan Bates, especially, invests the role of the vicious East End gangster with a camp knowingness that is entirely missing from Jack Higgins's somewhat glum novel.

Thus, in an over-the-top reworking of the warehouse 'crucifixion' in *The Long Good Friday*, Jack Meehan delivers a demented eulogy to his mother ('My father cleared off when I was only 4 years old. My mother was reduced to getting bits of cleaning when she could and, when she couldn't, she resorted to having sexual intercourse with perfect strangers up against the back wall of public lounges. Five shillings a time') while having his henchman, Bonati (Leonard Termo) nail to a blackboard an employee who has just defrauded an elderly lady customer (Mrs Orton). The scene then ends with Jack turning to his brother, telling him that he wants the man 'back at work' the following morning. This comic mood is reinforced by a more general play with stereotypes (the casting of Bob Hoskins against type as a priest seen hoovering the church and ironing in his underpants) and the extensive use of cinematic allusion and pastiche (that includes, *inter alia*, references to *I Confess*, *Strangers on a Train*, *White Heat*, Hammer horror and the spaghetti western). While such devices may contribute a certain comic élan, there is an absence of any clear ideological design – or parodic purpose – to them with the result that what claims the film may have had to moral and political seriousness are effectively undermined.

Gangsters and tradition: *Mona Lisa, Empire State* and *Stormy Monday*

A somewhat different take on the themes of *The Long Good Friday* is to be found in *Mona Lisa, Empire State* and *Stormy Monday*. It has already been noted how *The Long Good Friday* makes use of Bob Hoskins' gangster to allegorise the emergent enterprise culture of the 1980s. However, if this may also be linked to the rise of Thatcherism, then more than just the metaphor of 'enterprise' is involved. For Thatcherism was fuelled not only by economic neo-liberalism but by social conservatism and the economic themes of self-interest, competition and 'freedom' were combined with traditional themes of nation, family, personal morality and social order. This mix of radical economic impulses and social and moral conservatism is also evident in the figure of Harold Shand. For while he may be driven by the profit motive, he also maintains an ethical code, refusing to deal in drugs and showing his disdain for heroin use in the scene at Erroll's (Paul Barber) (where, on seeing a syringe, he complains of the lack of 'decency in this disgusting world'). Moreover, while he may be associated with a modernising project to internationalise the UK economy, he is also hugely patriotic. Thus, when he learns that Charlie is returning to the US, he derides America and mounts a spirited defence of British values:

> Us British, we're used to a bit more vitality, imagination, touch of the Dunkirk spirit....What I'm looking for is someone who can contribute to what England has given to the world....A little bit more than an 'ot dog, know what I mean?

The British cinema gangster of the 1980s more generally embodied this struggle between the 'old' and 'new' England. This is evident, for example, in *Mona Lisa*, in which Bob Hoskins plays a small-time gangster, George, who has been released from jail after seven years. On the outside, he discovers that the world he once knew has changed. Working as a driver for the black prostitute, Simone (Cathy Tyson), he undertakes a search for her friend, the heroin-addicted prostitute Cathy (Kate Hardie), that involves him in a night-mare journey through a new, exploitative underworld of crime characterised by sex clubs, pornography, drug-dealing and prostitution.

Like Shand in *The Long Good Friday*, George may be seen to stand for the traditional working-class gangster with an old-fashioned code of honour that is increasingly out of place in the contemporary era. In doing so, the film not only links George's disillusionment with a rising tide of 'permissiveness' but also the 'threat' posed by changing social roles (both sexual and racial) to his white working-class masculinity, a threat that is immediately evident at the film's beginning when George is rejected by his estranged wife and, in a reprise of a similar scene in *The Long Good Friday*, he expresses his surprise at the rising numbers of black residents in his old neighbourhood ('Where did they all come from?' he asks his friend Thomas (Robbie Coltrane)). So, while the film is at one level about the construction of an 'odd couple' in which the conventional barriers of age, outlook and race are overcome, the doomed romanticism of the film's noir plot ensures that George's infatuation ends in apparent betrayal (at the hands of a contemporary 'femme fatale') and a recoil from unorthodox identities ('I sold myself for a pair of dykes'). Moreover, just as drug-dealing is associated with the 'spades' in *The Long Good Friday*, so the unpleasant new world in which George becomes embroiled is implicitly linked to a growing participation of blacks, not only Simone herself ('a tall, thin, black tart') but the vicious black pimp, Anderson (Clarke Peters), who specialises in the provision of (white) under-age schoolgirls. Thus, in turning the working-class male gangster into an emblem of 'old England', and pitting him against a new – ethnically changing and increasingly sexualised – 'England', the film also locks into a strand of (Thatcherite) traditionalism preoccupied with the decline of family and nation. It is significant, therefore, that the film should end with an image of the 'reconstructed' white family from which the independent (and, thus, threatening) adult woman has now been excluded.

The contrast between old and new gangsterism which is manifest in *Mona Lisa*, is further developed in *Empire State*, a curious hybrid of film noir, melo-drama and social comment. As with *The Long Good Friday*, the plot revolves around the redevelopment of Docklands and the possibilities for making money that this offers. The British developers are also seeking the support of an American investor, Chuck (Martin Landau), who also has second thoughts as a result of the social divisions (and potential for social unrest) that redevel-opment is perceived to be creating. However, more clearly than in *The Long Good Friday*, there are distinct types of gangsters, symbolic of the social and economic changes around them.

Frank (Ray McAnally) represents the old East End, a club owner and gangster who, like Shand, maintains certain 'standards' and refuses to deal in drugs. His authority is challenged, in a semi-oedipal drama typical of American gangster films, by his protégé, Paul (Ian Sears), who has 'crossed over' into pimping and drug-dealing and, anticipating the profits to be made

Figure 14.2 No holds barred: Frank (Ray McAnally) presides over a fight between symbols of London's East End – new and old – in Ron Peck's *Empire State* (1987)

Source: British Cinema and Television Research Group archive, De Montfort University

following the American's investment in the area, has succeeded in obtaining the lease of Frank's club. In a key scene, he warns Frank of 'the new class of money' that is moving in and of the end of old-style gangster rule. 'I thought I'd have you stuffed' and 'put in a glass case', he declares. 'You put a coin in the slot and you hear it all pour out of your mouth – all the East End chat, the filthy language, and the threats of the old violence.'

The irony of the film, however, is that when the American departs, it is Paul who is left with a deal gone sour and a group of unhappy (yuppie) investors. Frank challenges him to recoup his losses by gambling on a no-holds barred bout between two fighters, which clearly symbolises the battle between the two East Ends. Frank's fighter wins and, thus, succeeds in upholding the 'traditional' values of the 'old' London. In this way, the film ends up (for all its savagery) reworking a theme that is typical of much of British cinema – the triumph of the small man, or small business, over impersonal economic forces. As such, the old-style British gangster not only becomes associated, as in *Mona Lisa*, with 'tradition' but also with the resistance of small-scale local capital to the globalising economic forces represented by the American ('drop sterling, buy yen'). This is a theme that emerges even more strongly in *Stormy Monday*.

Stormy Monday is set in Newcastle during 'America Week' when a shady American businessman, Cosmo (Tommy Lee Jones), is buying up city-centre property with the support of the local council. He is faced, however, with the obstacle of the local club owner, Finney (Sting) who is refusing to sell up (and by hiring the Polish Krakow Jazz Ensemble during America Week signals his independence of spirit). A key scene, in this regard, is the reception for Cosmo hosted by the city's Thatcherite mayor. Following her speech celebrating how American qualities will contribute to 'a re-emergence of this once great nation', Cosmo himself addresses the assembled gathering. Quoting the maxim 'when the going gets tough the tough get going', he declares it is time for the tough to get going in Newcastle. As he speaks, the film inter-cuts shots of two London gangsters, hired by Cosmo, arriving at Finney's office ready to force him to sign the papers that will give Cosmo ownership of his club.

In this respect, Cosmo gives eloquent expression to the economic and cultural imperialism that the film sees as overwhelming Newcastle. Using the pretext of 'American Week', the city is recreated in the image of American popular culture: the bars based on Weegee and Hopper, the huge Coca Cola bottle in the square, the marching majorettes, the club bouncers in NYPD uniforms, the boys playing basketball, the vintage American cars on the streets. At the level of plot, however, this triumph of Americanism is upturned. Finney has been tipped off about the arrival of the gangsters and, uses his own men, to 'turn them around'. In this way, Cosmo is forced to negotiate with Finney and, following his attempt to blow up Brendan (Sean Bean) and Kate (Melanie Griffith), to leave Newcastle altogether. When the tough get going, it seems it is the locals who are the toughest. In this way, the film, like *Empire State*, belies the social and economic realities of the period and celebrates a symbolic victory of local over international forces. There is here a mirroring of similar tensions within Thatcherism. For while the free market economics of the Thatcher government clearly encouraged the integration of the 'national economy' into a global system, Thatcherite rhetoric nevertheless remained firmly attached to 'Little England' notions of national sovereignty and identity in a way that increasingly stood at odds with the realities of economic and cultural globalisation.

Conclusion

There is also an oddness about the ending of *Stormy Monday*. For while the film's plot may constitute a critique of US cultural imperialism, this is apparently belied by the film's own fascination with American film and musical genres. The resolution of this apparent contradiction probably lies in the film's use of the Krakow Jazz Ensemble who play an American form but imbue it with European influences. In a sense, this is true of the British gangster film more generally as it, too, has appropriated a Hollywood model but inflected it in a nationally specific direction. In the case of the 1980s, this involved a self-conscious concern to allegorise the nation as a way of commenting on the social and economic changes characteristic of the era. In some ways, such allegories may be counted 'progressive', critiquing the economic excesses of the era and counterpointing them to alternative value systems (such as the Polish community in *Stormy Monday*). In other respects, the films may be seen to be morally and politically conservative, identifying the gangster figure with the 'little man' under attack and, in doing so, turning him into an emblem of both 'tradition' and traditional conceptions of the 'nation'.

Bibliography

Gibbons, L. (1997) 'Framing history: Neil Jordan's *Michael Collins*', *History Ireland*, 5, 1: 47–51.

Hess, J. (1975) 'Godfather II: a deal Coppola couldn't refuse', *Jump Cut*, 7, 1: 10–11.

Hill, J. (1988) 'Images of violence' in K. Rockett, L. Gibbons and J. Hill *Cinema and Ireland*, London: Routledge.

Sarris, A. (1977) 'Big funerals: the Hollywood gangster, 1927–1933', *Film Comment*, 13, 3: 6–9.

Warshow, R. (1974) 'Movie chronicle: the westerner' (orig. 1954), in *The Immediate Experience*, New York: Atheneum.

15 From underworld to underclass
Crime and British cinema in the 1990s

Claire Monk

When *Face* (Antonia Bird, 1997) – an East End tale of robbery gone wrong, shot during the last months of Conservative government, and released in the changed political climate of Autumn 1997 – was praised as possibly 'the best British thriller since *The Long Good Friday*' (Quentin Curtis, *Daily Telegraph*, 26 September 1997), the comparison revealed more than its author might have intended.[1] The blend of imperialism and aspirational entrepreneurialism embodied by *The Long Good Friday*'s yacht-owning gang boss, Harold Shand, had uncannily prefigured the values that would dominate the 1980s. *Face*, by contrast, was one of a crop of late-1990s British films – from the comedies *Brassed Off* (Mark Herman, 1996) and *The Full Monty* (Peter Cattaneo, 1997) to Danny Boyle's heroin drama *Trainspotting* (1996) – whose subtext was the economic and social damage that Thatcherism and longer-term industrial decline had wrought on the once-working classes. In the eighteen years separating the two films, *everything* – socially, culturally and politically – had changed. The fact that, in the face of such transformations, *Face*'s makers and critics were able to enhance its cultural value and commercial appeal by claiming similarities not just with *The Long Good Friday* but with a still older London gangster 'classic' – Mike Hodges' 1971 *Get Carter* – exposed a little-trumpeted trait of the film culture of 'Cool Britannia': its uncritical, backward-looking self-referentiality and unacknowledged nostalgia. Above all, it spoke of the endurance of the gangland film as the preferred model for what a British crime film 'should' be.

But, as *The Long Good Friday* had suggested, the traditional London gangster, with his attachment to obsolete social, sexual and racial hierarchies and open nostalgia for the vanished days of empire, was already an anachronism by 1979, let alone 1997. So too, I will argue, was the genre prototype provided for British cinema by the gangland films of the 1960s and 1970s. In particular, the real-life organisational and technological models of both crime and 'legitimate' business, as well as gender relations, public morality and the wider social formation, had been transformed almost beyond recognition since the 1960s heyday of the Richardsons and the Krays.

Although *Face* represented a genuine attempt to 'modernise' the London gangland film – by rejecting and feminising the gangster subculture's traditionally reactionary politics and offering a critique of 1980s and 1990s social changes from the Left – the difficulties it faced in doing so from within the genre are revealing. My analysis will argue that the 1990s British films that responded best to the social realities shaping 1990s crime were those that departed from traditional genre models. It will also seek to illustrate why the gangland film's continuing appeal (for parts of the male audience in particular) may lie precisely in its celebration of regressive ideologies and obsolete models of criminal, gender and social organisation.

Gender politics and the gangster

As the celebrations of the gangster's explosive, anti-rational male aggression in films such as *Get Carter* and *Villain* (Michael Tuchner, 1971) testify, the 'classic' British villain has been centrally defined by his contempt for women as well as his reactionary politics. The villain's reputation for misogyny is, of course, far older than these films and is firmly rooted in biographical fact (Pearson, 1995: 31–32, 37). Indeed, it is possible to go further and read this vehement opposition to the 'feminine' spheres of home life and 'respectable' society as the primary organising logic explaining the peculiar character of the underworld as an inherently homosocial subculture, in which male rituals, hierarchies and rivalries often seem to take precedence over gangland's ostensible business of illegal money-making.[2] The gang or 'firm' itself is likewise a homosocial space; in both cases, the intrusion of women – or, conversely, in *Performance* (Nicolas Roeg and Donald Cammell, 1970), the entry of the gangster into a zone of sexual and gender ambiguity – is always a threat.

In the 1970s British gangland films, this masculinist dynamic and the corresponding subordination/exclusion of women had been accepted traits of the genre. However, the shifting perceptions of gender power and actual shifts in gender relations that had taken place in Britain since 1979 (not least due to the rule of a powerful woman Prime Minister) made this genre blueprint less feasible in the 1990s. It seems significant that Margaret Thatcher's final year in power brought two British films – Peter Greenaway's *The Cook, the Thief, His Wife and Her Lover* and Peter Medak's *The Krays*, released in the UK in October 1989 and April 1990, respectively – which deployed the London gangland milieu in ways that were not only read by some as allegories of Thatcherism (Desjardins, 1993; Walsh, 1993) but also rendered transparent, dissected and critiqued ganglord's misogyny and subjugation of women. However, as their timing (and allegorical slant) indicate, these films represented a closing comment on the Thatcherite 1980s rather than the beginnings of its aftermath and the art-cinema characteristics of both films increase their distance from the crime genre. After *The Krays*, the masculinist gangster vanished from British cinema until 1993, when he returned in Danny Cannon's *Young Americans* as a Krays-era veteran who steps in at the last minute to gun down the film's London-based American drug-lord villain. By 1997, he had metamorphosed into a sensitive character open to female influence in *Face*; and a deflationary self-parody in J.K. Amalou's ultraviolent, and less successful, thriller *Hard Men* (1997).

Gender, work and crime: social change and the 1990s British cinema

During the Thatcher and Major years' changes relating to gender, the organisation and technologies of work, and attitudes to crime had implications for how crime would be represented by the 1990s British cinema. In the 1990s women made increasingly confident inroads into the workforce, especially in the white-collar and service industries. Although the desirability of women as employees was in many cases due to their 'flexibility' in tolerating work that was part-time, insecure and ill-paid, the impression grew of a society in which women were in the ascendancy in the workplace and beyond. By contrast, masculinity – particularly young, skill-less, goal-less working-class masculinity – was increasingly defined as a problem.

As the 1990s progressed, male unemployment and social exclusion, and broader problems of masculinity, became the subtexts or themes of an increasing number of British films. Some of the most commercially successful of these – *Brassed Off* and *The Full Monty* – transformed this material into feel-good comedy. But the predicament of the jobless underclass male was also a taken-as-read ingredient in a number of more pessimistic social dramas and crime thrillers beginning with Mike Leigh's *Naked* (1993). British cinema's youth-orientated crime dramas – *Shopping* (Paul Anderson, 1994), *Twin Town* (Kevin Allen, 1997) – and gang thrillers – *Face* – took a less-than-complex stance on the underclass male. For Antonia Bird, *Face* was simply about 'the choices that you have if you come from a working-class background in inner-city London and you're bright.…There's no work, so either you go into crime or you give in' (quoted in McCabe 1997: 11).

The working woman who is more clued-up than her male counterparts was a recurrent figure in these films. In *Face*, the mother and girlfriend of lapsed Communist armed robber, Ray, committed activists who have kept the political faith, function as critics of the futility and unprofitability of his lifestyle. By contrast, in *Twin Town*, the working female (like much else in the film) is cynically caricatured: the teenage sister of the two young car-nicking protagonists sees herself as several cuts above them because she *works*, but it is no shock when her job as a massage-parlour receptionist proves to be less respectable than she claims.

A second change taking place in the 1980s and 1990s workplace was the restructuring and 'downsizing' of organisations, producing structures that were ostensibly less hierarchical than the traditional firm. In eliminating unskilled workers and middle-management, this trend was one of the root causes of 1990s male unemployment and disempowerment. The death of the old business structures had profound implications for the conceptual viability of the gangland model as a blueprint for a contemporary crime cinema. The organised crime 'family' or 'firm' has always modelled itself on 'legitimate' business, and the structures of the Richardson and Kray gangs had a clear (if parodic) relationship to the authoritarian/paternalistic management hierarchies of their 1960s heyday. Lines of command were dictatorial and rigid, but the 'workers' felt secure and cared for, breeding loyalty and a sense of belonging.

This model was a standard genre ingredient in the British gangland films of the 1960s and 1970s; but the transformations of the 1980s and 1990s severed its roots in social reality. It is no coincidence that at this moment of male insecurity and loss, the old-school London gangster, and the films that had paid him homage, were reappropriated as comforting nostalgia. The one *new* 1990s British film to exploit this mood directly was the transatlantic policier *Young Americans*. Although it was aggressively targeted at the US market and a young UK multiplex audience, its themes and narrative resolution – in which an ageing London gangster emerges as the eleventh-hour hero – yearned for an idealised, parochial 1960s gangland in which codes of behaviour were honoured and crime was, above all, a British affair. Its implication was that the old-school gangster was a figure from the past who was nevertheless sorely missed, and needed, in the present. For the most part, however, this wistful nostalgia for 'olde gangland' was a media rather than cinematic phenomenon. Images of the 1960s Michael Caine and profiles of the septuagenarian ex-gangster 'Mad' Frankie Fraser became typical fare in men's monthly magazines such as *Loaded* and *GQ*; and the gangland films of more optimistic eras, from *Get Carter* to *The Long Good Friday*, were canonised as genre classics by the taste-makers of 'lad' culture.

The social factor that had the most visible impact on 1990s British cinema's treatment of crime was the increased complexity of public attitudes to crime. There was not merely a lack of consensus in public opinion regarding certain areas of activity defined by the law as 'criminal' – most obviously on questions around the distribution and use of illegal drugs – but also an increasingly evident gulf between the law and the actual behaviour of the public. In many working-class communities where the closure of local industries had brought multi-generational unemployment, theft and drug-dealing became normalised as strategies for survival. Among the clubbers who discovered Ecstasy from the late 1980s onwards and the broader, cross-class section of society who followed them, the blanket illegality of a diverse spectrum of recreational substances fostered a certain contempt for the law, and brought millions of people into direct or indirect contact with the criminal black market. In 1990s Britain, the boundaries between underworld and underclass, petty and organised crime and criminality and mainstream society came to seem increasingly blurred.

This blurring of moral boundaries, coupled with a degree of cynical disillusion with the law, was reflected in a considerable number of 1990s British films in which crime was portrayed as a matter-of-fact aspect of life. Certain figures recur across these films: slow, ineffectual police (*Shopping*; *Face*); the viciously bent cop who controls his local organised crime scene with a ruthlessness unmatched by the nominal career criminals; and the equally ruth-less all-powerful criminal top-dog, who functions on a corporate scale, abides by no codes of honour, and seeks to dominate or eliminate the small fry by any means possible. In *Twin Town* and *Face*, these last two figures are effectively one and the same. They represent an equal threat to the former film's teenage car thieves and the latter's professional armed robbers. In both cases, the activ-ities of the (relatively powerless) lawbreakers are presented as legitimated by the power abuses and/or organised corruption of the law.

In the context of this disillusioned relativism, the fact that few 'crime films' of the traditional kind (i.e. primarily concerned with the subculture of organ-ised/career crime or the battle between law and disorder) were made in Britain in the 1990s is both revealing and deceptive. Crime in society had, in effect, entered the mainstream. In keeping with this, much of the 'criminal' activity taking place in 1990s British cinema could be found dispersed into genres or genre mixes in which the law-breaking nature of the activity was not always the central issue at stake. Crime in the 1990s was also characterised by its multifaceted links with youth and style subcultures: indeed, in the sense that certain types of crime in 1990s Britain were predominantly the province of juveniles, crime *was* a youth subculture. In this regard, it is highly significant that the portrayal of crime as 'normal' in a succession of 1990s British films was closely associated with the emergence of young film-makers who aspired to compete with Hollywood on its own terms by making commercial films that would play to the tastes of an under-25 (and, implicitly, largely male) audience.

Shopping

Although it was a critical and commercial failure, Paul Anderson's *Shopping* was important in relation to these trends in that it marked the emergence of a strand of British films that combined an empathetic or 'insider' stance on crime with an attempted appeal to a young audience whose interests and subcultures were being ignored by the early-1990s British cinema. Uninterested in emulating the small-scale realist and magical–realist social dramas that had won praise in Britain since the 1980s, Anderson and contem-poraries like *Young Americans'* director Danny Cannon embraced the Hollywood action thriller as their aesthetic model. Their films, notable for their 'un-English' violence, sought mass audiences above critical respectability.

The audience Anderson envisaged for *Shopping* was one weaned on play-station computer games, brand-name trainers and the hi-tech spectacle and excitement of Hollywood cycles such as the *Terminator* films. Without a Hollywood budget to play with, however, his film's construction of an (implicitly near-future) British urban dystopia makes do with lower-tech strategies: aerial shots of cooling towers; London location-shooting in derelict buildings around Whitechapel, Bermondsey and the Isle of Dogs; expression-istic use of dark streets and dry ice. In place of optimistic visions of a gleaming futuristic metropolis, the film substitutes post-industrial urban decay. This aesthetic was one of the most successful things about *Shopping*, and set it apart from most British films of the time – as Ben Thompson noted in *Sight and Sound* (July, 1994: 167): 'This mythic city with its wastelands and skeletal concrete structures actually looks more like London than many more overt representations of the capital.'

Shopping's claims to contemporaneity and credibility nevertheless rested on a narrative rooted in a specific UK social reality. Since the late 1980s, the British media had begun to report on, and analyse, an apparent epidemic of novel forms of car crime among teenagers – usually in deprived areas of regional cities remote from the South-East – whose lives seemed increasingly divorced from the hopes or moral norms of 'mainstream' society. While adolescent car theft and joyriding were not new crimes, 1990s concerns about 'twoccing' (police jargon for 'taking without owner's consent') stemmed from its compulsive, subcultural character. For the underclass teenager, who might nick and dump scores of cars in a year, the adrenalin rush of illicit motoring was a way of life, a source of identity more than a means to profit. *Shopping*'s title referred to a related (and more genuinely new) early-1990s phenomenon – ram-raiding – in which large-scale shoplifting (usually of 'designer' goods) is achieved by ramming a stolen vehicle through a shop-front – a method combining flamboyance with the grab-and-go tactics of the heist. Newcastle-upon-Tyne achieved a particular reputation for twoccing and ram-raiding. It was also Anderson's home city. *Shopping*, then, tried to transform material with very specific local origins into a film with broad generic appeal.

Shopping's urban youth are beyond police or parental control, but their self-sufficiency, live-for-the-day nihilism and coruscating contempt for adults and the law are presented in the film as morally superior to the unreliability of parents and the unconvincing platitudes and threats of the police. The film opens with the release of its joyrider 'hero', Billy (Jude Law), from jail. Asked by ineffectual police chief Conway (Jonathan Pryce) what prison has taught him, Billy replies: 'Don't get caught'. Billy is met from jail by his friend Jo (Sadie Frost) a tough, androgynous young Ulsterwoman. Although the pair's closeness and chemistry raise expectations that they are (or will become) lovers, Jo retains an asexual autonomy, and denounces Billy's gestures of courtship as 'romantic crap'. Almost immediately, the pair trade up from Jo's stolen car by ramming a BMW. When the angry owner gets out to remonstrate, they drive off in it at high speed, sneeringly tossing him the keys to the cheaper model they have abandoned. Billy, a respected figure in the community of car thieves, is welcomed back by his peers, but Tommy (Sean Pertwee), an older rival gang-leader who in Billy's absence has gained ascendancy as a drug-dealer and fence by controlling younger criminals, is less pleased, seemingly because Billy's revered status, maverick unpredictability and refusal to be anyone's employee threaten his power.

However, the film shows this power to be largely delusory. We eventually learn that Tommy is just one ambitious entrepreneur among many competing

Figure 15.1 Consumer terrorists: Billy (Jude Law) and Jo (Sadie Frost) go joy-riding
in Paul Anderson's teen pic *Shopping* (1994)
Source: British Cinema and Television Research Group archive, De Montfort University

to work for Venning (Sean Bean), a *bona fide* gangster-made-good. Tommy has
a hard time persuading Venning to hire him to steal to order from the Alaska,
a hip department store. Venning beats down his price (as Tommy is shown
to do with his own reluctant underlings), and the job fails when Billy and Jo
ram-raid the store before Tommy can get there. The alarm system alerts the
police, but the officers are ambushed by Billy's supporters from a rooftop, with
horrific results. Tommy is now determined to gain revenge against Billy.
Lusting after Jo, he unsuccessfully tries to persuade her to switch loyalties. Jo,
whose enthusiasm for Billy's activities is waning, asks Billy to leave town with
her and start a new (although not necessarily law-abiding) life, but he can see
no point. Eventually Billy, determined to ram-raid a high-security upmarket
shopping centre to show Tommy who's boss, is set up by Tommy and killed by
the police, along with Jo.

  Shopping was the first 1990s British film to focus on distinctly contemporary forms of crime and to do so from the perspective of those engaged in it.
Despite its cautionary ending, its stance on Billy and his friends is non-judg-
mental. The conclusion it encourages us to draw is that it is exploiters like
Tommy (and, on a larger scale, Venning and the consumer provocation offered
by the Alaska) who are to be condemned rather than Billy, who ram-raids
mainly out of a desire for excitement and challenge. The film values

autonomy (represented by Billy) and despises dependency: an index of Tommy's moral turpitude is that he part-pays his young subcontractors – against their will – in drugs for resale, thus fleecing them of their full payment in cash while tempting them into future addiction.

Primarily, however, *Shopping* lays the blame on society and authority, including the parents who seek to keep the teenage car-thieves out of trouble – all of them working-class women, portrayed without exception as slatterns or screeching harpies. It is this obsequious pandering to what it imagines to be a youths'-eye view that proves (along with weak characterisation and dialogue) to be the film's downfall. Far from suggesting a coherent social critique, *Shopping*'s socially aware posturing collapses under the weight of its own contradictions. The film tries to present Billy and Jo as living critiques of capitalist consumer culture while simultaneously flattering a brand-obsessed young audience by mirroring their own fetishisation of designer labels and the 'right' models of car: 'I can't believe people pay that much!' cries Billy as he shoplifts a £90 Alessi kettle. Its credibility is further scuppered by its misjudged attempts to signal its own hipness. 'Cutting-edge' youth-cultural signifiers (Jo constantly plays with a car-chase computer game, even during actual car chases) are brandished with a crassness that confirms the film's exploitation status. Fittingly, *Shopping*'s fiercest attacks on 'straight' society are reserved for its consumption of the 'wrong' products: the BMW's owner is declared by Jo to 'deserve' to have his car stolen because it contains a Dire Straits audio tape and a box of Ferrero Rocher chocolates.

Shallow Grave

For all its failings, *Shopping* did at least break with the gender conventions of more traditionalist crime films by granting Jo an autonomous central role. Her lean, androgynous allure and aggressively asexual aloofness, although often compromised by the absurdities of the script and crudeness of Frost's performance, make her a more interesting and less predictable figure than Billy. More importantly, the film made Jo the moral equal of her male counterparts: neither saviour nor betrayer, angel nor whore, her gender does not make her any better or worse than the men.

The figure of the active, confident, unidealised female protagonist recurred in a more successful British (or, more accurately, Scottish) film released early the following year, although in a social and class setting far removed from that of *Shopping*. If *Shopping* had 'updated' the social-deviancy crime film only to end up as youth-culture exploitation, *Shallow Grave* (1994) – the debut feature from director Danny Boyle, producer Andrew Macdonald and writer John Hodges, who would later make *Trainspotting* – jettisoned conventional crime genre models (and moralisations) entirely. Generically, *Shallow Grave* is a black comedy, although one clearly influenced by the crime/humour/viscera mix and studied amorality of Quentin Tarantino's

Reservoir Dogs. Nevertheless, its narrative – and cinematic effect – depend on the background presence of a world of professional crime, only briefly glimpsed on screen and therefore all the more startling in its sudden, violent incursions into the equally vicious middle-class professional milieu which is the film's main setting.

Highly stylised, in its structure and dialogue as much as in its richly coloured baroque art direction, Boyle's film's success in attracting a hip, sophisticated young audience had much to do with its formal innovation: its success in creating a fast-moving, rhythmic visual language equivalent to the techno music on its soundtrack raised considerable excitement about what British films could achieve. But *Shallow Grave* also succeeded where *Shopping* had failed because of its more basic virtues of sharp dialogue and meticulous, heightened characterisation. Its most startling trait, however, was the cool, gleefully amoral gaze it cast on its protagonists.

Shallow Grave charts a tale of escalating ruthlessness, greed and betrayal among three preposterously arrogant late-20s Edinburgh yuppies who find that they can achieve instant wealth by concealing an unexpected death. Journalist Alex (Ewan McGregor), accountant David (Christopher Eccleston) and junior doctor Juliet (Kerry Fox) share a huge, stylish flat in Edinburgh's Georgian New Town. They are seeking a fourth flatmate, but no applicant meets their standards – except for the urbane Hugo (Keith Allen), who claims to be writing a novel and has no apparent job but plenty of money. Soon after moving in, however, Hugo is found dead from a drug overdose. With him is a suitcase containing a huge sum of cash. After a process of mutual goading, Alex, Juliet and David agree to keep it, and conceal the death by burying Hugo's body in the woods. The task of dismembering the corpse to prevent identification falls to David, and his resulting disturbance opens a rift between him and Alex and Juliet. By contrast, Alex's conviction that their actions are undetectable increases his arrogance, and he and Juliet go on a spending spree.

However, brief flashes inter-cut into this narrative give the viewer 'God's-eye' access to events elsewhere (a violent cashpoint robbery, vicious beatings and murders), which suggest that the direct or indirect source of Hugo's money is professional crime, and establish that two hard men are on the trail of the cash and are happy to torture and kill to discover Hugo's whereabouts. Eventually, the pair reach the flat and attack Alex and Juliet, but David kills them. The bodies are disposed of near Hugo's.

Despite a denouement in which Juliet stabs David to death and sets off for Rio de Janeiro with the suitcase – only to find that it contains no money – *Shallow Grave*'s ending nevertheless suggests the possibility that the unrepentantly amoral can get away with murder. Alex, the ringleader in covering up Hugo's death and the one participant untouched by qualms throughout, emerges with the money. Left pinned to the floor by kitchen knives, he is treated as dead by the police – but the film's ending shows him smiling as they depart, knowing that the cash is safe (if bloodstained) under the floorboards beneath him. In its apparent celebration of the triumph of the shameless, this conclusion has unpalatable Social Darwinist overtones, but its extreme ambiguity offers only tenuous closure. It is unclear whether Alex is dead or alive; and if alive, whether he will magically unpin himself once the camera stops rolling and get away with keeping the money, or bleed slowly to death. And if Alex is dead, his hovering smile nevertheless suggests that he expects to be reunited with the money in eternity beyond the grave.

Shallow Grave stands apart as the one 1990s British film in which this discomfiting amoral distance was fully achieved. A less-discussed aspect of the film is the equation it tacitly constructs between its criminal young professionals and the professional criminals who unexpectedly impinge on their world. Viewed from this perspective, the film sketches the 1990s breakdown of boundaries between 'straight' society and the underworld more slyly than any other British film of the decade, and it is through this relationship that it delivers the social and moral critiques teasingly deferred at the level of plot.

In the 1990s context, it is hugely significant that it is violent, professional crime, not the law, that disrupts the three protagonists' chances of remaining undetected and precipitates their slide from concealing death to committing murder. Traits associated with their elevated status as 'professionals' – arrogance and a winner-takes-all ethos – make possible their near-fascistic conviction that they are above the law; but their consequent willingness to kill places them on the same *moral* level as the film's professional thugs. At the same time, the apparent distance of the flatmates' lifestyle from the underworld makes them blind to its closeness. Their bourgeois misreading of the signs of Hugo's criminal connections serves as an ironic condemnation of their values: his vagueness about his occupation and his easy way with cash are read as signs of creativity and 'cool' rather than anything more sinister.

Such details suggest that *Shallow Grave* is capable of being read as a critique; but the post-political (and often irony-blind) culture within which it circulated suggest that the likelihood of it being widely received as such was small. It was a film bred of cynical times, and its appeal for audiences rested substantially on its gleeful, self-conscious surface celebration of greed.

Face

Shallow Grave was the film in which the mid-1990s British cinema's drive towards an almost Nietzschean anti-morality reached its apotheosis. Some later British films of the decade attempted to trade on an anti-moral stance towards crime – from con-trickery (*Shooting Fish*, Stefan Schwartz 1997) to the sadism of the Shankhill Butchers (*Resurrection Man,* Marc Evans, 1997). But there was also a return to a moral framework in which actions had consequences and some were seen as clearly 'wrong', although involvement in crime continued to be seen as a rational, and defensible, choice.

The heist-gone-wrong thriller *Face* fitted this latter pattern. Filmed shortly before New Labour's landslide General Election victory in May 1997 and released in September that year, it was a strange film to have emerged from the post-*Trainspotting* moment of confidence and innovation. On the one hand, it was a genre crime thriller, marketed at the 'core' 18–25 audience as aggressively as *Shallow Grave* had been.[3] Compliant pre-release media coverage emphasised its realist take on criminal morality and 'un-English' visceral appeal, while seeking to equate it both with London gangland 'classics' and with recent US 'cult classics' appealing to a young male audience. In a typical wording, *Time Out* hailed *Face* for its 'graphic violence…closer in style to *Goodfellas* and *Reservoir Dogs*' than to some hypothetical 'typical' British film (Dessau, 1997). On the other hand, *Face* also presented itself as an overtly political film, and was promoted as such in some media coverage. Moreover, its politics and political memory were very specifically rooted in the 'hard'-left politics of the 1980s: the struggles in support of the miners' strike and against union-breaking and the introduction of new technology at Rupert Murdoch's News International plant at Wapping.

Face's politics, target market and late-1990s setting made updating and ideological reorientation of its genre model necessary. However, its discrepant aspirations made it an object lesson in the problems involved in re-routing the gangster's reactionary politics in a 'progressive' direction; and in addressing revolutionary left ideas to a young audience at a moment in which socialist ideas had been evacuated from mainstream discourse. As a political film, *Face*'s central concerns are the 1990s loss of political faith and belief in the possibility of change, the defeat of collective values by individualism and greed and the widespread nihilism and cynicism that it sees as resulting from these losses. As a genre thriller, it seeks to express these concerns at the level of allegory. Its main protagonist, Ray (Robert Carlyle), a former Communist, disillusioned after the mid-1980s defeat of the miners, has abandoned the class struggle and become a professional armed robber. Ray's partner in crime, Dave (Ray Winstone), is by contrast an 'old-style face' – an East End criminal-made-good and family man who embodies patriarchal, apolitically conservative values and enjoys a comfortable lifestyle in a middle-class Victorian suburb. In keeping with his status as patriarch, Dave's wife is never seen, and his daughter, Sarah (Christine Tremarco), is a classic 'Essex girl', fun-loving and unreflective, whose relationship with her boyfriend, Chris (Andrew Tiernan), arouses Dave's jealous overprotectiveness. By contrast, the women in Ray's life embody the idealism he has abandoned. His semi-estranged mother, Alice (Sue Johnston), is still a Communist Party member; his girlfriend Connie (Lena Headey) runs a home for teenagers.

Face opens with Ray and Dave's preparations for their next job – an armed heist at a security depot near Heathrow in which they expect to net £2 million. While the sum involved reinforces our impression that they are engaged in professional crime because it is a more efficient and lucrative earner than the alternatives, the film works hard to persuade us that they are unenthusiastic participants in a high-risk and barely profitable profession. Ray, trying to dissuade the gang's youngest recruit Jason (Damon Albarn) from following their example, reflects: 'I'm 35 years old....All told, I've done five years inside, and any money I've had, I could have earned double driving a van'. Ray and Dave's two other accomplices have been scripted with rather obvious allegorical intent: Stevie (Steven Waddington) is a mentally slow innocent whom Ray has taken under his wing despite the risk that he will be a liability in a crisis; Julian (Philip Davis) is a recent father besotted with his new baby, but also an unstable psycho obsessed with maximising his personal profit by exploiting fellow gang members.

The haul in the raid proves far smaller than hoped for. Ray is in favour of making the best of things and sharing the proceeds equally, but Dave is infuriated: he had hoped to retire on his cut. Julian tries to extort an extra £40,000 in expenses, but retracts after the gang beat him as a punishment. Each participant stashes their share of the cash − but over the next 24 hours, the stashes are stolen one by one, Dave is attacked, and Jason and an elderly couple who had agreed to hide some of the money are murdered. Eventually, confronted by Ray, Dave confesses to the thefts and killings. It transpires that the job − and all his recent work − has been initiated and controlled by his daughter's boyfriend Chris, who is a bent cop. Beaten by the gang and about to be strangled by Dave, Chris sneers at their powerlessness and delivers his own 'moral': 'There is no public service...just money and the people who have it.' Ray shoots Dave; Julian gets away with the cash (which Chris had stashed in a police locker); but Ray and Stevie slip away and escape up the motorway to a new life. At a Midlands service station, they are joined (against Ray's expectations) by Connie.

Given the juncture at which it was released, it is unsurprising that *Face's* politics were dismissed by many critics as irrelevant to the times: 'When is Bird going to let her nostalgia for the old agitprop 1980s go the same way as the 1980s?' bemoaned Tom Shone of the (Murdoch-owned) *Sunday Times*. On the contrary, it could be argued that *Face's* gesture of reviving the memory of 'unfashionable' 1980s protest politics was an extremely timely step to take. Its sour critique was important precisely because it contradicted the ideological double-think of 1997, which presented 'New Britain' as a caring nation at a moment when the realities of Government policy for asylum-seekers, the poor and the disabled were becoming harsher.

A more salient criticism of *Face* is that its contradictory aspirations produced a confused address. It wanted to sell itself to a politicised, 30-plus audience as an uncompromising lament for the death of the Left, but this lament was of limited interest to its main target market, the post-political under-25s. Furthermore, its strategies for conveying its political messages − notably a highly strategic use of music from British artists associated with the Left oppositional cultures of the 1980s, such as Billy Bragg, Paul Weller and The Clash − raised doubts about the extent to which these messages would be readable by this target audience. For the under-25s and others resistant to left-wing ideas, *Face* was marketed as a somewhat different film: 'A violent, bloody, nut-in-the-face of a movie [with] gallons of claret...gutsy, gritty and hard-boiled' (Nick Fisher, *Sun*, 26 September 1997).

Face's attempts to feminise and modernise its genre model were equally problematic. Its rationalisation of white male involvement in professional crime as the only option, or as a last-ditch act of despair, failed to ring true on several levels – not least in its disregard for the psychic and gendered dimensions of the criminal subculture's appeal. The relatively powerful roles played by its female characters appear to mark a more persuasive break with genre tradition; but even here, sketchy characterisation and the problematic function assigned to Alice and Connie seem only to confirm the rule that the gangland film can only accommodate women in strictly defined roles, and as catalysts rather than central agents. Both women are presented as autonomous, 'strong' and unabused, and neither dumbly supports Ray's criminal activities. On the contrary, these activities have contributed to Ray's estrangement from Alice, and threaten to end his relationship with Connie. The problem is that Alice's and Connie's function as Ray's moral critics and conscience is virtually their only narrative function: they exist in order to 'save' Ray from himself. In contrast with the idiosyncratic and morally murky female protagonists of *Shopping* and *Shallow Grave*, they are given screen time in order to be better than men; to show what Ray has fallen from, and could aspire to be.[4]

While *Face* sought to both revive British gangster genre traditions and to use them to comment on the malaise of the 1990s, the position from which it did so was untenable. Its vision was as nostalgic and idealised as that of its predecessors, not least in its mythologisation of a 'decent', white male working-class criminality. Above all, the conflict between the requirements of representing late-1990s reality and the needs of the genre caught *Face* between a rock and a hard place. While it rejected the gangland milieu's misogyny, and took pains to 'feminise' and domesticate its villains – giving Ray a caring conscience, making Dave a protective dad, and emphasising Julian's enchantment with his new baby – its main business, violence and retribution, remained, as in any classic gangster narrative, a matter between men.

Smalltime

Made on video for £5,000, writer/director Shane Meadows' mini-feature *Smalltime* has become something of a cult since its first festival screenings in 1996. An observant social comedy of petty crime, acted by Meadows, his (untrained) mates and some drama students, it was co-funded by the BFI on the basis of short films that Meadows had made with a borrowed video camera. *Smalltime's* production ethos and brightly coloured camcorder-made looks located it light-years away from the TV-subsidised British film-making epitomised by *Face*. And while *Smalltime* (in common with Meadows' 1997 feature *TwentyFourSeven*) was not overtly 'political', it marked a renewed belief in community and a kind of social morality that seemed to herald a new, anti-nihilistic fighting spirit in British cinema as the 1990s drew to a close.

Smalltime had genuine origins in the (non-)working-class community it depicted rather than observing it with the gaze of the socially concerned outsider. One consequence is that it never idealises, sanitises or aggrandises its protagonists: their swearing, sexual behaviour and limited criminal and intellectual horizons are all presented in hilariously unbowdlerised fashion. In contrast with *Face*'s lofty apologia for its armed gang, Meadows' engagement with his twenty-something small-time thieves is sympathetic but mercilessly debunking.

Smalltime is set in Sneinton – a dead-end urban area of red-brick terraced houses on the edge of Meadows' home city of Nottingham – which, like the Edinburgh fringe-estates of *Trainspotting*, feels parochially marooned from the metropolitan centre. The film opens with a motormouth voice-over by the main character, Jumbo (Meadows), which explicitly states this marginality before the titles, or any images, have appeared on screen:

> There's one thing you've godda understand, right, this ain't fuckin' London. This ain't even Nottingham, man; this is Sneinton. And all that matters in Sneinton is having a tenner in your pocket, you know what I mean? It don't matter how you get it.

While *Smalltime* never challenges this aspect of Jumbo's criminal philosophy, this doesn't prevent Meadows from portraying the gang as a bunch of self-deluding no-hopers. As Jumbo's monologue continues, his credibility is swiftly undermined both by his subtly absurd self-regard and by the disparities between his words and the deflationary accompanying images:

> See, in the beginning, it was just me and Malc, y' know he's like my kid brother....Now he's like a fully fledged partner in the business....We all just started out as mates, and now we're a family. A family business. That's what I believe in, see. There's my missus and Malc's missus, right, who just sit around watching telly all day, and I don't care, you know what I mean, as long as my tea's on the table that's fine with me. We've got kids, and we ain't fuckin' going anywhere....You can trust us. We're not into anything heavy. We rob from the rich, and we sell it to the poor at half price. We're just smalltime.

As Jumbo speaks, we see Malc scrambling very visibly over some back walls, Jumbo stealing a cheap-looking coat-stand and Jumbo's girlfriend Ruby (Gena Kawecka) making a 'small willie' gesture with her little finger while discussing Jumbo with Malc's partner Kate (Dena Smiles). We soon learn that, far from 'watching telly all day', Ruby spends much of her time masturbating with a vibrator, an activity to which Jumbo is oblivious despite the noise made by it (and Ruby) and her refusal to have sex with him. His assertion

Figure 15.2 The underclass tools up in Shane Meadows' low-budget *Smalltime*
Source: British Cinema and Television Research Group archive, De Montfort
   University. Courtesy of Alliance Atlantis Releasing

that 'you can trust us' and his comparison of himself to local Nottingham
legend Robin Hood are richly ironic in their debased moral relativism. Yet
even as a thief, Jumbo is unsuccessful. His activities are indeed 'smalltime': so
unintelligently plotted, so intrinsically unlikely to produce a profit, that they
verge on the pointless. A theft of dog food from the yard of a corner shop fails
to yield any cans of the premium 'Butcher's Tripe' flavour that Jumbo is
convinced will make the job an earner. The gang openly walk off with most
of the goods at a car-boot sale, but do not even seem surprised when the
items are re-stolen.

   Smalltime initially seems to be little more than a primitive, episodic one-
joke account of these failed scams. However, its greater interest lies in its
unexpected expansion into a social comedy of gender that hinges on exactly
the questions of masculinity, misogyny and crime that *Face* side-stepped. Its
central narrative impetus stems from the disparate aspirations of its male and
female characters but, in contrast with *Face*, this impetus is rooted in the frus-
trations and actions of Ruby and Kate more than those of their male
counterparts. Ruby initially seems little brighter than Jumbo, yet it becomes
apparent that her sexual rejection of him is a symptom of wider frustration
with his shortcomings. Jumbo's mimicry of the classic gangster 'family'
includes emulating its sexism and exclusion of women; but Ruby refuses to
accept this, resulting in strife and physical violence. Kate, a more aspirational
and 'middle-class' figure who is studying at college, is as strong-willed as Ruby

but more goal-directed. The narrative's central drive derives from Kate's attempts to, on the one hand, stem Jumbo's violence towards Ruby and, on the other, to persuade the weak Malc to resist Jumbo's influence and go straight. Conversely, Jumbo resents Kate's 'intrusion' into the all-male gang and sees her influence on Malc as malign.

At the structural level, then, *Smalltime* is about the power struggle between Jumbo and Kate – or between self-justificatory masculinist/criminal values and female respectability. What its narrative seeks to resolve is whose will will prevail. *Smalltime* is particularly interesting, in other words, because it explicitly plays out a gendered dynamic that is always present, but usually dormant, in the professional crime film. It seems especially apposite that it should do so in the 1990s, at a time when the gender dominance that working-class masculinity used to take for granted is increasingly insecure; but what makes the film exceptional is that it responds by exploring this insecurity rather than reacting against it. While Meadows makes as much fun of the women as he does of the men, they are shown to have a capacity to take action to change their lives that the self-deluded men lack. Ruby may be a battered woman, but her confident, self-contained sexuality and indifference to Jumbo make it clear that his violence towards her is an expression of impotence rather than power.

Smalltime's conclusion reverses the gendered logic of gangland and, in doing so, legitimates the 'feminine' sphere and brings gender relations in line with 1990s realities. Jumbo's perception of the 'intrusion' of women into the male 'space' of his gang as a threat is presented as clearly absurd. Rather, it is Jumbo's intrusions into Malc's relationship with Kate – exercising a non-existent male-bonding prerogative – that are shown to be embarrassing and dysfunctional. Fittingly, the film ends with Malc escaping with Kate, their kids and Jumbo's mentally disabled getaway driver to run a doughnut stall in Skegness, leaving Jumbo in the lurch on his last job (a fruitless raid on a charity shop), and leading to his arrest. Ruby, happy with her vibrator, doesn't notice.

Smalltime's focus on petty crime made it almost unique in 1990s British cinema. Yet, its depiction of criminal activity as undramatic and unimpressive surely had more in common with the everyday realities of much 1990s crime than did the glamorised dystopia of *Shopping* or the efficiently orchestrated armed heist of *Face*. Equally rare was its overt interest in crime as a gendered phenomenon and as a source of tension between women and men. Most curiously of all, *Smalltime* was one of very few 1990s British films dealing with crime to be fully rooted in 1990s conditions rather than remaining in one sense or another preoccupied with, or in thrall to, the 1980s. All three of these achievements necessitated a departure from the usual conventions of the professional crime film. In an apparent paradox, *Smalltime* – like Meadows' earlier short film, *Where's the Money, Ronnie?* (1995) – owed obvious debts to the gangland genre; yet, crucially, the relationship of both to its mythologies was entirely deflationary. By contrast, it seems telling that *Face*'s attempts to

work *within* the gangster rubric – with all its gendered and ritualistic implications – and in particular to incorporate credible 1990s female characters into
it, produced problems of unreality that the more generically hybrid 1990s
films discussed in this chapter had on the whole left behind.

Notes

1 Bird herself instigated the comparison, telling journalists: 'I quite consciously
 wanted to make a *Long Good Friday* for the '90s.' (Dessau, 1997: 21).
2 Pearson gives several examples of Ronnie Kray's perverse destruction of the profitability of clubs and casinos with which he became involved that support this
 reading (Pearson 1995, 117–20, 144–9, 156–62).
3 Alice Rawsthorn reported on a whole package of marketing strategies that were
 used to build pre-release awareness of *Face* among its 'target audience of students
 and under-25s' during the summer of 1997, including 'giving away 500,000
 promotional postcards at pop festivals, clubs and pop concerts' (Rawsthorn,
 'British filmmakers battle to avoid cult movie label', *Financial Times*, 22 September
 1997, p. 17).
4 For a further discussion of some of these problems, see the review of *Face* by
 Adam Mars-Jones, 'Let's face it, villains ain't wot they used to be', *Independent*, 'The
 Eye' section, 26 September 1997, p. 7.

Bibliography

Desjardins, M. (1993) 'Free from the apron strings: representations of mothers in the
 maternal British state', in L. Friedman (ed.) *British Cinema and Thatcherism*, London:
 University College Press, pp. 130–44.
Dessau, B. (1997) 'Antonia Bird: Tarantino meets "Goodfellas"', *Time Out*, 3–10
 September, p. 21.
Dyja, E. (ed.) (1997) *BFI Film and Television Handbook 1998*, London: British Film
 Institute.
Keeffe, B. (1995) 'Haunting Friday', *Sight and Sound*, August, pp. 20–1.
McCabe, B. (1997) 'East End *Heat*', *Sight and Sound*, October, pp. 10–12.
Pearson, J. (1995) *The Profession of Violence: The Rise and Fall of the Kray Twins*, 4th edn,
 London: HarperCollins.
Walsh, M. (1993) 'Allegories of Thatcherism: the films of Peter Greenaway', in L.
 Friedman (ed.) *British Cinema and Thatcherism*, London: University College Press,
 pp. 255–77.
Wollen, P. (1993) 'The last new wave: modernism in the British films of the Thatcher
 era', in L. Friedman (ed.) *British Cinema and Thatcherism*, London: University
 College Press, pp. 35–51.

Filmography, 1939–1997

Compiled by Andrew Clay and Steve Chibnall, assisted by Sumay Helas and Kevin Waite

The following is a chronological listing of British films featuring the activities of professional criminals as a significant element in a narrative which is

(a) set mainly within the period since 1939
(b) not primarily comedic in character
(c) more than 45 minutes in length

The filmography reflects the book's focus on representations of a British criminal underworld in which crime is motivated chiefly by the desire for money, and on this basis it excludes espionage thrillers and films about political terrorism. The concern with the ideas of Britishness and the underworld has led us to divide the films into primary and secondary classifications.

The primary filmography is composed of films in which underworld-based crime is a central activity and in which most of the narrative takes place in Britain, but also includes a few marginal texts that might be excluded on one or other of these criteria but which are discussed as crime films in the book.

The secondary filmography is composed of films in which crime is a more minor element, takes place abroad or is white collar in character.

Abbreviations
ABPC: Associated British Picture Corporation
B: book
BLPA: British Lion Production Assets
C: characters
(Col.) colour
N: novel
P: play
RS: radio serial
RSs: radio series
S: story
TVP: television play
TVS: television serial
TVSs: television series

Title (Year[1])	Director	Production company (Producer)	Screenwriter (Story)	Leading players	Crime interest
The Mind of Mr Reeder (USA *The Mysterious Mr Reeder*) (1939)	Jack Raymond	Jack Raymond (Charles Q. Steele)	Bryan Wallace, Marjorie Gaffney, Michael Hogan (N: Edgar Wallace)	Will Fyffe, John Warwick	Forgery
The Spider (1939)	Maurice Elvey	Admiral Wembley (Victor M. Greene)	Kenneth Horne, Reginald Long (N: Henry Holt)	Derrick de Marney, Diana Churchill	Jewel theft
There Ain't No Justice (1939)	Penrose Tennyson	Ealing (Sergei Nolbandov)	Penrose Tennyson, Sergei Nolbandov, James Curtis (N: James Curtis)	Jimmy Hanley, Edward Chapman	Boxing, racketeering
Too Dangerous to Live (1939)	Anthony Hankey, Leslie Norman	Warner Bros (Jerome Jackson)	Paul Gangelin, Connery Chappell, Leslie Arliss (N: David Hume)	Sebastian Shaw, Greta Gynt	Jewel theft
They Came By Night (1940)	Harry Lachman	Twentieth Century (Edward Black)	Frank Launder, Sidney Gilliat, Michael Hogan, Roland Pertwee (P: Barre Lyndon)	Will Fyffe, Phylis Calvert	Jewellery and bullion robbery
Two for Danger (1940)	George King	Warner Bros (A.M. Salomon)	Brock Williams, Basil Woon, Hugh Gray (Brock Williams)	Barry K. Barnes, Greta Gynt	Art theft

Title (Year[1])	Director	Production company (Producer)	Screenwriter (Story)	Leading players	Crime interest
The Flying Squad (1940)	Herbert Brenon	(ABPC) (Walter Mycroft)	Doreen Montgomery (N: Edgar Wallace)	Sebastian Shaw, Phyllis Brooks	Drug smuggling
Fingers (1940)	Herbert Mason	Warner Bros (A.M. Salomon)	(Brock Williams)	Clifford Evans, Leonora Corbett	Dealing in stolen property
Once a Crook (1941)	Herbert Mason	Twentieth Century (Edward Black)	Roger Burford (P. Evadne Price, Ken Attiwill)	Gordon Harker, Sydney Howard	Jewel robbery
The Saint Meets the Tiger (1941)	Paul Stein	RKO (William Sistrom)	Leslie Arliss, Wolfgang Wilhelm, James Seymour (N: Leslie Charteris *Meet the Tiger*)	Hugh Sinclair, Jean Gillie	Bullion robbery
The Missing Million (1942)	Phil Brandon	Signet (Hugh Perceval)	James Seymour (N: Edgar Wallace)	Linden Travers, John Warwick	Kidnapping
Suspected Person (1942)	Lawrence Huntington	ABPC (Warwick Ward)	(Lawrence Huntington)	Clifford Evans, Patricia Roc	Bank robbery
Late at Night (1946)	Michael Chorlton	Bruton Films (Herbert Wynne)	(Henry C. James)	Daphne Day, Barry Morse	Black marketeering
Appointment With Crime (1946)	John Harlow	British National (Louis H. Jackson)	(Michael Leighton, Vernon Sewell)	William Hartnell, Robert Beatty	Jewel robbery

Title (Year[1])	Director	Production company (Producer)	Screenwriter (Story)	Leading players	Crime interest
Send For Paul Temple (1946)	John Argyle	Butcher's (John Argyle)	Francis Durbridge, John Argyle (RS: Francis Durbridge)	Anthony Hulme, Joy Shelton	Jewel robbery
Dancing With Crime (1947)	John Paddy Carstairs	Coronet-Alliance (James A. Carter)	Brock Williams (Peter Fraser)	Richard Attenborough, Barry K. Barnes	Black marketeering
They Made Me A Fugitive (USA *I Became A Criminal*) (1947)	Cavalcanti	Gloria-Alliance (Nat Bronstein, James Carter)	Noel Langley (N: Jackson Budd *A Convict has Escaped*)	Sally Gray, Trevor Howard	Black marketeering and drug dealing
Black Memory (1947)	Oswald Mitchell	Bushey (Gilbert Church)	(John Gilling)	Michael Atkinson, Myra O'Connell	Robbery and black marketeering
It Always Rains On Sunday (1947)	Robert Hamer	Ealing (Henry Cornelius)	Robert Hamer, Henry Cornelius (N: Arthur la Bern)	Googie Withers, Jack Warner	Black marketeering
Brighton Rock (USA *Young Scarface*) (1947)	John Boulting	ABPC (Roy Boulting)	Grahame Greene, Terence Rattigan (N: Graham Greene)	Richard Attenborough, Hermione Baddeley	Protection racketeering
Night Beat (1948)	Harold Huth	BLPA (Harold Huth)	T.J. Morrison, Roland Pertwee, Robert Westerby (Guy Morgan)	Anne Crawford, Maxwell Reed	Black marketeering

Title (Year[1])	Director	Production company (Producer)	Screenwriter (Story)	Leading players	Crime interest
The Flamingo Affair (1948)	Horace Shepherd	Inspiration (Horace Shepherd)	(Maurice Moisiewitsch)	Denis Webb, Colette Melville	Robbery and black marketeering
River Patrol (1948)	Ben R. Hart	Knightsbridge (Hal Wilson)	(James Corbett)	John Blythe, Lorna Dean	Black marketeering
The Dark Road (1948)	Alfred Goulding	Marylebone (Henry Halstead)		Charles Stuart, Joyce Linden	Robbery
Escape (1948)	Joseph L. Mankiewicz	Twentieth Century (William Perlberg)	Phillip Dunne (John Galsworthy)	Rex Harrison, Peggy Cummins	Escaped convict
Good Time Girl (1948)	David Macdonald	Triton (Sydney Box, Samuel Goldwyn Jr)	Muriel Box, Sydney Box, Ted Willis (N: Arthur la Bern *Night Darkens the Street*)	Jean Kent, Dennis Price	Racketeering
No Orchids For Miss Blandish (1948)	St John L. Clowes	Tudor-Alliance (A.R. Shipman)	St John L. Clowes (N: James Hadley Chase)	Jack la Rue, Linden Travers	Kidnapping
A Gunman Has Escaped (1948)	Richard Grey	Condor Films (Harry Goodman, Richard Grey)	(John Gilling)	John Harvey, John Fitzgerald	Robbery
Noose (USA *The Silk Noose*) (1948)	Edmond T. Greville	Edward Dryhurst	Richard Llewellyn, Edward Dryhurst (P: Richard Llewellyn)	Carole Landis, Derek Farr	Black marketeering

Title (Year[1])	Director	Production company (Producer)	Screenwriter (Story)	Leading players	Crime interest
Held in Trust (1949)	Cecil H. Williamson	Productions No 1 (Cecil H. Williamson)	(Cecil H. Williamson)	Ian Proctor, Dorothy Shaw	Robbery
Man on the Run (1949)	Lawrence Huntington	ABPC (Lawrence Huntington)	(Lawrence Huntington)	Derek Farr, Joan Hopkins	Robbery and army desertion
Third Time Lucky (1949)	Gordon Parry	Kenilworth–Alliance (Mario Zampi)	Gerald Butler (N: Gerald Butler, *They Cracked Her Glass Slipper*)	Glynis Johns, Dermot Walsh	Illegal gambling
No Way Back (1949)	Stefan Osiecki	Concanen Recordings (Derrick de Marney)	Stefan Osiecki, Derrick de Marney (S: Thomas Burke, *Beryl and the Croucher*)	Terence de Marney, Eleanor Summerfield	Robbery and black marketeering
The Adventures of PC 49 – The Case of the Guardian Angel (1949)	Godfrey Grayson	Exclusive-Hammer (Anthony Hinds)	Alan Stranks, Vernon Harris (RS: Alan Stranks)	Hugh Latimer, Patricia Cutts	Lorry hijacking
Bait (1950)	Frank Richardson	Advance	Mary Bendetta, Francis Miller (P: Frank Richardson)	Diana Napier, John Bentley	Jewel theft
The Blue Lamp (1950)	Basil Dearden	Ealing (Michael Relph)	T.E.B. Clarke, Alexander Mackendrick (Jan Read, Ted Willis)	Jack Warner, Jimmy Hanley, Dirk Bogarde	Robbery

Title (Year[1])	Director	Production company (Producer)	Screenwriter (Story)	Leading players	Crime interest
Night and the City (1950)	Jules Dassin	Twentieth Century (Samuel G. Engel)	Jo Eisinger (N: Gerald Kersh)	Richard Widmark, Gene Tierney	Sports racketeering
Blackout (1950)	Robert S. Baker	Tempean (Robert S. Baker, Monty Berman)	(Robert S. Baker, John Gilling)	Maxwell Reed, Dinah Sheridan	Smuggling
Dangerous Assignment (1950)	Ben R. Hart	Target (Miriam Crowdy)	(Chuck Messina)	Lionel Murton, Pamela Deeming	Stolen car racketeering
The Second Mate (1951)	John Baxter	Elstree Independent (John Baxter)	Barbara K. Emary, Jack Francis (Anson Dyer)	Gordon Harker, Graham Moffatt	Jewel smuggling
The Dark Man (1951)	Jeffrey Dell	Independent Artists (Julian Wintle)	(Jeffrey Dell)	Edward Underdown, Maxwell Reed	Robbery, theft and black marketeering
Pool of London (1951)	Basil Dearden	Ealing (Michael Relph)	(Jack Whittingham, John Eldridge)	Bonar Colleano, Susan Shaw	Jewel robbery and smuggling
The Quiet Woman (1951)	John Gilling	Tempean (R. Baker, M. Berman)	John Gilling (Ruth Adam)	Derek Bond, Jane Hylton	Smuggling
Assassin For Hire (1951)	Michael McCarthy	Merton Park (Julian Wintle)	Rex Rienits (TVP: Rex Rienits)	Sydney Tafler, Ronald Howard	Professional killing
The Dark Light (1951)	Vernon Sewell	Hammer (Michael Carreras)	(Vernon Sewell)	Albert Lieven, David Greene	Bank robbery

Title (Year[1])	Director	Production company (Producer)	Screenwriter (Story)	Leading players	Crime interest
Scarlet Thread (1951)	Lewis Gilbert	Nettlefold-International Realist (Ernest G. Roy)	A.R. Rawlinson (P: A.R. Rawlinson, Moie Charles)	Kathleen Byron, Laurence Harvey	Jewel theft
Calling Bulldog Drummond (1951)	Victor Saville	MGM British (Hayes Goetz)	Gerard Fairlie, Howard Emmett Rogers, Arthur Wimperis (N: Gerard Fairlie)	Walter Pidgeon, Margaret Leighton	Robbery
Home to Danger (1951)	Terence Fisher	New World (Lance Comfort)	(John Temple-Smith, Francis Edge)	Guy Rolfe, Rona Anderson	Drug peddling
The Six Men (1951)	Michael Law	Planet Productions (Roger Proudlock)	Reed de Rouen, Michael Law, Richard Eastham (E. and M.A. Radford)	Harold Warrender, Reed de Rouen	Jewel robbery
Blind Man's Bluff (1952)	Charles Saunders	Present Day (Charles Reynolds)	(John Gilling)	Zena Marshall, Sydney Tafler	Robbery
Judgement Deferred (1952)	John Baxter	Group 3 (John Baxter, John Grierson)	Geoffrey Orme, Barbara K. Emary, (Herbert Ayres, *Doss House*)	Hugh Sinclair, Helen Shingler	Drug racketeering
The Frightened Man (1952)	John Gilling	Tempean (R. Baker, M. Berman)	(John Gilling)	Dermot Walsh, Barbara Murray	Theft

Title (Year[1])	Director	Production company (Producer)	Screenwriter (Story)	Leading players	Crime interest
Whispering Smith Hits London (USA *Whispering Smith Versus Scotland Yard*) (1952)	Francis Searle	Hammer-Lesser (Anthony Hinds, Julian Lesser)	John Gilling (Steve Fisher)	Richard Carlson, Greta Gynt	Blackmail, racketeering
13 East Street (1952)	Robert Baker	Tempean (R. Baker, M. Berman)	John Gilling (Robert Baker)	Patrick Holt, Sandra Dorne	Robbery
Wings of Danger (1952)	Terence Fisher	Hammer-Lippert (Anthony Hinds)	John Gilling (N: Elleston Trevor *Dead on Course*)	Zachary Scott, Robert Beatty	Counterfeit dollar smuggling
King of the Underworld (1952)	Victor M. Gover	Bushey (Gilbert Church)	(John Gilling)	Tod Slaughter, Patrick Barr	Blackmail and theft
My Death is a Mockery (1952)	Tony Young	Park Lane (David Dent)	(N: Douglas Baber)	Donald Houston, Kathleen Byron	Smuggling
The Gambler and the Lady (1952)	Pat Jenkins, Sam Newfield	Hammer (Anthony Hinds)		Dane Clark, Kathleen Byron	Gambling and protection racketeering
The Yellow Balloon (1952)	J. Lee-Thompson	Marble Arch (Victor Skutezky)	J. Lee-Thompson, Anne Burnaby (Anne Burnaby)	William Sylvester, Kenneth More	Robbery, blackmail
The Lost Hours (USA *The Big Frame*) (1952)	David Macdonald	Tempean (R. Baker, M. Berman)	John Gilling (Steve Fisher)	Mark Stevens, Jean Kent	Racketeering

Title (Year[1])	Director	Production company (Producer)	Screenwriter (Story)	Leading players	Crime interest
The Ringer (1952)	Guy Hamilton	London-BLPA (Hugh Perceval)	Val Valentine, Lesley Storm (P: Edgar Wallace)	Herbert Lom, Donald Wolfit	Master criminal
Murder at Scotland Yard (1952)	Victor M. Gover	Bushey (Gilbert Church)	(John Gilling)	Tod Slaughter, Patrick Barr	Robbery
Wide Boy (1952)	Ken Hughes	Merton Park (William H. Williams)	Rex Rienits	Sydney Tafler, Susan Shaw	Blackmail, black marketeering
The Long Memory (1953)	Robert Hamer	Europa (Hugh Stewart)	Robert Hamer, Frank Harvey (N: Howard Clewes)	John Mills, John McCallum	Perjury
The Broken Horseshoe (1953)	Martyn C. Webster	Nettlefold (Ernest G. Roy)	A.R. Rawlinson (TVS: Francis Durbridge)	Robert Beatty, Elizabeth Sellars	Drug racketeering
Turn the Key Softly (1953)	Jack Lee	Chiltern (Maurice Cowan)	John Brophy, Maurice Cowan (N: John Brophy)	Yvonne Mitchell, Terence Morgan	Burglary, shoplifting and prostitution
Recoil (1953)	John Gilling	Tempean (R. Baker, M. Berman)	(John Gilling)	Kieron Moore, Elizabeth Sellars	Jewel robbery
Blood Orange (1953)	Terence Fisher	Hammer (Michael Carreras)	(Jan Read)	Tom Conway, Mila Parely	Jewel robbery
The Saint's Return (USA *The Saint's Girl Friday*) (1953)	Seymour Friedman	Hammer (Julian Lesser, Anthony Hinds)	Allan Mackinnon (C: Leslie Charteris)	Louis Hayward, Sydney Tafler	Gambling, racketeering

Title (Year[1])	Director	Production company (Producer)	Screenwriter (Story)	Leading players	Crime interest
The Intruder (1953)	Guy Hamilton	Ivan Foxwell	Robin Maugham, John Hunter (N: Robin Maugham, *The Line on Ginger*)	Jack Hawkins, Michael Medwin	Burglary
Flannelfoot (1953)	Maclean Rogers	E.J. Fancey	Carl Heck (Jack Henry)	Ronald Howard, Mary Germaine	Jewel theft
Behind the Headlines (1953)	Maclean Rogers	E.J. Fancey	(Maclean Rogers)	Gilbert Harding, John Fitzgerald	Lorry theft
Park Plaza 605 (1953)	Bernard Knowles	B and A Productions (Bertram Ostrer, Albert Fennell)	Bernard Knowles, Albert Fennell, Bertram Ostrer, Clifford Witting (N: Berkeley Gray, *Daredevil Conquest*)	Tom Conway, Eva Bartok	Jewel smuggling
Three Steps to the Gallows (USA *White Fire*) (1953)	John Gilling	Tempean (R. Baker, M. Berman)	John Gilling (Paul Erickson)	Scott Brady, Mary Castle	Jewel smuggling
The Floating Dutchman (1953)	Vernon Sewell	Merton Park (W.H. Williams)	Vernon Sewell (N: Nicolas Bentley)	Dermot Walsh, Sydney Tafler	Jewel robbery
Stryker of the Yard (1953)	Arthur Crabtree	Republic (William N. Boyle)	Guy Morgan, Lester Powell	Clifford Evans, Jack Watling	Bank robbery and forgery

Title (Year[1])	Director	Production company (Producer)	Screenwriter (Story)	Leading players	Crime interest
Escape by Night (1954)	John Gilling	Tempean (R. Baker M. Berman)	(John Gilling)	Bonar Colleano, Andrew Ray, Sid James	Vice racketeering
Companions in Crime (1954)	John Krish	Republic (William N. Boyle)	Kenneth Hayles, Patricia Latham	Clifford Evans, George Woodbridge	Smuggling
River Beat (1954)	Guy Green	Insignia (Victor Hanbury)	(Rex Rienits)	Phyllis Kirk, John Bentley	Diamond smuggling
The Good Die Young (1954)	Lewis Gilbert	Remus (Jack Clayton)	Lewis Gilbert, Vernon Harris (N: Richard Macauley)	Laurence Harvey, Gloria Grahame, Richard Basehart	Robbery
The Diamond (USA *The Diamond Wizard*) (1954)	Montgomery Tully	Gibraltar (Steven Pallos)	John C. Higgins (N: Maurice Procter)	Dennis O'Keefe, Margaret Sheridan	Bullion robbery and synthetic diamond racketeering
Johnny on the Spot (1954)	Maclean Rogers	E.J. Fancey	Maclean Rogers (N: Michael Cronin)	Hugh McDermott, Elspeth Gray	Criminal gang
Dangerous Cargo (1954)	John Harlow	ACT Films (Stanley Haynes)	Stanley Haynes (S: Percy Hoskins)	Susan Stephen, Jack Watling	Bullion robbery
Forbidden Cargo (1954)	Harold French	London Independent (Sydney Box)	(Sydney Box)	Nigel Patrick, Elizabeth Sellars	Drug smuggling

Title (Year[1])	Director	Production company (Producer)	Screenwriter (Story)	Leading players	Crime interest
The Sleeping Tiger (1954)	Joseph Losey	Insignia (Victor Hanbury)	Carl Foreman (N: Maurice Moisiewitsch)	Dirk Bogarde, Alexis Smith	Robbery
Devil's Point (USA *Devil's Harbour*) (1954)	Montgomery Tully	Charles Deane	(Charles Deane)	Richard Arlen, Greta Gynt	Cortisone theft
Radio Cab Murder (1954)	Vernon Sewell	Insignia (George Maynard)	Vernon Sewell (Pat McGrath)	Jimmy Hanley, Lana Morris	Bank robbery
The Green Buddha (1954)	John Lemont	Republic Productions (William N. Boyle)	(Paul Erickson)	Wayne Morris, Mary Germaine	Jewel theft
The Passing Stranger (1954)	John Arnold	Harlequin (Anthony Simmons, Leon Clore, Ian Gibson–Smith)	Anthony Simmons, John Arnold (Anthony Simmons)	Lee Patterson, Diane Cilento	Robbery and gun running
The Delavine Affair (1954)	Douglas Pierce	Croydon-Passmore (John Croydon, Henry Passmore)	George Fisher (N: Robert Chapman, *Winter Wears a Shroud*)	Peter Reynolds, Honor Blackman	Jewel robbery
The Brain Machine (1955)	Ken Hughes	Merton Park (Alec Snowden)	(Ken Hughes)	Patrick Barr, Elizabeth Allen	Cortisone theft
Track the Man Down (1955)	R.G. Springsteen	Republic Productions (William N. Boyle)	(Paul Erickson, Kenneth R. Hayles)	Kent Taylor, Petula Clark	Robbery

Title (Year[1])	Director	Production company (Producer)	Screenwriter (Story)	Leading players	Crime interest
Impulse (1955)	Charles de la Tour, Cy Endfield	Tempean (R. Baker M. Berman)	Lawrence Huntington, 'Jonathan Roach' (Carl Nystrom, R. Baker)	Arthur Kennedy, Constance Smith	Jewel theft
The Gilded Cage (1955)	John Gilling	Tempean (R. Baker M. Berman)	Brock Williams (Paul Erickson)	Alex Nicol, Veronica Hurst	Art smuggling
Tiger by the Tail (USA *Crossup*) (1955)	John Gilling	Tempean (R. Baker M. Berman)	Willis Goldbeck, John Gilling (N: John Mair *Never Come Back*)	Larry Parks, Constance Smith	Counterfeiting
Police Dog (1955)	Derek Twist	Westridge Fairbanks (Harold Huth)	(Derek Twist)	Joan Rice, Tim Turner	Robbery
The Ship That Died of Shame (1955)	Basil Dearden	Ealing (Michael Relph)	Michael Relph, Basil Dearden, John Whiting (S: Nicholas Monsarrat)	Richard Attenborough, George Baker	Smuggling
Confession (1955)	Ken Hughes	Anglo-Guild (Alec Snowden)	Ken Hughes (P: Don Martin)	Sydney Chaplin, Audrey Dalton	Theft
The Secret (1955) (col.)	C. Raker Endfield	Laureate-Golden Era (S. Benjamin Fisz)	C. Raker Endfield (P: Robert Brenon)	Sam Wanamaker, Mandy Miller	Jewel theft
Cross Channel (1955)	R.G. Springsteen	Republic Productions (William N. Boyle)	(Rex Rienits)	Wayne Morris, Yvonne Furneaux	Jewel smuggling

Title (Year[1])	Director	Production company (Producer)	Screenwriter (Story)	Leading players	Crime interest
The Gold Express (1955)	Guy Fergusson	Gaumont (Frank Wells)	(Jackson Budd)	Vernon Gray, Ann Walford	Gold robbery
One Way Out (1955)	Francis Searle	Major (John Temple-Smith, Francis Edge)	Jonathan Roche (J. Temple-Smith, Jean Scott-Rogers)	Jill Adams, Eddie Byrne	Jewel theft and blackmail
Joe Macbeth (1955)	Ken Hughes	Film Locations (M.J. Frankovich, George Maynard)	Philip Jordan (P: William Shakespeare *Macbeth*)	Paul Douglas, Ruth Roman	Racketeering
Portrait of Alison (USA *Postmark for Danger*) (1955)	Guy Green	Insignia (Frank Godwin)	Guy Green, Ken Hughes (TVS: Francis Durbridge)	Robert Beatty, Terry Moore	Jewel smuggling
Dial 999 (USA *The Way Out*) (1955)	Montgomery Tully	Merton Park (Alec Snowden)	Montgomery Tully (N: Bruce Graeme *The Way Out*)	Gene Nelson, Mona Freeman	Aiding and abetting
Assignment Redhead (1956)	Maclean Rogers	Butchers W.G. Chalmers	Maclean Rogers	Richard Denning, Carole Matthews, Ronald Adam	Counterfeit money, International criminal
Johnny, You're Wanted (1956)	Vernon Sewell	Anglo-Amalgamated (George Maynard)	Michael Leighton, Frank Driscoll (TVSs: Maurice McLoughlin)	John Slater, Alfred Marks	Drug smuggling

Title (Year[1])	Director	Production company (Producer)	Screenwriter (Story)	Leading players	Crime interest
The Gelignite Gang (1956)	Terence Fisher	Cybex (Geoffrey Goodheart)	(Brandon Fleming)	Wayne Morris, James Kenney	Robbery
Soho Incident (USA *Spin a Dark Web*) (1956)	Vernon Sewell	Film Locations (M.J. Frankovitch, George Maynard)	Ian Stuart Black (N: Robert Westerby *Wide Boys Never Work*)	Faith Domergue, Lee Patterson	Gambling racketeering
The Long Arm (USA *The Third Key*) (1956)	Charles Frend	Ealing (Tom Morahan)	Janet Green, Robert Barr, Dorothy and Campbell Christie	Jack Hawkins, Richard Leech	Theft
Eyewitness (1956)	Muriel Box	Rank (Sydney Box)	Janet Green	Donald Sinden, Nigel Stock	Robbery
Find the Lady (1956)	Charles Saunders	Major (J. Temple-Smith, Francis Edge)	Kenneth R. Hayles	Beverly Brooks, Donald Houston	Bank robbery
House of Secrets (1956)	Guy Green	Rank (Julian Wintle, Vivian A. Cox)	Robert Buckner, Bryan Forbes (N: Sterling Joel)	Michael Craig, Brenda de Banzie	Counterfeiting
They Never Learn (1956)	Denis Kavanagh	Edwin J. Fancey (E.J. Fancey)	Denis Kavanagh, E.J. Fancey	Adrienne Scott, Jackie Collins	Forgery
Tiger in the Smoke (1956)	Roy Baker	Rank (Leslie Parkyn)	Anthony Pelissier (N: Margery Allingham)	Tony Wright, Muriel Pavlow	Hidden loot

Title (Year[1])	Director	Production company (Producer)	Screenwriter (Story)	Leading players	Crime interest
The Hideout (1956)	Peter Graham Scott	Major (J. Temple-Smith, Francis Edge)	Kenneth R. Hayles	Dermot Walsh, Ronald Howard	Theft
Yield to the Night (1956)	J. Lee Thompson	ABPC (Kenneth Harper)	Joan Henry, John Cresswell (N: Joan Henry)	Diana Dors, Yvonne Mitchell, Michael Craig	Crime passionelle
The Counterfeit Plan (1957)	Montgomery Tully	Merton Park (Alec Snowden)	(James Eastwood)	Zachary Scott, Reggie Castle	Counterfeiting
No Road Back (1957)	Montgomery Tully	Gibraltar (Steven Pallos, Charles Leeds)	Charles Leeds, Montgomery Tully (P: Falkland Cary, Philip Weathers)	Skip Homier, Paul Carpenter	Robbery
The Secret Place (1957)	Clive Donner	Rank (John Bryan, Anthony Perry)	(Linette Perry)	Belinda Lee, Ronald Lewis	Jewel theft
Booby Trap (1957)	Henry Cass	Jaywell (Bill Luckwell, Derek Winn	Peter Bryan, Bill Luckwell (Peter Bryan)	Sydney Tafler, Patti Morgan	Drug dealing
The Crooked Sky (1957)	Henry Cass	Luckwin (Bill Luckwell, Derek Winn)	Norman Hudis (Lance Z. Hargreaves, Maclean Rogers)	Wayne Morris, Karin Booth	Counterfeiting
Kill Me Tomorrow (1957)	Terence Fisher	Delta (Francis Searle)	Robert Falconer, Manning O'Brine	Pat O'Brien, Lois Maxwell	Diamond smuggling

Title (Year[1])	Director	Production company (Producer)	Screenwriter (Story)	Leading players	Crime interest
The Key Man (1957)	Montgomery Tully	Insignia (Alex Snowden)	J. McLaren Ross (P: J. McLaren Ross)	Lee Patterson, Hy Hazell	Robbery
Date With Disaster (USA *Thunder Over Tangier*) (1957)	Charles Saunders	Fortress (Guido Coen)	(Brock Williams)	Tom Drake, William Hartnell	Theft
Man From Tangier (1957)	Lance Comfort	Butcher's (W.G. Chalmers)	(Manning O'Brine)	Robert Hutton, Lisa Gastoni	Forgery
Hell Drivers (1957)	C. Raker Endfield	Rank-Aqua (B.S. Fisz)	C. Raker Endfield, John Kruse (S: John Kruse)	Stanley Baker, Herbert Lom	Racketeering
The Heart Within (1957)	David Eady	Pennington-Eady (Jon Pennington)	Geoffrey Orme (John Baxter)	James Hayter, Earl Cameron	Drug dealing
The Flesh is Weak (1957)	Don Chaffey	Raystro (Raymond Stross)	(Leigh Vance)	John Derek, Milly Vitale	Prostitution, racketeering
The Long Haul (1957)	Ken Hughes	Marksman (Maxwell Sutton)	Ken Hughes (N: Mervyn Mills)	Victor Mature, Diana Dors	Fur smuggling
The Flying Scot (USA *Mailbag Robbery*) (1957)	Compton Bennett	Insignia (Compton Bennett)	Norman Hudis (Ralph Smart, Jan Read)	Lee Patterson, Kay Callard	Robbery
Morning Call (1957)	Arthur Crabtree	Winwell (Bill Luckwell, Derek Winn)	(Leo Townsend)	Ron Randell, Greta Gynt	Kidnapping

Title (Year[1])	Director	Production company (Producer)	Screenwriter (Story)	Leading players	Crime interest
Death Over My Shoulder (1958)	Arthur Crabtree	Vicar (Frank Bevis)	Norman Hudis (Alyce Canfield)	Keefe Brasselle, Bonar Colleano	Insurance fraud and hired killing
Undercover Girl (1958)	Francis Searle	Bill and Michael Luckwell (Kay Luckwell, Derek Winn)	Bernard Lewis, Bill Luckwell (Bernard Lewis)	Paul Carpenter, Kay Callard	Blackmail and drug dealing
On the Run (1958)	Ernest Morris	Danziger (E & H. Danziger)	(Brian Clemens, Eldon Howard)	Neil McCallum, Susan Beaumont)	Boxing racketeering
Gideon's Day (USA *Gideon of Scotland Yard*) (1958) (Col.)	John Ford	Columbia British (Michael Killanin)	T.E.B. Clarke (N: J.J. Maric (John Creasey))	Jack Hawkins, Dianne Foster	Racketeering and police corruption
Blind Spot (1958)	Peter Maxwell	Butcher's (R. Baker M. Berman)	Kenneth R. Hayles (R. Baker, John Gilling)	Robert Mackenzie, Delphi Lawrence	Gem smuggling
Man With a Gun (1958)	Montgomery Tully	Merton Park (J. Greenwood)	(Michael Winner)	Lee Patterson, Rona Anderson	Protection racketeering
Tread Softly Stranger (1958)	Gordon Parry	Alderdale (Denis O'Dell)	George Minter, Denis O'Dell (P: Jack Popplewell *Blind Alley*)	Diana Dors, George Baker	Embezzlement and robbery

Title (Year[1])	Director	Production company (Producer)	Screenwriter (Story)	Leading players	Crime interest
Three Crooked Men (1958)	Ernest Morris	Danziger (E. & H. Danziger)	(Brian Clemens, Eldon Howard)	Gordon Jackson, Sarah Lawson	Bank robbery
The Bank Raiders (1958)	Maxwell Munden	Film Workshop (Geoffrey Goodhart)	(Brandon Fleming)	Peter Reynolds, Sandra Dorne	Bank robbery
Nowhere to Go (1958)	Seth Holt	Ealing (Eric Williams)	Seth Holt, Kenneth Tynan (N: Donald Mackenzie)	George Nader, Maggie Smith	Theft
The Great Van Robbery (1959)	Max Varnel	Danziger (E. & H. Danziger)	(Brian Clemens, Eldon Howard)	Denis Shaw, Kay Callard	Robbery
Passport to Shame (USA Room 43) (1959)	Alvin Rakoff	United Co-Productions (John Clein)	(Patrick Alexander)	Odile Versois, Diana Dors	Prostitution racketeering
Robbery With Violence (1959)	George Ivan Barnett	GIB Films (George Ivan Barnett)	David Cumming (Edith M. Barnett)	Ivan Craig, Sally Day	Bank robbery
No Safety Ahead (1959)	Max Varnel	Danziger (E. and H. Danziger)	(Robert Hurst)	James Kenney, Susan Beaumont	Bank robbery
High Jump (1959)	Godfrey Grayson	Danziger (E. and H. Danziger)	(Brian Clemens, Eldon Howard)	Richard Wyler, Lisa Daniely	Jewel robbery

Title (Year[1])	Director	Production company (Producer)	Screenwriter (Story)	Leading players	Crime interest
Model For Murder (1959)	Terry Bishop	Parroch (C: Jack Parsons, Robert Dunbar)	Terry Bishop, Robert Dunbar (Peter Fraser)	Keith Andes, Hazel Court	Gem smuggling
Wrong Number (1959)	Vernon Sewell	Merton Park (J. Greenwood)	James Eastwood (P: Norman Edwards)	Peter Reynolds, Lisa Gastoni	Mail van robbery
Man Accused (1959)	Montgomery Tully	Danziger (E. H. Danziger)	(Mark Grantham)	Ronald Howard, Carol Marsh	Jewel theft
Naked Fury (1959)	Charles Saunders	Coenda (Guido Coen)	Brock Williams (Guido Coen)	Reed de Rouen, Kenneth Cope	Robbery
The Desperate Man (1959)	Peter Maxwell	Merton Park (J. Greenwood)	James Eastwood (N: Paul Somers *Beginner's Luck*)	Jill Ireland, Conrad Phillips	Jewel theft
The Price of Silence (1960)	Montgomery Tully	Eternal (Maurice J. Wilson)	Maurice J. Wilson (N: Laurence Meynall *One Step From Murder*)	Gordon Jackson, June Thorburn	Blackmail
The Shakedown (1960)	John Lemont	Ethiro (Norman Williams)	(John Lemont, Leigh Vance)	Terence Morgan, Hazel Court)	Pornography and blackmail
Moment of Danger (USA *Malaga*) (1960)	Laslo Benedek	Cavalcade (Thomas Clyde)	David Osborn, Donald Ogden Stewart (N: Donald MacKenzie)	Trevor Howard, Dorothy Dandridge	Jewel theft

Title (Year[1])	Director	Production company (Producer)	Screenwriter (Story)	Leading players	Crime interest
Hell is a City (1960)	Val Guest	Hammer (Michael Carreras)	Val Guest (N: Maurice Proctor)	Stanley Baker, John Crawford	Robbery and illegal gambling
The Challenge (1960)	John Gilling	Alexandra (J. Temple-Smith)	(John Gilling)	Jayne Mansfield, Anthony Quayle	Bullion robbery
Jackpot (1960)	Montgomery Tully	Eternal (Maurice J. Wilson)	Maurice J. Wilson, Montgomery Tully (John Sherman)	William Hartnell, Betty McDowell	Robbery
The League of Gentlemen (1960)	Basil Dearden	Allied Film Makers (Michael Relph)	Bryan Forbes (N: John Boland)	Jack Hawkins, Nigel Patrick	Bank robbery
The Professionals (1960)	Don Sharp	Independent Artists (Norman Priggen)	(Peter Barnes)	William Lucas, Andrew Faulds	Bank robbery
Never Let Go (1960)	John Guillermin	Independent Artists (Peter de Savigny)	Alun Falconer (John Guillermin, Peter de Savigny)	Richard Todd, Peter Sellars	Stolen-car racketeering
Dead Lucky (1960)	Montgomery Tully	ACT Films (Ralph Bond, Robert Dunbar)	(Sidney Nelson, Maurice Harrison)	Vincent Ball, Betty McDowall	Gambling, racketeering

Title (Year[1])	Director	Production company (Producer)	Screenwriter (Story)	Leading players	Crime interest
The Man Who Couldn't Walk (1960)	Henry Cass	B. & M. Luckwell (Jock Macgregor, Umesh Mallik)	(Umesh Mallik)	Peter Reynolds, Eric Pohlmann	Jewel theft
Piccadilly Third Stop (1960)	Wolf Rilla	Ethiro (Norman Williams)	(Leigh Vance)	Terence Morgan, Yoko Tani	Robbery
The Criminal (USA *The Concrete Jungle*) (1960)	Joseph Losey	Merton Park (J. Greenwood)	Alun Owen (Jimmy Sangster)	Stanley Baker, Margit Saad	Robbery
Too Hot to Handle (USA *Playgirl After Dark*) (1960) (Col.)	Terence Young	Wigmore (Selim Caltan, Ronald Rietti)	Herbert Kretzmer (Harry Lee)	Jayne Mansfield, Leo Genn	Vice racketeering
Crossroads to Crime (1960)	Gerry Anderson	AP Films (Gerry Anderson, John Read)	(Alun Falconer)	Anthony Oliver, Patricia Heneghan	Lorry hijacking
The Unstoppable Man (1960)	Terry Bishop	Argo (Jack Lamont, John Pellatt)	Alun Falconer, P. Manning O'Brine, Terry Bishop (N. Michael Gilbert *Amateur in Violence*)	Cameron Mitchell, Harry H. Corbett	Kidnapping
The Gentle Trap (1960)	Charles Saunders	Butcher's (Jack Parsons)	Brock Williams, Alan Osborne (Guido Coen)	Spencer Teakle, Felicity Young	Jewel theft

Title (Year[1])	Director	Production company (Producer)	Screenwriter (Story)	Leading players	Crime interest
Marriage of Convenience (1960)	Clive Donner	Merton Park (J. Greenwood)	Robert Stewart (N: Edgar Wallace, *The Three Oak Mystery*)	John Cairney, Harry H. Corbett	Escaped convict
The Man Who Was Nobody (1960)	Montgomery Tully	Merton Park (J. Greenwood)	James Eastwood (N: Edgar Wallace)	Hazel Court, John Crawford	Diamond smuggling
Feet of Clay (1960)	Frank Marshall	Danziger (Brian Taylor)	(Mark Grantham)	Vincent Ball, Wendy Williams	Drug racketeering
Compelled (1960)	Ramsey Harrington	Danziger (Brian Taylor)	(Mark Grantham)	Ronald Howard, Beth Rogan	Jewel robbery
Echo of Barbara (1961)	Sidney Hayers	Independent Artists (Arthur Alcott)	John Kruse (N: Jonathan Burke)	Mervyn Johns, Maureen Connell	Racketeering
Offbeat (1961)	Cliff Owen	Northiam (E.M. Smedley Aston)	(Peter Barnes)	William Sylvester, Mai Zetterling	Robbery
Rag Doll (1961)	Lance Comfort	Blakeley's Films (Tom Blakeley)	Brock Williams, Derry Quinn (Brock Williams)	Jess Conrad, Hermione Baddeley	Burglary
Payroll (1961)	Sidney Hayers	Lynx-Independent Artists (Norman Priggen)	George Baxt (N: Derek Bickerton)	Michael Craig, Francoise Prevost	Robbery

Title (Year[1])	Director	Production company (Producer)	Screenwriter (Story)	Leading players	Crime interest
The Fourth Square (1961)	Allan Davis	Merton Park (J. Greenwood)	James Eastwood (N: Edgar Wallace *Four Square Jane*)	Conrad Phillips, Natasha Parry	Jewel theft
The Man in the Back Seat (1961)	Vernon Sewell	Independent Artists (Julian Wintle, Leslie Parkyn)	(Malcolm Hulke, Eric Paice)	Derren Nesbitt, Keith Faulkner	Robbery
The Frightened City (1961)	John Lemont	Zodiac (John Lemont, Leigh Vance)	Leigh Vance (John Lemont, Leigh Vance)	Herbert Lom, John Gregson	Protection
Man at the Carlton Tower (1961)	Robert Tronson	Merton Park (J. Greenwood)	Philip Mackie (N: Edgar Wallace, *The Man at the Carlton*)	Maxine Audley, Lee Montague	Jewel robbery
Information Received (1961)	Robert Lynn	United Co-Production (John Clein, George Maynard)	Paul Ryder (Berkeley Mather)	Sabina Sesselman, William Sylvester	Robbery
Jungle Street (1961)	Charles Saunders	Theatrecraft (Guido Coen)	Alexander Dore (Guido Coen)	David McCallum, Kenneth Cope	Robbery
Pit of Darkness (1961)	Lance Comfort	Butcher's (Lance Comfort)	Lance Comfort (N: Hugh McCutcheon *To Dusty Death*)	William Franklyn, Moira Redmond	Jewel robbery
Man Detained (1961)	Robert Tronson	Merton Park (J. Greenwood)	Richard Harris (N: Edgar Wallace *A Debt Discharged*)	Bernard Archard, Elvi Hale	Burglary and counterfeiting

Title (Year[1])	Director	Production company (Producer)	Screenwriter (Story)	Leading players	Crime interest
Enter Inspector Duval (1961)	Max Varnel	Bill and Michael Luckwell (Bill Luckwell, Jock MacGregor)	J. Henry Piperno (Jacques Monteux)	Anton Diffring, Diane Hart	Jewel theft
Never Back Losers (1961)	Robert Tronson	Merton Park (J. Greenwood)	Lukas Heller (N: Edgar Wallace *The Green Ribbon*)	Jack Hedley, Jacqueline Ellis	Gambling racketeering
Cash on Demand (1961)	Quentin Lawrence	Hammer-Woodpecker (Michael Carreras)	David T. Chantler, Lewis Greifer (TVP: Jacques Gillies *The Gold Inside*)	Peter Cushing, Andre Morell	Robbery
Bomb in the High Street (1961)	Terence Bishop, Peter Bezencenet	Foxwarren-Elthea (Ethel Linder Reiner, T.B.R. Zichy, Henry Passmore)	(Benjamin Simcoe)	Ronald Howard, Terry Palmer	Bank robbery
Freedom to Die (1962)	Francis Searle	Bayford (Charles A. Leeds)	(Arthur la Bern)	Paul Maxwell, Felicity Young	Robbery
Crosstrap (1962)	Robert Hartford-Davis	Newbery Clyne Avon (Michael Deeley, George Mills)	Philip Wrestler (N: John Newton Chance)	Laurence Payne, Jill Adams	Jewel theft

Title (Year[1])	Director	Production company (Producer)	Screenwriter (Story)	Leading players	Crime interest
The Devil's Daffodil (Britain/West Germany, 1962)	Akos Rathany	Omnia-Rialto (Steven Pallos, Donald Taylor)	Donald Taylor, Basil Dawson (N: Edgar Wallace *The Daffodil Mystery*)	Christopher Lee, Marius Goring	Drug smuggling
Ambush in Leopard Street (1962)	J. Henry Piperno	B. & M. Luckwell (Bill Luckwell, Jock MacGregor)	Bernard Spicer, Ahmed Faroughty (Bernard Spicer)	James Kenney, Michael Brennan	Robbery
A Prize of Arms (1962)	Cliff Owen	Inter-State (George Maynard)	Paul Ryder (Nicholas Roeg, Kevin Kavanagh)	Stanley Baker, Helmut Schmidt	Payroll robbery
The Share Out (1962)	Gerard Glaister	Merton Park (J. Greenwood)	Philip Mackie (N: Edgar Wallace *Jack O' Judgement*)	Bernard Lee, Alexander Knox	Blackmail, racketeering
The Break (1962)	Lance Comfort	Blakeley's Films (Tom Blakeley)	(Pip and Jane Baker)	Tony Britton, William Lucas	Smuggling
The Painted Smile (1962)	Lance Comfort	Blakeley's Films- Doverton (Tom Blakeley)	Jane Baker, Pip Baker (Brock Williams)	Liz Fraser, Kenneth Griffith	Prostitution, racketeering
Number Six (1962)	Robert Tronson	Merton Park (J. Greenwood)	Philip Mackie (N: Edgar Wallace)	Ivan Desny, Nadja Regin	Robbery
Gaolbreak (1962)	Francis Searle	Butcher's (Francis Searle, Ronald Liles)	(A.R. Rawlinson)	Peter Reynolds, Avice Landone	Theft

Title (Year[1])	Director	Production company (Producer)	Screenwriter (Story)	Leading players	Crime interest
Strongroom (1962)	Vernon Sewell	Theatrecraft (Guido Coen)	Richard Harris, Max Marquis (Richard Harris)	Derren Nesbitt, Colin Gordon	Bank robbery
Night Without Pity (1962)	Theodore Zichy	Parroch (Jack Parsons)	(Aubrey Cash)	Sarah Lawson, Neil McCallum	Robbery
Gang War (1962)	Frank Marshall	Danziger (Brian Langslow)	(Mark Grantham)	Sean Kelly, Eira Heath	Jukebox racketeering
Time to Remember (1962)	Charles Jarrett	Merton Park (J. Greenwood)	Arthur la Bern (N: Edgar Wallace *The Man Who Bought London*)	Yvonne Monlaur, Harry H. Corbett	Jewel theft
Danger By My Side (1962)	Charles Saunders	Butcher's (John I. Phillips)	(Ronald C Liles, Aubrey Cash)	Anthony Oliver, Maureen Connell	Robbery
Tomorrow At Ten (1962)	Lance Comfort	Blakeley's Films (Tom Blakeley)	(Peter Millar, James Kelly)	John Gregson, Robert Shaw	Kidnapping
A Guy Called Caesar (1962)	Frank Marshall	B. & M. Luckwelll (Bill Luckwell, Umesh Mallik)	Umesh Mallik, Tom Burdon (Umesh Mallik)	Conrad Phillips, George Moon	Jewel theft
The Primitives (1962)	Alfred Travers	Border (O Negus–Fancey)	(Alfred Travers, Moris Farhi)	Jan Holden, Bill Edwards	Jewel robbery

Title (Year[1])	Director	Production company (Producer)	Screenwriter (Story)	Leading players	Crime interest
Kill (1962)	Arnold Louis Miller	Searchlight (Stanley Long, Arnold Miller)	(Bob Kesten)	Ronald Howard, Jess Conrad	Fraud and theft
Touch of Death (1962)	Lance Comfort	Helion (Lewis Linzee)	Lyn Fairhurst (Aubrey Cash, Wilfred Josephs)	William Lucas, David Sumner	Robbery
The Small World of Sammy Lee (1963)	Ken Hughes	Elgin (Ken Hughes, Frank Godwin)	Ken Hughes (TVP: Ken Hughes *Sammy*)	Anthony Newley, Robert Stephens	Low-life milieu
The Set-Up (1963)	Gerard Glaister	Merton Park (J. Greenwood)	Roger Marshall (S: Edgar Wallace)	Maurice Denham, John Carson	Jewel robbery
Incident at Midnight (1963)	Norman Harrison	Merton Park (J. Greenwood)	Arthur la Bern (S: Edgar Wallace)	Anton Diffring, William Sylvester	Drug dealing
Calculated Risk (1963)	Norman Harrison	McLeod (William McLeod)	(Edwin Richfield)	William Lucas, John Rutland	Bank robbery
Impact (1963)	Peter Maxwell	Butcher's (John I. Phillips)	(Peter Maxwell, Conrad Phillips)	Conrad Phillips, George Pastell	Robbery and diamond smuggling
On the Run (1963)	Robert Tronson	Merton Park (J. Greenwood)	Richard Harris (S: Edgar Wallace)	Emrys Jones, Sarah Lawson	Hidden loot
The Switch (1963)	Peter Maxwell	Philip Ridgeway (Philip Ridgeway, Lance Comfort)	Philip Ridgeway, Colin Fraser (Philip Ridgeway)	Anthony Steel, Zena Marshall	Watch smuggling

Title (Year[1])	Director	Production company (Producer)	Screenwriter (Story)	Leading players	Crime interest
The Rivals (1963)	Max Varnel	Merton Park (J. Greenwood)	John Roddick (N: Edgar Wallace *Elegant Edward*)	Jack Gwillim, Erica Rogers	Car theft and kidnapping
The Marked One (1963)	Francis Searle	Planet (Tom Blakeley)	(Paul Erickson)	William Lucas, Zena Walker	Counterfeiting
Girl in the Headlines (1963)	Michael Truman	Viewfinder (John Davis)	Vivienne Knight, Patrick Campbell (N: Laurence Payne *The Nose on My Face*)	Ian Hendry, Ronald Fraser	Drug racketeering
A Place to Go (1963)	Basil Dearden	Excalibur (Michael Relph)	Michael Relph, Clive Exton (N: Michael Fisher *Bethnal Green*)	Rita Tushingham, Mike Sarne	Robbery
The Informers (1963)	Ken Annakin	Rank (William MacQuitty)	Alun Falconer, Paul Durst (N: Douglas Warner *Death of a Snout*)	Nigel Patrick, Margaret Whiting	Bank robbery and police informants
Panic (1963)	John Gilling	Ingram (Guido Coen)	John Gilling (Guido Coen, John Gilling)	Janine Gray, Glyn Houston	Robbery
Five to One (1963)	Gordon Flemying	Merton Park (J. Greenwood)	Roger Marshall (S: Edgar Wallace, *Thief in the Night*)	Lee Montague, Ingrid Hafner	Robbery
The Hi-Jackers (1963)	Jim O'Connolly	Butcher's (John I. Phillips)	(Jim O'Connolly)	Anthony Booth, Jacqueline Ellis	Lorry hijacking

Title (Year[1])	Director	Production company (Producer)	Screenwriter (Story)	Leading players	Crime interest
Clash By Night (USA *Escape By Night*) (1963)	Montgomery Tully	Eternal (Maurice J. Wilson)	Maurice J. Wilson, Montgomery Tully (N: Rupert Croft-Cooke)	Terence Longdon, Jennifer Jayne	Prison escape
Act of Murder (1964)	Alan Bridges	Merton Park (J. Greenwood)	(Lewis Davidson)	John Carson, Anthony Bate	Confidence tricking
Face of a Stranger (1964)	John Moxey	Merton Park (J. Greenwood)	John Sansom (N: Edgar Wallace)	Jeremy Kemp, Bernard Archard	Hidden loot
The Main Chance (1964)	John Knight	Merton Park (J. Greenwood)	Richard Harris (N: Edgar Wallace)	Gregoire Aslan, Edward de Souza	Jewel theft
Traitor's Gate (1964)	Freddie Francis	Summit (Ted Lloyd)	John Sansom (N: Edgar Wallace)	Albert Lieven, Gary Raymond	Robbery of Crown Jewels
Bunny Lake is Missing (1965)	Otto Preminger	Wheel (Otto Preminger)	John Mortimer, Penelope Mortimer (N: Evelyn Piper)	Laurence Olivier, Carol Lynley	Kidnapping
He Who Rides a Tiger (1965)	Charles Crichton	David Newman (David Newman)	(Trevor Peacock)	Tom Bell, Judi Dench	Burglary
Kaleidoscope (1966) (Col.)	Jack Smight	Winkast (Elliott Kastner, Jerry Gershwin)	(Robert and Jane Howard-Carrington)	Warren Beatty, Susannah York	Gambling and racketeering

Title (Year[1])	Director	Production company (Producer)	Screenwriter (Story)	Leading players	Crime interest
The Trygon Factor (1967) (Col.)	Cyril Frankel	Rialto-Preben Phillipsen (Ian Warren, Brian Taylor)	(Derry Quinn, Stanley Munro)	Stewart Granger, Susan Hampshire	Robbery and smuggling
Robbery (1967) (Col.)	Peter Yates	Oakhurst (Michael Deeley, Stanley Baker)	(Peter Yates, Edward Boyd, George Markstein)	Stanley Baker, James Booth	Mail train robbery
The Strange Affair (1968) (Col.)	David Greene	Paramount (Howard Harrison, Stanley Mann)	Stanley Mann (N: Bernard Toms)	Michael York, Jeremy Kemp	Drug dealing and police corruption
Strip Poker (USA *The Big Switch*) (1968) (Col.)	Pete Walker	Pete Walker	(Pete Walker)	Sebastian Breaks, Virginia Weatherall	Racketeering
Only When I Larf (1968) (Col.)	Basil Dearden	Beecord (Len Deighton, Brian Duffy)	John Salmon (N: Len Deighton)	Richard Atten- borough, David Hemmings	Confidence tricking
The File of the Golden Goose (1968) (Col.)	Sam Wanamaker	Theme- Caralan- Dador (David E. Rose)	John C. Higgins, James B. Gordon (John C. Higgins)	Yul Brynner, Charles Gray	Counterfeiting
The Italian Job (1969) (Col.)	Peter Collinson	Oakhurst- Paramount (Michael Deeley)	(Troy Kennedy Martin)	Michael Caine, Noel Coward	Robbery, Italy
Man of Violence (1970) (Col.)	Peter Walker	Peter Walker (Peter Walker)	(Peter Walker, Brian Comport)	Michael Latimer, Luan Peters	Gold smuggling

Title (Year[1])	Director	Production company (Producer)	Screenwriter (Story)	Leading players	Crime interest
Perfect Friday (1970) (Col.)	Peter Hall	Sunnymede-DeGrunwald (Jack Smith)	C. Scott Forbes, Anthony Greville-Bell (C. ScottForbes)	Ursula Andress, Stanley Baker	Bank robbery
Performance (1970) (Col.)	Donald Cammell, Nicolas Roeg	Goodtimes Enterprises (Sanford Lieberson)	(Donald Cammell)	James Fox, Mick Jagger	Protection racketeering
Get Carter (1970) (Col.)	Mike Hodges	MGM British (Michael Klinger)	Mike Hodges (N: Ted Lewis, *Jack's Return Home*)	Michael Caine, Ian Hendry	Pornography and racketeering
Villain (1971) (Col.)	Michael Tuchner	Atlantic United/Anglo-EMI (Alan Ladd Jr, Jay Kanter)	Dick Clement, Ian La Frenais, Al Lettieri (N: James Barlow *The Burden of Proof*)	Richard Burton, Ian McShane	Protection racketeering and payroll robbery
All Coppers Are ... (1972) (Col.)	Sidney Hayers	Peter Rogers (G.H. Brown)	(Allan Prior)	Martin Potter, Julia Foster	Cigarette robbery
Sitting Target (1972) (Col.)	Douglas Hickox	Peerford (Barry Kulick)	Alexander Jacobs (N: Laurence Henderson)	Oliver Reed, Jill St John	Escaped convict
The Fast Kill (1972) (Col.)	Lindsay Shonteff	Shonteff (Lindsay Shonteff)	(Martin Gillman)	Tom Adams, Susie Hampton	Diamond robbery
Blue Movie Blackmail (Italy *Servizio di Scorta*) (Britain/ Italy, 1973) (Col.)	Massimo Dellamano	Monymusk/ Clodio/Italian International (Ross Mackenzie, Leonardo Pescardo)	(Massimo Dellamano, Sandy MacRae)	Ivan Rassimov, Stephanie Beacham	Drug racketeering and blackmail

Title (Year[1])	Director	Production company (Producer)	Screenwriter (Story)	Leading players	Crime interest
Dead Cert (1974) (Col.)	Tony Richardson	Woodfall (Neil Hartley)	Tony Richardson, John Oaksey (N: Dick Francis)	Judi Dench, Scott Anthony	Racehorse doping
Eleven Harrowhouse (1974) (Col.)	Aram Avakian	Harrowhouse (Elliott Kastner)	Charles Grodin, Jeffrey Bloom (N: Gerald Browne *Eleven Harrowhouse Street*)	Charles Grodin, Candice Bergen	Diamond robbery
Brannigan (1975) (Col.)	Douglas Hickox	Wellborn (Jules Levy, Arthur Gardener)	Christopher Trumbo, Michael Butler, William McGiven, William Norton (C. Trumbo, M. Butler)	John Wayne, Richard Atten-borough)	Gang warfare
Freelance (1975) (Col.)	Francis Megahy	Freelance Films (Francis Megahy)	(Francis Megahy, Bernie Cooper)	Ian McShane, Gayle Hunnicutt	Racketeering
Sweeney! (1977) (Col.)	David Wickes	Euston Films (Ted Childs)	Ronald Graham (TVSs: Ian Kennedy Martin *The Sweeney*)	John Thaw, Dennis Waterman	Conspiracy
The Squeeze (1977) (Col.)	Michael Apted	Martinat (Stanley O'Toole)	Leon Griffiths (N: David Craig)	Stacy Keach, David Hemmings	Robbery

Title (Year[1])	Director	Production company (Producer)	Screenwriter (Story)	Leading players	Crime interest
The Black Panther (1978) (Col.)	Ian Merrick	Impics (Ian Merrick)	Michael Armstrong (Joanne Leighton)	Donald Sumptor, Debbie Farrington	Kidnapping
Sweeney 2 (1978) (Col.)	Tom Clegg	Euston Films (Ted Childs)	Troy Kennedy Martin (TVSs: Ian Kennedy Martin *The Sweeney*)	John Thaw, Dennis Waterman	Robbery
Give Us Tomorrow (1979) (Col.)	Donovan Winter	Donwin (Donovan Winter)	(Donovan Winter)	Sylvia Sims, Derren Nesbit	Bank robbery
McVicar (1980) (Col.)	Tom Clegg	The Who Films (Roy Baird, Bill Curbishley, Roger Daltrey)	John McVicar, Tom Clegg (B: John McVicar, *McVicar By Himself*)	Roger Daltrey, Adam Faith	Prison breaking and burglary
The Long Good Friday (1981) (Col.)	John Mackenzie	Calendar/ Black Lion (Barry Hanson)	Barrie Keefe	Bob Hoskins, Helen Mirren	Racketeering
Loophole (1981) (Col.)	John Quested	Brent Walker (Julian Holloway, David Korda)	Jonathan Hales (N: Robert Pollock)	Albert Finney, Martin Sheen	Bank robbery
Slayground (1983) (Col.)	Terry Bedford	Jennie & Co/EMI (John Dark, Gower Frost)	Trevor Preston (N: Donald E. Westlake)	Peter Coyote, Billie Whitelaw	Robbery and contract killing
The Hit (1984) (Col.)	Stephen Frears	Central/Zenith /Recorded Picture Co (Jeremy Thomas)	(Peter Prince)	Tim Roth, John Hurt, Terence Stamp	Contract killing

Title (Year[1])	Director	Production company (Producer)	Screenwriter (Story)	Leading players	Crime interest
Mona Lisa (1986) (Col.)	Neil Jordan	Handmade Films (Stephen Woolley, Patrick Cassavetti)	Neil Jordan, David Leland	Bob Hoskins, Cathy Tyson, Michael Caine	Prostitution and drug racketeering
Empire State (1987) (Col.)	Ron Peck	British Screen/ Cine-Film/ Film Inter-national (Norma Heyman)	Ron Peck, Mark Ayres	Ray McAnally, Cathryn Harrison	Corruption
Bellman and True (1987) (Col.)	Richard Loncraine	Handmade Films/ Euston Films (Michael Waring, Christopher Neame)	Desmond Lowden, Richard Loncraine, Michael Wearing (N: Desmond Lowden)	Bernard Hill, Derek Newark	Bank robbery
Stormy Monday (1987) (Col.)	Mike Figgis	Moving Picture Company (Nigel Stafford-Clark)	Mike Figgis	Melanie Griffith, Tommy Lee Jones, Sean Bean	Money laundering
A Prayer For the Dying (1988) (Col.)	Mike Hodges	PFD Films (Peter Snell)	Edmund Ward, Martin Lynch (N: Jack Higgins)	Mickey Rourke, Bob Hoskins	Contract killing
Buster (1988) (Col.)	David Green	Buster Films (Norma Heyman)	Colin Shindler	Phil Collins, Julie Walters	Train robbery

Title (Year[1])	Director	Production company (Producer)	Screenwriter (Story)	Leading players	Crime interest
For Queen and Country (Britain/USA, 1989) (Col.)	Martin Stillman	Zenith/Atlantic Entertainment/ Working Title (Tim Bevan)	Martin Stillman, Trix Worrell	Denzel Washington	Milieu of petty crime
The Krays (1990) (Col.)	Peter Medak	Fugitive Features (Paul Cowan)	Philip Ridley	Billie Whitelaw, Tom Bell, Gary & Martin Kemp	Protection
The Big Man (1990) (Col.)	David Leland	Palace Productions (Harvey and Bob Weinstein)	Don MacPherson (N: William McIlvanney)	Liam Neeson, Joanne Whalley	Drug racketeeing and illegal prizefighting
Smack and Thistle (1991) (Col.)	Tunde Ikoli	Working Title Films/ Channel Four (Sarah Cellan Jones, Alison Jackson)	Tunde Ikoli	Charlie Caine, Patrick Malahide	Illegal gambling, drugs and racketeering
Double X. (1992) (Col.)	Shani S. Grewal	String of Pearls (Shani S. Grewal)	Shani S. Grewal (S: David Fleming *Vengeance*)	Simon Ward, William Catt, Norman Wisdom	Robbery and racketeering
The Young Americans (1993) (Col.)	Danny Cannon	Polygram Film/Line Entertainment (Paul Trijbits, Alison Owen)	Danny Cannon, David Hilton	Harvey Keitel, Iain Glen	Drug racketeering
Shopping (1994) (Col.)	Paul Anderson	Impact Pictures/ Channel Four Films (Jeremy Bolt)	Paul Anderson	Sadie Frost, Jude Law	Ram-raiding and drug racketeering

Title (Year[1])	Director	Production company (Producer)	Screenwriter (Story)	Leading players	Crime interest
Shallow Grave (1995) (Col.)	Danny Boyle	Channel Four Films (Andrew Macdonald)	John Hodge	Kerry Fox, Christopher Eccleston, Ewan McGregor	Drug racket proceeds
The Innocent Sleep (1995) (Col.)	Scott Michell	Timedial (Matthew Vaughn, Scott Michell)	Ray Villis	Rupert Graves, Michael Gambon	Police corruption and masonic conspiracy
i.d. (1995) (Col.)	Philip Davies	BBC Films/The Sales Company (Sally Hibbin)	Vincent O'Connell (S: James Bannon)	Reece Dinsdale, Warren Clarke, Claire Skinner	Police infiltration of football gang
Hard Men (Britain/ France, 1997) (Col.)	J.K. Amalou	Venture Movies/ Dacia Films (J.K. Amalou, Georges Benayoun)	J.K. Amalou	Vincent Regan, Ross Boatman, Lee Ross	Protection racketeering
Smalltime (1997) (Col.)	Shane Meadows	A Big Arty Production/ BFI (Shane Meadows)	Shane Meadows	Mat Hand, Dena Smiles	Petty theft
Face (1997) (Col.)	Antonia Bird	BBC/Distant Horizon (David M. Thompson, Elinor Day)	Ronan Bennett	Robert Carlyle, Ray Winstone	Robbery

Title (Year[1])	Director	Production company (Producer)	Screenwriter (Story)	Leading players	Crime interest

Secondary filmography

Title (Year[1])	Director	Production company (Producer)	Screenwriter (Story)	Leading players	Crime interest
On the Night of the Fire (USA *The Fugitive*) (1939)	Brian Desmond Hurst	G and S Films (Josef Samlo)	Brian Desmond Hurst, Terence Young, Patrick Kirwin (N: F.L. Green)	Ralph Richardson, Diana Wynyard	Theft
The Briggs Family (1940)	Herbert Mason	Warner Bros (A.M. Salomon)	John Dighton (Brock Williams)	Edward Chapman, Jane Baxter	Burglary
The Hundred Pound Window (1943)	Brian Desmond Hurst	Warner Bros (Max Milder)	Abem Finkel, Brock Williams, Rodney Ackland (Mark Hellinger)	Anne Crawford, David Farrar	Black market-eering
The Voice Within (1945)	Maurice J. Wilson	GN Film Productions (Isadore Goldsmith)	Stafford Dickens, Herbert Victor, B. Charles Deane (Michael Goldsmith)	Barbara White, Kieron O'Hanrahan	Smuggling
The Shop at Sly Corner (USA *The Code of Scotland Yard*) (1947)	George King	Pennant Pictures (George King)	Katherine Strueby (P. Edward Percy)	Oscar Homolka, Derek Farr	Burglary and handling stolen goods

Title (Year[1])	Director	Production company (Producer)	Screenwriter (Story)	Leading players	Crime interest
The Mysterious Mr Nicholson (1947)	Oswald Mitchell	Bushey (Gilbert Church)	Francis Miller, Oswald Mitchell (Francis Miller)	Anthony Hulme, Lesley Osmond	Theft
Journey Ahead (1947)	Peter Mills	Random (Peter Mills)	(Warren Tute)	Ruth Haven, John Stevens	Smuggling
My Brother's Keeper (1948)	Alfred Roome, Roy Rich	Gainsborough (Anthony Darnborough)	Frank Harvey (Maurice Wiltshire)	Jack Warner, Jane Hylton	Prison escape
London Belongs to Me (USA *Dulcimer Street*) (1948)	Sidney Gilliat	IP-Individual (Frank Launder, Sidney Gilliat)	Sidney Gilliat, J.B. Williams (N: Norman Collins)	Richard Atten-borough, Alastair Sim	Low-life milieu
The Small Voice (USA *Hideout*) (1948)	Fergus McDonnell	Constellation (Anthony Havelock-Allan)	Derek Neame, Julian Orde, (N: Robert Westerby)	Valerie Hobson, James Donald	Escaped convicts
Dick Barton – Special Agent (1948)	Alfred Goulding	Marylebone (Henry Halstead)	Alan Stranks, Alfred Goulding (RS: Edward J. Mason)	Don Stannard, George Ford	Smuggling and master criminal
The Calendar (1948)	Arthur Crabtree	Gainsborough (Anthony Darnborough)	Geoffrey Kerr (P: Edgar Wallace)	Greta Gynt, John McCallum	Horse race racketeering
Now Barabbas was a robber … (1949)	Gordon Parry	Anatole de Grunwald	Gordon Parry (P: William Douglas Home)	Richard Greene, Cedric Hardwicke	Various lives of convicts
Vengeance is Mine (1949)	Alan Cullimore	Cullimore-Arbeid (Ben Arbeid)	(Alan Cullimore)	Valentine Dyall, Anne Forth	Contract killing

Title (Year[1])	Director	Production company (Producer)	Screenwriter (Story)	Leading players	Crime interest
The Third Man (1949)	Carol Reed	London-BLPA (David O. Selznick, Alexander Korda)	Graham Greene (S: Graham Greene)	Joseph Cotten, Alida Valli, Orson Welles	Black marketeering
Boys in Brown (1949)	Montgomery Tully	Gainsborough (Anthony Darnborough)	Montgomery Tully (P: Reginald Beckwith)	Jack Warner, Richard Attenborough	Robbery by juveniles
A Matter of Murder (1949)	John Gilling	Vandyke (Roger Proudlock, Sam Lee)	(John Gilling)	John Barry, Charles Clapham	Embezzlement
Stranger at My Door (1950)	Brendan J. Stafford, Desmond Leslie	Leinster Films (Paul King)	(Desmond Leslie)	Valentine Dyall, Joseph O'Connor	Burglary and blackmail, Dublin
Once a Sinner (1950)	Lewis Gilbert	John Argyle	David Evans (N: Ronald Marsh, *Irene*)	Pat Kirkwood, Jack Watling	Forgery
Cairo Road (1950)	David Macdonald	Mayflower (Aubrey Baring)	Robert Westerby	Eric Portman, Laurence Harvey	Drug smuggling, Egypt
I'll Get You For This (USA *Lucky Nick Cain*) (1951)	Joseph M. Newman	Kaydor-Romulus (Joseph Kaufman)	George Callahan, William Rose (N: James Hadley Chase *High Stakes*)	George Raft, Collen Gray	Forgery
There is Another Sun (USA *Wall of Death*) (1950)	Lewis Gilbert	Nettlefold (Ernest G. Roy)	Guy Morgan (James Raisin)	Maxwell Reed, Laurence Harvey	Robbery and racketeering

Title (Year[1])	Director	Production company (Producer)	Screenwriter (Story)	Leading players	Crime interest
Cloudburst (1951)	Francis Searle	Hammer (Anthony Hinds, Alexander Pal)	Leo Marks, Francis Searle (P: Leo Marks)	Robert Preston, Elizabeth Sellars	Theft
Another Man's Poison (1951)	Irving Rapper	Daniel Angel (D. Angel, Douglas Fairbanks Jr)	Val Guest (P: Leslie Sands, *Deadlock*)	Bette Davis, Gary Merrill	Bank robbery
Files from Scotland Yard (1951)	Anthony Squire	Parthian (Henry Hobhouse)		John Harvey, Moira Lister	Three police cases
I Believe in You (1952)	Basil Dearden	Ealing (Michael Relph)	M. Relph, B. Dearden, Jack Whitting-ham, Nicholas Phipps (B: Sewell Stokes, *Court Circular*)	Celia Johnson, Cecil Parker	Juvenile crime
Salute the Toff (1952)	Maclean Rogers	Nettlefold (Ernest G. Roy)	(N: John Creasey)	John Bentley, Carol Marsh	Insurance fraud
Hammer the Toff (1952)	Maclean Rogers	Nettlefold (Ernest G. Roy)	(N: John Creasey)	John Bentley, Patricia Dainton	Robbery
Hot Ice (1952)	Kenneth Hume	Present Day–SWH Piccadilly (Charles Reynolds)	Kenneth Hume (P: Alan Melville *A Weekend at Thrackley*)	John Justin, Barbara Murray	Jewel theft
Cosh Boy (1953)	Lewis Gilbert	Daniel Angel–Romulus	Lewis Gilbert, Vernon Harris (P: Bruce Walker *Master Crook*)	James Kenney, Joan Collins	Robbery

Title (Year[1])	Director	Production company (Producer)	Screenwriter (Story)	Leading players	Crime interest
The Man Who Watched Trains Go By (USA Paris Express) (1953) (Col.)	Harold French	Raymond Stross (Joseph Shaftel)	Harold French (N: Georges Simenon)	Claude Rains, Marta Toren	Embezzlement, Holland
Street Corner (USA Both Sides of the Law) (1953)	Muriel Box	London Independent (Sydney Box, William MacQuitty)	Muriel Box, Sydney Box (Jan Read)	Anne Crawford, Peggy Cummins	Crime compendium
Desperate Moment (1953)	Compton Bennett	Fanfare (George H. Brown)	George H. Brown, Patrick Kirwan (N: Martha Albrand)	Dirk Bogarde, Mai Zetterling	Racketeering
The Fake (1953)	Godfrey Grayson	Pax (Steven Pallos, Ambrose Grayson)	Patrick Kirwan, Bridget Boland (James Daplyn)	Dennis O'Keefe, Coleen Gray	Art forgery and theft
The Limping Man (1953)	Charles de la Tour, Cy Endfield	Banner (Donald Ginsberg)	Ian Stuart Black, Reginald Long (Anthony Verney)	Lloyd Bridges, Moira Lister	Smuggling
The Blue Parrot (1953)	John Harlow	ACT Films (Stanley Haynes)	Allan Mackinnon (S: Percy Hoskins Gunman)	Dermot Walsh, Jacqueline Hill	Underworld milieu
Dangerous Voyage (USA Terror Ship) (1954)	Vernon Sewell	Merton Park (W.H. Williams)	Julian Ward (Vernon Sewell)	William Lundigan, Naomi Chance	Theft

Title (Year[1])	Director	Production company (Producer)	Screenwriter (Story)	Leading players	Crime interest
The Embezzler (1954)	John Gilling	Kenilworth–Mid-Century (R. Baker, M. Berman)	John Gilling	Charles Victor,	Bank robbery
Delayed Action (1954)	John Harlow	Kenilworth (R. Baker M. Berman)	(Geoffrey Orme)	Robert Ayres, Alan Wheatley	Robbery
Beautiful Stranger (USA *Twist of Fate*) (1954)	David Miller	Marksman (Maxwell Setton, John R. Sloan)	Robert Westerby, Carl Nystrom (David Miller, Rip Van Ronkel)	Ginger Rogers, Stanley Baker	Forgery, Cannes
Diplomatic Passport (1954)	Gene Martel	Rich & Rich-Princess (Burt Balaban, Gene Martel)	(Paul Tabori)	Marsha Hunt, Paul Carpenter	Jewel smuggling, Paris
A Prize of Gold (1955) (Col.)	Mark Robson	Warwick (Irving Allen, Albert Broccoli, Phil Samuel)	Robert Buckner, John Paxton (N: Max Catto)	Richard Widmark, Mai Zetterling	Gold robbery, Berlin
Tangier Assignment (1955)	Ted Leversuch	Rock Pictures (Cyril Parker)	(Ted Leversuch)	Robert Simmons, June Powell	Gun running, Tangier
Contraband Spain (1955) (Col.)	Lawrence Huntington	Diadem (Ernest Gartside)	(Lawrence Huntington)	Richard Greene, Anouk Aimée	Forgery, Spain
Barbados Quest (USA *Murder on Approval*) (1955)	Bernard Knowles	Cipa (R. Baker M. Berman)	(Kenneth R. Hayles)	Tom Conway, Delphi Lawrence	Private investigator and forgery

Title (Year[1])	Director	Production company (Producer)	Screenwriter (Story)	Leading players	Crime interest
Bond of Fear (1956)	Henry Cass	Mid-Century (R. Baker M. Berman)	John Gilling, Norman Hudis (Digby Wolfe)	Dermot Walsh, Jane Barrett	Escaped convict
The Secret Tent (1956)	Don Chaffey	Forward (Nat Miller, Frank Bevis)	Jan Read (P: Elizabeth Addeyman)	Donald Gray, Andrée Melly	Burglary
Guilty? (1956)	Edmond T. Greville	Gibraltar (Charles A. Leeds)	Maurice J. Wilson, Ernest Dudley (N: Michael Gilbert)	John Justin, Barbara Laage	Counterfeiting
Fortune is a Woman (USA *She Played With Fire*) (1957)	Sidney Gilliat	John Harvel (Frank Launder, Sidney Gilliat)	F. Launder, S. Gilliat, Val Valentine (N: Winston Graham)	Jack Hawkins, Arlene Dahl	Forgery and fraud
West of Suez (USA *Fighting Wildcats*) (1957)	Arthur Crabtree	Winwell (Bill & Kay Luckwell, Derek Winn)	(Lance Z. Hargreaves)	Keefe Brasselle, Kay Callard	Contract killing
Hi-Jack (retitled *Action Stations*) (1957)	Cecil H. Williamson	Cecil H. Williamson	Cecil H. Williamson	Paul Carpenter, Mary Martin	Counterfeiting, Spain
Interpol (USA *Pickup Alley*) (1957)	John Gilling	Warwick (Irving Allen, Albert Broccoli, Phil C. Samuel)	John Paxton (B: A.J. Forrest)	Victor Mature, Anita Ekberg	Drug smuggling
That Woman Opposite (USA *City After Midnight*) (1957)	Compton Bennett	Monarch (William Gell)	Compton Bennett (N: John Dickson Carr *The Emperor's Snuffbox*)	Phyllis Kirk, Dan O'Herlihy	Jewel theft, France

Title (Year[1])	Director	Production company (Producer)	Screenwriter (Story)	Leading players	Crime interest
The Big Chance (1957)	Peter Graham Scott	Major (John Temple-Smith)	Peter Graham-Scott (N: Pamela Barrington)	Adrienne Corri, William Russell	Embezzlement
Sail Into Danger (1957)	Kenneth Hume	Patria (Steven Pallos)	(Kenneth Hume)	Dennis O'Keefe, Kathleen Ryan	Art theft, Spain
Chase a Crooked Shadow (1957)	Michael Anderson	Associated Dragon (Douglas Fairbanks Jr, Thomas Clyde)	(David D. Osborn, Charles Sinclair)	Richard Todd, Anne Baxter	Theft, Costa Brava
A Woman of Mystery (1958)	Ernest Morris	Danziger (E. & H. Danziger)	(Brian Clemens, Eldon Howard)	Dermot Walsh, Hazel Court	Counterfeiting
Mark of the Phoenix (1958)	Maclean Rogers	Butcher's (W G Chalmers)	Norman Hudis (Desmond Cory)	Julia Arnall, Sheldon Lawrence	Jewel theft
The Man Inside (1958)	John Gilling	Warwick (Irving Allen, Albert Broccoli)	Richard Maibaum, John Gilling, David Shaw (N: M.E. Chaber)	Jack Palance, Anita Ekberg	Jewel theft
Subway in the Sky (1959)	Muriel Box	Orbit (Sydney Box, John Temple-Smith, Patrick Filmer-Sankey)	Jack Andress (P: Ian Main)	Van Johnson, Hildegarde Neff	Drug dealing, Berlin

Title (Year[1])	Director	Production company (Producer)	Screenwriter (Story)	Leading players	Crime interest
Breakout (1959)	Peter Graham Scott	Independent Artists (Julian Wintle, Leslie Parkyn)	Peter Barnes (B: Frederick Oughton)	Lee Patterson, Hazel Court	Embezzlement and jail break
The White Trap (1959)	Sidney Hayers	Independent Artists (Julian Wintle, Leslie Parkyn)	(Peter Barnes)	Lee Patterson, Conrad Phillips	Escaped convict
A Woman's Temptation (1959)	Godfrey Grayson	Danziger (F. & H. Danziger)	(Brian Clemens, Eldon Howard)	Patricia Driscoll, Robert Ayres	Mail-van robbery
The Witness (1959)	Geoffrey Muller	Merton Park (J. Greenwood)	Julian Bond (John Salt)	Dermot Walsh, Greta Gynt	Robbery
Too Young to Love (1959)	Muriel Box	Beaconsfield/ Welbeck (Herbert Smith)	Muriel Box, Sydney Box	Pauline Hahn, Thomas Mitchell	Prostitution, Brooklyn
So Evil So Young (1961) (Col.)	Godfrey Grayson	Danziger (Brian Taylor)	(Mark Grantham) (P: Elsa Shelley)	Jill Ireland, Ellen Pollock	Juvenile robbery
Transatlantic (1961)	Ernest Morris	Danziger (Brian Taylor)	(Brian Clemens, James Eastwood)	Pete Murray, June Thorburn	Jewel theft
Two Living One Dead (Britain/ Sweden, 1961)	Anthony Asquith	Swan (Karl E. Mosley, Teddy Baird)	Lindsey Galloway (N: Sigurd Christianssen)	Virginia McKenna, Bill Travers	Robbery, Sweden
The Secret Partner (1961)	Basil Dearden	MGM British (Michael Relph)	(David Pursell, Jack Seddon)	Stewart Granger, Haya Harareet	Embezzlement, blackmail and theft

Title (Year[1])	Director	Production company (Producer)	Screenwriter (Story)	Leading players	Crime interest
Attempt to Kill (1961)	Royston Morley	Merton Park (J. Greenwood)	Richard Harris (N: Edgar Wallace, *The Lone House Mystery*)	Derek Farr, Tony Wright	Confidence tricking
Dangerous Afternoon (1961)	Charles Saunders	Theatrecraft (Guido Coen)	Brandon Fleming (P: Gerald Anstruther)	Ruth Dunning, Nora Nicholson	Escaped convict
Backfire! (1962)	Paul Almond	Merton Park (J. Greenwood)	Robert Stewart (N: Edgar Wallace)	Alfred Burke, Zena Marshall	Arson fraud
Seven Keys (1962)	Pat Jackson	Independent Artists (Julian Wintle, Leslie Parkyn)	(Jack Davies, Henry Blyth)	Jeannie Carson, Alan Dobie	Hidden loot
Breath of Life (1962)	J. Henry Piperno	Norcon (Norman Cohen, Bill Luckwell)	(J. Henry Piperno)	George Moore, Larry Martyn	Bank robbery
Cairo (1963)	Wolf Rilla	MGM (Lawrence P. Bachmann, Ronald Kinnoch)	Joanne Court (N: W.R. Burnett, *The Asphalt Jungle*)	George Sanders, Richard Johnson	Theft, Cairo
Return to Sender (1963)	Gordon Hales	Merton Park (J. Greenwood)	John Roddick (S: Edgar Wallace)	Nigel Davenport, Yvonne Romain	Illegal financial speculation
The Moon-Spinners (1964) (Col.)	James Neilson	Walt Disney (Bill Anderson)	Michael Dyne (N: Mary Stewart)	Hayley Mills, Eli Wallach	Jewel robbery, Crete

Title (Year)[1]	Director	Production company (Producer)	Screenwriter (Story)	Leading players	Crime interest
The Sicilians (1964)	Ernest Morris	Butcher's (John I. Phillips, Ronald Liles)	(Ronald Liles, Reginald Hearne)	Robert Hutton, Reginald Marsh	Kidnapping, Paris
Twenty-Four Hours to Kill (1965) (Col.)	Peter Bezencenet	Grixflag (Bernard Coote, Harry Alan Towers)	Peter Yeldham (Peter Welbeck)	Lex Barker, Mickey Rooney	Gold smuggling, Beirut
Circus of Fear (1966)	John Moxley	Circus (Harry Alan Towers)	Peter Welbeck	Christopher Lee, Leo Genn	Robbery
Death is a Woman (1966) (Col.)	Frederic Goode	AB-Pathe (Harry Field)	(Wally Bosco)	Patsy Ann Noble, Mark Burns	Drug smuggling, Malta
Maroc 7 (1966) (Col.)	Gerry O'Hara	Cyclone (John Gale, Leslie Phillips, Martin C. Chute)	(David Osborn)	Gene Barry, Elsa Martinelli	Theft, Morocco
Poor Cow (1967) (Col.)	Kenneth Loach	Fenchurch–Vic (Joseph Janni)	Nell Dunn, Kenneth Loach (N: Nell Dunn)	Carol White, Terence Stamp	Robbery
Hell is Empty (Britain/ Czechoslo- vakia, 1967) (Col.)	John Ainsworth, Bernard Knowles	Dominion (Michael Eland)	John Ainsworth, Bernard Knowles, John Fowler (N: J.F. Straker)	Martine Carol, Anthony Steel	Robbery, Prague
Deadfall (1967) (Col.)	Bryan Forbes	Salamanda (Paul Monash)	Bryan Forbes (N: Desmond Cory)	Michael Caine, Giovanni Ralli	Theft

Title (Year[1])	Director	Production company (Producer)	Screenwriter (Story)	Leading players	Crime interest
Clegg (1969) (Col.)	Lindsay Shonteff	Sutton–Shonteff (Herbert Alpert, Lewis Force)	(Lewis J. Hagleton)	Gilbert Wynne, Garry Hope	Private investigator and embezzlement
The Walking Stick (1970) (Col.)	Eric Till	Winkast–Gershwin–Kastner (Alan Ladd Jr)	George Bluestone (N: Winston Graham)	David Hemmings, Samantha Eggar	Antiques robbery
Puppet on a Chain (1970) (Col.)	Geoffrey Reeve, Don Sharp	Big City (Kurt Unger)	Alistair MacLean, Don Sharp, Paul Wheeler (N: Alistair MacLean)	Sven Bertil-Taube, Barbara Parkins	Drug smuggling, Holland
A Touch of the Other (1970) (Col.)	Arnold Louis Miller	Global (Leslie Berens, Arnold L. & Sheila Miller)	(Frank Wyman)	Kenneth Cope, Shirley-Anne Field	Prostitution and protection racketeering
Gumshoe (1971) (Col.)	Stephen Frears	Memorial (Michael Medwin)	Neville Smith	Albert Finney, Billie Whitelaw	Private investigation and racketeering
Pulp (1972) (Col.)	Mike Hodges	Three Michaels (Michael Klinger, Mike Hodges, Michael Caine)	(Mike Hodges)	Michael Caine, Mickey Rooney	Gangster milieu
The Ragman's Daughter (1972) (Col.)	Harold Becker	Harpoon Penelope (Harold Becker)	Alan Sillitoe (S: Alan Sillitoe)	Simon Rouse, Victoria Tennant	Theft

Title (Year[1])	Director	Production company (Producer)	Screenwriter (Story)	Leading players	Crime interest
Redneck (Italy *Senza Ragione*) (Britain/Italy, 1972) (Col.)	Silvio Narizzano	Sterle/ Alessandra (Michael Lester, Silvio Narizzano)	Win Wells, Masolino D'Amico (Rafael Sanchez Campoy)	Franco Nero, Telly Savalas	Kidnapping, Italy
The Marseille Contract (USA *The Destructors*) (Britain/ France, 1974) (Col.)	Robert Parrish	Kettledrum/P ECF/SARL/ AIP (Judd Bernard)	Judd Bernard	Michael Caine, Anthony Quinn	Drug smuggling, France
Shatter (Britain/- Hong Kong, 1974) (Col.)	Michael Carreras	Hammer/ Shaw Brothers (Michael Carreras, Vee King Shaw)	(Don Houghton)	Stuart Whitman, Ti Lung	Drug racketeering, Hong Kong
Juggernaut (1974) (Col.)	Richard Lester	United Artists (Richard DeKoker)	Richard DeKoker, Alan Plater	Richard Harris, Omar Sharif	Extortion
Double Exposure (1977) (Col.)	William Webb	Westwind (William Webb)	(William Webb)	David Baron, Anouska Hempel	Illegal arms dealing
The Disapp- earance (Britain/ Canada, 1977) (Col.)	Stuart Cooper	Trofer/ Tiberius (David Hemmings, Gerry Arbeid)	Paul Mayersberg (N: Derek Marlowe *Echoes of Celandine*)	Donald Sutherland, Francine Racette	Contract killing
Silver Bears (1978) (Col.)	Ivan Passer	Raleigh (Arlene Sellars, Alex Winitsky)	Peter Stone (N: Paul Erdman)	Michael Caine, Cybill Shepherd	Fraud, Iran

Title (Year[1])	Director	Production company (Producer)	Screenwriter (Story)	Leading players	Crime interest
The Bitch (1979) (Col.)	Gerry O'Hara	Spritebowl/Bitch (John Quested)	Gerry O'Hara (N: Jackie Collins)	Joan Collins, Michael Coby	Diamond smuggling
North Sea Hijack (1980) (Col.)	Andrew V. McLagen	Cinema Seven (Elliott Kastner)	Jack Davies (N: Jack Davies *Esther Ruth and Jennifer*)	Roger Moore, James Mason	Extortion
Green Ice (1981) (Col.)	Ernest Day	Pimlico/ ITC Entertainment (Jack Wiener)	Edward Anhalt, Ray Hassett, Anthony Simmons, Robert De Laurentiis (N: Gerald Browne)	Ryan O'Neal, Anne Archer	Robbery, Mexico
Parker (Britain/ West Germany, 1985) (Col.)	Jim Goddard	Moving Picture Co (Nigel Stafford-Clark)	(Trevor Preston)	Bryan Brown, Cherie Lunghi	Kidnapping and drug racketeering
Billy the Kid and the Green Baize Vampire (1986) (Col.)	Alan Clarke	Zenith Productions (Simon Mallin)	Trevor Preston	Phil Daniels, Alun Armstrong	Criminal milieu
Chicago Joe and the Showgirl) (1990) (Col.)	Bernard Rose	Chicago Joe Ltd (Tim Bevan)	David Yallop	Kiefer Sutherland, Emily Lloyd	Robbery
Let Him Have It (1991) (Col.)	Peter Medak	Vivid Productions (Luc Roeg, Robert Warr)	Neal Purvis, Robert Wade	Chris Eccleston, Paul Reynolds	Robbery

Title (Year[1])	Director	Production company (Producer)	Screenwriter (Story)	Leading players	Crime interest
London Kills Me (1991) (Col.)	Hanif Kureishi	Working Title (Tim Bevan)	Hanif Kureishi	Justin Chadwick, Steven Mackintosh	Drug dealing
Trainspotting (1996) (Col.)	Danny Boyle	Channel Four (Andrew Macdonald)	John Hodge	Ewan McGregor, Robert Carlyle	Drug dealing
The Near Room (1997) (Col.)	David Hayman	British Screen/ Glasgow Film Fund/Inverclyde Productions	Robert Murphy	Adrian Dunbar, David O'Hara	Drugs, prostitution and blackmail

Note:

The year given for each film up to and including 1985 is the year of registration as a British film. From 1986 onwards, the year given is the year of release in Britain.

Index

999 (scenario) 17
A Convict has Escaped (scenario) 18, 19
A Hill in Korea 85
A Place to Go 101
A Prayer for the Dying 13, 166
A Prize of Arms 4, 9, 54, 56, 58, 64, 91
A Question of Silence 66
A Sense of Freedom 4, 26
Adam, Ronald 99
Affluent Society, The 106
Albarn, Damon 183
Aldabra Productions 110
Aldrich, Robert 37, 38, 39
Alfie 124, 126
All the Night and All the Way Home 214
Allegret, Marc 46
Allen, Keith 180
Allen, Kevin 174
Allen, Lewis 46
Allen, Patrick 62
Allen, Richard 137
Alliance 148
Anderson, Lindsay 95
Anderson, Paul 14, 174, 176, 177
Anderson, Rona 56
Andrews, Nigel 127
Angels from Hell 142
Anglo-Amalgamated 83, 89
Annakin, Ken 4, 104, 105
Appointment with Crime 9, 18, 52, 81
Apted, Michael 4, 5, 24, 134, 136
Armchair Cinema 138
Armes, Roy 95
Armitage, George 127
Armstrong, Alun *128*, 129
Aslan, Gregoire 89
Asphalt Jungle, The 107
Asquith, Anthony 41
Associated British Pathé 72

Attenborough, Richard 18, 19, *20*, 28, 31, 52 123
Audley, Maxine 87
Avec Avec (script) 110

Bacon, Francis 131
Baker, George 51, 58, 62, 84, 85
Baker, Roy 9
Baker, Stanley 10, 22, 54, 58, 81, 85–91, *102*, 103, 105
Balcon, Jill 69
Bannen, Ian 139
Barber, Paul 167
Barlow, James 23
Barnes, Barry K. 28, 29, 57
Barnes, Peter 100
Barr, Charles 1
Bartholomew, Ian 166
Basehart, Richard 54
Bass, Alfie 85
Bates, Alan 166
BBC 13, 125, 134, 141
BBFC 7, 8, 16–25, 40, 72, 120
Bean, Sean 5, 155, 156, 157, 170, 178
Beat Girl 106
Beauty Jungle, The 126
Bell, Tom *12*, 58
Benson, Martin 56, 63
Berkeley, Ballard 31
Betts, Ernest 23
Bevan, Tim 110
Beyond this Place 84, 148
Bezencenet, Peter 100
BFI 184
Big Breadwinner Hog 13
Big Heat, The 131, 149
Billion Dollar Brain 126
Billson, Anne 129, 132
Bird, Antonia 3, 172, 174, 183

Bird, Norman 55
Bird, Richard 5
Bishop, Terence 100
Black, Ian Stuart 35
Black Lion/Calendar 25
Black Memory 82
Black Rainbow 122
Blanche Fury 46
Blind Date 87, 96
Blue Lamp, The 21, 43, 83, 96, 123, 134
Blue Velvet 127
Bogarde, Dirk 21, 83, 85, 123
Bogart (Humphrey) 47
Bomb in the High Street 100
Boorman, John 123
Boulting, John 3, 19, 31, 123
Boulting, Roy 19
Box, Muriel 32
Box, Sydney 32, 68
Boyd, Don 110
Boyd, Stephen 4, 143
Boyle, Danny 5, 14, 172, 179, 180
Bracewell, Michael 129
Bragg, Billy 183
Brambell, Wilfred *121*
Branche, Derrick 162
Brassed Off 172, 174
Brecht-Weill 34
Brief Encounter 41, 42
Brighton Rock 3, 4, 5, 6, 17, 19, *20*, 31, 43,
    82, 102, 120, 123
British Lion 77
Brooks, Dawn 61
Brosnan, Pierce 165
Brunsdon, Charlotte 11, 12
Budd, Roy 117–18
Burden of Proof, The 23
Burroughs, William 112
Burton, Richard 23, *24*, 115, 135
Buscombe, Ed 139, 140
Butcher's 98, 101

Caine, Michael 5, 12, 13, 23, 117, 126,
    128, 129, 132, 135, 175
Calculated Risk 105
Calleia, Joseph 29
Calvi, Robert 124
Cammell, Donald 3, 12, 105, 110–16,
    124, 173
Campbell's Kingdom 85
Cannon, Danny 13, 173, 176
Capone, Al 161, 166
Captain Horatio Hornblower RN 82

Cardiff, Jack 148
Careless, ex-Detective Inspector Sidney
    107
Carlyle, Robert 5, 182
Carstairs, John Paddy 16, 18, 28, 52
Casey, Bernie 127
Cassavetes (John) 12
Cattaneo, Peter 172
Cavalcanti, Alberto 3, 7, 30, *31*, 52, 81,
    123
Chadder, Viv 10
Chaffey, Don 10, 75
Challenge, The 5, *6*, 106
Chapman, Edward 33
Chaplin, Sydney 94
Charity, Tom 1
Charteris, Leslie 16
Chase, James Hadley 17, 37, 38, 39, 44,
    45, 47, 94, 125
Checkpoint 85
Cheyney, Peter 21, 94, 125
Chibnall, Steve 11
Childs, Ted 139
City of Dreadful Night, The 27
Clark, Dane 83
Clash, The 183
Clay, Andrew 8, 9
Clayton, Jack 95
Clowes, St John L. 7–8, 48
Clegg, Tom 4, 13, 136
Clement, Dick 23, 134
Clements, John 9
Clowes, St John L. 20, 37, 47, 94
Coduri, Camille 166
Cohen, Nat 124
Collinson, Peter 4, 12
Coltrane, Robbie 168
Columbia Studios 83
Comfort, Lance 101
Confession 94, 95
Connery, Sean 85, 108, 134, 144
Constantine, Eddie 77, 163
Cook, the Thief, his Wife and her Lover, The
    14, 162, 163, 173
Corbett, Harry H. 106
Cornelius, Henry 32
Coward (Noel) 41, 48
Cox, Alex 123
Craig, Michael 62
Crawford, Anne 54
Crawford, John 12, 87–8, 102
Crichton, Charles 4, 8, 12

Criminal, The 3, 4, 5, 10, 11, 12, 22,
    88–90, 96, 101, 102–3, 123
Crippen 33
Crisham, Walter 47
Crofts, Frank 21
Croupier 119, 122
Cruel Sea, The 85
Cul de Sac 124
Cummins, Peggy 86
Curtis, James 94, 125

Dancing with Crime 18, 28, 29, 33, 52, 54,
    57, 58, 59, 64
Danziger brothers 83, 98
Darby, Kim 39
Dark Eyes of London 5
Dassin, Jules 3, 7, 33, 81, 94, 123, 148,
    152
Davenport, Nigel 135
Davies, Russell 145
Davis, John 8
Davis, Philip 4, 183
Dawson, Anthony 99
Day, Peter 124
Daybreak 72
de Banzie, Brenda 77
de Marney, Terence 9, 60, 81
Deadfall 12
Dead of Night 32
Dearden, Basil 9, 21, 22, 54, 58, 96, 101,
    123, 134
Death Wish 132
'Decline of the English Murder' 33
Deerhunter, The 158
Delany, Maureen 153
Dennington and Tulloch 135
Derek, John 76
Dickens (Charles) 14, 41
Dimes, Albert 7, 89, 103
Dirty Dozen, The 39
Dirty Harry 123, 129, 132, 134
Dixon of Dock Green 134
Doctor Faustus 32
Doctor in the House 83
Domergue, Faith 35, 56
Donner, Clive 107
Dors, Diana 11, 28, 32, 62, 69, 72, 73, 74,
    77, 78, 84
Douglas, Paul 60, *61*
Downhill 9
Dreigoschenoper, Die 34
Dryhurst, Edward 29
Duffy (script) 110

Duncan, Paul 126
Durgnat, Raymond 96
Dyer, Richard 91

Ealing Studios 7, 11, 21, 32, 84, 149, 150
Eastwood, Clint 132
Eccleston, Christopher 180
Eisenstein 114
Eisinger, Jo 33
Ekland, Britt 23, 121, 130
Elliott, Denholm 141
Ellis, Ruth 71, 72, 73
Elsaesser, Thomas 128, 129, 131, 132
Empire State 13, 166, 167, 168–70
Endfield, Cy (C. Raker) 4, 10, 85, 87
Escape 9
Eureka! 122
Euston Films 13, 124, 137, 138
Evans, Marc 181

Fabian, (of the Yard) 78
Face 3, 4, 5, 14, 172–4, 175, 176, 181–4,
    186–8
Faith, Adam 104
Falconer, Alun 104
Fallen Idol, The 41
Fanny by Gaslight 47
Fantoni, Barry 12
Farewell, My Lovely 118
Farr, Derek 29, 30, 53
Faulkner, Keith 64
Faulkner, William 38
Ferman, James 24, 25
Field, Shirley Ann 76
Fields, Gracie 95
Figgis, Mike 3, 148, 155, 160, 166
Finlay, Frank 105
Finney, Albert 90
Flamingo Affair, The 9, 52, 53, 55, 58
Flash Gordon 122
Fleetwood-Wilson, Lieutenant-Colonel
    A. 18, 19, 21
Flesh is Weak, The 10, 11, 75, 76
Forbes, Bryan 12, 55
Force of Evil 161
Ford, Glenn 149
Ford, John 8, 105
Foster, Barry 139
Foulkes, R. A. 132
Four Feathers, The 9
Fox, Edward 143, 145
Fox, James 112, *113*
Fox, Kerry 180

Fraser, 'Mad' Frankie 175
Frears, Stephen 5, 13, 14, 160, 162
Freeman, Paul 163
French Connection, The 134
Frend, Charles 8
Friedkin, William 134
Frightened City 3, 11, 107–8, 123
Frightened Man, The 62, 63, 64
Frost, Sadie 177, *178*, 179
Fugitive 53, 54, 57
Fulford, Christopher 166
Full Monty, The 172, 174
Funeral in Berlin 126
Furie, Sidney J. 126

Gail, Zoe *43*, 46
Gainsborough Studios 2, 45, 68, 82
Galbraith, G. K. 106
Gambit 12
Gambler and the Lady, The 83
Gambon, Michael 162
Gangsters 13
Gans, Herbert 84
Gaolbreak 98
Garden of Eden, The 22
Garfield, John 81
Garnett, Tony 141
Gaunt Stranger, The 27
Gentle Gunman, The 22
Gentle Trap, The 61, 64
George, Susan *3*, 12
Get Carter 2, 3, 4, 5, 13, 23, 102, 117–33,
    134, 135, 144, 172, 173, 175
Gibbons, Luke 164
Gideon's Day 8, 88, 105
Gifford, Denis 1, 14, 98
Gilbert, Lewis 4, 22, 54, 106, 126
Gilling, John 5, 62, 106
Ginsberg, Alan 120
Glass Key, The 17
Glenville, Peter 32
Glover, David 91
Godfather, The 165, 166
Godfather, Part II, The 161, 164, 165
Godsell, Vanda 87
Gold, Jack 124
Good Die Young, The 4, 9, 22, 54, 55, 59,
    64, 106
Good Time Girl 10, 11, 32, 33, 48, 68–71,
    73
Goodfellas 182
Gorer, Geoffrey 83
Gorris, Marlene 66

Gosling, ex-Detective Superintendent
    John 105
GPO Film Unit 7
Grade, Lew 134
Grahame, Gloria 131
Granada Television 13, 124
Grant, Arthur 101
Gray, Sally 30, 54
Great Expectations 34, 41
Greenaway, Peter 14, 162, 173
Greene, David 3, 12, 124, 134
Greene, Graham 17, 19, 31, 32, 41, 45, 82
Greenstreet, Sydney 42
Greenwood, Jack 89
Gregson, John 107
Greville, Edmond T. 3, 20, 29, 30, 52,
    106, 123
Grierson, John 30
Griffith, Melanie 12, 148, 155, 156, 157,
    158, 170
Griffiths, Jane 62
Griffiths, Leon 134, 137
Grissom Gang, The 37, 39
Guest, Val 10, 37, 87, 101, *102*, 126
Guillermin, John 4, 5, 104
Gysin, Brion 112

Hamer, Robert 7, 9, 32, 149, 150
Hamilton, Guy 53, 126
Hammer Films 1, 2, 48, 83, 87, 88, 167
Hammett, Dashiel 38, 125
HandMade Films 13
Hard Men 174
Hardie, Kate 168
Harlow, John 9, 18, 52
Harman, Jympson 43
Harris, Sir Sidney 20
Harrison, George 13
Harrison, Norman 105
Harrison, Rex 9
Hartford-Davis, Robert 124
Hartnell, William 8, 9, 81, 86, 107
Harvey, Laurence 54
Hawkins, Jack 55, 58, 88
Hawks, Howard 16
Hayers, Sidney 4, 62
He Who Rides a Tiger 4, 5, 12
Headey, Lena 182
Heisler, Stuart 17
Hell Drivers 4, 10, 11, 85–7
Hell is a City 10, 11, 12, 84, 87–8, 101,
    102, 103, 105
Hemingway (Ernest) 12, 157

Hemmings, David 24, 143
Hendry, Ian 117, 126
Herman, Mark 172
Hess, John 161
High Noon 104
Higson, Andrew 95
Hi-Jackers, The 101
Hill, Billy 6, 7
Hill, John 13, 14, 95, 96
Hindley, Myra 71
Hinxman, Margaret 136
Hit, The 5, 13, 160
Hitchcock, Alfred 9, 27
Hit Man 127
Hodges, John 179
Hodges, Mike 2, 13, 23, 117–22, 123–7,
    129, 131, 134, 166, 172
Holiday Camp 42
Holloway, Stanley 29
Holt, Seth 101
Hopkins, John 134
Hoskins, Bob 13, 25, 163, 166, 167
House of the Arrow 27, 35
House of Whipcord 137
Howard, Ronald 28, 34, 52
Howard, Trevor 9, 30, 31, 53, 82
Hughes, Ken 3, 34, 51, 60, *61*, 83, 94, 95,
    123
Hunt, Leon 13
Huston, John 17
Huth, Harold 28, 52

I Confess 167
i.d. 4
Ibsen 48
Impact 98
In the Wake of a Stranger 84
Independent Artists 98
Informer, The 166
Informers, The 4, *10*, 11, 104–6
Intruder, The 53, 55, 59, 64
Ipcress File, The 126
Ireland, John 54
It Always Rains on Sunday 7, 11, 32, 33,
    34, 42, 149–52, 155, 158
Italian Job, The 4, 12, 126

Jack's Return Home 118, 124–5
Jackson, Gordon 85
Jagger, Mick 112, 114
Jailbreak 142
James Bond 14, 91
James, Sidney 42, 85

Janson, Hank 125
Joe Macbeth 3, 51, 60, 64, 95
Johnston, Sue 182
Jones, Barry 29, 57
Jones, Brian 112
Jones, Griffith 30, 32, 53, 82, 123
Jones, Tommy Lee 12, 148, 156, 158, 170
Jordan, Neil 13, 160, 166
Jordan, Philip 95
Jungle Street 106

Kawecka, Gena 185
Kazan, Elia 102
Keach, Stacy 5, 24, 136, 143
Kennedy Martin, Ian 138
Kent, Jean 32, 68, 71
Kersh, Gerald 125
King, Dave 163
Kitchener, Madge 19, 20
Kitchener, Lord 19
Klinger, Michael 124, 126, 127
Koestler, Arthur 73, 74
Korda, Zoltan 9
Krasker, Robert 89
Kray, Reggie 2, 22, 25, 115, 124, 135,
    137, 166, 172, 175
Kray, Ronnie 4, 22, 23, 25, 115, 124, 135,
    137, 166, 172, 175
Krays, The 4, 25, 173
Kruger, Hardy 87
Kureishi, Hanif 162

La Bern, Arthur 32, 125
La Frenais, Ian 23, 134
La Rue, Jack 44, 47
Ladykillers, The 8
Landau, Martin 168
Landis, Carole 5, 29, 30, 54
Lang, Fritz 34, 131
Langley, Noel 30
Last Video, The (script) 110
Lavender Hill Mob, The 8
Law and Order 13, 141
Law, Jude 177, *178*
Lawson, Wilfrid 85
League of Gentlemen, The 9, 54, 55, 56, 58,
    64, 95, 96
Leahy, James 96
Lean, David 14, 41, 47
Lee, Bernard 148
Leigh, Mike 174
Lejeune, C. A. 40, 44
Lemont, John 3, 22, 106, 107, 123

LeRoy, Mervyn 16
Lewis, Jay 126
Lewis, Ted 118, 119, 121, 124–7, 131
Little Caesar 16, 161
Little Welsh Girl, The 124
Live Now Pay Later 126
Llewellyn, Richard 19, 29
Loach, Ken 125
Loaded 121
Lock, Stock & Two Smoking Barrels 1
Lockwood, Margaret 45
Lom, Herbert 33, 70, 77, 85, *86*
Loneliness of the Long Distance Runner 124
Long Arm, The 8, 88
Long Good Friday, The 1, 2, 3, 4, 5, 13, 14,
   25, 134, 163–8, 172, 175
Long Haul, The 84
Long Memory, The 9, 83
Look Back in Anger 126
Loot 166
Lorre, Peter 42
Losey, Joseph 3, 10, 12, 22, 85, 87, 88, 89,
   90, 96, 102, 103, 107, 123
Love Story 128
Lovel, Terry 95
Lucas, William 62, *63*
Lumet, Sidney 134
LWT 141

M 34
McAnally, Ray 168, *169*
Macbeth 60
McCabe, Colin 105
McCallum, David 85
McCallum, John 32, 149, 151
McDermott, Hugh *43*, 47
Macdonald, Andrew 179
Macdonald, David 10, 32, 68
MacDonald, Robert David 37
McFarlane, Brian 8
McGoohan, Patrick 85
McGregor, Ewan 180
Macgregor, Scott 103
Mackendrick, Alexander 8
Mackenzie, John 2, 3, 4, 25, 134, 165
McLaren, John 42
McLaughlin, Gibb 153
Macmillan 97
Macphail, Angus 32
MacQuitty, William 105
McShane, Ian 23
McVicar 4, 26
Magee, Patrick 89, 103

Major (John) 174
Malcolm, Derek 141
Maltese Falcon, The 17
Man in Grey, The 47
Man in the Back Seat, The 62, 64, 98
Man of Violence 12
Man Who Fell to Earth, The 122
Mankiewicz, Joseph L. 9
Mansfield, Jayne *6*
Manvell, Roger 95
Mark, Commissioner Robert 97, 138
Marked Woman 32
Markham, Petra 23
Marks, Laurence 71
Marmont, Percy 47
Marsden, Frances 42
Marshall, Bryan 163
Mason, A. E. W. 27
Mason, James 47
Maxwell, Peter 98
Maybrick 33
Mayersberg, Paul 122
Meadows, Shane 14, 184, 185, 187
Medak, Peter 4, 25, 173
Medwin, Michael 53
Melachrino, George 48
Melly, George 128
Melville, Colette 53
Merchant, Vivien 144
Merton Park 98
Messina, Eugenio 15, 29
MGM 44, 120, 124, 127
Middleton 132
Mildred Pierce 149
Millions Like Us 42
Mills, John 9, 83
Minder 105, 137
Mine Own Executioner 44
Minter, George 84
Minter, James G. 44, 48
Molnar, Lily 46
Mona Lisa 13, 160, 166–8, 170
Monk, Claire 14
Morgan, Terence 22, 62, 106
Morons From Outer Space 122
Morris, Ernest 106
Morris, Wayne 35
Morrison, T. J. 28
Mosley, Leonard 40
Mrs Miniver 47
Murdoch, Rupert 182
Murphy, Robert 13, 47, 96, 98, 148, 152
Murphy, Stephen 21, 24

Murray, Barbara 63
My Beautiful Laundrette 14, 162, 163

Naked 174
Naked City, The 152
Naked Fury 98
Naughton, Bill 124
Neame, Ronald 12
Nelson, Gene 35
Nesbitt, Derren *10*, 64, 105
Nesbitt, Robert 37
Never Let Go 4, 5, 11, 104
Newley, Anthony 120, *121*
Newman, Gordon 141
Newton, Robert 39
Night and Day 45
Night and the City 3, 4, 5, 6, 7, 8, 11, 33, 34, 81, 94, 123, 148, 152–5, 158
Night Beat 28, 30, 34, 35, 52, 54, 55, 57
No Orchids for Miss Blandish 7, 8, 17, 20, 37–50, 84, 94
No Way Back 9, 60, 81
Noose 3, 4, 5, 6, 9, 14, 19, 20, 29, 30, 48, 52, 53, 54, 57, 123
Norden, Christine 29, 55
Norman, Mick 142, 143
Nothing But the Best 107
Novello, Ivor 9
Nowhere to Go 84, 101
Nozzeck, Max 22
Nygh, Anna *142*

O'Brien, Alan 141
O'Connolly, Jim 101
Odd Man Out 89, 166
Offbeat 4, 11, 94, 98–100, 102, 104, 105, 106
Offence, The 134, 144
Oliver Twist 14, 41
Olivier (Laurence) 41
Orton, Joe 166
Orwell, George 33, 38
Osborne, John 117, 126
Osiecki, Stefan 9, 60
Our Friends in the North 119, 129
Out 13
Owen, Alun 88, 103
Owen, Bill 8, 28, 52
Owen, Cliff 4, 54, 94, 98, *99*

Pacino, Al 161
Palance, Jack 87
Pale Rider 132

Pallenberg, Anita 112, 114, 115
Panic in the Streets 102
Parke, MacDonald 42, 47
Parry, Gordon 61
Pasolini 48
Patrick, Nigel 29, 105
Patterson, Lee 35, 54
Passport to Shame 10, 11, 75, 76, 77, 79
Payroll 4, 62, *63*, 64, 84
Performance 3, 12, 13, 14, 105, 110–16, 124, 134, 164, 173
Peace, Charles 7
Peck, Ron 13, 166
Peeping Tom 39
Penry, Ken 23, 25
Pertwee, Roland 28
Pertwee, Sean 177
Peters, Clarke 168
Petley, Julian 1
Petrie, Hay 29
Piccadilly Third Stop 11, 106–7
Pidgeon, Walter 47
Point Blank 123
Polanski, Roman 124
Pollak, Otto 67–8, 71
Pool of London 96
Pope John Paul I 124
Poulson 124
Powell, Dilys 7, 40, 152, 155
Powell, Michael 39
Power, Hartley 39
Prayer for the Dying 122
Prevost, Francoise 62, *63*
Price, Dennis 107
Proctor, Maurice 102
Professionals, The 141
Pryce, Jonathan 177
Public Enemy (scenario) 16
Public Enemy, The 16, 161
Pulleine, Tim 7, 8
Pulp 122

Quayle, Anthony *6*
Queen's Pawn 135
Quentin, Shirley 60

Radclyffe, Sarah 110
Raft, George 7
Rag Doll 101
Raimo, Addie 7
Raine, Jack 60
Rakoff, Alvin 10, 75, *78*
Random Harvest 44

Rank 8, 85, 87, 148
Rattigan, Terence 31, 41
Rawlings, Gwen 11
Ray, Nicholas 45
Raymondo, Derek 106
Reckoning, The 124
Red Harvest 136
Reed, Carol 5, 41, 89
Reed, Maxwell 29, 53
Regan 135, 138
Reisz 95
Relph, Michael 96, 101
Rennie, Michael 21
Renown Pictures 44, 48, 84, 148
Repulsion 124
Reservoir Dogs 180, 182
Resurrection Man 181
Revenger's Tragedy, The 132
Rhys Jones, Griff 122
Richards, Jeffrey 2, 97
Richardson 95
Richardson (gang) 22, 23, 124, 137, 172,
   175
Richie, Guy 1
Rientis, Rex 34
Rilla, Wolf 11, 106, 107
Ringer, The 27, 35
RKO 148
Robbery 4, 12, 136
Robertson, James 7, 8
Robinson, David 136
Robson, Flora 69
Roeg, Nicolas 3, 12, 105, 114, 115, 124,
   173
Roman, Ruth 60
Room at the Top 95
Ross, Hector 28, 52
Rourke, Mickey 166
Rumour 118, 124
Russell, Ken 126

Saad, Margit 89
Sabini, Darby 7
Saint in London, The 16
Salo 48
San Demetrio, London 42
Sanders, George 16
Sangster, Jimmy 88
Sapphire 96
Sarris, Andrew 161
Saturday Night and Sunday Morning 90,
   124
Saunders, Charles 61, 98, 106

Savage, Jon 12
Scarface 16, 44, 161
Schlesinger, John 95
Schlondorff 115
Schmid, Helmut 58
Schwartz, Stefan 181
Scorsese, Martin 129
Scotland Yard 89
Sea Fury 87
Searl, Frances 98
Sears, Ian 168
Sellers, Peter 4, 104, 105
Serious Charge 82
Sewell, Vernon 9, 21, 35, 54, 62, 94, 98
Shakedown, The 22, 106, 107
Shakespeare (William) 41, 60, 95
Shallow Grave 5, 14, 179–82, 184
Shane 132
Sharp, Ian 141
Shaw, Susan 34
Shepherd, Horace 9, 52
Ship That Died of Shame, The 54, 56, 58,
   64
Shooting Fish 181
Shopping 14, 174, 175, 176–9, 180, 184,
   187
Shone, Tom 183
Shulman, Milton 40
Siegel, Don 123, 134
Sillitoe, Alan 124
Sim, Sheila 28, 52
Sinden, Donald 23
Skurry, Arthur 7
Small World of Sammy Lee, The 3, 12, 95,
   120, *121*, 123
Smalltime 14, 184–7
Smart, Carol 67, 68
Smiles, Dena 185
Smith, Dan T. 124
Smith, Mel 122
So Evil My Love 46
Soho Incident 9, 35, 54, 56, 59, 64
Soho Racket (scenario) 16
South East Five (scenario) 18
Spencer, Neil 123
Spicer, Andrew 9, 10, 11
Spillane 136
Spin a Dark Web 35
Spivs in Love 124
Spot, Jack 7
Squeeze, The 4, 5, 24, 134, 136, 143–7
Stamp, Terence 5
Stark, Rosemary 24

Starr, Freddie 144, 145
Steel, Anthony 85
Stevens, George 132
Sting 156, 158, 170
Stormy Monday 3, 5, 11, 12, 13, 148,
    155–60, 166–7, 170–1
Strange Affair, The 3, 4, 5, 12, 124, 134
Strangers on a Train 167
Strasberg, Lee 164
Streatfield, D. 45
Street, Sarah 136
Strip Tease Murder 106
Stross, Raymond 76
Sullivan, Francis L. 33
Summerfield, Eleanor 60
Summers, Walter 5
Summerskill, Dr. Edith 40, 48
Summertime 47
Suschitsky, Wolfgang 120
Suspect 118, 124
Sweeney, The (series) 10, 88, 105, 124,
    134–47
Sweeney! 5, 13, 135–40, 143
Sweeney 2 5, 13, 135, 136, 138, 140–3
Sylvester, William 100

Tafler, Sydney 34, 83
Tarantino, Quentin 180
Taxi Driver 129, 132
Teakle, Spencer 61
Tekli-Compton 124
Tempean 83
Tempo 124
Tennyson, Pen 94
Tenser, Tony 124
Terminal Man, The 119, 122
Terminator (films) 176
Termo, Leonard 166
Terror, The 5
Thames Television 124, 134, 138
Thatcher (Margaret) 14, 161, 162, 173,
    174
Thaw, John 10, 88, 135
There Ain't No Justice 94
They Drive by Night 4, 5, 27, 85, 94, 148
They Live by Night 45
They Made Me a Fugitive 3, 4, 5, 6, 7, 8, 9,
    19, 20, 30, *31*, 32, 33, 43, 48, 52, 53,
    81, 82, 123, 148
Thin Lizzy 142
Third Man, The 5, 41, 82, 89, 152
This Man is News 28
This Sporting Life 95

Thomas, W. I. 67
Thompson, Ben 177
Thompson, Derek 163
Thompson, J. Lee 10, 11, 71, *72*
Thomson, James 27
Tibbs gang 137
Tiernan, Andrew 182
Tierney, Gene 33, 94, 148, 152
Tiger in the Smoke 9
Todd, Richard 104
Too Hot to Handle 106
Trainspotting 172, 179, 182
Travers, Linden 39, 44, 45, 47
Tread Softly Stranger 61, 64, 84
Tremarco, Christine 182
Trevelyan, John 22, 23, 24
Tuchner, Michael 4, 23, 124, 173
Twentieth Century Fox 33, 81, 152
TwentyFourSeven 184
Twin Town 174, 176
Tynan, Kenneth 124
Tyson, Cathy 167

Uneasy Terms 21, 94
Uninvited, The 44

Van Den Berg, Toby 71
Vance, Leigh 76, 106–8
Versois, Odile 77, 78
Vesselo, Arthur 7, 40
Victim 96
Victor, Charles 63
Villain 4, 5, 13, 23, *24*, 124, 134, 135, 140,
    173
Vincendeau, Ginette 149
Violent Playground 84, 96
Vitale, Milly 76

Waddington, Steven 183
Walker, Alexander 95, 128
Walker, Peter 12, 137
Wallace, Edgar 16, 27
Walsh, Dermot 63
Walsh, Raoul 46, 85
Wanamaker, Sam 12, 89
Warnecke, Gordon 162
Warner Bros 8, 81, 82, 148
Warner, Jack 21
Warshow, Robert 161
Watch the Lady (scenario) 17
Waterman, Dennis 135
Watkins, Arthur 20, 21
Watson, Colin 38

Waxman, Franz 33
Webb, Denis 53
Webb, Duncan 15
Webster 132
Wednesday Play 125
Welland, Colin 135
Weller, Paul 183
Wellman, William 16
Westerby, Robert 28, 35, 125
When the Gangs Came to London
　(scenario) 16
Where's the Money, Ronnie? 188
White, Alf 7
White, Carol 64, 98, 104, 143, 144
White Devil, The 132
White, Dorothy 23
White Heat 46, 167
Whitehouse (Mary) 41
Whitley, Reg 19
Whitting, Margaret *10*
Who Dares Wins 141
Wicked Lady, The 45
Wickes, David 13, 136
Wide Boy 34, 83
Widmark, Richard 33, 94, 148, 152, *154*
Williams, Brock 28
Williams, Harcourt 31

Williams, Norman 106
Willis, Ted 32
Willman, Noel 89
Wilson, Elizabeth 51
Wilson, Harold 1
Wilson, Scott 39, 47
Winner, Michael 132
Winstone, Ray 182
Withers, Googie 32, 33, 149, 151, 153
Woods, Arthur 4, 94
Working Title 110
World in Action 118, 119, 124
Wrong Box, The 126

Yates, Peter 4, 12, 136
Yellow Teddy Bears, The 124
Yesterday's Enemy 87
Yield to the Night 10, 11, 71–4
York, Michael *3*
Young Americans 13, 173, 175, 176
Young, Felicity 61
Young Scarface 31
Young, Terence 106

Z Cars 134, 135
Zimmerman, Fred 104

The
Moonshine
Dragon

Cornelia Funke

With illustrations by
Mónica Armiño

Barrington Stoke

First published in Great Britain in 2014 by
Barrington Stoke Ltd
18 Walker Street, Edinburgh, EH3 7LP

www.barringtonstoke.co.uk

Title of the original German edition:
Lesepiraten Champion – Der Mondscheindrache
© 2011 Loewe Verlag GmbH, Bindlach

Illustrations © 2014 Mónica Armiño
Translation © 2014 Barrington Stoke

A CIP catalogue record for this book is available
from the British Library upon request

ISBN: 978-1-78112-353-9

Printed in China by Leo

This book has dyslexia friendly features

For Robin

Contents

1   A Dragon and a Knight   1

2   A Good Plan   31

3   The Iron Dragon   59

4   Moonlight Magic   81

Chapter 1

A Dragon
and a Knight

The moon shone into Patrick's room. It turned the carpet silver. Even Patrick's jeans on the chair looked as if they were woven out of silver threads.

Who could sleep on a night like this?

Patrick lay in his bed, stared out of the window and counted the stars.

Patrick had almost dropped off to sleep when he was startled by a soft rustling sound on the floor by his bed.

He peered down to see what it was.

There was a book on the floor.
Patrick had read the book earlier that
day. It was about dragons and knights.
Now it lay open on the carpet, even
though Patrick was sure he had closed it.

Strange.

Patrick reached down to close the book. Then he heard another sound. The white pages moved, as if an invisible hand had turned them over.

Then Patrick heard a soft snort. He was so startled that he hid under his blankets. After a moment, he peeped out and looked down at the book.

Now Patrick could hear a loud panting noise. As he watched, a scaly tail appeared from between the pages of the book. The tail was followed by two claws, then a silver body with wings and spikes on its back and then – THUD! A dragon slid out from the book and landed on Patrick's carpet.

"Oh dear, oh dear!" the dragon moaned. He looked around. "Where am I? I was in my den. Where have I ended up now?"

The dragon was very beautiful to look at. He had silver and blue scales and a great long tail. He was just like

the picture Patrick had always had in his mind of how a dragon would look. The only difference was that this dragon would fit inside a jam jar.

The pages of the book moved again, and this time Patrick heard the clatter of hooves and the clink of iron.

"He's coming!" the dragon whispered in horror. "He's following me. He's found me! I have to hide. But where? Where?"

The dragon twisted his long neck this way and that. In the end he spotted Patrick's toy castle, in the darkest corner of the room.

"Yes!" he cried. "That's perfect!"

The dragon spread his silver wings
as if he wanted to fly, but it seemed
he couldn't manage more than a tired
flutter.

"Well then, I shall just have to run,"
he said.

The dragon ran across the moonlit
carpet to the castle, as fast as his legs
could carry him.

The dragon was only a human-sized step away from the book when a horse sprang out of it. On the horse's back was a knight in armour with a plume of white feathers on his helmet. The horse reared up and the knight looked around.

Patrick ducked ever deeper under his blankets.

"Ha! I will get you, you evil fire-worm!" the knight roared when he spotted the dragon. "This time you will not escape!"

The knight galloped up to the dragon with his sword held high.

"Stop!" Patrick yelled. He pushed
his blankets off and jumped out of bed.
"Leave the dragon alone, OK?" he said to
the knight.

"Whoa!" the little knight cried and his horse stopped. The knight stared up at Patrick. The dragon looked too – at Patrick, the knight and the horse. He let out a cry of alarm and then disappeared into the toy castle.

"A giant!" the knight cried. "By God, we are in a land of giants!"

"Nonsense!" Patrick said. He leaned down to talk to the knight. "You're in my room and no dragons are hunted here. Is that clear?"

"Peace, hideous giant!" the knight roared. "The White Knight is not afraid of you!" He waved his lance, spurred his horse and galloped straight for Patrick's bare legs.

"Hey, stop that!" Patrick cried. "Put away that spear!"

But the knight had already poked his tiny spear into Patrick's shin.

"Ow!" Patrick cried. "Are you crazy?"

Patrick was furious. He snatched at the knight and lifted him off his horse.

And that's when it happened.

As soon as Patrick touched the knight, he began to shrink. Down, down, down he shrank – and fast! Patrick only just managed to pull the knight off his horse.

A few seconds later, he was down beside him on the carpet – and Patrick was even shorter than the knight!

The White Knight was the first to recover from the shock.

He jumped to his feet and drew
his sword. Clink, clink, clink went his
armour.

"Aha!" he growled. "You are a
wizard, a vile enchanter."

"What nonsense!" Patrick cried. He got to his feet.

"Liar!" the knight yelled. "Slimy devilish warlock!"

He lunged this way and that as he attacked Patrick with his sword.

Patrick had to make a wild leap to one side to stop his head being cut off. Then he ran. He ran towards the castle, faster than he had ever run before.

Patrick was in luck. The White
Knight's armour was so heavy that he
struggled to get back on his horse.

When at last he made it back into
the saddle, Patrick was almost at
the castle gate. But two crayons and
a rubber were lying on the carpet,
blocking his way.

Patrick struggled to climb over the crayons as the knight galloped closer and closer.

'Oh no!' Patrick thought. 'If only I'd listened to Mum when she told me to keep my room tidy.'

Patrick used all his strength to lift himself over the crayons and reach the drawbridge of the castle.

He stumbled inside and grabbed the handle that cranked up the bridge to close it. His arms shook as he turned the handle.

With a creak, the bridge began to lift. At the very last second it slammed shut and closed the castle door. Phew!

When he saw this, the angry White Knight beat his shield on the castle wall. It made a sound like thunder.

Chapter 2

A Good
Plan

"Oh man!" Patrick groaned. His legs trembled and he leaned against the inside wall of the castle.

"Are you a really a wizard?" a voice behind Patrick asked.

Patrick spun round. The dragon! He had forgotten about the dragon. It was crouched in the far corner of the castle yard.

"I'm not a wizard," Patrick said. "And I'm not a giant. I'm just a normal boy."

"You would say that," the dragon said. "But the boys I know are not as big as castle towers. And they do not change size all of a sudden."

"I've never changed size before," Patrick told him. "I have no idea how that happened."

"Must be moonlight magic," the dragon said. "I've heard of such a thing before. When the moonlight disappears, the magic disappears too."

"I'm glad to hear it!" Patrick said. "It's pretty dangerous to be so small! Can you see what that stupid bucket-head is doing out there?"

The dragon stretched his long neck, but the castle wall was too high for him to see over.

Patrick climbed the stairs that led to the top of the wall, and peered over the battlements.

"I see him," he whispered. "He has got off his horse and now he is looking at my toys. What's he up to?"

"Oh, he'll be looking for treasure," the dragon said. "If the White Knight isn't collecting dragon heads, then he's hunting for treasure."

"Well, he'll have his work cut out for him finding treasure in my bedroom," Patrick said.

"Maybe so, but he's still going to get us," the dragon wailed.

"Nonsense!" said Patrick.

"Don't be so sure. The White Knight is stronger and braver than you think!" the dragon said.

"He has killed more dragons and knights than anyone can count," the dragon went on. "So far I've always managed to escape, but now ..." He shook his beautiful head. "Now it seems I must die in this strange world, where I've only just arrived."

Patrick came back down the stairs. "You crawled out of a book," he told the dragon.

The dragon looked at him in surprise. "What book?" he asked.

"One with lots of stories in it about dragons," said Patrick.

"I'm not from a story!" the dragon said in a huff.

"You are so," Patrick said. "Anyway, why can't you fly?"

"The White Knight has chased me for so long and so far that I've not had time to eat," the dragon said. "A dragon cannot fly on an empty stomach. Perhaps if you gave me something to eat –"

The dragon stopped and his ears pricked up. "I think the knight's coming back!" he whispered.

Patrick scrambled to climb back up the steps to the top of the wall.

The White Knight was now heading
for the castle at full gallop. He no longer
held his lance in his hands. Instead,
he held a crayon. There was a terrible
crash as he rammed the crayon against
the closed drawbridge. The plastic
drawbridge shattered like a broken
eggshell and a hole appeared in the
middle. The White Knight laughed. He
threw the broken crayon on the carpet
and picked up a new one.

"Oh, no!" Patrick groaned. "The bridge didn't hold out for very long."

Patrick scanned the room in the hope he might spot something they could use

to stop the knight. The plastic lances from his toy knight would be no use. Then he saw the big digger he had got for his last birthday. It was made of metal and it worked by remote control.

'Where did I put the remote control?' Patrick thought. His eyes fell on the bookshelf. Of course – there was the

control, on the third shelf from the top.
There was no way someone as small as
him could get up there.

The White Knight rammed the bridge a second time. The hole he had made in the plastic was getting bigger.

And then Patrick had an idea.

"Hey, you!" he called down to the dragon. "Do you eat bread?"

"I'll eat anything!" the dragon called back.

Patrick ran to the tall castle tower. It looked very high and there were no stairs. But, at the top of the tower, there were pellets of bread that Patrick had made to fire from the castle's big cannon.

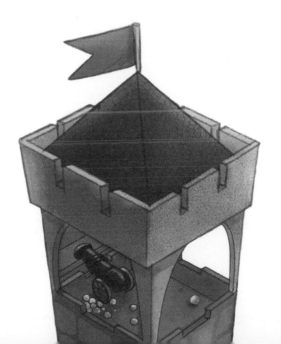

Patrick's fingers trembled as he pulled himself up the castle wall. Higher and higher he climbed. The knight pulled on his horse's reins to hold it still, and he watched Patrick climb.

With his very last bit of strength, Patrick pulled himself over the battlements of the tower and flopped onto the platform at the top. The bread pellets were there – some were dried-up, but most of them were all right.

"Catch!" Patrick shouted to the dragon.

The dragon opened his mouth and swallowed one pellet after another.

Chapter 3

The Iron Dragon

The White Knight and his horse stormed
the drawbridge again. Now it hung all
crooked on the thin chain that attached
it to the castle.

"S-s-s-s-s!" the dragon hissed as the last pellet of bread vanished into his belly. He licked his lips. Then he beat his powerful wings and flew up to Patrick on the castle tower.

"Miserable fire-worm!" the White Knight roared from below. "That will not save you and the wizard."

The dragon stuck out his tongue in reply.

"Where should I go?" he asked Patrick.

Patrick pointed to the bookshelf.

"Get on," said the dragon.

Patrick clambered onto the dragon's back and held onto his big spikes.

"Hold on!" the dragon called, and he spiralled up into the air.

The White Knight brandished his
sword and cursed. But Patrick laughed.
It was wonderful, flying on the dragon's

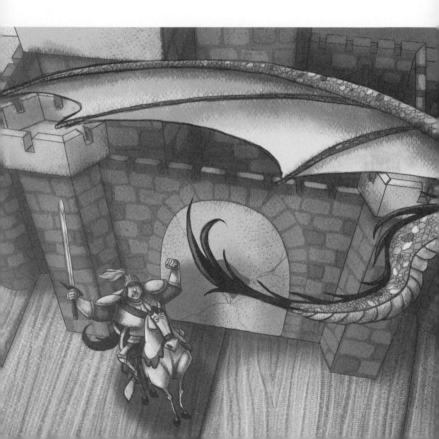

back. His room looked like a strange landscape below them as they flew across it in the moonlight.

The dragon rose higher and higher and landed on the shelf right next to the remote control.

"How was that?" he asked, as he folded his silver wings back together again.

"It was wonderful!" Patrick said.
"And now, watch this! We'll scare that
stupid knight back into his book."

Patrick and the dragon were both
so small that it was not easy for them
to point the huge remote control at the
giant digger, but together they managed
it.

"Let's go," Patrick whispered.

Patrick used his little hands to turn the switch and then moved the knob that steered the digger.

The digger began to jolt over the carpet. Straight towards the knight.

The knight's horse reared up when it saw the bucket of the giant digger coming towards it.

"Ha, a pathetic Iron Dragon!" the White Knight roared. "Attack!"

The knight spurred his horse on to attack, but it went wild. It reared and bucked and lashed out with its hooves until it threw the knight off its back. And then the horse galloped back to the book and, with one big leap, it disappeared between the pages.

The White Knight scrambled to his feet. With a bellow of rage, he charged at the digger.

"He's mad!" Patrick said. He pressed the button to lower the digger bucket, and the bucket scooped the knight up off the carpet. The knight kicked and screamed. He waved his sword at the digger, but he was trapped in the bucket.

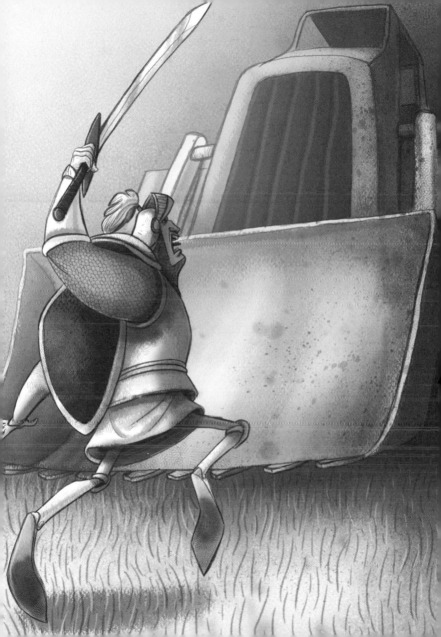

Patrick used the remote control to drive the digger straight at the book. "Off you go!" he shouted. "And don't come back!"

Then he shovelled the White Knight back into the book. The knight slipped between the pages and was gone.

"Thank goodness!" the dragon said. "He's gone! But what are you going to do with the Iron Dragon now?"

"I'm going to switch the Iron Dragon off," Patrick said.

"So you are a wizard!" the dragon cried.

"No, I'm not," Patrick told him. "Can you fly me down to the floor now, please?"

Patrick got up onto the dragon's back and off they flew.

Chapter 4

Moonlight Magic

The dragon flew over the room and set
Patrick down on his bed.

"What are you going to do now?"
Patrick asked the dragon. "You can't go
back to your story. That mad knight is
there."

The dragon shrugged. "Where else
can I go?"

"You could stay with me," Patrick said.

"You are very kind," the dragon said. "But I would rather go back to my own world."

"I've got it!" Patrick cried. "Why don't you go to another story? There are stories in my book with dragons and no knights."

"Really?" the dragon said, his eyes wide open.

"I promise," Patrick said. "Hold on."

Patrick slid down the bed sheets and ran over to the book. It seemed so huge now he was so small. He turned the big, heavy pages of the book.

"Yes, here," he said. "Page 123. This is the place for you."

"If you say so …" The dragon flapped his wings over the open page. "OK! Say goodbye. I'm going into this new story now …"

Then – whoosh! The dragon vanished in between the pages of the book.

"Thank you!" Patrick heard him call, from far, far away.

Then Patrick was alone again in his room. The moon still shone through the window.

Patrick yawned as he climbed back into his bed. He curled up on the pillow and covered himself with a corner of the blanket.

"Moonlight magic," he murmured. "Well, let's see."

When Patrick woke up the next morning, he was as big as ever. The same size as a normal boy. But the broken castle and the broken crayons proved that last night's adventure had not been a dream.

From then on, every moonlit night, Patrick left an open book next to his bed.

But as for the pages which told the story of the White Knight ... Patrick stuck those pages firmly together.

Our books are tested
for children and young people by
children and young people.

Thanks to everyone who consulted on
a manuscript for their time and effort in
helping us to make our books better
for our readers.

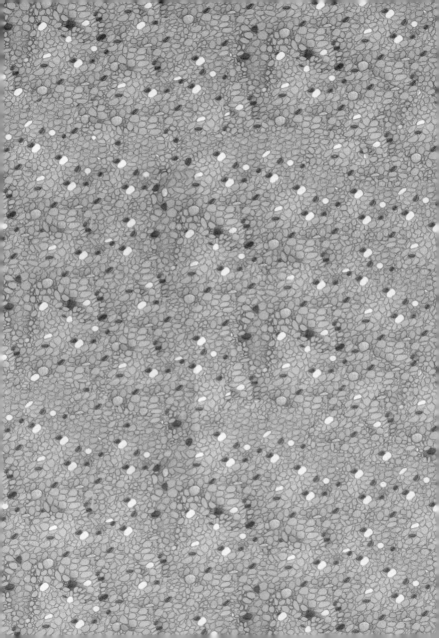